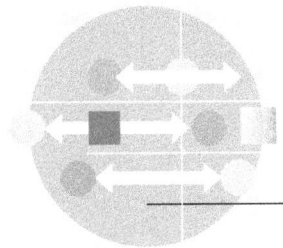

Trade and Transport Corridor Management Toolkit

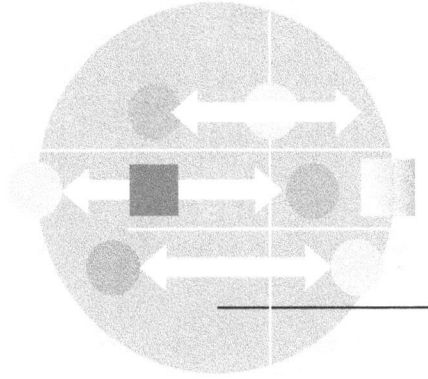

Trade and Transport Corridor Management Toolkit

Charles Kunaka
Robin Carruthers

THE WORLD BANK
Washington, D.C.

ISBN (paper): 978-1-4648-0143-3
ISBN (electronic): 978-1-4648-0144-0
DOI: 10.1596/978-1-4648-0143-3

Cover design: Debra Naylor, Naylor Design, Inc.

Library of Congress Cataloging-in-Publication Data

Kunaka, Charles.
  Trade and transport corridor management toolkit / Charles Kunaka, Robin Carruthers.
    pages cm
  Includes bibliographical references and index.
  ISBN 978-1-4648-0143-3—ISBN 978-1-4648-0144-0
  1. Transportation corridors—Planning. 2. Trade routes—Planning. 3. Business logistics. I. Carruthers, Robin. II. Title.
  HE323.K86 2014
  388.3'242—dc23

                                                                              2014001154

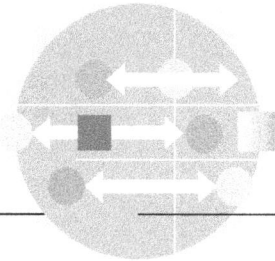

CONTENTS

PART II Improving Corridor Performance   139

Boxes

Figures

Tables

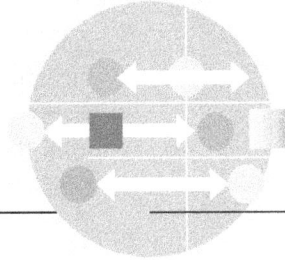

FOREWORD

Trade and transport corridors—major routes that facilitate the movement of people and goods between regions and between countries—have existed for millennia. They enable regions and countries to offer high-capacity transport systems and services that reduce trade and transport costs by creating economies of scale. Regional corridors are particularly important to landlocked countries, where they are economic lifelines, often providing the only overland routes to regional and international markets.

Despite the long history of corridors, there has been a lack of guidance on how to design, determine the components to include, and analyze the likely impact of corridor projects. The *Trade and Transport Corridor Management Toolkit* fills this void, making an important contribution to knowledge of corridors.

The *Toolkit* synthesizes the best knowledge available on the implementation of corridor projects. It presents in a succinct form the experiences of the World Bank and other development agencies in assessing, designing, implementing, and evaluating the impact of trade and transport corridor projects. Before now, this knowledge was spread out in disparate project documents, often beyond the reach of project teams preparing and implementing projects. By presenting this information in one volume, the *Toolkit* saves task managers the tedious task of looking for the best available tools. It also ensures greater consistency, which will also facilitate comparison and benchmarking of performance, which are of great value to the private sector.

The *Toolkit* should also be of immense value to policy makers in provincial and national governments as well as regional economic institutions, for several reasons. First, corridors affect the space economy of countries; they are best developed with clear estimates of what the spatial impacts are going to be. Second, a corridor is a system made up of several components, including infrastructure (roads, railways, ports), transport and logistics services and regulations (typically influenced by policy choices of and financing from the public sector). It is important that policy makers appreciate the linkages between these components, particularly as the overall performance of a corridor is determined by the weakest component. Third, the *Toolkit* deals with the concept of corridor management and the motivations of the various parties that may have interests in its development. It argues that both the public and private sectors should have a say in corridor development processes and operations.

Well thought-out corridor projects can have significant impacts, reducing trade costs and enhancing the competitiveness of cities, communities, regions, and countries, especially where they are landlocked. I hope the advice, guidelines, and general principles outlined in the *Toolkit* are of help to all who work on corridor projects and enable them to better appreciate both the importance of good corridor project design and the challenges of and possibilities for improving performance and reducing trade costs.

Mona E. Haddad
Sector Manager, International Trade
World Bank

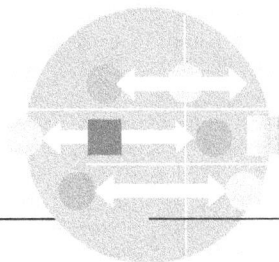

ACKNOWLEDGMENTS

This *Toolkit* is the product of a collaborative effort involving many colleagues at the World Bank and the African Development Bank, as well as practitioners in countries and regional economic communities. Its preparation was funded by the World Bank and a grant from the Multi-Donor Trust Fund for Trade and Development.

The project benefited immensely from the contributions of various people at the World Bank, particularly John Arnold, Jean-François Arvis, Henry Bofinger, Ranga Krishnamani, Jonathan Stevens, and Virginia Tanase, who drafted specific modules. Anca Dumitrescu, Olivier Hartmann, Tadatsugu (Toni) Matsudaira, Daniel Saslavsky, Jordan Schwartz, Graham Smith, and Maika Watanuki reviewed and commented on early drafts. Jean-François Marteau, Cordula Rastogi, and Tomas Serebrisky peer reviewed the *Toolkit* at the concept stage and helped shape the final product. Dorsati Madani, Jean-François Marteau, and Cordula Rastogi (World Bank); Jean Kizito Kabanguka and Tapio Naula (African Development Bank); and Tengfei Wang (United Nations Economic and Social Commission for Asia and the Pacific [UNESCAP]) reviewed and provided invaluable comments for the finalization of the draft.

The authors are also extremely grateful to members of the Sub-Saharan Africa Transport Policy Program Regional Economic Communities Transport Coordinating Committee, the Korea Transport Institute, officials of several governments, and participants at seminars held at the World Bank who provided comments at various stages during preparation and testing of the *Toolkit*. Their comments helped immensely in maintaining the practical relevance of the final product.

The authors would also like to acknowledge the support of several colleagues in the International Trade Unit of the World Bank who helped finalize the manuscript, in particular Cynthia Abidin-Saurman, who prepared the draft for publication, and Amir Fouad, who guided the publication process. Their generous and patient assistance is greatly appreciated.

Last and by no means least, special acknowledgment goes to Mona Haddad (Sector Manager, International Trade, World Bank) for her strong leadership, enthusiastic encouragement, insightful guidance, and provision of resources.

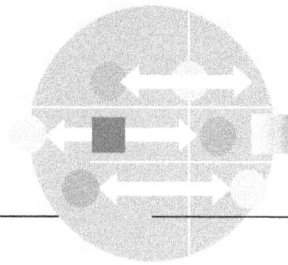

ABOUT THE AUTHORS

Robin Carruthers is a consultant on transport, trade, and infrastructure and a former lead transport economist at the World Bank. Before joining the Bank, he spent three decades as a partner of a transport consulting firm in Argentina, Australia, and the United Kingdom. He recently conducted a facilitation and infrastructure study of the Mashreq countries, evaluated the marine electronic highway planned for the Straits of Malacca and Singapore, advised the government of Paraguay on integrating its transport and logistics strategies, and assisted the Inter-American Development Bank on the design of a maritime corridor, logistics, and trade facilitation strategy for the Caribbean.

Charles Kunaka is a senior trade specialist in the World Bank's International Trade Unit. He has a background in transport economics and policy and is an expert on analyzing and designing trade and transport corridor projects. He recently coauthored a book on bilateral road transport agreements and a pioneering study on logistics services for small-scale producers in rural areas. As regional coordinator for the Bank-hosted Sub-Saharan Africa Transport Policy Program in East and Southern Africa, he led work on regional transport and integration. Before joining the Bank, he worked for the Southern African Development Community (SADC) as a senior transport policy officer, championing the integration of transport markets across SADC's 14 member countries.

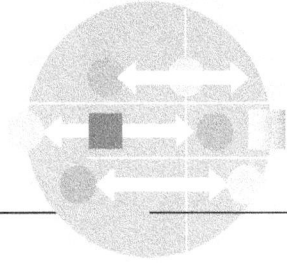

ABBREVIATIONS

ASEAN	Association of Southeast Asian Nations
CIF	cost, insurance, and freight
EFTA	European Free Trade Association
FOB	free on board
FTA	free trade agreement
GPS	Global Positioning System
HIV/AIDS	human immunodeficiency virus/acquired immune deficiency syndrome
ICT	information and communications technology
IRU	International Road Transport Union
NTM	nontariff measure
SIC	standard industrial classification
SPS	sanitary and phyto-sanitary
SSATP	Sub-Saharan Africa Transport Policy Program
TBT	technical barrier to trade
TEU	20-foot equivalent unit
TIR	transports internationaux routiers (international road transport)
TTFA	Trade and Transport Facilitation Assessment
UNECE	United Nations Economic Commission for Europe
UNESCAP	United Nations Economic and Social Commission for Asia and the Pacific
WTO	World Trade Organization

All amounts are presented in U.S. dollars unless otherwise indicated.

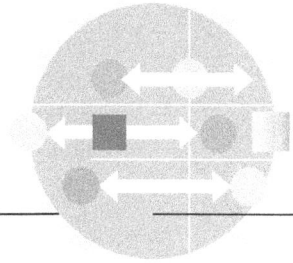

Purpose and Use of This Toolkit

Global trade moves along a few high-density routes. Partly as a result, trade and transport facilitation projects are increasingly designed around regional trade corridors.

Trade corridors are not a new phenomenon: they have been used for trade and transport for centuries. The ancient Silk Road is probably the best-known trade corridor in the world, one that has had an enduring impact on the social and economic development of the regions it crossed. It continues to be a source of learning even today.

A trade and transport corridor is a coordinated bundle of transport and logistics infrastructure and services that facilitates trade and transport flows between major centers of economic activity. A formal trade and transport corridor is typically coordinated by a national or regional body, constituted by the public or private sectors or a combination of the two.

Interest in exploiting the corridor approach to trade and transport facilitation has increased significantly in recent years. All regions of the world, developed and developing, have several trade and transport corridor initiatives.

The corridor agenda is increasingly widely adopted by governments, the private sector, and development agencies. There is a realization that poor corridor performance can hurt the economic prospects, especially of land-locked developing economies, with disproportionate impacts on their small and medium-size enterprises. Over the past three decades, the World Bank alone has financed more than 100 trade and transport corridor–based projects and studies, and many similar projects and studies are in the pipeline (box I.1). Other international agencies have also provided support to private sector organizations and governments in developing countries for building infrastructure, institutional and legal frameworks to improve corridor performance. Clearly, there is both recognition of the importance of corridors and emphasis on using this approach to meet trade and transport development objectives. Most projects focus on infrastructure development, typically road infrastructure. The soft dimensions, especially regulatory and procedural controls and the quality of logistics services, do not always receive the attention needed to maximize the benefits of investments in infrastructure.

There are several compelling reasons why the corridor approach is widely used:

- It is critical to providing landlocked countries in particular with basic access to maritime ports for their overseas trade.
- Regional integration improves the growth prospects of middle- and low-income countries, especially landlocked countries. Transport corridors provide a visible and direct opportunity to bring about regional integration.
- Regulatory and other constraints to trade facilitation attain practical relevance at the corridor level, enabling the design of appropriate interventions.
- Corridors provide a spatial framework for organizing cooperation and collaboration between countries and public and private sector agencies involved in providing trade and transport infrastructure and services.

For these and other reasons, there is a growing network of international transport corridors across the developing world.

Why a Toolkit?

Analyzing transportation and logistics performance along a corridor is a complex undertaking. Many components are involved, covering among others, technical issues concerning transport systems, policies, regulations governing service provision, and cooperation and collaboration between institutions. The information required for proper analysis of a corridor has to be acquired from many different sources. The task of assembling all

BOX I.1

Lessons from Corridor and Regional Projects by the World Bank

The World Bank has financed corridor projects across all regions of the world. Although most projects have a national focus, a large and growing number are regional, involving at least two countries. Most such projects have been in Sub-Saharan Africa and Europe and Central Asia, two regions with a large number of landlocked countries. Most projects in these regions in particular but also elsewhere seek to connect landlocked countries to external markets, typically through seaport gateways.

Corridor projects implemented by the World Bank often involve four main types of interventions:

- Infrastructure typically accounts for most of the funding, as much as three-quarters in some cases. The focus is typically on the rehabilitation and upgrading of transport infrastructure, including roads, rail, and seaports as well as airports, border facilities, and other inland cargo facilities. Road safety measures along trade and transport corridors can be part of infrastructure improvements.
- Transit and trade facilitation includes the transit regime, border-crossing improvements, transport services, and modernization of customs. In recognition of the fact that the incidence of human immunodeficiency virus/acquired immune deficiency syndrome (HIV/AIDS) is particularly high among truck drivers and commercial sex workers along transport corridors, one recent project included HIV/AIDS interventions along transport corridors.
- Institutional strengthening usually includes support for trade facilitation and capacity building for managing projects. In a few instances, this component may include efforts to promote private sector participation in the management of corridors.
- Analytical work and no-lending technical assistance help countries gather evidence in order to better understand corridor performance and design well-informed interventions.

In *The Development Potential of Regional Programs: An Evaluation of World Bank Support of Multi-country Operations*, the Independent Evaluation Group (IEG 2007) reviews regional projects, several of which

(box continues on next page)

BOX I.1 *continued*

were corridor projects. It reports a few important findings and makes some recommendations:

- Regional programs can deliver strong results.
- Success and sustainability depend on strong ownership of all participating countries.
- Analytical work and resource mobilization are often necessary to reconcile potentially conflicting interests of different countries.
- There is need for clear delineation and coordination of the roles of national and regional institutions, accountable governance arrangements, and planning for sustainability.
- Cooperation between development partners is often necessary to put together grant and loan financing packages for regional programs. Grant resources are often needed, especially at the beginning, to support analytical work and strengthen regional cooperation mechanisms.

relevant data and constructing a complete picture of the operation and performance of an entire corridor can be daunting, but it is precisely because the various components are interlinked that a holistic picture is needed. A corridor is a set of interconnected and complementary subsystems; this interconnectedness is fundamental to how it plays its role. Project managers and officials concerned with trade and transport should make judgments about bottlenecks and barriers and decide on strategies for improving overall system performance rather than simply optimizing parts of it.

This Toolkit is designed to help project managers in public and private sector agencies address the challenges associated with the design of corridor projects. Despite the volume of work on corridors, little guidance material is available on how to approach corridor projects. Task managers spend considerable time looking for the best available tools. They often find it difficult to ascertain what already exists and where to find it. Studies have been duplicated, because previous work is not always widely disseminated or easily discoverable. In addition, the lack of consistency in approaches makes it difficult to ensure that task managers are getting consistent advice even within individual organizations.

Providing a comprehensive guide to tools and techniques for corridor projects is important, as the volume of such projects is likely to increase. Corridors remain very important, especially to landlocked countries and postconflict countries and regions. Both the World Bank Group Trade Strategy (World Bank 2011) and its Transport Business Strategy

(World Bank 2008) emphasize trade and transport corridors as priorities for the Bank's work on trade facilitation and logistics. The Transport Business Strategy proposes "encouraging client countries to adopt corridor approaches to investing in transport infrastructure and improving transport services, especially along multicountry regional routes." It seeks to reduce the costs associated with moving goods along international supply chains, by enhancing "the performance of trade corridors used by land-linked developing countries, especially in Africa," among other measures. Other development agencies, such as the Asian Development Bank and the African Development Bank, have similar strategies.

Analytical work on corridors is widely dispersed. Examples of the few documents by the World Bank are two papers, "Best Practices in Management of International Trade Corridors" (Arnold 2006) and "Institutional Arrangements for Corridor Management in Sub-Saharan Africa" (Adzigbey, Kunaka, and Mitiku 2007), and a comprehensive book, *Connecting Landlocked Developing Countries to Markets: Trade Corridors in the 21st Century* (Arvis and others 2011), which provides the conceptual underpinnings to this Toolkit. Based on analytical research, the book uses numerous case studies to illustrate how landlocked countries can improve their connectivity to international markets. Some of the measures proposed include the following:

- reengineering transit regimes based on the well-established and successful regime used across most of Europe and Central Asia
- rethinking the approaches to transport service regulation by promoting quality-based regulation in road transport and developing multimodal transportation
- promoting comprehensive corridor management initiatives to build trust within and between countries.

Other organizations have also conducted studies, although most tend to be specific to a region or corridor. For example, the Islamic Development Bank's *A Study of International Transport Corridors in OIC Member Countries* (2011) assesses the role and contribution of transport corridors to economic growth and cooperation, trade, and regional integration in the 57 Organization of Islamic Cooperation (OIC) member countries and identifies priority transport corridors and challenges faced along them. The report notes that transport corridors are increasingly important, particularly in developing economies and emerging markets, because of their role in spurring economic development and facilitating trade.

This Toolkit provides a comprehensive and holistic compilation of approaches and techniques on corridor diagnostics, performance assessment, management, operations improvement, and impact evaluation.

It addresses many of the requests from task managers at international agencies for more holistic advice on corridor management. It brings together and updates existing knowledge and fills in gaps. It can be used for both international and national trade corridors. It also addresses capacity-building needs for corridor management and identifies the legal and trade agreements that determine the trade context within which a corridor functions.

Organization of the Toolkit

The Toolkit is designed for national and international public sector agencies and the private sector actors that have to design, develop, or provide services using a trade and transport corridor approach. It provides tools to answer four main questions:

- What are the approaches to identifying the main issues and constraints to movement of trade and transport along a corridor?
- How well is the corridor performing, and where are the weaknesses?
- What are the options for improving the performance of the corridor?
- What are the likely impacts of investments or improvements to the corridor?

These questions guide the iterative steps in designing and implementing a corridor project (figure I.1).

The Toolkit groups the four main questions into three parts, which comprise 13 modules (table I.1). Part I includes four modules on how to carry out a corridor diagnostic. These modules focus on the infrastructure, regulatory, and institutional framework for a corridor. Part I also includes a critical module on corridor performance indicators. Part II comprises eight modules on specific corridor components. It explains how performance can be improved through targeted interventions. Part III consists of a single module, on assessing the impact of a corridor.

What Goes into a Corridor Diagnostic?

International trade and transport corridor projects are complex to design and implement. They often take considerable time, involve several components, and require the involvement of different stakeholders, implementing agents, and impact indicators. Typically, preparatory work, including diagnostic studies and consultations with stakeholders in all corridor countries, starts a year or more before a project can be clearly articulated.

FIGURE I.1 Corridor Project Cycle

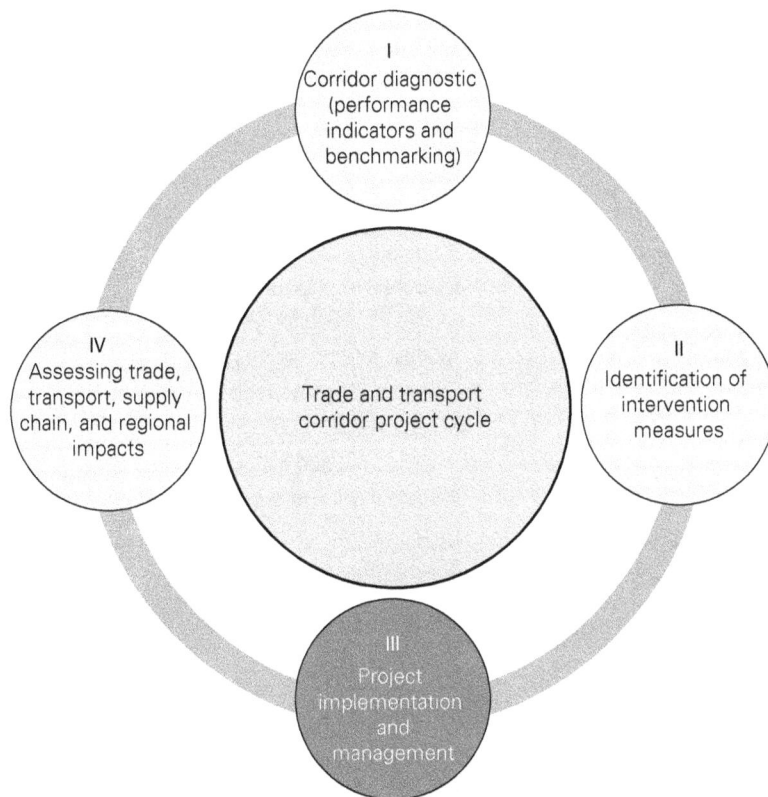

The Toolkit describes approaches to conducting a corridor diagnostic. A diagnostic takes three main forms: determining the development and trade context, assessing corridor-length performance, and conducting a detailed diagnostic at specific locations, or chokepoints, along a corridor to identify practical intervention measures (Raballand and others 2008).

The diagnostic process collects quantitative and qualitative data to identify the major impediments to trade facilitation and the capacity within the public and private sector for removing them. Quantitative data are collected on all corridor components and from various service providers. Qualitative data are collected through surveys of logistics service providers, shippers, and government officials involved in the logistics and transportation sectors. The diagnosis involves discussions with groups as well as individuals, normally conducted by technical experts familiar with trade and logistics or their representatives.

TABLE I.1 Contents of Trade and Transport Corridor Management Toolkit

Part	Modules
I: Corridor diagnostic and performance assessment	Module 1: Carrying out a corridor diagnostic
	Module 2: Assessing the legal and regulatory context of a corridor
	Module 3: Institutional arrangements for corridor management
	Module 4: Corridor performance indicators
II: Improving corridor performance	Module 5: Border management in a corridor
	Module 6: Customs transit regimes
	Module 7: Road freight transport
	Module 8: Rail transport
	Module 9: Shipping and maritime transport
	Module 10: Port operations
	Module 11: Land access to ports
	Module 12: Airfreight
III: Corridor impact evaluation	Module 13: Evaluating the economic impact of a corridor

How Is Corridor Performance Measured?

The Toolkit defines core corridor performance measures and explains how to interpret them. The proposed core indicators are volume, cost, time, reliability, and safety and supply chain security. Ultimately, trade corridors are about trade competitiveness. If a subregion has no strategy to benefit from the increased flows, it may not be worth developing a trade corridor.

How Can Corridor Performance Be Improved?

The Toolkit identifies mechanisms for improving the performance of the corridor through initiatives by the public and private sectors. These initiatives include investments in infrastructure and modification of policies and regulations, especially related to trade facilitation. It also considers the government's capacity to maintain the infrastructure and regulate the flow of goods along the corridor and the private sector's ability to provide a variety of levels and quality of services, as measured in terms of time and cost. As the interventions require interaction between the public and private sectors, the Toolkit proposes measures to enhance the involvement of a variety of stakeholders.

Corridor performance is affected by various parties, both public and private, which have to collaborate. The overall level of performance is determined by the weakest link among these parties. For this reason, it is important that corridor projects include a capacity enhancement component. The regulatory authorities may exhibit weaknesses or lack of awareness about what is needed to improve overall performance, or practices in the private sector may compromise performance. Corridor performance indicators are a valuable starting point in identifying areas in which capacity needs to be built and the type of support required.

The public and private sectors implement priority interventions using their own resources or support from development agencies. The World Bank; regional development banks (the Asian Development Bank, the African Development Bank, the Inter-American Development Bank, the Islamic Development Bank, and others); and other UN agencies (the United Nations Conference on Trade and Development [UNCTAD], the United Nations Economic and Social Commission for Asia and Pacific [UNESCAP], the United Nations Economic Commission for Africa [UNECA], the United Nations Economic Commission for Europe [UNECE], and others) support numerous corridor projects across the developing world. Implementation involves the procurement of goods, works, and services, as well as any environmental and social impact mitigation set out in agreed plans. A common challenge with international projects is how to synchronize processes and specifications across borders. Doing so calls for close interaction and at times the use of the same vendors for project components in different countries. Because of their complexity, corridor projects often experience delays, and unexpected events sometimes prompt the restructuring of the projects.

How Is the Impact of Corridor Interventions Estimated?

The economic evaluation of a corridor project attempts to determine whether the reductions in cost of current trade and the generation of new trade are worth the investment cost needed to bring them about. Although the development objective of the project may be expressed in terms of increasing export growth, the economic evaluation should also take account of the reduction in import costs. Questions that need to be answered include the following: How will improvements along the corridor affect trade competitiveness in regional and international markets? How do changes in transportation costs and the attractiveness of a region affect the location and relocation of enterprises? The same questions can be asked at the level of

FIGURE I.2 Structure of the Toolkit

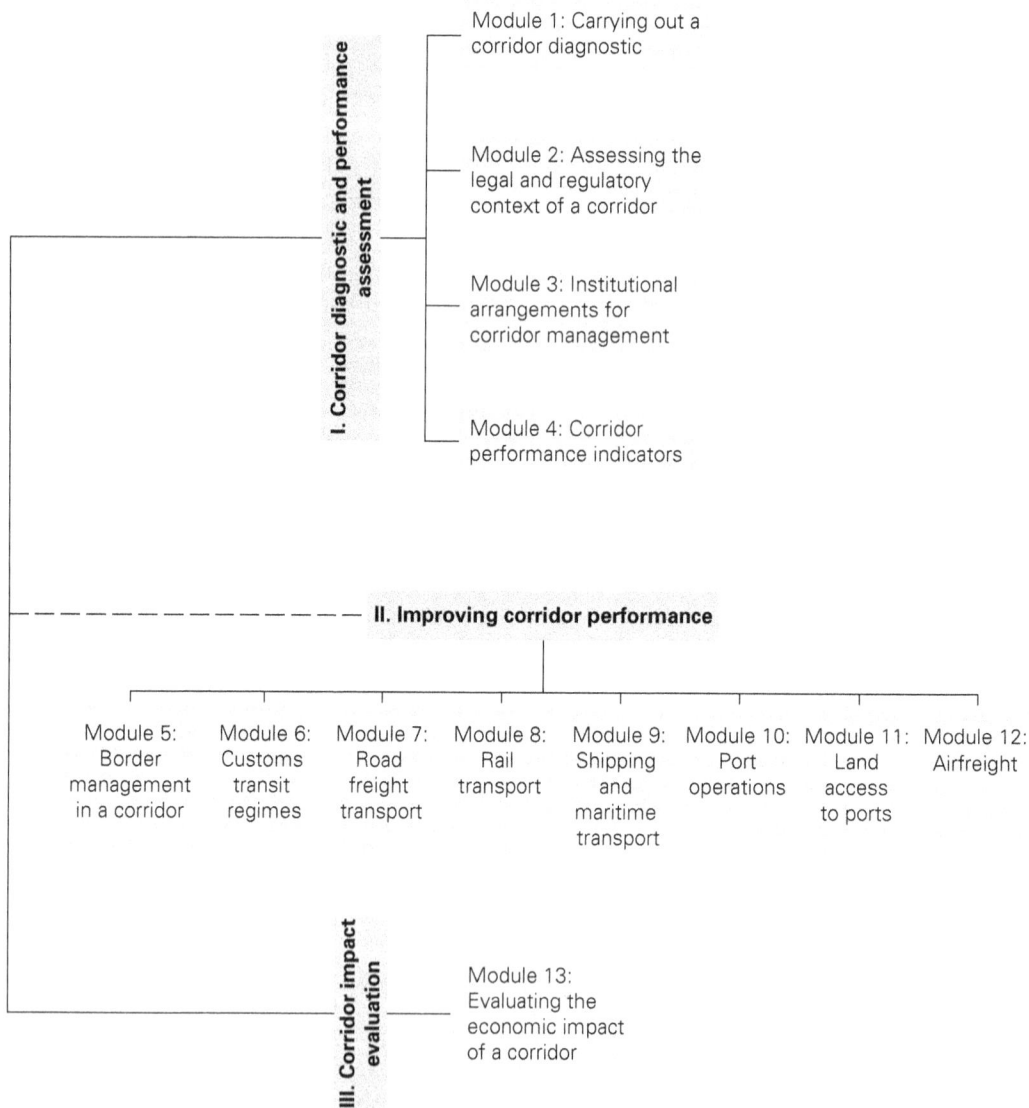

I. Corridor diagnostic and performance assessment

Module 1: Carrying out a corridor diagnostic

Module 2: Assessing the legal and regulatory context of a corridor

Module 3: Institutional arrangements for corridor management

Module 4: Corridor performance indicators

II. Improving corridor performance

Module 5: Border management in a corridor

Module 6: Customs transit regimes

Module 7: Road freight transport

Module 8: Rail transport

Module 9: Shipping and maritime transport

Module 10: Port operations

Module 11: Land access to ports

Module 12: Airfreight

III. Corridor impact evaluation

Module 13: Evaluating the economic impact of a corridor

a facility or component of a corridor, where isolating impact is probably much more complex.

The link between corridor improvements and trade impacts can be indirect. In some instances, it is possible to assess impact only in terms of estimates of time and cost savings. Translating these savings into trade and other developmental impacts tends to be difficult, but this kind of analysis is particularly informative to the design and execution of projects. Knowing when, where, and how to intervene within the corridor could have great potential in maximizing trade impacts.

How to Use the Toolkit

Parts I and III of the Toolkit cover the basic principles governing the analysis of trade corridors and the measurement of the impact of interventions. Both are essential reading. The modules in Part II are relevant depending on the components found on a specific corridor. Not all of the modules will be used for every corridor. Figure I.2 shows the structure of the Toolkit and how the different modules can be utilized.

References

Adzigbey, Y., C. Kunaka, and T. N. Mitiku. 2007. "Institutional Arrangements for Transport Corridor Management in Sub-Saharan Africa." SSATP Working Paper 86, World Bank, Sub-Saharan Africa Transport Policy Program, Washington, DC.

Arnold, J. 2006. "Best Practices in Management of International Trade Corridors." Transport Paper TP-13, World Bank, Washington, DC.

Arvis, J. F., R. Carruthers, G. Smith, and C. Willoughby. 2011. *Connecting Landlocked Developing Countries to Markets*: *Trade Corridors in the 21st Century*. Washington, DC: World Bank.

IEG (Independent Evaluation Group). 2007. *The Development Potential of Regional Programs*: *An Evaluation of World Bank Support of Multi-country Operations*. World Bank, Washington, DC.

Islamic Development Bank. 2011. A *Study of International Transport Corridors in OIC Member Countries*. Jeddah.

Raballand, G., O. Hartmann, J. F. Marteau, J. K. Kabanguka, and C. Kunaka. 2008. "Lessons of Corridor Performance Measurement." SSATP Discussion Paper 7, World Bank, Sub-Saharan Africa Transport Policy Program, Washington, DC.

World Bank. 2008. *Safe, Clean, and Affordable Transport for Development*: *The World Bank Group's Transport Business Strategy 2008–2012*. Washington DC.

———. 2011. *Leveraging Trade for Development and Inclusive Growth the World Bank Group Trade Strategy, 2011–2021*. Washington DC.

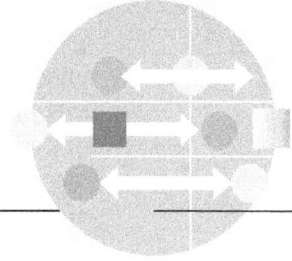

Primer

Moving goods and people is the basic function of trade and transport corridors. Common objectives of corridor projects include improving infrastructure connectivity, facilitating the efficient movement of freight, and promoting economic growth by improving the competitiveness of exports and reducing the costs of imports or developing clusters of economic activity along the corridor supported by efficient logistics. A corridor that has all the requirements for successful transport cannot be considered successful if it has no trade. But the trade function of a corridor differs according to its geographic context. A corridor that links a landlocked country to a port has a far more complex function than one that links the inland area of a coastal country to a port in the same country. A corridor that links two ports (in the same or adjacent countries) has yet another function.

Drivers of Corridor Development

In most low-income countries, corridors are defined and driven by the governments, regional economic communities, and international development agencies that support them. The spatial definition of a corridor therefore reflects the proponents. However, it is often at the regional or international level that governments are most conscious of the importance of corridors for trade and transport purposes and have the ability to engage in cooperation with their neighbors on what is actually a public good. Through infrastructure development and regulation of services, the public sector can be an important driver of corridor development, often leading market dynamics. The main objective is to create opportunities to trade or to enhance private sector competitiveness. Corridors can therefore emerge not as products of deliberate local level planning but of necessity to encourage trade.

In advanced economies and some coastal developing countries, the private sector has taken the lead in corridor development. It can have a clear sense of the benefits of developing a few key trade routes to help realize its objectives in supply chain organization or reduce trade costs.

Underlying the motives of either the public or private sectors in driving corridor development is an acknowledgement of the potential of scale effects. For instance, the government of South Africa (1999) emphasizes the ability of a corridor to connect major economic centers and to concentrate demand on a few routes between them. Such densification of demand can create conditions that attract the private sector to invest in large-scale infrastructure and services. Through a concentration of resources for development and demand, there can be greater returns on investment and benefits to firms and society.

In the development of international corridors, projects are most effective when they are prepared and launched in politically stable economies. The most thriving corridors are between countries that are linked not only geographically but also by the same willingness and commitment to develop the corridor. This commitment is important because each country entering into a corridor development arrangement does so with its national development as a primary objective but should recognize that this objective cannot be fully attained unless the common objective of collective welfare is also realized. For this reason, it is important to understand regional geopolitical and economic integration dynamics.

At the same time, trade and transport corridors are one of the priority strategies for opening up postconflict countries to trade with the outside world. In the immediate aftermath of conflict, it is more feasible to open up and secure a few trade routes to the outside world and to concentrate infrastructure investment and service provision on those routes than to design and implement a national transport program. During the civil war in Mozambique, for instance, the Southern African Development

Community (SADC) prioritized and mobilized resources to restore operations on one corridor at a time, starting with the Beira Corridor in 1985. The Beira Corridor links landlocked Malawi, Zambia, and Zimbabwe to the Port of Beira in Mozambique. Using this strategy, SADC was able to mobilize billions of dollars in the 1980s and 1990s to improve several corridors linking its landlocked member countries to ports in Angola, Mozambique, and Tanzania.

Corridor projects can be based on historical trade routes or greenfield developments (Sequiera 2013). Historical trade routes can date back decades or centuries. As a result of changes in economic and political circumstances, they may require new investments to modernize or increase capacity and operational efficiency. In various respects, improving historical trade routes is a bigger challenge than opening up new trade routes, as existing routes come with legacy issues of infrastructure, policies, and institutional jurisdictions. Yet at the same time, such routes would have a prima facie case for the need for the corridor, making estimates of demand and actions needed to improve performance easier to model and predict.

Greenfield developments aim to generate new productive capacity in previously undeveloped areas. They need new arrangements for agency cooperation capable of identifying needs and development planning. They require more robust analytical approaches to project demand and an optimal mix of components for a functional corridor.

Increasingly, the growth of cities and corridors is intertwined. Cities are shaped by good connections to domestic, regional, and international markets. Van Pelt (2003, p. 6) defines a corridor as a "stream of products, services and information moving within and through communities in geographical patterns." Corridors are an important conduit for such transmissions. Since the 19th century, corridors have been used to describe the systematic ordering of urban centers, with transport infrastructure serving as the main link between cities (Whebell 1969). Classical theory on the evolution of transport networks clearly shows the interaction between transport networks, development, and the growth of urban centers (Taaffe, Gauthier, and O'Kelly 1996). However, contemporary practice has been to approach corridor projects in isolation from the growth of urban centers. This practice has led to spatially linear development patterns in some countries along major trade routes, which can end up contributing to urban congestion by concentrating traffic flows on a few links. As a result, it becomes necessary to build by-passes around the most congested cities.

A common weakness in several corridor projects has been the tenuous or absent involvement of small centers and communities through which a corridor passes. The resultant corridors can have poor links to such communities, leading to a "bead" development pattern (Priemus 2001; Byiers 2013). In some instances, as trade corridors have thrived, the involvement of local communities has declined (Hall 2007). It is therefore important that all layers of government and communities be actively involved in corridor projects. Weak effects arise when regions accommodate infrastructure but do not benefit from it. Unless local communities are provided with access to international trade corridors and trade gateways (Kunaka 2010), the corridors are the equivalent of pipes, in that they may have restricted access. Corridors need to be supported by feeder routes, because local economic benefits can occur only if there are connections and goods can be offloaded or loaded or transshipped. Only when communities along a corridor are involved can a corridor play a transformative role.

Components and Functions of a Corridor

A corridor has three main categories of intertwined dimensions: infrastructure, services, and institutions for coordinating corridor activities (figure P.1).

In its most common configuration, a trade and transport corridor has an international gateway (for example, ports, airports, or a land border) at one end and a large metropolitan area or production cluster at the other. These gateways usually provide an intramodal or intermodal transfer (figure P.2). Additional gateways (for instance, regional airports or domestic seaports serving coastal or inland waterway corridors) may be located at an intermediate point in the corridor.

Gateways are included as part of a corridor because their capacity and quality of service can affect the cost of international movements.[1] In fact, as Arnold (2006) argues, some corridors are developed to increase traffic volumes at a gateway. For example, increasing utilization is the main objective of the Walvis Bay Corridor in Southern Africa. Similarly, there is a symbiotic relationship between the development of the Maputo Corridor and further investments in the Port of Maputo in Mozambique.

This Toolkit proposes that maritime transport should be explicitly modeled in corridor projects. Although improving port infrastructure on its own is essential, it is also important to consider the maritime shipping component as part of the international movement of goods. Hummels (2001) estimates that each day saved in shipping time is equivalent to about a 0.5 percent reduction in ad valorem tariffs. Although this figure differs by product, it underscores that corridor performance should include the total time it takes to ship goods from origin to destination. In most cases, the maritime

FIGURE P.1 The Infrastructure-Services-Institutions Nexus of Corridors

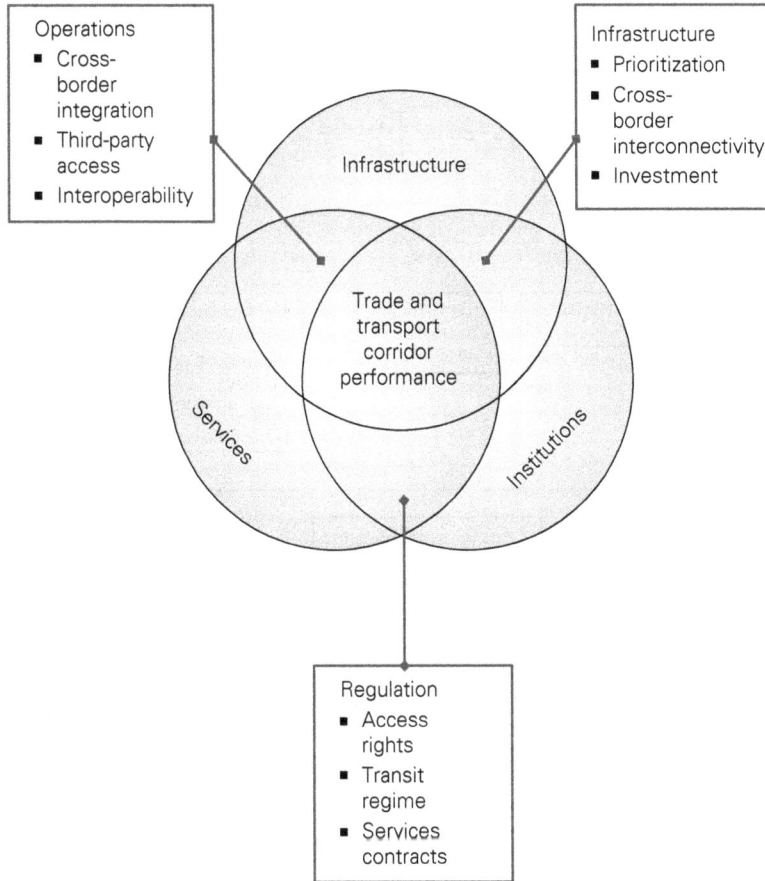

Operations
- Cross-border integration
- Third-party access
- Interoperability

Infrastructure
- Prioritization
- Cross-border interconnectivity
- Investment

Infrastructure

Trade and transport corridor performance

Services

Institutions

Regulation
- Access rights
- Transit regime
- Services contracts

shipping time is a significant proportion of the total time for the international delivery of goods. Although opportunities to improve international shipping may be limited, the choice of port gateway and how well connected it is to overseas ports can be a critical determinant of the attractiveness of a corridor.

Multimodal operations are common on most corridors. The Toolkit does not include a module dedicated to multimodal systems. Assessment of such systems is similar to that provided in the modules on different modes of transport. The main difference would be the performance and efficiency of the mode interface points. This aspect is addressed where mode interface facilities, such as dry ports, are dealt with in Part II of the Toolkit.

FIGURE P.2 Components of a Trade and Transport Corridor

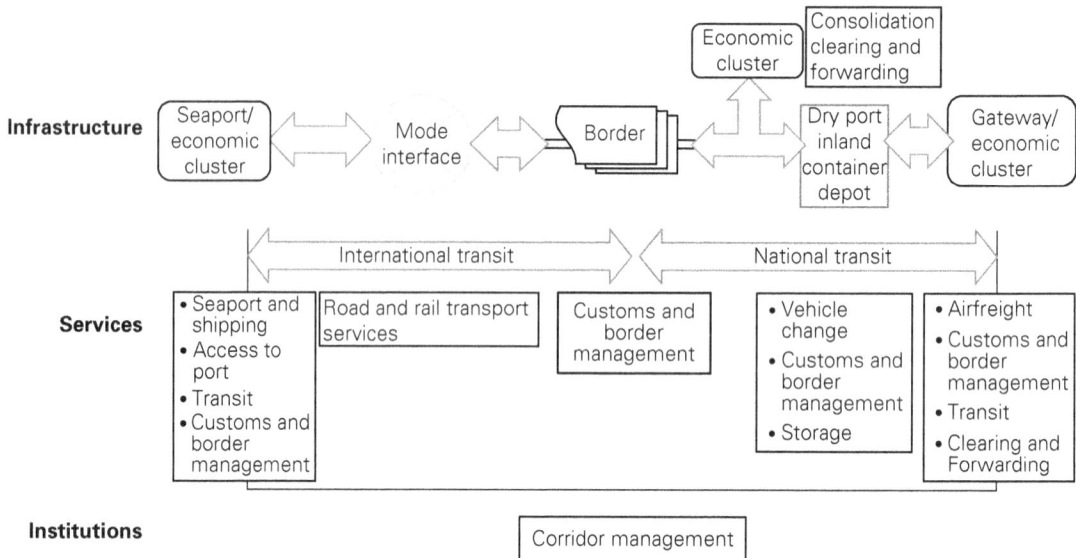

A corridor can play various functions. It can

- facilitate the prioritization of investments in infrastructure, policy reform, and services
- facilitate network effects, by promoting the consolidation of trade and transport volumes through a few links and nodes, which in turn can encourage improvement in quality of service
- influence spatial planning and development in subregions and countries served
- help enterprises optimize their production networks.

Prioritization of Interventions

Virtually every developing country and region wants a major trade route passing through it. Assigning different degrees of importance to such routes will aid in the allocation of resources. Transport and logistics infrastructure in a corridor can include all modes of transport and related facilities. This infrastructure includes roads (the main mode of carrying freight in cross-border trade in most countries), railways (which are particularly important in Europe and Central Asia), seaports, airports, border posts, and mode interchange facilities, such as dry ports. These elements typically account for about three-quarters of the project financing for a typical project.

Prioritization of infrastructure improvements should be carefully assessed along a corridor. It is important to verify the commitment of each party (country, agency) to realizing the corridor objectives by investing in critical infrastructure. Ideally, stretches of the corridor should have the same priority for each government concerned and be included as such in national programs and strategies for development (infrastructure, transport services, or trade, depending on the allocation of competencies among the ministries).

Interoperability is an imperative for efficient and effective trade. International corridors reduce fragmentation of jurisdictional, infrastructural, procedural, management, and other boundaries. Interoperability within and between transport modes is necessary for efficient and effective trade along a corridor; it can be achieved through harmonization of laws, institutional frameworks, norms, standards, and practices based on internationally agreed standards. The main goal of harmonization along corridors is to reduce to the extent possible the reasons for denied access to markets or for transportation purposes.

Analyzing priority ranking in connection with the availability of funding for corridor development gives an idea of the realism and capabilities of the government to plan and finance trade-related transport infrastructure. The analysis can lead to recommendations on the most appropriate measures for investment or actions by the corridor's management in cooperation with the governments concerned.

Infrastructure improvements have to be complemented by measures to improve the supply and quality of logistics services. Care should be taken to avoid significant discrepancies between theory and practice: in some cases, the regulatory framework is liberal, modern, and comprehensive but because of low or no enforcement, the market remains dominated by bad practices and its functioning continues to be unhealthy, impeding competition.

Transport and logistics services include all services related to the movement, handling, and processing of goods. They include transport services (road, rail, air, maritime); clearing and forwarding; customs and border management; warehousing; and other services. These services help move goods along a corridor. The transit and trade facilitation component usually includes the transit regime, modernization of customs, and improvements in border crossing. It could also include cargo tracking and tracing, improvement in intermodal surfaces, and other services. Most recent transport projects also include investments in port and airport safety improvements.

Network Effects

Corridors are subject to network effects: a critical mass of users is needed in order to lower costs for all users. There is a symbiotic relationship in that high-quality infrastructure and services can increase usage, which then encourages the provision of superior infrastructure and services, which in turn attract yet more traffic. In addition, indirect benefits are realized, as increased usage spawns the production of goods in regions served by the corridor. As a result, where corridor groups exist, one of their primary tasks is to promote and market a corridor. Consequently, assessing the impact of a corridor should extend beyond the direct effects to estimating wider impacts as well. (Module 13 covers approaches to assessing the impacts of corridor improvement or development.)

Spillover effects from developing international corridors are maximized when improvements on one side of a border encourage traffic generation or improvements in services on the other side. In most cases, the effects extend beyond the limits of the immediate area of the project. It is in this regard that spillover effects are a product of network effects and also give rise to transfers of costs and benefits to other regions. However, in most projects the estimation of such effects is still at a very nascent stage; estimates have been attempted in only a few developed regions, such as Europe.

One of the major challenges faced with corridors is determining the area or region that will be affected. Burghardt (1971) shows that corridors integrate the territorial functions of economic systems and the distribution functions of transport systems and that trade gateways have influence and control over a definable hinterland. It is therefore necessary to define the geographical region that forms a corridor's catchment area. However, most countries, including landlocked countries, have access to several competing corridors, complicating the assessment of effects of the development of any one corridor. Their catchment areas and therefore their impacts can overlap, complicating the process of attribution of effects from individual interventions.

Corridors serving landlocked countries are a special case. In low-income landlocked countries, the problem of distance is exacerbated by physical, bureaucratic, regulatory, and legal barriers associated with crossing borders. Low trade volumes limit the bargaining power of such countries with global logistics groups, often forcing them to rely on foreign intermediaries to consolidate shipments. As argued above, the corridor approach offers advantages to these countries in accessing higher-quality infrastructure that helps consolidate flows, which in turn justify higher-quality infrastructure and services.

Regional Development

Corridors are sometimes developed to promote growth in specific regions. Fundamental to the concept of development corridors is the presence of inherent economic potential, usually in the form of a natural resource, such as minerals, timber, or agriculture. Development or resource corridors seek to maximize public and private sector investments and related actions in order to multiply economic returns and benefits. Investments typically have to include both hard and soft infrastructure. The emphasis has to be on the transformational impact of the corridor. In this regard, resource corridors seek to achieve a sequencing of investments to leverage a large investment by an extractive industry in infrastructure, goods, and services into viable economic development in a defined geographic region.

The few cases in which governments have tried to use the development corridor approach have not always been successful in attracting private sector investment, especially in Africa. They have not involved all key stakeholders in the definition of the projects from the beginning. Particularly in development corridors, it is critical to involve several sectors with stakes in the region and corridor. A key to success is to coordinate across borders and involve small-scale enterprises, in order to increase volumes. The development corridor approach has to be holistic in promoting efficient integrated production. It must nurture supply chains that are regionally and globally competitive.

Most successful development corridors also have an "anchor" project and a champion, who leads their definition and promotion. According to Sequiera (2013), having a viable anchor project with significant backward and forward linkages in the economy is critical to the success of a developmental corridor. Without such a project, the corridor may fail to reach the critical mass of economic activity that makes further transport investments viable.

Feeder connections through secondary and tertiary networks are important to extend the impact of a corridor into neighboring areas. In their study of India, Ghani, Goswami, and Kerr (2013) find that the region of direct impact of road improvements was 10 kilometers on either side of the improved network (see Module 13). The extent of the area depends largely on the quality of the secondary networks and the availability of services to connect to the core network.

A corridor can therefore become both a product and an instrument of spatial planning in a country and a region (box P.1). As such, a corridor necessarily has to change with the changing character of transport, trade, and its impact on countries, communities, and institutions. There has been much debate about whether there is progression from purely transport to trade to development corridors. Corridors evolve over time as a result of changes in technology, planning, infrastructure, and policy initiatives. However, evidence and experience suggest that the evolution is not as linear as implied in some regional strategies.

Integrated Corridor Development in Maputo

The Maputo Corridor comprises the port, road, rail, pipeline, border post, and logistics services connecting northern Swaziland and the industrial core region of South Africa and the Port of Maputo in Mozambique. It links several intermediate centers in northeast South Africa (Witbank, Middleburg, Nelspruit, and Komatipoort) and the main sugar cane–growing region regions of Swaziland to Maputo.

The corridor has gone through several phases of development. It is now one of the most successful corridors in Africa, in terms of both the quality of its infrastructure and service and its development impact. At its peak, in the mid-1970s, the Maputo Corridor handled more than 14 million tonnes of cargo a year, most of it from South Africa. Following a protracted civil war in Mozambique, traffic volumes fell to 1 million tonnes by 1992, when all South African traffic had to be diverted to domestic ports.

Since the mid-1990s, the governments of South Africa and Mozambique have worked closely to reopen the corridor to South African and Swazi shippers. The two countries have promoted the rehabilitation of core infrastructure (road, rail, border post, port and dredging of the port, power, and information and communications technology [ICT]) using private sector financing and joint concessioning, particularly of the road. The initiative has led to more than $5 billion worth of investments along the corridor in both countries.

In addition, the governments have promoted exploitation of economic opportunity along the corridor, making Maputo a development corridor in the proper sense. There has been a deliberate effort to connect communities along the path of the corridor, especially communities that are economically disadvantaged. Estimates are that more than 15,000 direct jobs have been created in transport, logistics, agriculture, and mining ventures along the corridor. The infrastructure and service improvement has been accompanied from the beginning by related institutional mechanisms culminating in the Maputo Corridor Logistics Initiative in 2004. The initiative emphasizes maximizing the investment potential of the corridor and exploiting all opportunities that rehabilitation of infrastructure creates. It also serves as a private sector–led corridor management and facilitation organization.

Source: Based on Sequeira 2013.

Supply Chain Organization

At its core a corridor is about facilitating supply chains. A corridor connects locations using different modes of transport to link production and distribution centers. PriceWaterhouseCoopers (2010) maintains that mapping a corridor is in essence mapping a series of connected clusters of economic activity. Corridors can therefore be visualized as reflecting the decisions made by different parties on how to organize production, distribution, and supply to capture regional specialization. As such, a corridor is not just a physical concept; it also represents the strategic decisions and choices developed and made by firms, municipalities, and governments to attract increased flows of commodities to particular regions generated by deepening economic integration (Van Pelt 2003). The success of a corridor is thus in part a function of the coalitions that parties are able to form to attract investments and improve performance. How the parties collaborate to manage a corridor is a key dimension of the definition of a corridor. Institutional and economic relationships are part and parcel of a corridor, especially in the presence of competing trade routes (box P.2).

Framework for Institutional Collaboration

The institutional component covers the arrangements for cooperation and collaboration by the parties involved in a corridor. Bender (2001) rightly points out that corridors provide a spatial context for analyzing and organizing development support, which transcends institutions and international boundaries. There are several multidonor initiatives on corridor development, such as the TradeMark East Africa or the Central Asia Regional Economic Cooperation (CAREC) initiatives in Central and South Asia. Such initiatives cut across traditional political, social, and economic boundaries. The institutional arrangements of a corridor include mechanisms to support trade facilitation, strengthen corridor logistics capacity, and build capacity for managing projects. In some instances, this component may include efforts to promote private sector participation in the management of roads.

Corridors are about cooperation between public agencies, between the public and private sectors, and between private sector enterprises. Multisectoral representation and participation of the private sector are sine qua non conditions for successful trade and transport corridors. A corridor is therefore a spatial structure for overcoming the fragmentation of legal, institutional, physical, and practical boundaries. There are many different types of institutional and administrative arrangements for corridors;

Example of Impact of a Corridor on Supply Chain Organization

Most countries are served by competing trade routes. Corridor users therefore often have a choice of corridor. In South Africa, the main citrus-growing area is 480 kilometers closer to Maputo, in Mozambique, than it is to the domestic port of Durban. Despite this advantage, only 8 percent of citrus exports are shipped on the Maputo Corridor; the rest are shipped via domestic routes to Durban.

Two main problems explain this pattern. First, delays at the border post between South Africa and Mozambique negate the lower transport costs by road. Second, and more important, Maputo has fewer shipping lines servicing the port. The Port of Durban, the largest and busiest port on the continent, has shipping access to all key citrus markets. Currently, the only markets serviced from Maputo on a dedicated shipping schedule are Europe and the Mediterranean markets. In order to increase the throughput of Maputo, shipping access to other key markets, such as the Russian Federation and the Middle East, need to be serviced on a dedicated schedule.

This example illustrates two important issues, which influenced the design and content of this Toolkit. First, corridor design has to explicitly reflect the behavior of likely users. With competing trade routes, the decisions of shippers and their ability to reorganize their supply chains will influence the magnitude of the impact of corridor interventions. Second, maritime shipping services affect overland traffic assignment across a corridor network.

some are voluntary, others are legally binding commitments between authorities of the countries crossed by the corridor.

The ideal arrangement is one in which each of the parties involved has the same level of willingness, commitment, power, and influence over developments and interventions. The concept of heterarchy is probably closest to the essence of corridor management. Heterarchy is "self-organized steering of multiple agencies, institutions, and systems that are operationally autonomous from one another yet structurally coupled as a result of their mutual interdependence" (de Vries and Priemus 2003, p. 226). Command and control type approaches, though common, are less effective, because corridor components are spatially and institutionally distributed and complex. The ability to build coalitions is therefore probably more important than geography in improving a trade and transport corridor.

The soft aspects of corridor projects may not cost a lot of money, but they can be the most important. Financing of components related to trade facilitation in a corridor project represents about 10 percent of the total for trade and transport corridor projects financed by the World Bank. Both the East Africa Trade and Transport Facilitation Project and the Southern Africa Trade and Transport Facilitation Project have separate components on trade facilitation. Another measure that can reduce costs but is not costly to implement is the monitoring of corrupt and other informal practices, which can be prevalent on some corridors, affecting cost, time, and reliability. Corrupt practices are most visible at border-crossing points and checkpoints en route. The checkpoints are typically mounted by the uniformed officials from security or regulatory agencies, including customs. However, often it is not easy to obtain data on who is responsible or how much it costs (in money and time) to obtain clearance to proceed.

Note

1. For example, providing faster and more reliable turnaround for international conveyance will stimulate growth in trade and attract larger, more efficient conveyances.

References

Arnold, J. 2006. "Best Practices in Management of International Trade Corridors." Transport Paper TP-13, World Bank, Washington, DC.

Bender, S. 2001. "Trade Corridors: The Emerging Regional Development Planning Unit in Latin America." Organization of American States, Unit for Sustainable Development and Environment, Washington, DC.

Burghardt, A. F. 1971. "A Hypothesis about Gateway Cities." *Annals of the Association of American Geographers* 61 (2): 269–85.

Byiers, B. 2013. "Corridors of Power and Plenty? Lessons from Tanzania and Mozambique and Implications for CAADP." Discussion Paper 138, European Center for Development and Policy Management, Maastricht.

de Vries, J., and H. Priemus. 2003. "Megacorridors in North-West Europe: Issues for Transnational Spatial Governance." *Journal of Transport Geography* 11: 225–33.

Ghani, E., A. Grover Goswami, and W. R. Kerr. 2013. "Highway to Success in India: The Impact of the Golden Quadrilateral Project for the Location and Performance of Manufacturing." Policy Research Working Paper WPS6320, World Bank, Washington, DC.

Government of South Africa. 1999. *Moving South Africa: The Action Agenda: A 20-year Strategic Framework for Transport in South Africa*. Pretoria: Government of South Africa.

Hall, P. 2007. "Global Logistics and Local Dilemmas." Paper presented at the International Conference on Gateways and Corridors, Vancouver, May 2–4.

Hummels, D. 2001. "Time as a Trade Barrier." GTAP Working Paper 1152, Center for Global Trade Analysis, Department of Agricultural Economics, Purdue University, Lafayette, IN.

Kunaka, C. 2010. *Logistics in Lagging Regions*. Washington, DC: World Bank.

PriceWaterHouseCoopers. 2010. *Transport & Logistics 2030. Volume 3: Emerging Markets—New Hubs, New Spokes, New Industry Leaders?* http://www.pwc.com /en_GX/gx/transportation-logistics/tl2030/emerging-markets/pdf/tl2030_vol3 _final.pdf.

Priemus, H. 2001. "Corridors in the Netherlands: Apple of Discord in Spatial Planning." *Tijdschrift voor Economische en Sociale Geografie* 92 (1): 100–07.

Sequiera, S. 2013. "Transport Corridors and Economic Growth in Africa: Evidence from the Maputo Corridor." World Bank, Sub-Saharan Africa Transport Policy Program, Washington, DC.

Taaffe, E. J., H. L. Gauthier, and M. E. O'Kelly. 1996. *Geography of Transportation*. Englewood Cliffs, NJ: Prentice-Hall.

Van Pelt, M. 2003. *Moving Trade: An Introduction to Trade Corridors*. Hamilton, Canada: World Research Foundation.

Whebell, C. F. J. 1969. "Corridors: A Theory of Urban Systems." *Annals of the Association of American Geographers* 59 (1): 1–26.

Resources

Adzigbey, Y., C. Kunaka, and T. N. Mitiku. 2007. "Institutional Arrangements for Transport Corridor Management in Sub-Saharan Africa." SSATP Working Paper 86, World Bank, Sub-Saharan Africa Transport Policy Program, Washington, DC.

Arvis, J. F., R. Carruthers, G. Smith, and C. Willoughby. 2011 *Connecting Landlocked Developing Countries to Markets: Trade Corridors in the 21st Century*. Washington, DC: World Bank.

Blank, S. 2006. "North American Trade Corridors: An Initial Exploration in Notes and Analyses on the USA." Université de Montreal, Lubin School of Business, Montreal.

Brunner, H.-P., and P. M. Allen. 2000. *A Sub-Regional Development Approach— Transport, International Trade, and Investment Modeled in Space*. December. http://ssrn.com/abstract=258429 or doi:10.2139/ssrn.258429.

Chapman, D., D. Pratt, P. Larkham, and I. Dickins. 2003. "Concepts and Definitions of Corridors: Evidence from England's Midlands." *Journal of Transport Geography* 11: 79–191.

Darren, F., and T. Notteboom. 2012. "Corridor Strategies: The Integration of the Southern African Container Port Hubs and Intermediate Hubs with Port Hinterlands." Paper presented at the Asian Logistics Roundtable and Conference, Vancouver, June 14–15.

Hummels, D., and G. Schaur. 2012. "Time as a Trade Barrier." NBER Working Paper 17758, National Bureau of Economic Research, Cambridge, MA.

Molnár, A., X. Gellynck, and B. Kühne. 2007. "Conceptual Framework for Measuring Supply Chain Performance: An Innovative Approach." Paper presented at the First International European Forum on Innovation and System Dynamics in Food Networks Officially endorsed by the European Association of Agricultural Economists, Innsbruck-Igls, Austria, February 15–17.

Norling, N., and N. Swanström. 2007. "The Virtues and Potential Gains of Continental Trade in Eurasia." *Asian Survey* 47 (3): 351–73.

Pain, K. 2011. "'New Worlds' for 'Old'? Twenty-First-Century Gateways and Corridors: Reflections on a European Spatial Perspective." *International Journal of Urban and Regional Research* 35 (6): 1154–74.

Pelletier, J.-F., and Y. Alix. 2011. "Benchmarking the Integration of Corridors in International Value Networks: The Study of African Cases." In *Integrating Seaports and Trade Corridors*, edited by P. Hall, R. J. McCalla, C. Comtois, and B. Slack, 173–92. Farnham, United Kingdom: Ashgate.

Priemus, P., and W. Zonneveld. 2003. "What Are Corridors and What Are the Issues? Introduction to Special Issue: The Governance of Corridors." *Journal of Transport Geography* 11: 167–77.

Söderbaum, F., and I. Taylor. 2001. "Transmission Belt for Transnational Capital or Facilitator for Development? Problematising the Role of the State in the Maputo Development Corridor." *Journal of Modern African Studies* 39 (4): 675–95.

UEMOA (Union Economique et Monétaire Ouest Africaine). Various years. *Road Governance Reports*. http://www.watradehub.com/activities/calendar/borderless-2013-connecting-markets.

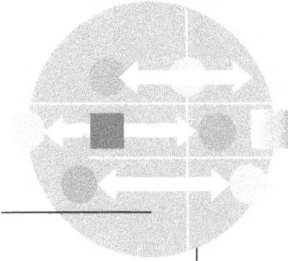

PART I

Corridor Diagnostic and Performance Assessment

Carrying out a detailed diagnostic of a corridor is an important first step in determining its operational performance, identifying bottlenecks to the flow of traffic, and recommending potential improvement measures. The assessment should cover the quality and performance of corridor infrastructure logistics services and institutions. It should include all agencies and parties that provide infrastructure and services in the corridor, as well as agencies that formulate and implement policies and regulations that affect corridor operations. It should identify the critical data that should be collected during assessment, including key performance indicators. The collection of primary data is often required, as data on corridors are generally not readily available. The output of a diagnostic should be a detailed report describing the corridor and its component parts, the services it offers, the parties and agencies involved, and the level of performance and prioritizing interventions to improve corridor performance.

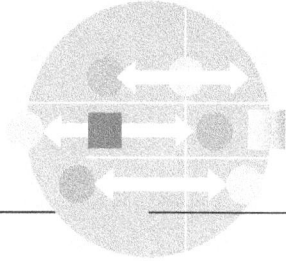

Carrying Out a Corridor Diagnostic

An important first step in developing a corridor project is the initial diagnostic to determine operational performance, diagnose impediments, and identify potential improvement measures. This diagnostic requires that both quantitative and qualitative data be collected. The diagnostic is carried out in consultation with logistics service providers, importers, shippers, and government agencies involved in the logistics and transportation sectors.

This module describes the approaches to executing a corridor diagnostic, which should cover all components of a corridor using robust, reliable, repeatable, and cost-effective techniques. Comprehensive assessments of corridor performance and operation are needed by nearly all development institutions and national authorities as part of their planned or ongoing work. The component-specific assessments are discussed in Part II of the Toolkit.

A corridor assessment is typically originated by a government, private agency acting on behalf of the government, financing agency, or private sector stakeholders. From a government perspective, it could be a ministry of trade, a ministry of transport, a trade and transport facilitation committee, or a corridor body. Information on actual transport and logistics performance is also generated by international development agencies, such as the World Bank and regional development banks. Such information is collected to deepen understanding of the current situation and to help identify opportunities for investment.

This module is organized as follows. The first section emphasizes the importance of setting an appropriate objective for a corridor assessment. The nature of the assessment depends on the expected use of the resultant report. The second section identifies sources of data and approaches for setting the macro-level context of a corridor. The third section examines the key considerations in analyzing corridor infrastructure. The fourth section examines logistics services. The last section provides a suite of tools used to understand how a corridor is performing and its main components. It also presents approaches to continuous monitoring of performance. Annex 1A elaborates the various issues that have to be considered in carrying out a corridor assessment.

Setting the Objective

The first step in carrying out a diagnostic is to clarify the purpose. Different parties may have very different objectives, which need to be recognized at the outset of the planning of the collection of data to minimize later discussions. The specific objective is determined by the organization for which the assessment is conducted. Examples of objectives can be to

- identify bottlenecks and their impact on the efficiency and reliability of logistics services
- promote regional corridors in order to promote regional cooperation and coordination of infrastructure and services
- identify opportunities for reform as advocated by corridor stakeholders.

Information is categorized as either general contextual information or specific information on the corridor and its components. The coverage of the assessment will depend in part on whether the assessment is a one-off effort or will be repeated. Repeat assessments are usually needed to monitor the impact of any corridor interventions. Table 1.1 summarizes the types of information collected.

Conducting a Strategic Assessment

Table 1.2 summarizes the main approaches to a strategic assessment of a corridor. Several tools and techniques can be combined for a holistic assessment.

Assessing a corridor should start by establishing the general national and regional context in terms of infrastructure, services, institutions, and policies.

TABLE 1.1 Key Data Collected for a Corridor Assessment

Item	Infrastructure		Trade and transport institutions	Transport operators	Services	
	Facilities	Terminal operators			Logistics services	Shippers
Scope of functional role	Planning, implementation, maintenance, public-private partnerships	Operations, equipment, superstructure	Regulatory responsibilities, enforcement role	Type of services provided, cargo type, hinterland served	Scope of services provided	Control of supply chain
Performance parameters	Capacity, demand, condition, size of transport units, cost of use, reliability	Capacity, terminal charges, reliability, equipment	Number of facilities, regulatory capacity	Fleet size, age distribution, vehicle capacity, traffic level, availability	Number and size of shipments, facilities, structure of industry	Volume, shipment size
Level of performance	Utilization	Average productivity, delay and dwell times (time it takes to pass through each component)	Average delay and processing times	Transit times, unit vehicle operating costs	Cost of service as percent of delivered value	Delivery times, order fulfillment, logistics costs
Extent of supply chain integration, document simplification	Intermodal connections	Downstream storage and transport services	Subcontracts, integration of information communications technology (ICT)	Multimodal services, distribution/ collection storage	House bills, regional and international shipments	Linkage to suppliers and final markets
Agreements, regulations, and policies	Standards, sources of funds	Concessions, leases, economic regulation	Regional and international legal instruments	Weight restrictions, certifications, quotas	Certification of service providers, multimodal transport operators, right to issue house bills	Cost of compliance
Impediments to efficiency	Planning and budgeting, dispersed responsibility	Weak access and poor coordination with regulators	Poor documentation, misrepresentation, weak ICT systems	Levels of duties and taxes, geographic restrictions, inadequate market information	Weak ICT connectivity with regulatory authorities and clients	Unpredictable times for transport and border crossings
Opportunities for improvement	Increase investment, harmonize standards, establish public-private partnerships, review user fees, remove bottlenecks	Improve ICT systems and services	Better coordinate border management, improve route management systems, reengineer transit regimes, make greater use of ICT	Improve financing, performance contracts; replace equipment, ICT	Improve ICT, supply chain management	Expand bonded storage, expedite clearance

TABLE 1.2 Tools and Techniques Used in a National or Regional Strategic Corridor Assessment

Purpose	Data sources, tools, and techniques
• Determine trade flows within corridor countries and between corridor countries and rest of the world	• International and regional freight flow modeling (using gravity models, for example)
• Compare performance relative to other countries	• International indices (for example, Logistics Performance Index) and benchmarking
• Determine extent of global connectivity	• Connectivity indices (for example, Liner Shipping Connectivity Index)
• Identify major constraints and opportunities for improvement	• Trade and Transport Facilitation Assessment

The purpose of this step is to understand the environment, which can explain current performance and prospects for its improvement. Information on the trade facilitation environment in a country or set of countries can usually be gleaned from published sources of the relevant agencies or from associations of service providers involved in the corridor. Sources of published data that are relevant to corridor assessment include the United Nations (COMTRADE); the World Bank; the International Monetary Fund (IMF); and international governmental and nongovernmental transport organizations, such as the International Road Transport Union (IRU), the Airports Council International, the International Civil Aviation Organization, and the International Union of Railways. Other sources of data include trade and transport publications, such as *Containerisation International* and *Air Cargo World*, and the websites of the operators of gateways (seaports, airports, inland terminals) and the government agencies responsible for corridor infrastructure. Additional information can be obtained from studies by multinational or bilateral aid agencies or government committees.

Data from secondary sources need to be complemented by other sources and techniques. Some important sources of data include the following:

- United Nations (UN) agencies and the World Trade Organization (WTO)
- international indexes, such as the Logistics Performance Index, Doing Business indicators, and the World Economic Forum's *Global Enabling Trade Report*
- firm-level survey (for example, from World Bank's Enterprise Survey)
- connectivity indexes.

UN Agencies and the World Trade Organization

One of the first tasks in conducting a corridor diagnostic is to determine the volume and types of current and future traffic in the corridor. At a minimum, estimates of traffic are based on projections of the volume of trade between corridor countries and with third countries. Estimates of the growth of the trade that may move along the corridor of interest should be made.

Trade corridors are developed to facilitate the movement of trade and transport traffic between centers of demand or countries. Trade flows are the basic demand for transport and logistics services.

Trade data can be obtained from various sources, including the following:

- The COMTRADE database, maintained by the UN Statistics Division, provides data on exports and imports by detailed commodity and partner country.
- The Trade Analysis Information System (TRAINS), maintained by UN Conference on Trade and Development (UNCTAD), provides data on imports, tariffs, para-tariffs, and nontariff measures at the national level.
- The Integrated Data Base (IDB) and Consolidated Tariff Schedule (CTS) databases, maintained by the WTO, provide data on most favored nation (MFN) applied, preferential, and bound tariffs at the national level.

Estimating Future Volumes of Traffic

A widely used approach to estimating volumes of traffic or trade in the future is gravity modeling (figure 1.1 shows a flow diagram used for a corridor study in East and Southern Africa). Transport (rather than trade) gravity models can be used to assess the change in the volume of freight that might result from transport time or cost savings as a result of corridor improvements. This growth might stem from trips diverted from other routes or corridors or from newly generated trips. The approach is best applied to the infrastructure components of a corridor project. It is more difficult to apply to the policy components. It is rarely used to evaluate a package of corridor improvements. More frequently, it is applied to individual components of such a package.

Gravity models are not perfect. Although they can be used to estimate the impact of trade growth, most trade gravity models do not rely on estimates of reductions in transport costs and times as the basis for those impacts. Moreover, the models can be difficult and time consuming to apply and rely on massive trade and transport cost databases for their application. Few corridor projects have the resources to develop and apply such models.

FIGURE 1.1 Flow Diagram of Methodology for Scenario Trade Flow Forecasting Using a Gravity Model

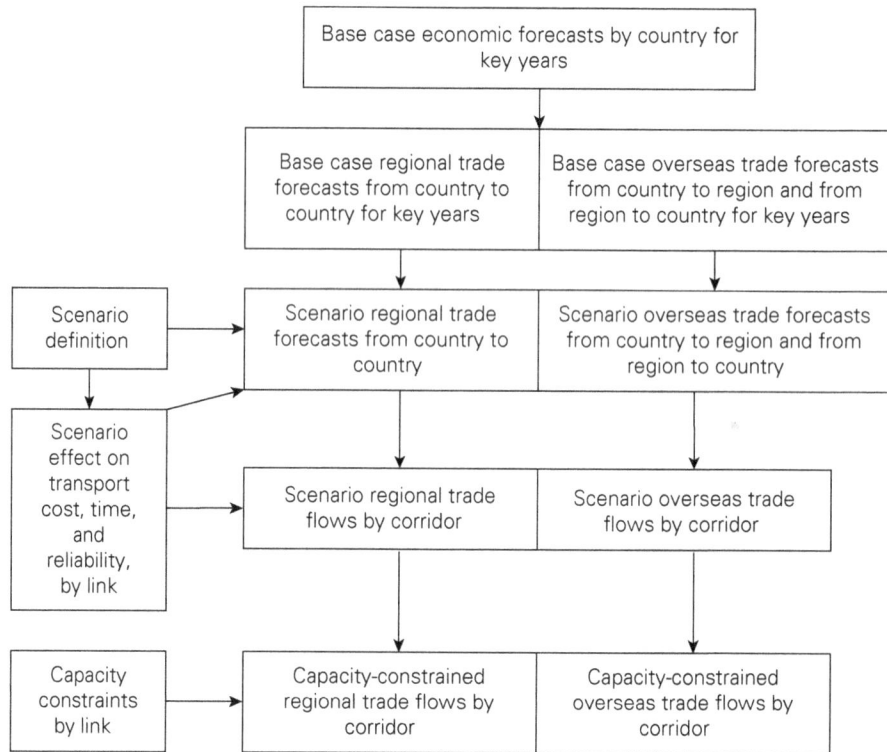

Source: Nathan Associates 2011.

Data from International Indices

International indices can be good sources of data to describe the general context of a corridor. The two most relevant indices are the Logistics Performance Index (LPI) and the Trading Across Borders component of Doing Business, both generated and maintained by the World Bank.

The LPI comprises a set of parameters that measure the logistics performance of countries. The data for the LPI are gathered from managerial-level personnel of international freight forwarding firms worldwide. They can therefore be considered to represent the experience of a large range of logistics providers and buyers.

The LPI consists of international and domestic components. The international LPI is based on the assessment of foreign operators located in the country's major trading partners. It is a weighted average of six components:

- the efficiency of the clearance process (the speed, simplicity, and predictability of formalities) by border control agencies, including customs
- the quality of trade- and transport-related infrastructure (ports, railroads, roads, information technology)
- the ease of arranging competitively priced shipments
- the competence and quality of logistics services (transport operators, customs brokers)
- the ability to track and trace consignments
- the timeliness of shipments in reaching their destination within the scheduled or expected delivery time.

The domestic LPI is based on logistics professionals' assessments of the country in which they work. It contains detailed information on individual aspects of logistics performance, such as

- the quality of trade-related infrastructure
- the competence of service providers
- the efficiency of border procedures
- the time and cost of moving goods across borders.

Taken together, the two parts of the LPI provide a picture of the structural and other issues affecting trade facilitation and logistics in a country. They also indicate the relative logistics performance of corridor countries. The highest level of performance of a corridor is typically influenced by the weakest component and the performance of the weakest country. Figure 1.2 displays the LPI of four countries in Southeast Asia. An assessment of the North-South corridor in the Greater Mekong subregion would reveal that the Lao People's Democratic Republic has the weakest performance of the four countries in the corridor. It would therefore be expected that improvements there, compared with other countries, would have a greater impact on overall corridor performance.

A different approach to strategic-level indicators has been used by the World Bank in its Doing Business surveys. The Doing Business database provides indicators of the cost of doing business by identifying specific regulations that enhance or constrain business investment, productivity, and growth. The data are collected from the study of existing laws and regulations in each economy and from targeted interviews with regulators or private sector professionals, donor agencies, private consulting firms, and business and law associations. Other datasets that can provide complementary information include the European Bank for Reconstruction and Development's

FIGURE 1.2 Comparative Logistics Performance in Southeast Asia, Based on the Logistics Performance Index

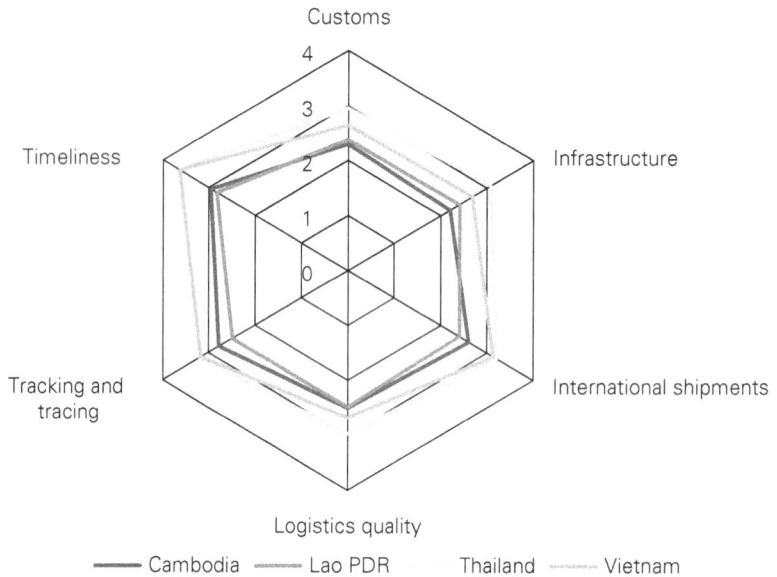

Source: World Bank estimates, based on data from World Bank 2012.

Transition Report, the World Economic Forum's *Global Competitiveness Report*, and the Fraser Institute's *Economic Freedom of the World*.

The most directly relevant component of Doing Business is Trading Across Borders (TAB), which provides information relevant to the strategic context of a corridor. Freight forwarders, shipping lines, customs brokers, and port officials provide information on the required documents, cost, and time to complete each procedure. TAB is based on a few assumptions about the business (size, ownership, location, exports) and the traded products. It compiles procedural requirements for exporting and importing a standardized cargo of goods. Every official procedure for exporting and importing the goods is recorded, along with the time and cost necessary for completion. All documents required for clearance of the goods across the border are also recorded. For exporting goods, TAB covers all procedures from the packing of the goods at the factory to their departure from the port of exit. For importing goods, TAB covers all procedures from the vessel's arrival at the port of entry to the cargo's delivery at the factory warehouse.

TAB is valuable to understanding the time and cost of trading. The data are published annually, so they can be used to determine a general trend in trade facilitation. TAB can also be used to monitor major reforms. However, the TAB data reflect de jure legal reforms and are not always provided by people directly involved in international logistics.

Assessing Corridor Infrastructure

Various types of infrastructure in a corridor should be included in the assessment. Technical parameters are particularly important in assessing the continuity and homogeneity of the corridor (table 1.3). It is difficult, for instance, for a rail corridor with more than one gauge, a road corridor with several low clearances, or an inland waterway with narrow locks or unpredictable depth to attain sound facilitation objectives.

When developing a corridor, it is usually helpful if the countries concerned are contracting parties to international multilateral agreements

TABLE 1.3 Main Issues in Assessing Corridor Infrastructure

Parameter	Main issue
Length and condition of core infrastructure (ports, roads, rails, inland waterways)	What is the extent and condition of transport infrastructure in each country, including inland container depots and dry ports? Are there missing links or links in poor condition?
Geographical alignment of core corridor transport infrastructure between economic centers in corridor countries	Are the corridor link alignments optimal in linking existing or planned economic centers (cities, mines, dry ports, sea ports, and so forth)?
Technical parameters (national or international harmonization and interoperability)	What is the degree of technical harmonization of infrastructure standards along the corridor?
Delineation of corridor hinterland, including branches (length, formalization, inclusion in the corridor, priority ranking)	How well is the corridor connected to surrounding regions and offline centers? What is the potential of the corridor to evolve from a transport to an economic and development corridor?
Modal complementarities and competition	Does the corridor infrastructure permit intermodal or multimodal operations? Is there appropriate equipment for the transfer of cargo between modes?
Funding availability (commitment, national budget, joint funds, grants, and so forth)	Do the corridor governments attach the same priority to financing and maintaining the corridor infrastructure?
Border infrastructure	Is there appropriate border-crossing infrastructure along the corridor?
Node and link capacity	What is the capacity of the different components of the corridor? Are there parts of the corridor in which demand exceeds infrastructure capacity? What are the node-related costs and charges?
Road safety performance (road safety audits, parking places and other facilities, and so forth)	How safe is the corridor? Can accident "blackspots" be identified and addressed? What health and other infrastructure is available along the corridor?

that define technical norms, standards, and parameters for infrastructure.[1] An alternative is for the parties to agree on specific technical parameters at the corridor level. If this path is taken, the parameters should be at least at the level of the international ones, in order to integrate the corridor into a regional network and avoid missing opportunities from technological development, prevent incompatibility with imported transport means, and ensure good safety performance.

The collection of data on transport infrastructure in the corridor can be from secondary sources, such as publications or annual reports of the different infrastructure operators, as well as interviews with the responsible government and private sector entities. Some of the data for highways can be obtained from a combination of official sources. For instance, highway departments normally collect and keep data used in planning models such as the Highway Development and Management Model (HDM4). Those data can be directly relevant to assessing corridor infrastructure improvements and their likely impact. Data should be collected on three aspects of the corridor:

- the physical characteristics of infrastructure and its condition
- quantitative data on individual infrastructure components of the corridor
- plans for proposed developments and maintenance of the infrastructure.

Data needs are often well defined for core infrastructure for ports, roads, railways, and inland waterways. They also need to be collected for facilities such as inland container depots (see Module 10).

Assessing Logistics Services

A common approach to collecting data for assessing logistics services in a corridor involves interviews with government agencies, traders, freight forwarders, and transport operators. Data can be collected in the form of a Trade and Transport Facilitation Assessment (TTFA) that is focused on a corridor.

The TTFA is a tool developed by the World Bank to evaluate the competitiveness of trade and the quality of logistics services used for trade. It has two components. The first focuses on public policy that affects trade and logistics. The second examines the performance of the supply chains used by importers and exporters. Both components draw on background research and interviews to identify constraints to and opportunities for improving competitiveness and the quality of service.

Interviews are carried out with the parties responsible for managing gateways, providing cargo-handling services, and regulating trade through these gateways. These are the same people who are best able to provide the information needed for putting together corridor monitoring indicators, so it is relatively straightforward to ensure that the relevant questions and answers are included in the structured interviews. Also interviewed for the same reasons are shippers, both importers and exporters. Among the groups able to provide information are chambers of commerce; trade, exporters, and shippers councils; and associations of freight forwarders, air cargo agents, and customs clearance agents. Discussions are held with senior officials involved in customs policy, border terminal management, agricultural and phyto-sanitary controls, and trade agreements. These interviews are normally conducted by technical experts familiar with trade and logistics or their representatives.

The TTFA can be used to collect information on the scope of activities, which identifies both the sequential activities the respondent is involved in (for example, transport and storage, forwarding and transport, long-distance transport and local distribution) and the variety of services offered in terms of different combinations of time and cost for movement through the corridor, including the gateway. The information collected on performance is primarily quantitative, concerning the time, cost, and reliability of the services provided in the corridor, including information on delays and discretionary use of storage. Data are also collected on freight rates and operating costs for transport services to assess the importance of factors other than costs on setting rates.

Information on the scale of activities includes the size of the transport units used for movement within the corridor and for international movement.

Information on documentary requirements identifies the extent to which the format has been simplified, standardized, and harmonized. It also determines the extent to which these documents are exchanged electronically. Coordination between sequential activities is examined by questions regarding the extent to which prior or subsequent activities are scheduled or coordinated through exchange of information on the status of these activities in real time.

Questions regarding regulations affecting services examine the impact on competition, availability, efficiency, and reliability of those services. Regulations in trade and transport agreements that affect the efficiency and reliability of cross-border movements include the following:

- restrictions on the cross-border movement of vehicles
- bilateral quotas and qualifications (bonds) affecting transport operators

- limitations on third-country transport operators transiting the country
- documentation and guarantee required for temporary admission of cargo
- duties, taxes, and transit fees applied to vehicles and cargo moving on the corridor
- arrangements for clearance of cargo behind the border
- acceptance of multicountry vehicle insurance and guarantees for potential liabilities with regard to duties and taxes.

Data from TTFA interviews can be used to provide an holistic assessment of a corridor. As such, a TTFA can be used to generate baseline values on the performance of a corridor. Another valuable contribution of a TTFA is its ability to provide information on competing routes that serve the same hinterland (box 1.1). This information can be valuable in identifying the characteristics of any one trade corridor that give it a competitive advantage or place it at a disadvantage.

BOX 1.1

Conducting a Trade and Transport Facilitation Assessment of a Regional Program in the Mashreq

A regional cross-border trade facilitation and infrastructure study was carried out for the Mashreq[a] using a TTFA. The study provided a number of recommendations for each country, as in effect it was a series of national studies. Although the recommendations were country based, many were deemed to offer greater benefits if implemented in a coordinated manner and monitored at the regional level. As a result, the study proposed coordinated and phased policy and regulatory changes, as well as investments in transport and border-crossing infrastructure that would benefit trade in the following transport corridors:

- a North-South corridor that links the European Union to Saudi Arabia and the Gulf states via Turkey, Syria, and Jordan, with a connecting link to Egypt
- an East-West corridor that links the Mashreq ports of Latakia, Tartous, Tripoli, and Beirut via Syria to Iraq
- an East-West corridor that links the same ports to Iraq via Syria and Jordan.

BOX 1.1 *continued*

The Mashreq work confirmed the versatility of the TTFA as a diagnostic tool and the utility of its findings in designing corridor-based
projects. Although many of the recommendations were similar to those
previously presented by the countries themselves, by regional agencies,
or by international institutions, several proposals were new. One called
for a regional hub port in the Eastern Mediterranean, possibly in Syria
or Lebanon, to serve as a distribution center for goods from both
Europe and Asia to the northern part of the Mashreq. Another called for
the creation of a corridor management agency, which has proven successful in some other corridors with characteristics similar to those of
the North-South Mashreq corridor. The assessment also suggested that
the impact of the recommendations could be enhanced if the region
served as a link between the broader community of Gulf States and the
European Union.

a. Iraq, Jordan, Lebanon, Syria, and West Bank and Gaza.

Executing a Corridor-Level Assessment

A corridor-level diagnostic can examine an entire corridor or it can focus on
specific chokepoints within a corridor. Corridor-wide assessment takes the
form of data collection and surveys covering the length of a corridor, typically between a gateway and an inland destination. It has been carried out
on some corridors in Africa and Central Asia. Chokepoint monitoring takes
the form of detailed surveys at specific locations that constrict movement.
Detailed micro-scale monitoring has been conducted in Southern Africa and
Southeast Asia.

Table 1.4 summarizes the approaches to corridor-level diagnostics. Often
several approaches and techniques have to be used together in order to
collect all relevant data and information. Often, while a TTFA could be a first
step in a corridor level diagnostic, its cost can proscribe its use or frequent
repetition. Rather, a survey with a narrower geographical scope may be
required. Such a survey would be similar to a TTFA but would have a narrower focus, only on the corridor. This makes it possible to have detailed
discussions on the specific corridor issues. As with the TTFA, a series of
questionnaires is used in discussions and interviews with corridor stakeholders (see annex 1B).

The information collected from corridor surveys and interviews includes
quantitative data on performance and costs as well as information on

TABLE 1.4 Examples of Approaches to Corridor-Level Diagnostics

Level of analysis	Purpose	Tools and techniques
Entire length of a corridor	• Benchmark performance against regional and international corridors • Identify main bottlenecks and their impact on cost, time, and reliability • Collect baseline data	• Surveys of public and private sector agencies • Travel diaries • Supply chain analyses • Time release studies at main ports of entry • Trucking studies
Corridor component	• Obtain detailed information to aid project design, especially at apparent chokepoints • Collect component-level baseline performance data • Design intervention measures	• Detailed surveys and assessments of border, road, rail, trucking, port, inland container depot, dry port, and other facilities • Facility modeling

procedures, the exchange of information, and constraints to improving efficiency. This information can be grouped into seven categories:

- the role of the component in terms of the scope of activities performed for goods moving through the corridor and the infrastructure used for these movements
- the scale of activities and limitations on that scale imposed by infrastructure and the capacity of service providers
- the level of performance in terms of the efficiency of operations, the level of utilization of facilities and services, and the delays that result from congestion
- documentary requirements and the extent of coordination among service providers and between service providers and regulatory agencies through the use of electronic data interchange
- trade and transport agreements, regulations, and policies that affect the efficiency and quality of services
- other impediments to improving efficiency and quality of services
- opportunities to improve the efficiency and quality of services.

Tools for Conducting a Corridor Assessment

Supply Chain Analysis

From the earlier definition, a corridor can be visualized as reflecting the movement patterns of bundles of supply chains. As such, supply chain analytical techniques can be applied to examine four aspects of relevance to overall corridor performance:

- the time, cost, and reliability performance of end-to-end movements of the supply chains
- uncertainties associated with individual activities in the supply chain
- flexibility and transparency of the supply chains
- transactions generated by supply chain activities and the transfer of risks between chain actors.

These aspects would offer valuable insights into how the corridor ought to operate to optimize the topology of the supply chain networks.

Corridor analysis can therefore be based on value chain or supply chain analysis—but with critical caveats. Supply chains combine the services associated with the movement of goods through the trade corridor and activities that directly affect the value of these goods, a dimension that would normally not be included in a corridor diagnostic. Activities that directly affect the value of these goods include sourcing and the intermediate processing of inputs, the customization of finished products, and the distribution channels for the finished products. They also include the transactions associated with the change in ownership of goods moving through the supply chain and the procurement and coordination of services and processing activities. The key is to understand the likely impact of corridor performance on chain performance and organization. Baldwin (2012) argues that a fundamental tradeoff in supply chains is between gains from specialization and the coordination costs of distributed plants. He observes that at least in Europe and North America, supply chains tend to be regional. As the push for increased intraregional trade in low-income regions takes hold, it is possible that similar patterns will emerge there. Such patterns would increase the importance of trade corridors in the evolution and integration of supply chains. Supply chains can be restructured to increase the value of the finished products, including through adjustments that take advantage of improvements in the performance of the trade corridors (figure 1.3).

Supply chain analyses provide an opportunity to add other logistics and production costs to the transport costs used in most other assessment methods. They can also provide estimates of the volume of additional trade that might be generated by reducing these logistics and production costs.

However, supply or value chain analysis typically analyzes only a sample of the chains that would benefit from implementation of the corridor project, and it does not provide measures of benefits that can be easily compared with estimates of investment costs. Use of supply or value chain

FIGURE 1.3 Relationship between Supply Chain and Corridor Performance

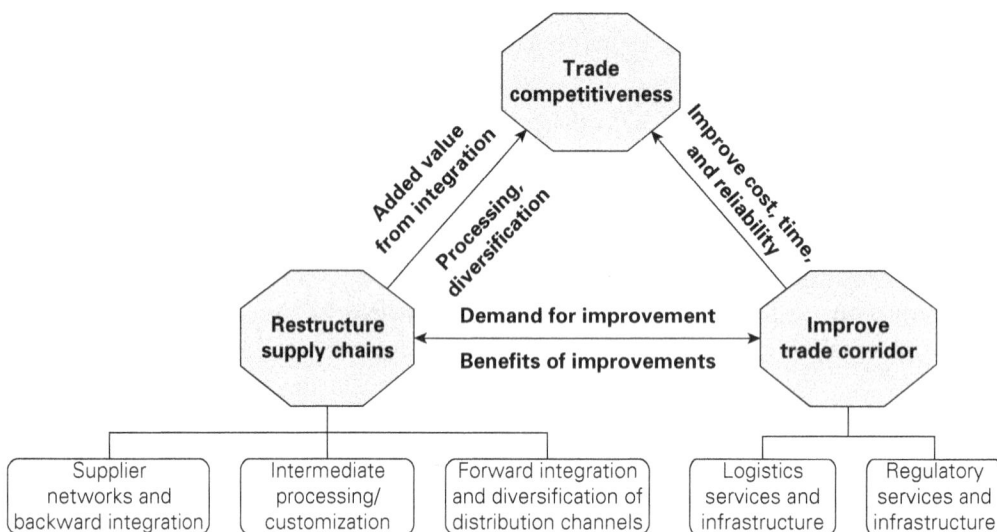

Source: Arnold 2012.

analysis in economic evaluation thus requires a quite different approach from that of cost-benefit analysis. Supply chain analysis should include the corridor investment costs as a component of the costs of the supply or value chain, but finding these costs is not easy; such costs are therefore rarely included. Thus, although supply or value chain analysis can add to the understanding of how the benefits of the corridor investment might be realized, it is not usually part of the economic evaluation of proposed corridor improvements.

Firm-Level Surveys

Enterprise Surveys are firm-level surveys of a representative sample of a country's private sector. The surveys, which have been conducted since 2002, now include more than 130 low- and middle-income countries. They cover a broad range of business environment topics, including access to finance, corruption, infrastructure, crime, competition, and performance measures. The findings are intended to be used by policy makers to identify, prioritize, and implement reforms of policies and institutions that support efficient private economic activity. Questions relating to transport and logistics can help provide perspective on the significance of transport and logistics constraints in a country and the magnitude of the challenges faced. The publicly available Enterprise Survey data can be a useful starting point for understanding the context of corridor analysis.

Trip Diaries

Trip diaries are a valuable source of information on how a corridor is performing from the point of view of drivers and truck operators. They help overcome the difficulty of obtaining information to paint a complete picture of performance of a corridor from the point of view of users. Trip diaries include information on origin and destination; vehicle registration and type; type and value of cargo; transit time and cost; reason for stop, duration, and cost (the reason will identify the agency responsible for the stop and what formal and informal fees were paid.) They can be used to generate both qualitative and quantitative data on stops, costs, time, and explanations of what happens during the movement of a vehicle along a corridor. These diaries have helped improve conditions along the Silk Road (box 1.2).

Specialized Surveys

Various surveys can be commissioned on the components of a corridor. They can include trucking surveys, to obtain information on the structure of the trucking industry in corridor countries, operational practices, costs, and the regulatory environment; border surveys, to obtain detailed disaggregated information on clearance processes; port surveys, to collect information on clearance processes, port performance, and disaggregated data on cargo dwell time in ports; and surveys of clearing and forwarding industries. The most pertinent surveys are covered in relevant modules of this Toolkit.

Corridor Observatories

The above techniques can be part of an organized system for regular information gathering and processing on a corridor, in the form of what is called a corridor observatory. An observatory is a set of tools for regular corridor data collection, analysis, and dissemination designed to aid decision making about improving corridor performance. It is typically supported by a national, regional, or corridor body. Observatories are a loop process in which each assessment feeds a new round of political dialogue and reforms. Performance measurement is typically from the perspective of the user but is also relevant to policy makers and service providers who have to design and implement a supply response.

Using Trip Diaries to Improve Trade along the Silk Road

The most extensive use of trip diaries has been as part of the New Eurasian Land Transport Initiative (NELTI), an International Road Transport Union (IRU) project in Central Asia. Over the past 15 years, the IRU has been contributing to reviving the ancient Silk Road as a major trade route between Europe and Asia. The NELTI was launched in September 2008, with the support of major international organizations and national governments. The project monitors data on commercial deliveries of industrial and consumer goods across the Eurasian landmass by independent transport companies from Eurasian countries along five different routes.

During their trips, drivers using the routes collect data on road conditions, waiting times at border-crossing points, the quality of the road infrastructure, administrative barriers, and other features. These data are analyzed to develop road maps identifying the issues to be solved and the measures required to reduce the time and cost of road transport haulage between China and Europe.

BOX FIGURE B1.2.1 Breakdown of Time Spent by Haulers en Route from Europe to Central Asia

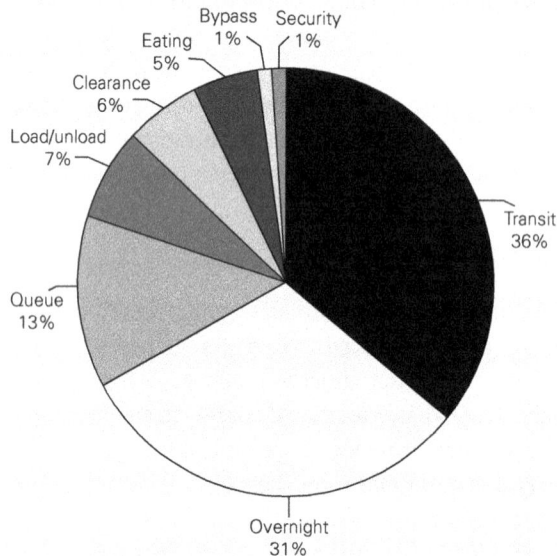

Source: Saslavsky 2012.

BOX 1.2 *continued*

NELTI monitoring has shown that 40 percent of road transport time along the routes of the Silk Road is spent at borders. As a result, it can be postulated that border-crossing procedures impede trade growth along the entire Eurasian landmass. About 30 percent of transport costs are unofficial payments, borne by haulers en route and at border-crossing points. Intervention measures can be targeted at border posts where most delays are experienced.

A critical consideration in the design of an observatory is the ability to pull together different streams of data into a coherent performance monitoring system. Two issues are particularly important: the availability of the data on each of the events in the movement sequence and the ability to join the pieces of data from the discrete events into a chain, so that a single consignment can be tracked between a gateway and an inland destination.

Computerized data sources can be complemented by primary data collection to satisfy both conditions. Successful observatories use as much existing and mainly computerized data sources as possible. Automated data sources are ideal for corridor performance assessment and diagnostics. They are replicable and once established can offer data for the duration of project, thus enabling impact evaluations.

Increasingly, various agencies involved in corridor operations have automated data gathering, chief among them ports and customs and other border management agencies as well as from some private sector stakeholders. For example, trucking companies in most regions now use Global Positioning Systems for tracking movement of their fleets (box 1.3). Partnering with these corridor players can result in a win-win situation, as project designers have access to operational data and data contributors will benefit from any improvements to the corridor.

Automated sources are important also to understanding the extent of integration of activities along a corridor. The extent of integration of sequential activities in the corridor is determined from data collected on the use of electronic data interchange between the parties involved in sequential activities. Information should be collected from all stakeholders on their use of information and communications technology (ICT) to coordinate movement of goods through the corridor. Integration can be accomplished through vertical integration of service providers and regulatory agencies, but the modern approach has been to use ICT systems to coordinate activities, including the interactions between the public and private sectors, generally referred to as *trade facilitation*. This information is used to identify

BOX 1.3

Using Global Positioning System Data in Corridor Monitoring

In the past, lack of road transport data was a constraint. As a result of rapid changes in technology, road transport data are now widely available. One of the most promising sources of data for corridor performance monitoring is the Global Positioning System (GPS). GPS tracking systems are widely used by the private sector, especially truck and train operators, who provide information on the location of vehicles and therefore consignments. GPS data can be used to obtain detailed information on vehicle utilization, speed, transaction times at various points, and so forth.

GPS provides regular, low-cost data that are highly comparable and can even be extrapolated to the past. For example, GPS tracking is used in Southern Africa to provide insight into dwell times at border posts. Huge amounts of data on thousands of truck movements are analyzed. GPS data are used to determine how long it takes to cross a border based on the direction of movement of a truck. From this information it is possible to ascertain how long trucks and consignments spend on each side of the border. The main weakness is the absence of explanatory detail on the causes of any hold-ups to movement.

GPS monitoring can complement other border survey methods, including data from time release studies (TRS). It does not compete with other approaches: it gives a bird's eye view of trends at the border or other logistics node. The results will guide dialogue and highlight where more focused monitoring should be applied (at chokepoints, for example). In some countries, customs authorities are also relying on GPS to track movement of goods in transit. However, GPS is most appropriate when operators already use the technology for their fleet management, cargo tracking, or other purposes.

opportunities for improving performance changes in management, operations, and regulation.

However, while taping into automated data sources can minimize data gathering costs, data from automated sources may not always be in a form or format that can contribute directly to calculating corridor performance indicators. Such data may have to be processed and validated. Most data are usually quantitative, missing qualitative aspects to explain what process or impediment to movement may be encountered along the corridor. It is therefore important to complement such data with qualitative information, which may necessitate a survey. The conceptual design for an observatory on the northern corridor of East Africa shows the importance of such linkage (box 1.4).

The most comprehensive corridor performance monitoring system (equivalent to an observatory) is by Transport Canada.[2] Its system collects

BOX 1.4
Conducting Corridor Observatory Work in Africa

Beginning in 2001, the Sub-Saharan Africa Transport Policy Program (SSATP) sponsored a series of corridor observatories on the main transport corridors in Sub-Saharan Africa. The observatories are intended to contribute to policy dialogue in the corridor countries. It is expected that they will be sustained by the management entities of each corridor.

The observatory initiative was implemented in partnership with several other agencies. It uses the following tools:

- surveys of border-crossing delays, which have been used by the Japan International Cooperation Agency (JICA), the World Bank, and TradeMark East Africa
- observatories of abnormal practices, which measure the impact of delays and informal payments at checkpoints on roads (this work is supported by the U.S. Agency for International Development [USAID] in West Africa [through the West Africa Trade Hub] and by the European Union in Central Africa)
- transport observatories for corridors, based on the integration of operational data from computer systems for logistics operators and regulatory agencies.

Lessons learned during the SSATP program have recently been developed into guidelines on transport corridor observatories (Hartmann 2013).

BOX FIGURE B1.4.1 Basic Design of a Transport Corridor Observatory

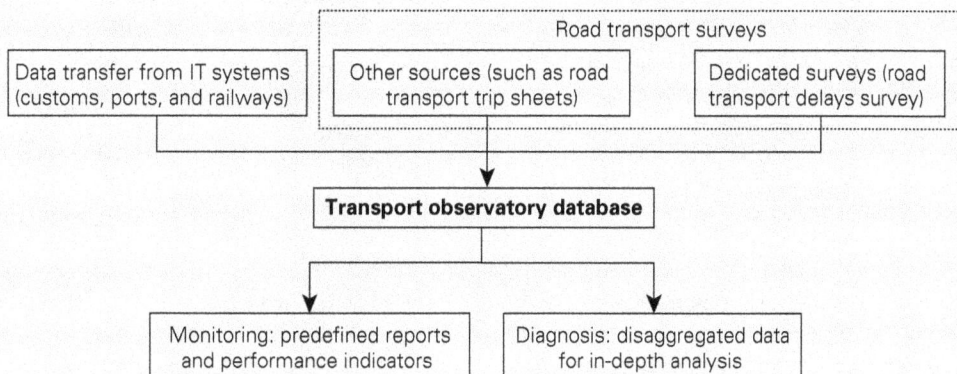

Source: Hartmann 2007.
Note: IT = information technology.

data from all corridor players and major shipping lines. The system helps it understand domestic logistical flows and identify infrastructure needs on strategic gateways and trade corridors. One of the system's objectives is to optimize the movement of goods through the major trade corridors.

The system comprises tools and databases for monitoring the performance of Canada's main trade corridors in terms of fluidity and supply chain resilience. The system generates aggregate indicators based on data on seaport performance; vessel movement on the high seas; overland transport systems (road, rail); and air cargo. The fluidity measure is complemented by an estimate of total logistics costs that takes a broader look at time to market and the reliability of the logistics system. The total logistics costs approach is similar to that described in Module 13. It combines various costs, direct transport, in-transit inventory, ordering, inventory, and costs associated with system uncertainties.

Summary of Corridor Assessment Techniques

Table 1.5 summarizes the techniques for assessing a corridor presented in this module.

TABLE 1.5 Summary of Corridor Assessment Techniques

Scale of analysis	Purpose	Tools and techniques	Indicative cost
National or regional	• Determine impact of logistics performance on trade competitiveness • Compare performance against other countries • Identify major constraints and opportunities for improvement	• Trade and Transport Facilitation Assessment (TTFA) • Trade modeling • Regional freight flow modeling (such as gravity models)	> $200,000
Entire length of a corridor	• Benchmark performance against regional and international corridors • Identify main bottlenecks and their impact on cost, time, and reliability • Collect baseline data	• Survey of public and private sector agencies • Travel diaries • Supply chain analysis • Time release studies at main ports of entry • Trucking study	$50,000–$200,000
Corridor component	• Obtain detailed information to aid project design • Collect component-level baseline performance data • Design intervention measures	• Detailed border, road, rail, trucking, port, inland container depot, and dry port survey or assessment • Facility modeling	< $50,000

Prioritizing Interventions

A diagnostic assessment of a corridor should culminate in a prioritized intervention plan intended to improve performance. Such plans are often multisectoral and, in the case of international corridors, multicountry. There is nearly always a range of possible actions that could be taken; the challenge is to identify interventions that can have a significant impact and are economically, technically, and politically feasible. Possibilities include infrastructure improvements; changes in policies, regulations, or procedures; training and capacity building for corridor actors; and better coordination mechanisms. Significant changes in performance often require interventions covering several corridor components at the same time.

The selection of priority interventions is the result of an iterative process that may be the product of a modeling process. Several criteria can be applied, including the following:

- the gravity of constraints and the magnitude of the economic impact (based on methods outlined in Module 13)
- the technical feasibility of proposed changes
- the political feasibility of proposed changes
- management capacity
- environmental considerations
- the availability of resources to finance the proposed changes.

The prioritized action plan should be costed and the agencies responsible for implementation and coordination clearly identified.

Annex 1A Defining and Collecting Data for a Corridor Diagnostic

This annex identifies the main considerations in collecting data for a corridor assessment. It outlines the possible objectives, sources of data, and questions that can be asked of the various stakeholders of a typical corridor. The sources are varied as they should cover all parties involved in developing, managing, and providing transport and logistics services in a corridor. Corridor development is associated with planning and constructing infrastructure to increase the capacity, efficiency, and reliability of services operating in the corridor. Corridor management involves coordinating activities of stakeholders to improve efficiency of services along corridor.

Objectives

The goal of the trade corridor assessment is to improve the quality of corridor infrastructure and logistics services so as to allow for more efficient and reliable movement of foreign trade along the corridor. The objectives of the assessment are set out as described in the module.

Often information for a diagnostic has to be collected from a combination of secondary sources and through surveys of stakeholders. Both are important as quantitative and qualitative information is needed to properly understand the level of performance and the nature of constraints. In addition an institutional assessment is also necessary. Sustainable efforts to maintain the infrastructure and eliminate bottlenecks require some form of corridor management to coordinate the efforts of government and reflect the aspirations of private sector stakeholders. The Toolkit uses a stakeholder survey to examine the effectiveness of the current organizational structure and produce a set of baseline indices with which to monitor progress

Collection of Data

Published data. Among sources of published data concerning traffic volumes are the UN (Comtrade); international transport organizations, for example, International Road Transport Union, Airports Council International, and transports internationaux routiers (international road transport, or TIR); and trade journals such as *Containerisation International* and *Air Cargo World*.

Sources of data on the physical characteristics of corridor infrastructure include trade publications from, for example, Fairplay, International Civil Aviation Organization (ICAO), and International Union of Railways, regarding the ports, airports, and railroads. There is also data from the websites of the operators of the gateways and the government agencies responsible for corridor infrastructure. Additional information can be obtained where there have been studies done by multinational or bilateral aid agencies or government committees.

Information on trade and transport regulations can usually be obtained from the websites of the relevant agencies or from the associations whose members are affected by these regulations. Information on the introduction of modern procedures for the regulation of trade and management of public infrastructure can be obtained from reports prepared by government committees or aid agencies prepared as part of efforts to improve the performance of the relevant agencies.

Traffic surveys. It is anticipated that most of the baseline data related to traffic volumes and level of utilization of the corridor infrastructure can be obtained from published statistics. However, it may be necessary to collect more detailed data using standard instruments such as traffic counts, origin-destination surveys, driver diaries, and time-release studies. Traffic counts can provide information on the split between freight and nonfreight vehicle movements at critical bottlenecks.

Origin-destination surveys may be needed for corridors that have a large number of access points used by a significant portion of the corridor traffic. There is usually unpublished data on traffic movements at intermediate nodes on the corridor such as inland terminals and tollbooths, but these do not provide information on the time spent or costs incurred while on the corridor. Some data can be obtained directly from transport companies but it will be limited in scope. It can be supplemented with driver diaries that can be used to collect this information in greater detail. This method is especially useful when attempting to determine sources of delay and informal costs en route.

Stakeholder surveys. More detailed information on traffic volumes and performance levels for transport and logistics must be collected through interviews with stakeholders involved in the movement of goods through the corridor. These include the parties responsible for management of the gateways, for providing cargo-handling services, and for regulating trade through these gateways. Also interviewed will be the shippers, both importers and exporters. A series of questionnaires covering these stakeholders are provided in the annexes.

The information collected from these surveys includes quantitative data on performance and costs as well as information on procedures, exchange of information and constraints on improving efficiency. This information can be grouped into seven categories:

- role of the respondent in terms of the scope of activities performed for goods moving through the corridor and the infrastructure used for these movements
- scale of these activities and the limitations on this scale as a result of available infrastructure and the capacity of the service providers
- level of performance in terms of efficiency of operations, level of utilization of facilities and services, and the delays that result from congestion
- documentary requirements and extent of coordination among service providers and with regulatory agencies through the use of electronic data interchange
- trade and transport agreements, regulations, and policies that affect the efficiency and quality of services
- other impediments to improving efficiency and quality of services
- opportunities to improve the efficiency and quality of services.

Some of the topics covered in each of these categories are shown in annex table 1A.2. Although these topics are similar to those used in the Trade and Transport Facilitation Assessment (TTFA), there are substantial differences as mentioned above. In particular the geographical scope is limited to the domestic or regional corridor and does not include

- overseas movements—the only international movements are those between adjoining countries,
- door-to-door movements except for those with a final origin or destination within the corridor, and
- value-added logistics services other than storage and consolidation (the exception would, of course, be when the assessment is for an economic development corridor).

The information collected on the scope of activities identifies both the sequential activities that the respondent is involved in, for example, transport and storage, forwarding and transport, long distance transport, and local distribution, and the variety of services offered in terms of different combinations of time and cost for movement through the corridor including the gateway.

The information collected on the scale of activities includes the size of the units used for transportation within the corridor.

Information on the volume of traffic and size of shipments helps identify opportunities for capturing economies of scale.

The information collected on performance is primarily quantitative data concerning the time, cost, and reliability of the services provided in the corridor. This includes information on delays and on discretionary use of storage. Data is also collected on freight rates and operating costs for transport services to assess the importance of factors other than costs on setting the rates.

The information collected on documentary requirements identifies the extent to which the format has been simplified, standardized, and harmonized. It also determines the extent to which these documents are exchanged electronically. Coordination between sequential activities is examined using questions regarding the extent to which prior or subsequent activities are scheduled and/or coordinated through exchange in real time of information on the status of these activities.

Questions regarding regulations affecting services examine the impact on competition, availability, efficiency, and reliability on those services. Some of these regulations are shown in table 1A.1. These include regulations in trade and transport agreements that affect the efficiency and reliability of cross-border movements. These include documents describing

- restrictions on cross-border movement of vehicles
- bilateral quotas and qualifications (bonds) affecting transport operators
- limitations on third-country transport operators transiting the country
- documentation and guarantee required for temporary admission of cargo
- duties, taxes, and transit fees applied to vehicles and cargo moving on the corridor
- arrangements for clearance of cargo behind the border
- acceptance of multicountry vehicle insurance and guarantees for potential liabilities with regard to duties taxes.

The last section of the questionnaires is a subjective ranking of the performance of the other stakeholders in the corridor. The responses would

TABLE 1A.1 Additional Information Collected from Questionnaires

Participant	Demand	Policies/procedures
Terminal operators	Cargo form, shipment size, schedules	Concessions and other public-private partnership (PPP) arrangements
Transport services providers	Cargo form, shipment size, schedules	Market entry, range of services and liabilities, equipment standards
Forwarders and clearance agents	Shipment sizes,	Market entry, range of services and liabilities
Regulators	Prearrival and postrelease	Trade restrictions, tax collection

be limited to those parties that the respondent interacts with and should be based on that interaction rather than a general assessment of the performance of those parties.

Sample Frame

The stratified sample would be used for the stakeholder survey. The sample frame for the interviews would be structured as shown in table 1A.2. This also indicates the criteria used to stratify the same. The number of stakeholders from each category to be interviewed would be limited by the budget allocated for the assessment. Preliminary numbers are shown in the rightmost column.

TABLE 1A.2 Survey Sample Frame

Type of entity	Selection criteria	Number
Developers of corridor infrastructure		
Port and airport authorities	At gateway	1
Public railways	Headquarters	1–2
Highway department	Headquarters	1
Transport service providers		
Road	Long-distance trucking companies operating on the corridor with medium to large fleets, specifically companies providing cross-border transport	2–5
Rail	Railway department responsible for freight operations and any subsidiary responsible for unit train operations, private operators of unit trains	1–3
Air	International passenger and airfreight carriers	1–2
Inland water transport (IWT) or coastal	Larger container barge and coaster operators	2–3
Terminal operators for gateways		
Port	Container terminal operator	1–2
Airport	Air cargo terminal operator	1
Inland container depot (ICD)	Terminal operator	1
Government agencies involved in trade regulation		
Customs	Headquarters, senior officers at gateways and border crossings	2–3
Health and safety	Senior officers at gateways and border crossings	2–4
Logistics services providers		
Forwarding and clearance agents	Both domestic and foreign companies handling significant volumes of corridor traffic	2–3
Providers of warehousing	Facilities located in major clusters near the gateways and terminus of the corridor	2–3

Diagnosis

The diagnosis of corridor performance uses the data collected from published sources, the stakeholder survey, and additional traffic surveys. The data collected from the stakeholder survey is organized to perform the following types of analysis:

- assess corridor performance (time, cost, variability)
- benchmark performance
- identify bottleneck including regulatory impediments
- evaluate scale economies (facilities, vehicle size, fleet size)
- assess integration of sequential activities
- review policies related to trade and transport.

The mapping uses the cost and time data provided by the shippers, transport and logistics service providers, and terminal operators to develop a flow chart for a typical movement through the corridor. This would indicate the time and cost for the various activities as well as any factors contributing to the variation in time to complete the activity. This information would be used to identify activities that account for a majority of the time and cost for movement through the corridor.

The benchmarking uses the performance data provided by the logistics service providers, terminal operators, and regulators to evaluate the efficiency of services at the gateways and borders. Their efficiency is compared with the industry standards or that of comparable corridors.

The identification of bottlenecks uses the data provided by all stakeholders regarding congestion and resulting delays on the links and nodes of the corridor. These bottlenecks are generally caused by insufficient infrastructure, low throughput, and/or regulatory impediments.

The evaluation of economies of scale applies to the size of shipments and the size of transport units used to transport them on the corridor. It also applies to the physical characteristics of the gateways and the size of vessels/aircraft that use them. For the latter the size of conveyance may also be limited by total traffic through the gateway. The data for this evaluation is obtained from shippers, transport and terminal operators.

The extent of integration of sequential activities in the corridor is determined from data collected on the use of electronic data interchange between the parties involved in sequential activities. This includes information collected from all the stakeholders on their use of information and communications technology (ICT) systems for coordinating movement of goods through the corridor.

Finally the impact of trade and transport regulation on the competitiveness of the transport and logistics services as well as the efficiency of terminal operations is determined from the review of these regulations and discussions with the parties affected.

The results of these analyses are combined into four reviews (figure 1A.1). The demand review determines the sensitivity of the cargoes moving through the corridor to the cost, time, and reliability of this movement including the transfer through the gateways and across the borders. This is used to weigh the importance of various proposed improvements.

The performance review compares the time, cost, and reliability of the sequential activities relative to available benchmarks. It also identifies the degree of integration of these activities. This integration can be accomplished through vertical integration of the service providers and regulatory agencies, but the modern approach has been to use information technology systems to coordinate their activities including the interactions between the public and private sector generally referred to as trade facilitation. This information is used to identify opportunities for improving performance changes in management, operations, and regulation.

FIGURE 1A.1 Example of Data Capture Points for the Kolkata-Kathmandu Corridor

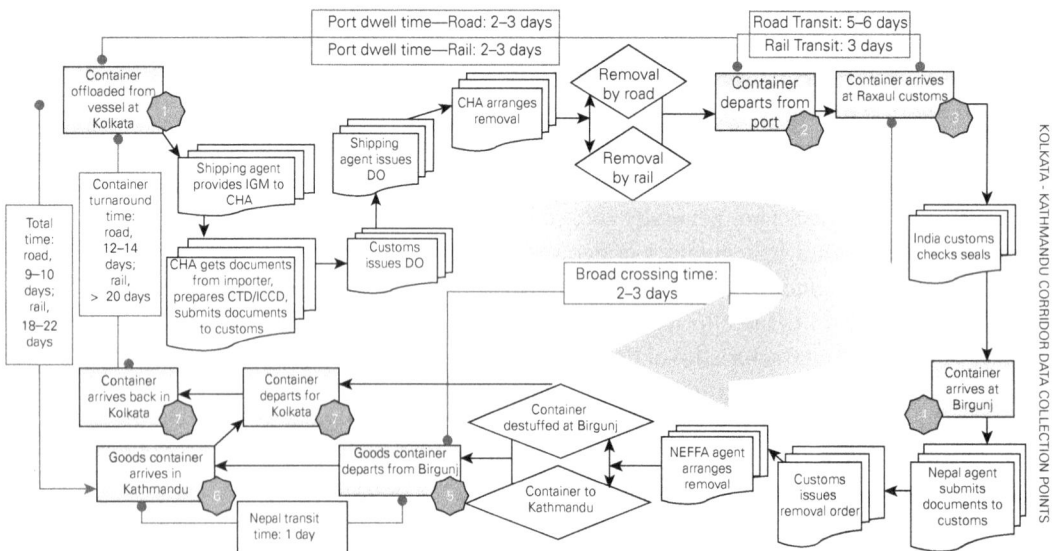

Source: World Bank 2013.

Note: CHA = Customs House Agent; CTD = Customs Transit Document; DO = Delivery Order; ICCD = Import Containerized Cargo Declaration; IGM = Import General Manifest; NEFFA = Nepal Freight Forwarders Association.

The capacity review determines the limitations on scale of transport services and bottlenecks introduced as a result of limits imposed by physical infrastructure and productivity of cargo handling operations. This is used for identifying opportunities for investment in infrastructure and cargo handling facilities. The final review examines the impact of regulation on the efficiency and competitiveness of the transport and logistics services including those at the gateways and border crossings.

The results of the mapping are used for both the demand analysis and the performance review. The findings from the analysis of benchmarks and integration are used in the performance review. The evaluation of scale economies and bottlenecks are used for the capacity review. The policy analysis is used as part of the regulatory review.

Annex 1B Questions for Discussions with Logistics Providers, Exporters, Importers, Distributors, and Wholesalers

A. Questions for Logistics Service Providers

1. What services are provided?
   - ☐ Warehousing
   - ☐ Consolidation
   - ☐ Cross docking
   - ☐ Distribution
   - ☐ Inventory management
   - ☐ Leasing space
   - ☐ Bonded storage
   - ☐ Cold storage
2. What kinds of trades are serviced?
   - ☐ Imports
   - ☐ Exports
   - ☐ Regional shipments
   - ☐ International shipments
3. What is the average dwell time?
   - ☐ For imports _____
   - ☐ For exports _____
4. What is the typical charge for handling and storage?
   - ☐ Of import cargoes _____
   - ☐ Of export cargoes _____
5. How much covered storage is on offer? _____

6. What are the principal commodities stored? _____

B. Questions for Exporters

7. What types of goods do you export?
   - ☐ Agricultural goods
   - ☐ Food products
   - ☐ Textiles and apparel
   - ☐ Other consumer goods
   - ☐ Machinery and equipment
   - ☐ Intermediate goods for manufacturing
   - ☐ Construction and project cargo
8. What are the major markets for your exports? _____
9. Who is the buyer of the exports?
   - ☐ Trader within country
   - ☐ Foreign brand manufacturer

- ☐ Foreign distributor
- ☐ Foreign retailer
- ☐ Overseas ethnic markets
- ☐ Foreign manufacturer/processor

10. For these buyers, what are the most import factors in selecting a supplier?
    - ☐ Product design or quality
    - ☐ Delivered cost
    - ☐ Delivery time
    - ☐ Order fulfillment
    - ☐ Order cycle (for introduction of new product or design)

11. What is the principal mode of transport for the international movement of your goods? _____

12. What are the terms of shipment?
    - ☐ Ex-works
    - ☐ Free on board (FOB)
    - ☐ Cost, insurance, and freight (CIF)
    - ☐ Delivered duty paid (DDP)/delivery duty unpaid (DDU)

13. What is the average amount of cargo that you ship in a year (in tonnes, 20-foot equivalent units [TEUs], truckloads)? _____

14. What is the extent of your involvement in the supply chain?
    - ☐ Provide own trucking
    - ☐ Arrange shipping up to international gateway or land border
    - ☐ Arrange international movement

15. For shipments that use the corridor, what are the principal cargoes?

16. Is the volume shipped?
    - ☐ Yes
    - ☐ No

17. What is the range of shipment size? _____

18. What is the mode of transport? _____

19. What is the average, minimum, and maximum time for delivery from the factory/warehouse to the following?
    - ☐ Seaport _____
    - ☐ Loaded on vessel _____
    - ☐ Airport _____
    - ☐ Loaded on aircraft _____
    - ☐ Land border _____

20. What are the principal causes of delays for shipments?
    - ☐ Arranging transport from factory
    - ☐ Clearing customs
    - ☐ Crossing borders

    ☐ Preparing documentation and obtaining approvals
    ☐ Arranging for payment
    ☐ Finding available transport
    ☐ Congestion at gateways or land borders
    ☐ Congestion along the corridor
    ☐ Connections with international transport

21. What is the cost for shipping goods up to the seaport, airport, or land border (per tonne and as percent of delivered cost)? _____

22. What is the cost of moving the goods through the airport or seaport or across the land border (per tonne and as percent of delivered cost)? _____

23. What percentage of the delivered cost is incurred from movement on the corridor? _____

24. What method of communication does the buyer use to place an order?
    ☐ Fax or e-mail
    ☐ Electronic data interchange
    ☐ Prearranged schedule in contract

25. To what extent do you use electronic data interchange in your transactions with the following?
    ☐ Suppliers _____
    ☐ Service providers _____
    ☐ Government agencies _____

26. What approvals must be obtained and documents submitted before goods can be shipped? _____

27. What is the typical time to process these approvals? _____

28. Where are goods cleared by customs for export?
    ☐ Factory
    ☐ Inland clearance facility or dry port
    ☐ International gateway

29. What percentage of shipments is physically inspected during clearance? _____

30. What is the average time for clearance of cargo, and how does it vary? _____

31. What impediments have the greatest impact on export competitiveness?
    ☐ Average delivery time
    ☐ Cost or reliability of inbound supply chains (delivery of inputs to production)
    ☐ Uncertainty of production time
    ☐ Cost or reliability of outbound supply chains up to gateway or land border

- ☐ Cost or reliability of international movements (beyond gateway or land border)
- ☐ Payment cycle (cash-to-cash cycle)
- ☐ Cost or time to complete regulatory procedures, including processing of documents

32. What initiatives related to the corridor would provide the greatest benefit in terms of competitiveness?
    - ☐ Investment in transport infrastructure
    - ☐ Increased competition in provision of transport services
    - ☐ Improvements in the quality and reliability of transport services
    - ☐ Simplification of documentation for shipping cargo
    - ☐ Simplification of clearance procedures at gateways and land borders
    - ☐ Greater use of electronic data interchange and information and communications technology
    - ☐ Greater frequency of service of international transport to export markets

33. Rate the following:
    - ☐ Port authority: ☐ Good ☐ Adequate ☐ Poor
    - ☐ Port terminal operator: ☐ Good ☐ Adequate ☐ Poor
    - ☐ Airport authority: ☐ Good ☐ Adequate ☐ Poor
    - ☐ Air cargo terminal operator: ☐ Good ☐ Adequate ☐ Poor
    - ☐ Truck operators: ☐ Good ☐ Adequate ☐ Poor
    - ☐ Rail operators: ☐ Good ☐ Adequate ☐ Poor
    - ☐ Clearing and forwarding agents: ☐ Good ☐ Adequate ☐ Poor
    - ☐ Customs: ☐ Good ☐ Adequate ☐ Poor

34. If poor, what are the reasons? _____

C. Questions for Importers, Distributors, and Wholesalers

35. What is your role as an importer?
    - ☐ Import inputs for production of finished products
    - ☐ Sell final products through own retail channels
    - ☐ Act as wholesaler of specific types of goods
    - ☐ Act as distributor of specific branded goods
    - ☐ Act as a trader selling shipments of goods purchased on speculation

36. What types of goods do you import?
    - ☐ Agricultural goods
    - ☐ Food products
    - ☐ Textiles and apparel
    - ☐ Other consumer goods
    - ☐ Machinery and equipment
    - ☐ Intermediate goods for manufacturing
    - ☐ Construction and project cargo

37. What are the major markets for your exports? _____
38. What are the most import factors in selecting a supplier?
    - ☐ Product design, quality, or both
    - ☐ Delivered cost
    - ☐ Delivery time
    - ☐ Order fulfillment
    - ☐ Order cycle (for introduction of a new product or design)
39. What is the principal mode of transport for the international movement of goods? _____
40. What are the terms of shipment?
    - ☐ Ex-works
    - ☐ FOB
    - ☐ CIF
    - ☐ DDP/DDU
41. What is the average amount of cargo you import in a year (in tonnes, TEU, or truckloads)? _____
42. What is the typical order size (in tonnes or TEU)? _____
43. What is the extent of your involvement in the supply chain?
    - ☐ Provide own trucking
    - ☐ Arrange shipping from international gateway or land border
    - ☐ Arrange shipping from foreign gateway
    - ☐ Arrange shipping from suppliers' warehouses
44. At what point in the supply chain from the supplier is ownership of the cargo transferred? _____
45. For shipments that use the corridor, what are the principal cargoes? _____
46. Is the volume shipped?
    - ☐ Yes
    - ☐ No
47. What is the range of shipment sizes? _____
48. What is the mode of transport? _____
49. What form of cargo is used for domestic shipment?
    - ☐ Full truck or wagon load
    - ☐ Less than truck or wagon load (groupage)
50. What is the average, minimum, and maximum time for delivery to the factory/warehouse of cargo landing at the seaport?
    Exiting the seaport: Average ___ Minimum ___ Maximum ___
    Unloading from the aircraft: Average ___ Minimum ___ Maximum ___
    Exiting the airport: Average ___ Minimum ___ Maximum ___
    Crossing the land border: Average ___ Minimum ___ Maximum ___

51. What are the principal causes of delays for shipments?
    - ☐ Delays in supplier's production activity
    - ☐ Supplier misses shipment dates
    - ☐ Preparation of documentation and obtaining approvals
    - ☐ Clearance procedures at gateway or land border
    - ☐ Arranging for payment
    - ☐ Availability of transport
    - ☐ Congestion at gateway or land border
    - ☐ Congestion along the corridor
52. What is the cost of shipping the goods from seaport, airport, or land border to the warehouse (per tonne and as percent of delivered cost)? _____
53. What is the cost for transferring the goods at the airport, seaport, or land border (per tonne and as percent of delivered cost)? _____
54. What percentage of the delivered cost is incurred from movement on the corridor? _____
55. What method of communication do you use to place an order with a buyer?
    - ☐ Fax or e-mail
    - ☐ Electronic data interchange
    - ☐ Prearranged schedule in contract
56. Do you use electronic data interchange for communication with any of the following parties?
    - ☐ Suppliers
    - ☐ Logistics service providers
    - ☐ Customs
    - ☐ Other government agencies
    - ☐ Ports, airports
    - ☐ Banks, financial institutions
57. What approvals must be obtained and documents submitted before ordering imports? _____
58. How long does it typically take to process these approvals? _____
59. What percentage of goods is cleared by customs at each of the following places?
    International gateway or land border: _____
    Warehouse: _____
    Inland clearance facility or dry port: _____
60. What is the average time for clearance of cargo, and how does it vary? _____
61. What percentage of shipments is subject to physical inspection by customs? _____

62. What percentage requires a certification for health, safety, standards, or other purposes? _____
63. What is the average time required to obtain the results from these tests, and how does it vary? _____
64. What impediments have the greatest impact on your competition with other suppliers?
    ☐ Average delivery time
    ☐ Cost or reliability of domestic component of inbound supply chains
    ☐ Cost or reliability of international component of inbound supply chains
    ☐ Payment cycle (cash-to-cash cycle)
    ☐ Cost or time to complete regulatory procedures including processing of documents
65. What initiatives related to the corridor would provide the greatest benefit in terms of competitiveness?
    ☐ Investment in transport infrastructure
    ☐ Increased competition in the provision of transport services
    ☐ Improvements in the quality and reliability of transport services
    ☐ Simplification of documentation for importing cargo
    ☐ Simplification of clearance procedures at gateways and land borders
    ☐ Greater use of electronic data interchange and information and communications technology
    ☐ Greater frequency of service of international transport to export markets
66. Rate the following:
    ☐ Port authority: ☐ Good ☐ Adequate ☐ Poor
    ☐ Port terminal operator: ☐ Good ☐ Adequate ☐ Poor
    ☐ Airport authority: ☐ Good ☐ Adequate ☐ Poor
    ☐ Air cargo terminal operator: ☐ Good ☐ Adequate ☐ Poor
    ☐ Truck operators: ☐ Good ☐ Adequate ☐ Poor
    ☐ Rail operators: ☐ Good ☐ Adequate ☐ Poor
    ☐ Clearing and forwarding agents: ☐ Good ☐ Adequate ☐ Poor
    ☐ Customs: ☐ Good ☐ Adequate ☐ Poor
67. If poor, what are the reasons? _____

Notes

1. Examples include the European agreements on main international transport routes (AGR), Main International Railway Lines (AGC), Important International Combined Transport Lines and Related Installations (AGTC), Main Inland Waterways of International Importance (AGN), the Trans-Asian Highway and

Trans-Asian Railway Agreements, and the International Agreements on Road/ Rail in the Arab Mashreq.

2. The Transport Canada Corridors and Gateway initiative is described at http:// www.canadasgateways.gc.ca/nationalpolicy.html.

References

Arnold, J. 2012. *Draft Vietnam: Trade and Transport Facilitation Assessment Report.* Washington, DC: World Bank.

Baldwin, R. 2012. "Global Supply Chains: Why They Emerged, Why They Matter, and Where They Are Going." Discussion Paper 9103, Centre for Economic Policy Research, London.

Hartmann, O. 2007. "Draft Development and Implementation of a Transport Observatory on the Northern Corridor for the SSATP." World Bank, Washington, DC.

———. 2013. "Corridor Transport Observatory Guidelines." Working paper 98, World Bank, Sub-Saharan Africa Transport Policy Program, Washington, DC.

Nathan Associates. 2011. "Definition and Investment Strategy for a Core Strategic Transport Network for Eastern and Southern Africa." Report for the World Bank, Washington, DC.

Saslavsky, D. 2012. "Draft Benchmarking Central Asian Corridors Using IRU Trip Diaries." World Bank, Washington, DC.

World Bank. 2012. *Connecting to Compete: Trade Logistics in the Global Economy.* Washington, DC: World Bank.

———. 2013. "Project Appraisal Document: Nepal-India Trade and Transport Integration Project." Washington, DC.

Resources

International Finance Corporation and World Bank. *Enterprise Surveys.* Washington, DC. http://www.enterprisesurveys.org/.
The International Finance Corporation (IFC) and the World Bank have conducted Enterprise Surveys since 2002. The surveys, conducted in more than 130 low- and middle-income countries, cover a broad range of business environment topics, including access to finance, corruption, infrastructure, crime, competition, and performance measures. The findings are intended to be used by policy makers to identify, prioritize, and implement reforms of policies and institutions that support efficient private economic activity.

UNCTAD (United Nations Conference on Trade and Development). *Liner Shipping Connectivity Index.* http://archive.unctad.org/templates/page.asp?intItemID =2618&lang=1.
UNCTAD's Liner Shipping Connectivity Index (LSCI) aims at capturing a country's level of integration into the liner shipping network. It can be considered a proxy for accessibility to global trade. The higher the index, the easier it is to access a high-capacity, high-frequency global maritime

freight transport system (and thus effectively participate in international trade). Countries that have high LSCI values are actively involved in trade. The LSCI can be considered as both a measure of connectivity to maritime shipping and a measure of trade facilitation. It reflects the strategies of container shipping lines seeking to maximize revenue through market coverage.

The index comprises four main components:

- containership deployment, based on the number of ships calling at a country's ports (normalized per capita)
- container carrying capacity (normalized per capita)
- the number of shipping companies, liner services, and vessels per company
- the average and maximum vessel size (a proxy for economies of scale).

Wilson, A. G. 1967. "A Statistical Theory of Spatial Distribution Models Transportation Research." *Transportation Research* 1 (3): 253–69.

Gravity models used in trade analyses are not generally directly applicable to the evaluation of corridor projects. Applications of the trade gravity model to trade facilitation measures include some work by the World Bank and Nathan Associates (a consulting firm).

World Bank. *Logistics Performance Index*. Washington, DC. http://lpi.worldbank.org.

The Logistics Performance Index (LPI) is based on a worldwide survey of operators on the ground (global freight forwarders and express carriers). It provides feedback on the logistics "friendliness" of the countries in which they operate and with which they trade. Respondents combine in-depth knowledge of the countries in which they operate, informed qualitative assessments of other countries with which they trade, and experience of the global logistics environment.

The LPI comprises both qualitative and quantitative measures. It measures the performance of the logistics supply chain within a country from two perspectives. An international LPI provides qualitative evaluations of a country by its logistics professionals working outside the country in six dimensions: the efficiency of customs and border management clearance, the quality of trade and transport-related infrastructure, the ease of arranging competitively priced shipments, the competence and quality of logistics services, the ability to track and trace consignments, and the frequency with which shipments reach the consignee within the scheduled time. A domestic LPI provides both qualitative and quantitative assessments of a country by logistics professionals working inside it. It includes detailed information on the logistics environment, core logistics processes, institutions, and performance time and cost data.

———. *Trade and Transport Facilitation Assessment*. Washington, DC. http://siteresources.worldbank.org/EXTTLF/Resources/Trade&Transport_Facilitation_Assessment_Practical_Toolkit.pdf.

The Trade and Transport Facilitation Assessment (TTFA) toolkit is intended for specialists interested in trade facilitation and logistics in developing countries, including policy makers; development practitioners, including staff of development agencies supervising the implementation of audits, such as country economists or operational task managers; and trade and transport facilitation consultants.

———. *World Integrated Trade Solution*. Washington, DC. http://wits.worldbank.org. The World Bank—in close collaboration with other international organizations, such as UNCTAD, the International Trade Center (ITC), the UN Statistical Division, and the World Trade Organization (WTO)—developed the World Integrated Trade Solution (WITS). This software accesses and retrieves information on trade and tariffs compiled in the COMTRADE and Trade Analysis Information System (TRAINS) databases.

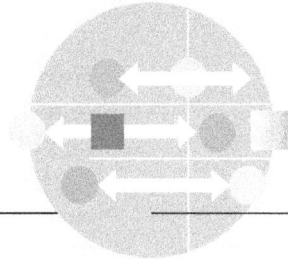

Assessing the Legal and Regulatory Context of a Corridor

At the initiation of a corridor project, it is often necessary to establish what international, regional, or bilateral legal instruments the corridor countries are party to that could affect the operation and performance of the corridor. Sharing the same instruments can be of great assistance in shaping a common vision and achieving smooth or seamless corridor operations. An extreme example is the European Union (EU), where the corridor approach is less relevant than elsewhere, because most of the basic legal instruments are in place and movement patterns are highly complex. In other regions, the legal foundations and agreements may not always allow the efficient and proper functioning of corridors, especially corridors connecting to third countries.[1] Generally, being a contracting party to international legal instruments and properly implementing their provisions are important because they ensure a degree of harmonization and simplification that facilitates transport and trade processes.

This module outlines why international legal instruments are relevant to corridors; describes the major instruments at the global, regional, and bilateral levels; and explains how to analyze the instruments and assess their implementation. It does not provide exhaustive coverage of the legal instruments that may affect trade corridors. It is intended to be used as a guide to identifying pertinent trade facilitation instruments that are relevant to the design of corridor projects.

The module is organized as follows. The first section reviews the major international and regional legal instruments that are of most relevance to corridor projects. International, regional, and domestic legal instruments often form a hierarchy. They have to be assessed to determine the extent to which they conform to one another, both on paper and in practice. The second section makes the case for the importance of proper coordination across the three levels to make sure they are coherent. Ultimately, of course, legal instruments are only as effective as their implementation. The last section therefore provides guidance on how to assess the extent to which an instrument conforms to international obligations and is being implemented. The module uses examples to illustrate how each of the steps might be executed.

Collaboration, Cooperation, and Management

Legal instruments are important to corridor development, as they are aimed at facilitating collaboration, cooperation, and management between corridor parties at different levels. *Collaboration* is the highest level of decision making. It involves political alliances between heads of state, parliaments, and governments along the corridor. *Cooperation* is mutual support by ministries and agencies. *Management* refers to the effective running of the corridor. An *agreement* refers to any form of document, binding or not, that reflects the willingness and commitment of the parties concerned by the development of the corridor and endorsed by them, including a memorandum of understanding, a convention, a treaty, or other types of agreements. Corridor instruments are the foundation for the management of international trade and transport corridors presented in Module 3.

It is also common to find corridor management arrangements embedded in other instruments, such as transit treaties. For example, Chile and Bolivia have a several decades–old agreement in place that regulates transit movement between the two countries. Pakistan and Afghanistan are negotiating a new bilateral agreement. Both agreements provide for the regulation of bilateral and transit traffic between the two pairs of countries.

In terms of collaboration, the success of a corridor depends on the extent to which national interests are subordinated in full willingness and commitment to the common stated objective, as formalized in an agreement. The agreement can be binding or voluntary, depending on cultural, historical, or economic and financial factors. Recommendations on the nature of the agreement can be formulated based on these general factors and on additional, more specific ones, such as whether sanctions for noncompliance are possible and enforceable in that environment, whether laws on mutual guarantee of investments are in force, whether double taxation is avoided, and so forth. Considering the importance of the coordinated allocation of national funds to ensure even development and coherent funding of the corridor, it would be beneficial to include ministers of finance in the collaboration and their mandated representatives in the cooperation.

Ideally, the collaboration agreement, which is supposed to be highly political, should contain the overall concept for coordinated development of the corridor—that is, the strategic perspective developed by the countries concerned on transport, logistics, and trade in the context of the corridor, as well as agreed upon benchmarks. The document should also contain the decision on the forms of cooperation and management of the corridor, aimed at implementing the strategic perspective. Given the high level at which collaboration occurs, it would be sensible to schedule regular meetings only every two or three years.

The cooperation agreement should detail all legal, economic, organizational, and social questions contributing to the implementation of the strategy and the benchmarks. As the document is a comprehensive one, it could be divided into chapters and cover all aspects related to infrastructure, services, and facilitation, such as but not limited to prioritization, the feasibility or technical design of specific maintenance, reconstruction, rehabilitation, upgrading and investment measures, transshipment facilities, equipment standards, improved logistics, enhanced safety and security, multinational data collection and analysis capability, cooperation in undertaking studies and creating a joint "library" of existing studies, and creation of conditions necessary for participation by international financial institutions and the private sector in the development and operation of the corridor.

Hierarchy of Instruments

Several levels of legal instruments affect corridor operations. Determining which international, regional, and bilateral instruments a country is party to helps in the assessment of the following:

- degree of harmonization and simplification
- likely legal costs (including sanctions) incurred for infringements or prior legal advice in cases of significant differences in legislation

- degree of cooperation and existence of/potential for partnerships along the corridor
- degree of freedom of movement for goods, people, services, and capital along the corridor.[2]

There are various considerations when assessing a country's use of international legal instruments:

- Which instruments is each corridor country party to at the multilateral, regional, and bilateral level? Most countries are members of a regional/subregional economic community and use such membership to improve and strengthen their domestic policy reform. Membership can also help consolidate market-oriented policy reforms.
- Are there any conflicts in the instruments at the international, regional, and bilateral levels? A proliferation of instruments can create confusion and compromise efficiency. Which instruments have supremacy in case of conflicts?
- What do the instruments cover?
- Are the instruments being properly implemented?
- Are any instruments used for reasons other than trade and transport facilitation, such as for security purposes?
- Is there any contribution to domestic policy reform. If so, what is it?

International Legal Instruments

An initial step in assessing the legal context of a corridor is to determine any instruments of relevance to trade and transport facilitation that corridor countries might be party to. Grosdidier de Matons (2013) identifies 19 general policy instruments applicable to all modes of transport (air, sea, land) that are relevant to trade and transport facilitation, as follows.

Five conventions protecting the interests of landlocked states:

- 1921 Barcelona Convention on freedom of transit
- 1947 General Agreement on Tariffs and Trade (GATT) (later the General Agreement on Trade in Services [GATS])
- 1965 New York Convention on Transit Trade of Landlocked Countries
- 1921 Convention and Statute on Freedom of Transit
- 1958 Geneva Convention on the High Seas.

Five conventions relating to the functioning of customs:

- 1950 Brussels Convention establishing a customs cooperation council
- 1973 Kyoto Convention on the simplification and harmonization of customs procedures, preceded by the 1923 Geneva Convention on the same matter

- 1977 Nairobi Convention on mutual administrative assistance for the prevention, investigation, and repression of customs offences
- 1982 Geneva Convention on the harmonization of frontier control of goods.

Five technical conventions relating to transport equipment:

- 1960 Brussels Convention on pallets
- 1956 and 1972 Geneva Customs Conventions on containers
- 1960 Brussels Convention on packings
- 1994 Geneva Convention on pool containers.

Four customs conventions relating to the temporary import of goods and equipment:

- 1961 Customs Convention on the temporary importation of professional equipment
- 1968 Customs Convention on the temporary admission of scientific equipment
- 1970 Customs Convention on the temporary admission of pedagogic material
- 1961 Customs Convention on the Admission Temporaire/Temporary Admission (ATA) carnet for the temporary admission of goods.

Most of the United Nations' legal instruments relating to transport facilitation have been elaborated under the auspices of the United Nations Economic Commission for Europe (UNECE). Countries from regions other than Europe can become parties to the vast majority of these legal instruments.

One of the major international instruments that is extensively used in Europe but has since been adopted globally is the 1975 Geneva Customs Convention on the International Transport of Goods under cover of the TIR carnets.[3] If adopted and properly implemented, carnets can have a significant impact on corridor performance. The TIR provides for a system of bonds, operated in nearly 70 countries, that guarantees that customs and other duties will be paid on goods transported in transit trucks. Its objective is both to improve transport conditions and to simplify and harmonize administrative formalities in international transport, particularly at frontiers. (Module 6 elaborates on the TIR.)

Other instruments that may be important are the conventions on the international carriage of goods by various modes of transport, including the following:

- Warsaw and Montreal Conventions on air transport
- Hague-Visby, Hamburg, and Rotterdam Conventions on sea transport

- Convention on the Contract for the International Carriage of Goods by Road
- Convention on International Carriage by Rail.

These conventions provide assurance to shippers that the means of transport are safe and that the goods will be delivered to the designated recipient at destination. They deal mainly with the risks and liabilities in the event that goods are damaged or lost during transport. Risks during transport are normally transferred through possession of transport documents such as bills of lading (airway bills in the case of air transport), which are fundamental to the international carriage of goods.

Major Regional Legal Instruments

Countries often prefer regional agreements and instruments to ratification of international instruments. Discovering all such agreements can be onerous.[4] Identifying the core set of international instruments is often easier than establishing instruments at the regional level. In general, some of the legal instruments in Central Asia, East Asia, and Latin America can be easily found in the respective UN commissions of these regions. The legal instruments of Africa, South Asia, and Middle East and North Africa are not always readily accessible. The concept of joining important regional and international conventions seems less appreciated in these regions.

East Asia and Pacific. The East Asia and Pacific region has several agreements of relevance to international trade corridors. They cover both infrastructure development and trade facilitation. Some of the main agreements include the following:

- *ASEAN Trade in Goods Agreement.* Signed in 2009 by Cambodia, Indonesia, the Lao People's Democratic Republic, Malaysia, Myanmar, the Philippines, Singapore, Thailand, and Vietnam, the agreement seeks to achieve the free flow of goods in the Association of Southeast Asian Nations (ASEAN) as one means of establishing a single market for regional integration. Article 12 of the agreement incorporates Article X of GATT 1994. Article 19 reduces or eliminates import duties. Chapter 5 identifies the scope of the trade facilitation work program. It promotes the transparency of policies, laws, regulations, administrative rulings, licensing, certification, and so forth at the regional and national level; communications and consultations between the authorities and the business and trading community; simplification, practicability, and efficiency of rules and procedures relating to trade; nondiscrimination rules and procedures relating to trade; the consistency and predictability of rules and procedures relating to trade; and so forth. Chapter 6 covers the rules on customs, including the expeditious clearance of goods.

- *ASEAN Comprehensive Investment Agreement.* Signed in 2009 by Cambodia, Indonesia, Lao PDR, Malaysia, Myanmar, the Philippines, Singapore, Thailand, and Vietnam, this agreement seeks to create a free and open investment regime in ASEAN to achieve economic integration and create a liberal, facilitative, transparent, and competitive investment environment in ASEAN. Article 7 requires ASEAN members that do not belong to the World Trade Organization (WTO) to abide by WTO provisions. The principle of fair and equitable treatment and full protection and security is stated in Article 11, which also provides for the free transfer of capital.

- *ASEAN Framework Agreement on the Facilitation of Goods in Transit.* This agreement was signed in 1998 by Indonesia, Lao PDR, Malaysia, the Philippines, Thailand, and Vietnam. Brunei Darussalam, Myanmar, and Singapore later also joined the agreement, which seeks to facilitate the transportation of goods in transit; simplify and harmonize transport, trade, and customs regulations requirements; and establish an effective, efficient, integrated, and harmonized transit transport system in ASEAN. Various provisions apply to transit transport. Part II regulates frontier facilities (designation frontier posts at border point); Part III regulates traffic regulations, transit transport services, road transport permits, technical requirements of vehicles, mutual recognition of inspection certificates, mutual recognition of driving licenses, and third-party insurance schemes for motor vehicles. Part IV regulates general conditions for rail transport. Part V regulates customs control, notably harmonization and simplification of customs procedures. The protocols analyze in detail the different themes of the agreement. For example, Protocol 1 governs the designation of transit transport routes and facilities, and Protocol 2 governs the designation of frontier posts.

- *Greater Mekong Subregion Cross-Border Transport Agreement of 2005.* Signed by Cambodia, China, Lao PDR, Myanmar, Thailand, and Vietnam, this agreement seeks to mitigate nonphysical barriers to the cross-border movement of goods and people, in order to increase efficiency, reduce costs, and maximize the economic benefits of improved subregional transport infrastructure. The agreement covers all relevant aspects of cross-border transport facilitation, including single-stop/single-window customs inspection; the cross-border movement of people; transit traffic regimes, including exemptions from physical customs inspection; bond deposit; escort; requirements regarding vehicle eligibility for cross-border traffic; and exchange of commercial traffic rights.

- *Ministerial Understanding on ASEAN Cooperation in Transportation.* This agreement was signed in 1996 by Indonesia, Malaysia, the Philippines, Thailand, and Vietnam. Brunei Darussalam and Singapore have since joined as contracting parties. The agreement establishes and develops a harmonized and integrated regional transportation system; enhances cooperation in the transport sector; establishes a mechanism to coordinate and supervise cooperation projects and activities in the transport sector; and promotes the interconnectivity and interoperability of national networks and access by linking islands, landlocked regions, and peripheral regions with the national and global economies. Articles 2, 3, and 4 deal with policy coordination, harmonization of laws, rules and regulations, development of multimodal transport, and trade facilitation.

- *Agreement on the Recognition of Commercial Vehicle Inspection Certificates for Goods Vehicles and Public Service Vehicles.* This agreement was signed by Indonesia, Lao PDR, Malaysia, the Philippines, Thailand, and Vietnam in 1998. Brunei Darussalam, Myanmar, and Singapore have also since joined this agreement, which seeks to facilitate the cross-border movement of commercial goods and public service vehicles by mutual recognition of commercial vehicle inspection certificates issued by the contracting parties.

- *Ministerial Understanding on the Development of the ASEAN Highway Network Project.* Adopted by the ASEAN countries in 1999, this understanding establishes the institutional mechanism for formalizing the strategic route configuration, formulates the ASEAN Highway Infrastructure Development Plan, promotes cooperation with other international and regional organizations to ensure technical compatibility of ASEAN's road standards, and intensifies cooperation in the facilitation of international road traffic throughout the region. Article 2 describes the ASEAN highway route configuration and technical requirements. Article 3 addresses the development strategy for implementation of the ASEAN Highway Network Project.

- Other agreements to facilitate free flow of goods in the region include the ASEAN Preferential Trading Arrangements (1977), the Agreement on the Common Effective Preferential Tariff Scheme for the ASEAN Free Trade Area (1992), the ASEAN Agreement on Customs (1997), the ASEAN Framework Agreement on Mutual Recognition Arrangements (1998), the e-ASEAN Framework Agreement (2000), the Protocol Governing the

Implementation of the ASEAN Harmonized Tariff Nomenclature (2003), the ASEAN Framework Agreement for the Integration of Priority Sectors (2004), and the Agreement to Establish and Implement the ASEAN Single Window (2005).

Europe and Central Asia. Europe and Central Asia has the second-largest number of landlocked countries in the world, after Africa. Not surprisingly, it has a long history of international cooperation in matters relating to trade and transport facilitation. Some of the major regional instruments include the following:

- *European Agreement on Main International Traffic Arteries (AGR) of 1975.* This agreement defines the main roads linking Albania, Armenia, Azerbaijan, Belarus, Kazakhstan, the former Yugoslav Republic of Macedonia, Moldova, the Russian Federation, Turkey, and Ukraine. Annexes to the agreement list relevant roads and standards to which the international arteries should conform.
- *European Agreement on Main International Railway Lines (AGC) of 1985.* This agreement seeks to facilitate and develop international railway traffic in Europe by adopting a common plan of railway network coordination. Annex I defines the railway lines of international importance. Annex II defines the technical characteristics of the international railway lines. Contracting parties include EU member states and some former Soviet republics.
- *European Agreement on Important International Combined Transport Lines and Related Installations (AGTC).* Signed in 1991 by EU member states and some former Soviet republics, this agreement seeks to facilitate the international transport of goods through combined transport to alleviate the burden on the European road network, make international combined transport in Europe more efficient and attractive to customers, and establish a legal framework to lay down a coordinating plan for the development of combined transport services. Annexes I and II define railway lines, installations, and border-crossing points of importance for international combined transport. Annex II defines the technical characteristics of the network.
- *Basic Multilateral Agreement on International Transport for Development of the Europe–the Caucasus–Asia Corridor.* This agreement, signed by Armenia, Azerbaijan, Bulgaria, Georgia, the Islamic Republic of Iran, Kazakhstan, the Kyrgyz Republic, Moldova, Romania, Tajikistan, Turkey, Ukraine, and Uzbekistan, is a key Transport Corridor Europe-Caucasus-Asia (TRACECA) document. It establishes

the legal basis for the development of economic relations, trade, and transport communication in Europe, the Black Sea, the Caucasus, the Caspian Sea, and Asia. It aims to regulate the international transport of goods and passengers and transport and transit through the territories of the parties.

Latin America and the Caribbean. More than 50 free trade agreements (FTAs) have been negotiated by the countries of Latin America and Caribbean (LAC), and more are in the process of being negotiated. Most of these bilateral/trilateral FTAs are modeled on the North American Free Trade Agreement (NAFTA) in terms of their structure, scope, and coverage.[5] Mexico alone has signed FTAs with more than 30 countries. Most bilateral FTAs have provisions on customs formalities (a single tariff mechanism, a single administrative document for imports and exports, harmonization of customs legislation and customs formalities) and on progressive if not immediate elimination of technical barriers to trade. The aim of these instruments is to facilitate the transit and transport of goods within corridors of member parties to these agreements.

Between 1961 and 2011, LAC countries signed more than 100 agreements that may affect trade in transport corridors. Some of the main agreements of relevance to trade corridors in the region include the following:

- *Cartagena Agreement of 1969.* This agreement was signed by Bolivia, Chile, Columbia, Ecuador, Peru, and República Bolivariana de Venezuela. The agreement creates a customs union and seeks to eliminate intraregional trade barriers. It provides for integrated border controls; the border integration and development policy, adopted in 1999, defines the areas for border integration. It establishes implementation and harmonization of customs procedures (codes, regulations, and a single manual for customs procedures); the united customs document and the harmonization of customs procedures entered into force June 1, 2010. It enhances or establishes regulations on customs transit; a new version of community customs transit regulations was completed in April 2010.
- *Central American Economic Integration Secretariat (SIECA).* Signed in 1960 by Costa Rica, El Salvador, Guatemala, Honduras, and Nicaragua, this agreement defines the technical and administrative role for the Central American economic integration process. The agreement includes six legal documents related to transport trade corridors: the Protocol to the General Treaty of Central American Economic Integration, the Central American Agreement on Road Transit, the Central American Agreement on Uniform Road Signals, the Regional

Agreement on the Temporary Importation of Road Vehicles, the Transportation Agreement between Central America and Panama 02-2007, and the COMITRAN Agreement.

- *Central America-4 Border Control Agreement.* Signed in June 2006 by El Salvador, Guatemala, Honduras, and Nicaragua, this agreement seeks to establish free movement across borders—no restrictions, no checks—for a maximum stay of 90 days. It establishes a harmonized visa regime for foreign nationals traveling within the contracting states. Although it has no specific provisions related to corridors, it has the same objectives as the Schengen Agreement in Europe.
- *Pacific Corridor of the Mesoamerican Integration and Development Project.* This project was launched by Belize, Costa Rica, El Salvador, Guatemala, Honduras, Nicaragua, Mexico, and Panama in June 2001; Columbia joined in 2006. It provides for measures to connect markets, reduce transport and trade costs, enhance trade competitiveness, improve the climate for foreign investment, and deliver goods and services to world markets more efficiently. It gives landlocked countries Bolivia and Paraguay access to oceans. The project comprises five corridors, including two major ones: the Pacific and Atlantic corridors are an overland link connecting the Atlantic and Pacific oceans via Chile, Brazil, and Bolivia.
- *Southern Common Market (MERCOSUR) of 1995.* Argentina, Brazil, Paraguay, and Uruguay are full members. Bolivia, Chile, Columbia, Ecuador, and Peru are associate members. The agreement provides for the creation of a customs union, eliminating intraregional barriers to the free movement of goods.

Middle East and North Africa. Various trade agreements affect corridor operations in the Middle East and North Africa:

- *Greater Arab Free Trade Agreement (GAFTA).* GAFTA covers 22 countries. It covers trade in both industrial and agricultural goods. With the exception of Somalia, most members are implementing the agreement.
- *Gulf Cooperation Council (GCC).* Created in 1981 by Bahrain, Kuwait, Oman, Qatar, Saudi Arabia, and the United Arab Emirates, the GCC had an ambitious program to establish a customs union and adopt a common currency. To date, neither goal has been achieved.
- *Convention of Cooperation in Transit and Road Transport between State Members of the Community Sahel-Saharan States (CEN-SAD).* The convention was agreed to in 2005. Article 2 defines its scope. Title II is related to interstate road transport. It applies to transportation and the transports of goods within the territories of member states.

- *Cooperation Agreement in Maritime Transport between Members of the Community of Sahel-Saharan States.* Concluded on June 1, 2006, this agreement seeks to organize maritime relations among member states; improve coordination of bilateral and multilateral maritime traffic; prevent all obstacles to the development of maritime transport among member states; coordinate efforts preventing illegal activities, such as piracy and terrorism; facilitate the port transport of merchandise in transit from the coastal to landlocked member states; develop technical cooperation in training personnel; and develop and assist in information sharing. The agreement is applicable to maritime transport among members of the community.

The Arab Maghreb Union has several instruments with potential impacts on regional trade and transport corridors, including the following:

- the Maritime Cooperation Agreement of 1991, revised in in 2009
- the Agreement on Road Transport and Transit of Passengers and Merchandises of 1990, revised in 2009
- the Agreement on Land Transport of Dangerous Products, 2009
- the Agreement on the Mutual Recognition of Driving Licenses in Member States, 1992.

South Asia. Major regional instruments and FTAs in South Asia include the following:

- *SAARC (South Asian Association for Regional Cooperation) Preferential Trading Agreement (SAPTA) of 1993.* SAPTA seeks to promote interregional trade and liberalize trade in the region through duty-free trade on certain products, tariff concessions, elimination of nontariff measures, and implementation of direct trade measures. It provides for special treatment for the least developed contracting states.
- *Bay of Bengal Initiative for Multi-Sectoral Technical and Economic Cooperation (BIMSTEC).* Signed in 1997 by Bangladesh, Bhutan, India, Myanmar, Nepal, Sri Lanka, and Thailand, BIMSTEC seeks to establish effective trade- and investment-facilitating measures, including simplification of customs procedures and elimination of tariff barriers. No agreement on the free trade area proposed in 2004 has yet been signed.
- *South Asia Free Trade Area (SAFTA) of 2004.* SAFTA seeks to strengthen intra-SAARC economic cooperation, eliminate barriers to trade, and facilitate the cross-border movement of goods. It also addresses the simplification and harmonization of customs clearance procedures and transit facilities for efficient intra-SAARC trade.

Bilateral agreements are more relevant to corridor operations in South Asia than multilateral instruments. More than 15 bilateral agreements directly affect trade and transit corridors. The agreements cover various issues, including trade, transit, road transport, and inland waterway transport. Examples of bilateral agreements include the following:

- *India-Bangladesh Trade Agreement*. Signed in 1972 and renewed in 2006, this agreement seeks to promote, facilitate, expand, and diversify trade between the two countries. It seeks mutually beneficial arrangements for the use of their waterways, roadways, and railways for the passage of goods between the two countries. The bilateral Protocol on Inland Water Transport and Trade, signed in 1999 and renewed in 2007, seeks to facilitate the passage of goods by using the two countries waterways. It provides a list of the routes involved. The two countries provide each other with handling and repair facilities and mutually recognize survey certificates and other documents.
- *Agreements between India and Nepal*. The Treaty of Trade, signed in 1991, provides transit access to Nepal, defines operational modalities, and provides a list of bilateral trade routes. Under the treaty, India provides maritime transit and supporting services and facilities to Nepal. The India-Nepal Rail Services Agreement governs the operation and management of rail services for Nepal's transit trade as well as bilateral trade between the two countries.
- *Bhutan-India Trade Agreement*. Signed in 1995, this agreement sets the broad basis for free trade between the two countries. It also specifies bilateral trade routes, including transit and trading procedures.

Sub-Saharan Africa. A comprehensive review of trade facilitation instruments in Sub-Saharan Africa was initially conducted in 2004 by the World Bank's Sub-Saharan Africa Transport Policy Program (SSATP), in partnership with African countries, regional economic communities (RECs), donors, and African institutions. The review, which was subsequently updated in 2013 (Grosdidier de Matons 2013) covers all worldwide, continental, and regional instruments that affect the facilitation of trade and transit along corridors. It identifies more than 90 subregional instruments in Sub-Saharan Africa.

The 2013 update found that at the world level, the trade framework under the WTO evolved following the Marrakech agreements, and the European Partnership Agreement renewed trade collaboration framework between the European Union and most developing countries previously covered by the Lomé agreements. However, at the continental level, there were no major new additions while at the regional level, new instruments continue to be drafted. A few corridor management groups have also been formalized over the intervening period.

Some of the pertinent instruments that were concluded over the past decade include the following:

- *Inter-State Convention on Road Transport of General Cargo.* In July 1996, the Council of heads of states of the members of the Economic Community of Central African States (UDEAC) agreed on the legal framework of road transport of general cargo in the subregion. This convention follows the wording of the Convention on the Contract for the International Carriage of Goods by Road of 1956.
- *The Economic and Monetary Community of Central Africa (CEMAC) Framework for Multimodal Transport Operations.* The Geneva Convention on international multimodal transport of 1980 did not come into force, because it was not ratified by a sufficient number of governments. CEMAC countries filled the gap in international law by providing member countries with a clear and undisputable framework for multimodal transport operations, the provisions of which were borrowed from the nonratified international convention.
- *Inter-State Regulation on Licensing of Road Carriers.* As of July 5, 1996, all road carriers, for transport for own account or for professional transport, need to be licensed and to adhere to the third-party liability insurance guarantee system (TIPAC). Licensing is handled by the ministries of transport of each member state. Licenses are issued for five years, for a specific road network or specific itineraries.
- *Northern Corridor Transit and Transport Agreement.* Signed in March 2007 by Burundi, the Democratic Republic of Congo, Kenya, Rwanda, and Uganda, this agreement extends the mandate and scope of the 1985 agreement, renews the protocols, and develops new ones. It has 11 protocols covering various aspects of transport infrastructure development, logistics services provision, and management of the corridor.
- *Central Corridor Transit Transport Facilitation Agency Agreement.* This agreement, signed by Burundi, the Democratic Republic of Congo, Rwanda, Tanzania, and Uganda in 2006, covers transit routes for cargo and passenger transport utilizing all Tanzanian roads connecting to the other countries as well as all roads and railway systems in these landlocked countries connecting to the Port of Dar es Salaam. The duration of the agreement is 10 years from the date of entry into force. No protocols have yet been issued. The depository of the agreement is the United Nations Economic Commission for Africa.

- *Regional Tripartite Program between COMESA, EAC, and SADC* is a joint tripartite initiative of the Common Market for Eastern and Southern Africa (COMESA), the East African Community (EAC), and the South African Development Community (SADC). It was born from the Tripartite Summit held in Kampala, Uganda, in October 2008. It is a comprehensive approach to corridor development, focusing on the North-South corridor linking Tanzania to South Africa, which passes through Botswana, Malawi, Mozambique, Zambia, and Zimbabwe.
- *Recommendation No. 02/2002/CM/UEMOA on the Simplification and Harmonization of the Administrative Procedures and Port Transit within the West African Economic and Monetary Union (UEMOA).* A program on simplification and harmonization of administrative procedures and transit in ports was issued in June 2002; the Ministers Council made a recommendation based on this program. Since this recommendation, several regulations and directives have been issued by the Ministers Council, with an emphasis on maritime transport. The transport maritime regulations are applicable to inland transport, intracommunity transport, and international maritime transport from and to a port of each member state.

Analysis of Legal Instruments

Conformity Analysis

The simplest form of evaluation is a "conformity table," in which national laws are compared with the regional or international legal instrument article by article. The result shows the degree of compliance of national laws with the international legal instrument. The table also provides details about the cost and time of implementing the international legal instrument. Detailed action plans can be elaborated based on the conformity table by each of the authorities responsible for implementing the international legal instrument.

This type of analysis yields a realistic assessment of the implications of implementing multilateral legal instruments and identifies (and subsequently eliminates) conflicting provisions, duplication, and overlap at the corridor level. The conformity table can also be a useful tool for assessing the performance of the corridor.

Table 2.1 is a hypothetical conformity table for a country considering becoming a party to the 1982 International Convention on the Harmonization of Frontier Controls of Goods.

TABLE 2.1 Assessment of Conformity with National Laws of the 1982 International Convention on the Harmonization of Frontier Controls of Goods

International legal instrument	Corresponding national law	Difference	Necessary adjustments	Impact of implementation	Time needed for compliance
Article 5: Resources of the services To ensure that the control services operate satisfactorily, the contracting parties shall see to it that, as far as possible and within the framework of national law, they are provided with the following:	Provisions of this article are specific requirements of the international legal instrument. They will therefore be introduced in national legislation through the law ratifying the convention.	No equivalent definition exists in the national law.	Introduce the provisions through the law of ratification of the convention.		
Qualified personnel in sufficient numbers, consistent with traffic requirements			Determine the border offices where the convention will apply and, based on traffic and human resources data, the necessary staff.	Recruitment of X numbers of personnel, costing $X, reassignment of personnel from other border offices, costing $X, or current staff is sufficient.	X months or by 201X
Equipment and facilities suitable for inspection, taking into account the mode of transport, the goods to be checked, and traffic requirements			Invest in facilities and acquisition of equipment if they are not already in place.	Minimum facilities (for example, X-ray scanner) would cost about $X.	X months/years or by 201X

Status and Extent of Implementation

Ratifying an international legal instrument or concluding a bilateral agreement is a very positive step, but it has little effect unless the instrument is implemented. Ideally, assessment of the degree of implementation should be based on documented comparison of laws, but in most cases, time and other resource constraints impose simpler solutions. Assessment should also include the technical readiness of countries to achieve the intended objectives of the instruments. One possible approach is to ask specific questions about the key provisions of the most important legal instruments, some of which are suggested below.

Becoming party to an international legal instrument requires careful analysis and evaluation at the national level. This process may call for adaptation of national laws and institutions, the adoption of new technical standards in transport infrastructure and equipment, and acceptance of new organizational and operational systems. Analysts must therefore evaluate the legal instrument to determine its benefits and implications for the government and the private sector, as well as its overall economic, social, and financial impact. Such an evaluation is carried out by the ministry most concerned (in transport facilitation matters it would be the ministry of transport) but normally requires multidisciplinary teamwork by several government agencies as well as consultation with representatives of the private sector, as almost all stages of the process concern both sectors. Assessment and evaluation should therefore be made jointly. It is important to ascertain the extent to which the content and provisions of regional and international instruments are known and respected by parties directly involved in corridor operations.

Table 2.2 provides an example of the questions that could be asked to assess the status of implementation of the 1968 Vienna Convention on Road Traffic.

Capacity building helps reduce transport costs by improving coordination at borders. Identifying linkages across borders and synergies between investments, policy choices, and practices in neighboring countries can help attract foreign investment in small countries and benefit larger countries by increasing their market share.

TABLE 2.2 Assessment of Implementation of the 1968 Vienna Convention on Road Traffic

Article	Questions
Article 3.3, 1949 Convention	Do customs offices and posts next to each other on the same international road have the same working hours?
Article 15, 1949 Convention and Article 33, 1968 Convention	Are vehicles required to have and turn on their front and rear lights during operation? How many and which color?
Article 17.4 and 17.5, 1949 Convention, and Article 4.d, 1968 Convention	Is it permissible to affix a notice (such as an advertising notice) to a traffic sign, obscuring or interfering with the sign?
Annex 7, 1968 Convention	Do vehicle weights and dimensions comply with Annex 7 of the 1968 Convention? If not, have countries concluded regional agreements allowing for increased weights?
Annex 10, 1949 Convention or Annex 7, 1968 Convention	Is the international driving permit in compliance?
Article 3.5, 1968 Convention	Does legislation lay down minimum requirements concerning the curriculum and qualifications of the staff of professional driving schools who provide driving instruction to student drivers?
Article 7.5, 1968 Convention	Is the wearing of safety belts compulsory for drivers and passengers of motor vehicles?
Article 8.6, 1968 Convention	Does national legislation prohibit the use by a driver of a motor vehicle or moped of a hand-held phone while the vehicle is in motion?
Article 35, 1968 Convention	Must every motor vehicle in international traffic be registered by a contracting party? Must the driver of the vehicle carry a valid certificate of such registration bearing the particulars specified?
Article 39, 1968 Convention	Are periodic technical inspections mandatory for motor vehicles used for the carriage of persons and having more than eight seats in addition to the driver's seat and motor vehicles used for the carriage of goods whose permissible maximum mass exceeds 3,500 kilograms and trailers designed to be coupled to such vehicles?
Article 41, 1968 Convention	Does national legislation foresee that driving permits are issued only after verification by the competent authorities that the driver possesses the required knowledge and skills?

Notes

1. An example is the Russia-Kazakhstan-Belarus customs union. Its product requirements affected the exports of the Kyrgyz Republic and therefore had a bottleneck effect on the flow of traffic.

2. An international agreement is a written instrument between two or more sovereign or independent public law entities, such as states or international organizations, intended to create rights and obligations between the parties that are governed by international law. Such instruments are designated as treaties, conventions, agreements, protocols, covenants, compacts, exchange of notes, memorandums of understanding, agreed minutes, letters, and so forth. Treaties may be bilateral or multilateral. Bilateral treaties are contracts in which two parties balance their claims on a specific matter. A multilateral treaty, usually titled a convention, sets rules of law to be observed by all parties, in their joint or

individual interest. A treaty can be regarded as a contract and must be interpreted as such. Enforcement of its terms and conditions by a government agency is more than the implementation of domestic law provisions. It is a contribution to international relations; it therefore has an impact on the signatories' reputation as partners in such relations (see Grosdidier de Matons 2013).

3. TIR stands for *transports internationaux routiers* (international road transport). It is an international customs transit system.

4. It is not unusual for regional agreements to contain provisions borrowed from international legal instruments. "Lite" versions of systems that have been successful in other regions of the world can be a solution for facilitation. It would be useful to establish the reasons why some developing countries in particular may not be keen on ratifying or implementing international instruments.

5. The main provisions common to these bilateral agreements are national treatment, market access for goods, customs procedures, cross-border trade in services, temporary entry for business people, administration of the agreement, and dispute settlement.

Reference

Grosdidier de Matons, J. 2013. "A Review of International Legal Instruments: Facilitation of Transport and Trade in Sub-Saharan Africa—Treaties, Conventions, Protocols, Decisions, Directives." SSATP Working Paper 73, World Bank, Sub-Saharan Africa Transport Policy Program, Washington, DC.

Resource

United Nations Treaty Collection. http://treaties.un.org/Pages/ParticipationStatus .aspx.
The collection includes UN and other treaties and provides information on the status of ratification of all instruments that have been deposited with the Secretary General of the United Nations. The site is a valuable first port of call to determine if corridor countries are party to the same international instruments. The most relevant chapters on trade and transport corridors are chapter X, which deals with international trade and development, and chapter XI, which deals with transport and communications. The online series is updated daily.

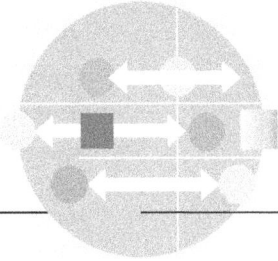

Institutional Arrangements for Corridor Management

In addition to cooperation and coordination in corridor development, a third pillar of the legal context of a corridor are the institutional arrangements for its management. Institutional arrangements are critical for the proper coordination of activities on a corridor. This module highlights the main functions and issues faced in corridor management and describes how to assess corridor institutional structures. Because institutions and the corridors they manage are by nature the products of complex geographical, political, historical, economic, and other forces, the module does not advocate for any particular mechanism for managing a corridor. Rather, it identifies the different types of management arrangements that exist on some corridors, the functions they play, and the stakeholders whose interests have to be considered.

Why Is Corridor Management Relevant?

The idea of managing a trade and transport corridor has become increasingly accepted as a component of trade and transport corridor projects. There are numerous parties involved in a corridor that require coordination to develop the corridor and ensure that it works efficiently.

They include the government agencies responsible for infrastructure (ports, roads, railways, border posts) and for regulation of services (transport, customs, immigration, security, health, agriculture, trade, and so forth) as well as private sector operators (roads, railways, ports, terminal operations, freight forwarding, cargo clearing, finance, and so forth). Above these, regional economic communities can be very influential in corridor development and trade and transport facilitation. Corridor management is about getting the various parties to co-produce plans and policies and to implement interventions that complement efforts to improve overall corridor performance. However, it can be a complex undertaking, as it often exists within the broad context of relations between countries.

Corridor management is as much about the relationships between different institutions and how they collaborate as it is about ensuring that the infrastructure and services are operational. Unless there is a mechanism for coordination, it may not always be apparent who should make the economic and technical decisions in a corridor and who is responsible for failures. Consequently, numerous corridors have institutional and administrative arrangements created for their management. Because of the large number of stakeholders, such management is not easy or efficient; decisions typically take a long time. Consultation and consensus are important to making sure solutions are acceptable to all parties and countries.

Capacity building has long been recognized as a necessary activity in trade facilitation. Aid-for-trade programs have been designed to enhance the capacity of low-income countries, in particular to improve their trade facilitation performance. This Toolkit is based on the premise that it is at the corridor level that many trade facilitation measures attain practical relevance. For this reason, the agencies and various players involved in corridor logistics must have the resources and capacity to maintain and continuously improve corridor performance.

Types of Corridor Management Mechanisms

The multiplicity of interested parties in a corridor often reflects the high degree of fragmentation in component laws, regulations, and institutions. A formalized corridor management structure may be a desirable mechanism to deal with pressing trade facilitation constraints in a structured and geographically restricted way. Generally, dedicated groups are found in corridors connecting landlocked countries to ports in neighboring countries.

The corridor groups seek to mitigate the negative consequences of being landlocked. A few other corridor initiatives in recent years have sought to exploit the corridor approach to meet other development objectives, such as regional development or health concerns (such as HIV/AIDS) that affect transient populations.

Groups may also be formed to manage a component of a corridor, such as a port or a border. The component to be managed explicitly is the one that is most critical to overall transport efficiency or one that poses special problems that require close cooperation among different parties.

Subnational corridor management efforts concentrate on how a region within a country can benefit from improved domestic and international connectivity. Although this Toolkit focuses on international trade and transport corridors, the same issues are relevant at the subnational level.

Whatever the level of the management structure, participants need to answer questions like the following:

- What best suits the corridor—a management structure or a monitoring structure?
- How should a management structure be formalized and empowered to manage the corridor, and what is the power of its decisions on governments?
- How will the management structure be financed (possibilities include national contributions based on a fixed budget, the secondment of experts from the country that provides the premises, and international grants)?
- Where will the structure be based, and what will its limit of competency (immunities) be?

Before addressing these and other questions, it is important to distinguish the characteristics of the management mechanism at different levels (table 3.1).

Main Activities of Corridor Management Bodies

Arnold (2006) identifies several activities in corridor management, including planning, financing, legislation, regulation, operation, monitoring, and promotion (table 3.2).

Key Considerations in Corridor Management

Regardless of the management arrangement, the independence and effectiveness of a corridor requires the support of all corridor countries.

TABLE 3.1 Characteristics and Examples of Corridor Management at the Regional, National, and Corridor Levels

Level	Management characteristics	Examples
Regional	Where a network of trade routes exists, it may not be feasible for each corridor to have a separate management structure. Instead, decision making is entrusted to a regional entity with oversight of all corridors. Typically, the regional body has a planning and monitoring role rather than a detailed management one. Corridor interventions are left to national players. In each country, responsibility is assigned to one ministry or to a multidisciplinary structure composed of line ministries, public agencies, and the private sector, usually under the direct supervision of a high-level official, such as the prime minister.	• Trans-European Transport Network (TEN-T) in Europe[a] • Corridors within the Economic Community of West African States (ECOWAS) • Corridors within Central Asia Regional Economic Cooperation (CAREC)
National	Corridor management is typically the responsibility of a national trade facilitation committee, which brings together public and private sector stakeholders concerned with international trade who serve as champions for change. These actors have the incentive to create, step by step, more constructive working relations with border control agencies and to join with them in seeking durable solutions. Experience suggests that consultation between the public and private sectors, and their working together toward a common goal, are crucial ingredients for the success of such bodies. But the formula for that cooperation—who takes the lead, whether the body should be larger or smaller, and who provides the funding—varies considerably from country to country, depending on the administrative culture and traditions regarding the roles of the public and private sectors. As the overriding objective is to build trust in settings where the point of departure is mutual mistrust, it is to be expected that some initiatives will fail or work for a while with one group of actors and then stumble when (for example) a government changes. This risk should not be grounds for giving up on the principle, although it may call for the reorganization or reconstitution of the committee. Committees tend to be very large, sometimes including more than 50 members and agencies. At this size, they are less effective in managing specific and largely technical tasks. To address this problem, some countries form smaller steering committees (with no more than five members).	• Bangladesh National Trade and Transport Facilitation Committee • Pakistan National Trade and Transport Facilitation Committee

TABLE 3.1 *continued*

Level	Management characteristics	Examples
Corridor	Management arrangements focused on a single corridor are much more common than national or regional arrangements. A single corridor structure reflects a need to concentrate on improving very specific trade routes, usually routes serving landlocked countries. Different models of single corridor management all share the same aim.	
	• Government-led management arrangements: In most instances, governments take the lead in corridor development and cooperation. Their role reflects both the international nature of corridors and the weakness of the private sector in collaborating and working across borders.	Northern Corridor Transit Transport Coordination Authority (NCTTCA) and Central Corridor Transit Transport Facilitation Agency (CCTTFA), both in East Africa
	• Private sector–led management arrangements: The private sector or autonomous state-owned enterprises may consider it necessary to exploit the corridor approach to develop business by growing volumes to support further investment or to create sufficient mass to advocate for the resolution of operational constraints.	Maputo Corridor Logistics Initiative (MCLI)
	• Management arrangements initiated by the public and private sectors	Walvis Bay Corridor Group, which actively promotes the use of the corridor linked to the Port of Walvis Bay in Namibia. The group engages in business development; commissions forward-looking research, feasibility studies, and new procedures; and gathers regional support for follow-up action on the corridor.
	• Project based corridor management arrangements	The Abidjan-Lagos Corridor Organization (ALCO) was formed to manage a World Bank–financed grant on HIV/AIDS in the Abidjan-Lagos corridor. Over time, ALCO has taken on more general corridor management functions, including serving as the project implementation unit for a trade facilitation project for the corridor.

a. The integration dimension of the networks rather than the role of management was the key objective.

Setting an Appropriate Objective

Establishing an appropriate objective for a corridor body is important to assessing its expected impact and its effectiveness. All corridor bodies aspire to enhance corridor performance and reduce costs. They may also have broader goals, such as promoting a supply chain in a specific sector, such as mining, agriculture, or industry. Ascertaining these nuances is important. Examples of objectives of some of the more famous corridor bodies are outlined below.

TABLE 3.2 Main Activities of Corridor Management Bodies

Activity	Objective
Planning, prioritizing, and financing corridor improvements	Coordinate development of infrastructure and facilities within a corridor by • prioritizing investments • ensuring the compatibility and complementarity of the planned assets, projecting demand and providing appropriate capacity, and maintaining a consistent level of quality • helping coordinate implementation of investments and improvements (for example, the Dar Corridor Committee under the Southern Africa Trade and Transport Facilitation project) • motivating and providing the regional linkages between infrastructure development in one country and related infrastructure that has to be developed in a neighboring country • advocating for and coordinating the maintenance and upgrading of corridor infrastructure and facilities • improving and expanding transport and logistics services within the corridor by appropriate agencies.
Advocating for legislative and regulatory reforms	• Either directly initiate legislation where the body has power (as in the case of Pakistan's National Trade and Transport Facilitation Committee) or advocate for legislation. • Advocate for simplification and harmonization of documentation and procedures related to standards and regulations. Typically, corridor bodies use lessons learned and experiences from other countries. In Zambia, advocacy by one of the regional corridor groups was instrumental to a review of national axle-load limits, leading to their standardization with neighboring countries. In some cases, proposals are based on international instruments. The main international and regional instruments of relevance to corridor performance are provided in Module 2.
Monitoring corridor performance	• Collect data on performance by coordinating efforts across all public and private sector stakeholders in the corridor. The data are evaluated to inform stakeholders of the level of service available as well as to quantify constraints, develop initiatives for improving performance, evaluate efforts to remove these constraints, and develop targets for future improvements.
Promoting corridor use	• Collect and disseminate information to potential users concerning the time and cost of moving goods through the corridor and the procedures to be followed at border crossings and gateways. • Disseminate information on current practices in corridor management, available legislation, and lessons learned from other corridor developments. Corridor marketing increases volumes, which can reduce costs for all users as well as help justify further investments in infrastructure and services.
Piloting reforms in trade facilitation and logistics	• Serve as pilot cases for reforms to better facilitate trade. It is not unusual for initiatives that start on corridors to be replicated nationally and regionally. In Southern Africa, the adoption of the Single Administrative Document for customs was first tested on the Trans-Kalahari Corridor before it was rolled out at the national level in several countries. The existence of a representative body makes it easy for all stakeholders to appreciate the rationale for proposed changes.

TABLE 3.2 *continued*

Activity	Objective
Giving voice to landlocked countries and the private sector	Through specific corridors, landlocked and coastal countries are able to engage each other in a concrete manner. Nearly all corridor groups draw their staff from all the countries served by the corridor. Several corridor groups also seek to achieve overall economic development along the corridor, based on the realization that transit corridors often have poor linkages to the local economies through which they pass. Making progress in this direction requires planning processes that are integrated with national and regional planning.
Supporting project implementation	Push for implementation of agreed actions to improve corridor performance. Well-established and mature corridor bodies can play an important role in facilitating and even serving as implementing units for corridor interventions. Examples of this include the Abidjan-Lagos Corridor Organization which is effectively a project implementation unit for a regional trade and transport facilitation project.

Source: Based on Arnold 2006.

Corridor groups in Africa have probably been much more effective in planning and monitoring than in meeting other objectives. They have tended to play an advocacy role, raising awareness of the investments that are required rather than getting involved in actual planning. Especially in groups where the private sector is active, the focus has been on marketing the corridors, in order to increase utilization. Doing so is important, especially where the private sector provides some of the infrastructure and services.

Striking a Balance between Public and Private Sector Interests

At one level, cooperation on international trade and transport corridors is about economic and political relationships between countries. As such, corridor management is typically based on interstate corridor bodies. Corridor groups are established as initiatives of either governments or the private sector. Often, cooperation on major interstate trade routes is based on legal instruments concluded between states. As a result, the majority of corridor management groups are dominated by governments.

Appropriate ownership and power sharing is critical to the effectiveness of the management function. In an ideal situation, each institution would share the same "horizontal" position of power and authority, a situation close to the concept of heterarchy (a situation in which all actors have the same power and influence). However, getting this balance right is not easy; in most corridor management bodies, either the public or the private sector dominates.

Some corridor bodies are making efforts to strike the right balance. The Northern Corridor Transit Transport Coordination Authority (NCTTCA) in East Africa now has a participatory stakeholders forum, in which the public and private sectors raise issues and exchange views. The Maputo Corridor Logistics Initiative (MCLI) has one of the more effective arrangements for the two sides to engage each other, largely as a result of its genesis and working modalities.

During corridor assessment, the constraints and priorities for improving a corridor are identified. As part of this assessment, a distinction should be made between infrastructure, services, and management priorities. Weaknesses in infrastructure or the regulatory environment are often easier to establish than weaknesses linked to the capacity of the different service providers, including the private sector. An assumption is usually made that service markets are competitive and service providers will compete on quality of service offered. This is not always the case, however: it is not unusual for corridor markets to operate at a suboptimal level. Under such circumstances, effort should be made to establish, from the interviews and other data collected as part of the assessment, what training and other capacity enhancement measures could be taken to improve the corridor.

The parties in a corridor have varying expectations of the benefits and costs associated with developing and using a corridor. Table 3.3 summarizes the main interests of the various stakeholders. Some costs and benefits are directly observable. For example, agencies involved in providing infrastructure incur very direct costs. In contrast, the costs of services incurred by corridor users may be less apparent. The stakeholder interests will affect how willing different players are to invest in management capacity.

Building Capacity

Capacity building for improved corridor management should be a critical component of any trade corridor project—but it is often neglected, because of the absence of sustainable financing mechanisms. Corridor projects are often not sustainable or fail to deliver on their intended development objectives as a result of lack of appropriate technical and management capacity. A corridor is only as strong as its weakest link; one underperforming component can compromise overall performance. It can also lead to the better-performing components incurring higher costs in an effort to compensate for the poorly performing component.

Defining a coherent and demand-driven capacity-building strategy for a corridor requires several steps:

- reaching consensus among corridor stakeholders on the main objectives and constraints and obtaining commitments from relevant institutions to address them

TABLE 3.3 Interests of Stakeholders in a Corridor

Stakeholder	Main interests
Shippers[a]	• Move consignment from origin to destination in shortest possible time and lowest cost. • Reduce shipping costs. • Ensure safe transportation and handling.
Transporters	• Reduce turnaround time. • Minimize opportunity cost of tying up truck on a particular route.
Clearing and forwarding agencies	• Reduce operating costs. • Handle increased volumes of cargo. • Increase the speed of the clearance process. • Reduce cross-border charges. • Harmonize documentation.
Customs authorities	• Promote overall economic development. • Increase customs duty collection. • Harmonize customs documents. • Improve throughput.
Port authorities	• Improve cargo throughput. • Increase port utilization. • Enhance port competitiveness.
Road authorities	• Preserve assets through axle-load control. • Recover the cost of infrastructure. • Improve road safety.
Security services	• Control illegal movement of goods and people. • Control illegal movement of goods and substances. • Manage the movement of plants and animals.
Service providers	• Increase traffic flows and therefore customers.
Consumers	• Reduce the cost of goods.
Health authorities	• Control and manage diseases and infections associated with mobile populations (HIV/AIDS, sexually transmitted diseases, and other communicable diseases).
Development partners	• Increase trade and regional integration and reduce poverty.

Source: Adzigbey, Kunaka, and Mitiku 2007.
a. In a study on cargo dwell time in ports in Africa, Raballand and others (2012) found that shippers can sometimes optimize their operations by storing cargo in ports rather than warehouses.

- identifying the component-specific capacity needs to improve performance
- determining the technical, human, and financial resources to enhance capacity
- designing a clear system of measurement to track the impact and results of the measures taken.

Capacity building on a corridor should not be a one-off exercise but an ongoing activity that should be part of the regular development plan for the corridor. As demands change, technology evolves; as people change, it is always necessary to cultivate capacity suited to the tasks at hand. Most of these issues should be identified as part of the assessment of a corridor, as outlined in Module 1.

Once the needs have been established, the next step is to identify the measures that can be taken to enhance the capacity of corridor agencies to improve performance. Several options are available. One of the main considerations is how to finance capacity-building measures. Financing is important, as the agencies that have to bear the costs of improvements often may not directly see the benefits; the rents accrue to other players and ultimately to the trading community.

One effective strategy to build corridor management capacity is training. Training can be based on international best practice. Materials and courses developed by international bodies—such as the World Customs Organization for customs and the International Federation of Freight Forwarders Association (FIATA) for clearing and forwarding agents—can be used. Agencies can also use in-house materials. Whatever materials are used, it is important that training responds directly to changes in the market.

Examples of well-managed corridors abound. Study tours are a valuable tool to expose corridor players to different approaches to management. Through such visits, stakeholders can learn lessons on how to deploy resources and identify new training needs.

Generally, corridor management requires an enthusiastic and strong champion. The champion provides strength and continuity to corridor development efforts. Donor funding may be needed to get the function off the ground. A champion serves as an anchor for dialogue and improvement efforts on a corridor.

The secondment of staff by one of the stakeholders can help build corridor management capacity. The Northern Corridor in East Africa started off with a secretariat that rotated among member countries. Europe has adopted a similar approach. Most countries have one ministry or agency that takes the lead in discussions on corridors. Such an agency could then be a natural home, especially in East and Southern Africa, which have already identified corridor stakeholders that can play such a function. Alternatively, a state or institution may designate some of its staff to manage business on a corridor. This approach is desirable at the stage at which definition of priorities and a corridor-wide perspective are needed. The Maputo Corridor Logistics Initiative was started when the major corridor users saw a need for such coordination.

The advantages of rotating top leadership include the following:

- Costs are spread among member states or institutions.
- There is greater commitment to ensure success, as sponsoring agencies would like to see their investments bear fruit.
- Partnerships can be consolidated through cost sharing and hence ownership.

The disadvantages of this approach include the following:

- There can be a lack of stability and continuity in terms of staff and action plans (especially where a rotating secretariat is used).
- The coordinating unit may promote domestic programs that may be suboptimal at the corridor level.
- The economically powerful states or sponsoring institutions may have greater representation in the secretariat or corridor institutions and hence more clout in decision making in favor of their interests.

Increasingly, corridor groups can share information on different aspects of corridor management. Programs such as the Sub-Saharan Africa Transport Policy Program (SSATP), port management associations, and regional programs such as Central Asia Regional Economic Cooperation (CAREC) provide opportunities for knowledge sharing that can help improve capacity on individual corridors. In Southern Africa, different organizations are working to establish knowledge platforms on corridors that will allow corridor groups to share experiences and learn from others.

Financing

A sustainable corridor management arrangement is paramount to viable corridor management. The best sustainable financing arrangements establish a direct link between investments in increased capacity and benefits to corridor service providers and users. Having reliable data on the level of performance of a corridor is important to all the functions of corridor management.

Across several corridors in Africa, there are now activities to collect data on a regular basis and to compute some core corridor performance indicators, often designed as observatories (see Module 1). These efforts are particularly important for landlocked countries, most of which have more than two alternative access routes to the sea. They would be interested in assessing which corridor is worth investing in for maximum returns. Being able to compare the relative performance of the corridors would be helpful to decision making, creating a virtuous cycle of corridor improvement. The most prevalent corridor management financing mechanisms are outlined below.

Self-financing. Management of a corridor can be financed by corridor stakeholders. The payment of contributions by stakeholders who choose to become members of a corridor management arrangement is one of the most common approaches to funding corridor management. Port operators in particular have traditionally shown a willingness to promote efficient corridor operations, which affect port utilization and throughput. Some of the contributions can be used for capacity-building purposes. The main advantage of self-financing is that it reveals the commitment of the stakeholders who are willing to make a contribution. It therefore exerts pressure to achieve tangible benefits.

Several lessons have been learned from corridor groups funded through member contributions:

- Stakeholders with budgetary constraints usually fall behind in meeting their contributions. Government ministries often have other competing demands that may have higher priority.
- Private sector membership subscriptions can be unreliable, especially when the benefits cannot be easily quantified and demonstrated.
- These systems usually demand roughly equal contributions, unrelated to benefits expected.

Usage levies. Another alternative is to levy a charge on traffic passing through a corridor. Such traffic is expected to benefit from improved performance. Therefore, the argument can be made that users should collectively contribute to the funding of management functions. A traffic-linked usage levy ensures sustainability of the corridor management arrangement while at the same time maintaining pressure on the corridor group to continue delivering benefits. Contributions should ideally reflect the proportion by which users benefit from handling the corridor tonnage. A levy based on the tonnage and distance that the traffic will move along the corridor can be introduced based on a rate per tonne-kilometer. Such a levy can be collected at a major gateway, such as a port of entry or some other intermediate point.

Given that most regions are trying to promote internal trade, it is also important to raise funding from traffic that does not originate or end at the port. Such levies can be collected by customs at international borders and transferred to the corridor management group.

The main advantage of the usage levy system is that it is directly linked to traffic volumes along the corridor. The more traffic there is and the more efficiently it is moved, the lower the levy. The weakness is that the levy can become complex and add to the cross-border charges that some stakeholders are seeking to eliminate or at least minimize. In addition, it is not unusual for there to be a time lag between making an investment in capacity and realizing the benefits. Still, if it is linked to demonstrated benefits accruing to the stakeholder group in general and economies at large, a usage levy is a sustainable way of generating funding for corridor management groups. It is the preferred mode of funding for corridor groups, as it achieves the twin objectives of ensuring sustainability of the trade facilitation interventions and providing funding for the corridor management institution.

Financing by corridor champions. Funding can come from contributions from different stakeholders based on the benefits they derive from improved corridor performance. The main contributors would be the corridor champions, such as port authorities and main shippers, with other stakeholders paying a percentage of the benefits they enjoy.

The advantages of this approach are similar to the membership contributory approach, in that the key beneficiaries largely foot the bill for improving corridor management. The main challenge is to demonstrate to each of the stakeholders the aspects of corridor improvement that can be attributed to interventions by the corridor group. As a corridor is a system with various players, each of which can affect the performance of the others. It would be difficult to allocate benefits in a way that different stakeholders would contribute different levels of support.

Donor funding. Some corridor management groups were initially funded by corridor champions or donors. Where corridor groups are new, it may be necessary to obtain some initial funding from other sources until stakeholders have reached a stage at which they can appreciate the key benefits and are able to fund the activities themselves. Donor funding is not sustainable in the long term, however; groups therefore need to establish revenue streams using one of the other approaches.

Summary. The guiding principles of funding described in this section are as follows:

- Membership contributions are the simplest approach to funding corridor management interventions. However, they can be problematic, because there is an element of unpredictability with regard to availability of funding from both the private and public sectors. Governments tend to have resource constraints and competing and more urgent priorities that can make it difficult for them to honor their obligations in a timely manner.

- User levies, when directly related to the benefits derived from enhanced corridor management, are the recommended mode of meeting corridor management costs. However, to be sustainable, they have to be lower than the derived benefits. It is generally easier to justify levies where there is result-based budgeting with clear targets for deliverables. The mode of collection of any levy must be simple to administer, so as not to adversely affect corridor transport operations.
- Some corridor institutions have been funded by donors in their formative stages. Donors tend to provide assistance where institutions demonstrate a commitment to sustain themselves after a brief period of initial support. Therefore, in most instances, donor funding remains critical to meeting the start-up costs of any corridor management arrangement before other more sustainable arrangements can be introduced.

Summary of Possible Interventions for Improving Corridor Management

Corridor management does not cost a lot of money and can be very useful in coordinating the actions of various parties in providing infrastructure and services. Without proper coordination, investments by one party can go to waste. The main issues to be considered in corridor management are summarized in table 3.4.

TABLE 3.4 Possible Interventions for Improving Corridor Management

Issue	Questions	Possible interventions
Existence of corridor management body	• Is there a corridor management mechanism? • If so, is it regional, bilateral, national, or corridor specific? • When was it formed? • Is it based on a formal legal instrument (treaty, Memorandum of Understanding, constitution, agreement)? • Does it have a registered office? • Does it have a permanent secretariat? • What is its governance structure? • How many staff does it have?	• Provide technical assistance to draft legal instrument.
Voice and representation within the corridor	• Who are the members? Do they include government agencies and private firms, including companies that provide transport, forwarding, clearing, storage, consolidation, integrated logistics services, and international third-party logistics providers? • Are decisions made by consensus? By majority?	• Encourage strong private sector participation. • Support formation of wide consultative forum.
Mandate of the corridor management body	• Is the body's mandate regional, national, or corridor specific? • What activities does the body review (customs, border management, security, special zones, trade finance and promotion, transport infrastructure, gateway concessions, regulation of pricing of services, regulation of routes operated, certification of logistics service providers)?	• Support clear objectives related to main constraints and linked to project outcomes.
Objective and priorities	• What are the priorities of the body (planning, regulatory reform, operations, monitoring, promotion, project implementation, and so forth)? • Are they aligned with project objectives?	• Support definition of clear objectives.
Funding	• How are staff, meetings, and activities of the corridor body financed? • Is the funding mechanism sustainable?	• Link funding to performance of corridor body. • Encourage user financing.
Data collection and performance monitoring	• What data are collected? • How are data collected? • What are the key performance indicators and benchmarks (cost, time, reliability, and so forth)? • How are reports disseminated?	• Provide technical assistance for a sustainable data management and reporting system. • Base data collection on sustainable mechanisms.
Technical capacity	• Does the body have task forces or working groups of specialists? • What are the principal problems and opportunities for addressing them? • What are the priority areas of action?	• Encourage formation of working groups of experts on specific topics.

References

Adzigbey, Y., C. Kunaka, and T. N. Mitiku. 2007. "Institutional Arrangements for Transport Corridor Management in Sub-Saharan Africa." SSATP Working Paper 86, World Bank, Sub-Saharan Africa Transport Policy Program, Washington, DC.

Arnold, J. 2006. "Best Practices in Management of International Trade Corridors." Transport Paper TP-13, World Bank, Washington, DC.

Raballand, G., S. Refas, M. Beuran, and G. Isik. 2012. *Why Does Cargo Spend Weeks in Sub-Saharan African Ports? Lessons from Six Countries.* Washington, DC: World Bank.

Resources

Abidjan-Lagos Corridor Organization (Project-Based Corridor Management Body). http://www.borderlesswa.com/sites/default/files/resources/feb12/RAPPORT _AN1_OCAL_PFCTAL_090212_Approved_Angl_pdf.pdf.

The Abidjan-Lagos Corridor Organization (ALCO) was formed in 2002 to manage a grant-funded project on HIV/AIDS in the corridor. The corridor connects five countries: Benin, Côte d'Ivoire, Ghana, Nigeria, and Togo. Its original purpose was to coordinate and manage the project across the five countries. The governing body included representatives of all five countries. ALCO has matured and taken on more general corridor management functions. It now includes a project implementation unit for a trade facilitation project for the corridor, for example.

CAREC Corridors Program (Horizontal Management Arrangement). http://www .carecprogram.org/index.php?page=carec-corridors.

The CAREC (Central Asia Regional Economic Cooperation) Corridors Program covers six corridors that link the region's key economic hubs to each other and connect the landlocked CAREC countries to other Eurasian and global markets. An Implementation Action Plan for the CAREC transport and trade facilitation strategy seeks to upgrade all six transport corridors to international standards by 2017. The aim is that as people and goods move faster and more efficiently through the corridors, significant improvements are seen in trade between the CAREC countries, with other regions, and in transit trade. Increased trade in turn supports business development, creates jobs, and brings a better quality of life to the people of the region.

Maputo Corridor Logistics Initiative (Private Sector–Led Corridor Management Body). http://www.mcli.co.za/.

The Maputo Corridor Logistics Initiative (MCLI) is a private sector body founded on a Memorandum and Articles of Association. It is a not-for-profit entity originally established by South African shippers interested in using the Port of Maputo in Mozambique. The South African Department of Transport has become one of the key members of MCLI, membership in which has grown to include shippers and service providers in Mozambique and Swaziland. The MCLI seeks to become a coordinator of logistics stakeholders, contributing to the aims and objectives of the Maputo development corridor. The corridor is one of the foremost success stories of the Spatial Development Initiative initiated by the South African government in the mid-1990s. MCLI focuses on making the corridor a cost-effective and reliable logistics route, with positive returns for all stakeholders. It also aims to create a favorable climate for investment and new opportunities for communities along the corridor.

Northern Corridor Transit Transport Coordination Authority (Government-Led Single-Corridor Management Body). http://www.ttcanc.org/.

The Northern Corridor Transit Transport Coordination Authority (NCTTCA) in East Africa is an interstate body. Formed in 1985 through a treaty signed by five countries (Burundi, the Democratic Republic of Congo, Kenya, Rwanda, and Uganda), it covers use of the corridor linked to the Port of Mombasa in Kenya. The NCTTCA and its activities are funded through a levy on tonnage passing through the port. Although the governments have a greater say in the Authority's decision making, there have been recent moves to consult with the private sector much more, mainly through a stakeholders forum. The NCTTCA has been particularly effective in advocating for implementation of regional transit instruments at the national level within the Common Market for Eastern and Southern Africa (COMESA), serving to test some of the initiatives before they are rolled out more broadly.

Pakistan National Trade and Transport Facilitation Committee (National Corridor Management Mechanism). http://www.nttfc.org.

The Pakistan National Trade and Transport Facilitation Committee (NTTFC) was created in 2001 to implement a trade facilitation program financed by the World Bank. It was established under the Ministry of Commerce, with the Pakistan Shippers Council providing secretariat services. Membership in the NTTFC is made up of both public and private sector representatives. It includes various government ministries, industry associations, and the main modes of transport (road, sea, air, rail). The NTTFC seeks to promote reforms to improve the trade facilitation environment in the country. Its terms of reference include the following:

- Continuously review trade and transport procedures and systems with a view to updating their simplification and harmonization.
- Coordinate the efforts of concerned organizations in the field of facilitation of international trade and transport.
- Collect and disseminate information on international trade and transport formalities, procedures, documentation, and related mailers.
- Simplify and align trade and transport documents on the basis of the United Nations' Layout Key, including documents designed for use in computer and other automated systems.
- Promote the adoption of standard trade and transport standard terminology and international codes for trade and transport information.

The NTTFC has tried to improve the legal framework for trade facilitation and logistics in Pakistan. Although it is dominated by public sector players, which would have been expected to more easily influence policy, it lacks the power to bring its initiatives to fruition. The problem may be that the NTTFC activities lack the practical orientation that a more focused body would bring. A regulatory authority proposed for the logistics services sector could help overcome this constraint. The NTTFC would then be a stakeholder consultation forum and a performance-monitoring body, relying on data from both the public and private sectors.

Walvis Bay Corridor Group (Public-Private Sector–Initiated Corridor Management Bodies). http://www.wbcg.com.na/.

The Walvis Bay Corridor Group (WBCG), a public-private body, is one of the most active and aggressive corridor promotion bodies in Africa. This business development–oriented body has commissioned various pieces of forward-looking research, feasibility studies, and new procedures. It also marshals regional support for follow-up action. The group is dominated by a few large stakeholders. It underscores the link between infrastructure development and the need to increase volumes to justify some of the investments that have been made or are being contemplated. WBCG was created by the port authority in Namibia and large transport operators who sought to derive benefits from efficiency improvements along the three corridors served by the Port of Walvis Bay. It brings together shippers; port, road, and rail operators; and national government departments to make the corridor competitive in a region where there are alternative trade routes. The port operator sees the corridor approach as a way of growing the port's market, justify further capacity improvements, and provide the benefits of economies of scale to all corridor users.

UNCTAD (United Nations Conference on Trade and Development). 2000. "Creating an Efficient Environment for Trade and Transport." Geneva. http://www.unece.org/fileadmin/DAM/cefact/recommendations/rec04/rec04_ecetr256e.pdf.

The document provides guidelines on establishing national trade and transport facilitation committees. They include defining the purpose of a national committee, its membership, and how it should be organized as well as assigning responsibilities to the various members of the committee and identifying how it should develop its work program.

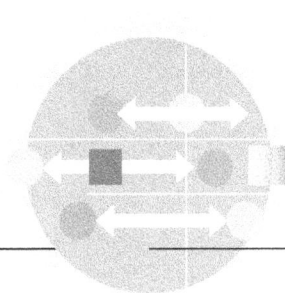

Corridor Performance Indicators

In recent years, the World Bank and other international agencies have received many requests for a method for measuring trade corridor performance.[1] These requests have come from diverse sources, and the proposed uses of the indicators have been quite different, depending on the source. The response to these requests has been positive and quite broad, from rather academic desk exercises to very pragmatic but conceptually limited user surveys. A range of methods and results have been able to address some specific needs, but a method for deriving generally acceptable and consistently measured indicators (with values) that address a broader range of topics and issues is still lacking.

This module provides a set of basic indicators that can be used to address a wide range of needs and to provide some initial values for a sample of transit corridors. The indicators described in this module do not meet all needs; specific indicators needed to identify potential locations of corridor improvements are found in the modules that deal with specific corridor components.

The module is structured as follows: The first section outlines the justification for corridor performance monitoring. The second section identifies the levels of decision making. The third and fourth sections examine the characteristics of indicators and the parameters to monitor, respectively. The last section provides a comparative analysis of corridor performance.

Uses of Corridor Monitoring and Indicators

There are three main uses of corridor performance measures:

- assessing how well a corridor is performing and where the main deficiencies are
- tracking changes in corridor performance over time and determining whether changes made to improve performance have had measurable impact
- determining performance relative to other corridors serving the same or different origins and destinations of traded goods.

Assessing Corridor Performance

Exporters and importers are concerned with the competitiveness of their products in the markets they are destined for. The time and cost of getting products to those markets often determine whether they will remain competitive once they are delivered. The reliability of supply is also critical to maintaining a foothold in a market.

As it is timeliness, reliability, and the delivered price in the market that determine whether the product is competitive or not, the corridor cost, time, and reliability should be for transit from the factory (or other production site) to the customer. Such a comprehensive measure is too product and producer specific to be a measure of corridor performance, however. The scope of the corridor performance measurement is therefore limited to transit from the point at which the product is loaded onto a truck (or rail wagon or waterway barge) to the point at which it is offloaded at the destination port (for exports transported by sea) or from the point at which the product leaves the dockside in the port of origin to the point at which it is offloaded from the truck (or rail wagon or waterway barge) for final delivery to the customer (for imports transported by sea). Similar limitations apply to airfreight (with the airport and aircraft replacing the port and ship). For goods transported only by land, the equivalent origin and destination are the loading onto a truck in the origin country and the offloading in the destination country. Performance should be assessed for different lengths of shipments, domestic and international. Although most corridors carry both types of traffic, some are clearly configured to carry specific types of traffic, which should be reflected in performance assessment.

These specifications of a corridor are broader than are generally used. Most corridor specifications apply only to the land transport part of the transit from origin to destination, ignoring the sea or air part of the transport. As such, they do not fully inform on the competitiveness of the product at its final destination.

To be useful in describing how products traded through a corridor can be made more competitive in their destination markets, the indicators need to identify the times and costs of transport and transactions at each stage of transit through the corridor, as well as through the corridor as a whole. Monitoring indicators are provided for each of the major stages of transit through the corridor, but not in as much detail as would be needed for evaluation of a project to reduce times and costs at specific locations. For example, the performance indicators identify transit through a port as a specific activity, whereas for evaluation of improvements at the port, the times and costs at each specific location and for each specific activity need to be known.

Tracking Performance over Time

There is great interest in knowing whether the performance of a corridor is improving or deteriorating and whether measures to improve performance are having the desired impact. The ability to monitor either the performance of a whole corridor or that part of a corridor where changes in performance are believed to have occurred or where changes have been made that should produce such changes is a powerful investigative tool.

Performance of a corridor can change over time for reasons that have little or nothing to do with the quality of infrastructure or logistics services in the corridor itself. Factors include the terms of trade of the products traded in the corridor, the political relationship between or within countries or regions that make up the corridor, and changes in the trade regime of the country or countries trading in the corridor, such as a reform of the customs agency or simplification of the tariff regime. The impact of many such changes will be apparent at the national level of trade before it becomes apparent in a particular corridor, but the corridor monitoring will easily pick up changes if they have not been previously found.

Another use of time series data is to monitor deviations of performance from the norm. When deviations occur the data can be used to trigger remedial action to set it back on course before the trade impacts become too grave. Deterioration in performance will be detectable in monitoring parameters before it is apparent in trade statistics, allowing preemptive action to be taken. Systems for continuous monitoring of performance thus become important.

But the main use of corridor indicators over time is to see whether measures to improve performance in the corridor itself have had the desired effect. There will usually be a time lag between the taking of an action to improve performance and a detectable indication that performance has changed, so a suitable time interval should pass before monitoring can be expected to show a result. Although some interventions can have an impact in the short term, a time interval of two years between measures should allow for the changes in performance to be noticeable, even if the impact on volumes of trade takes longer.

Comparing with Other Corridors

A relatively new use of corridor monitoring indicators is in the comparison of performance of a particular corridor with that of other corridors in which similar goods destined for the same final markets are traded. This application of the indicators derives from consideration of the competitiveness of the goods traded via the corridor to their final market. For this use of the indicators, it is necessary that they cover the whole corridor, not only the land part, as is the case with many indicators. The total rather than the partial values of the parameters should be used for the corridor. If it is found that the goods traded in the corridor are no longer competitive when transport and trade facilitation costs and times are taken into account, then the parameter values for specific parts of the corridor or specific activities within the corridor can be used. To determine whether the products are competitive, the total values are relevant.

For the comparison of total and partial parameter values between corridors to be useful they need to measure the same parameters, defined and measured in comparable ways. Comparability has not been satisfied by most corridor monitoring efforts until now. Monitoring has been aimed largely at assessing the performance of a single corridor at one point in time or comparison of performance at different points in time, applications for which consistency is not needed (although for comparison over time, consistency between the measurements each time they are taken is just as important as consistency of the measurements between corridors).

Only a few countries (particularly landlocked countries) are connected to trade markets by a single main corridor. But most countries have several corridors linking them to such markets. The performance of each corridor has to be considered relative to the performance of alternative corridors. Although such performance can be a result of overland infrastructure, services, and systems, at times it is a result of factors removed from the immediate environs of the corridor. An example is the recent development of a new port at Cai Mep in Vietnam, which affected the volume of freight and costs on the domestic corridor between Phnom Penh and Sihanoukville in Cambodia. Similarly, expansion of the Panama Canal will affect east-west traffic flows across the United States, as some cargo will be shipped directly to ports on the East Coast and in the Gulf of Mexico or transshipped in the Caribbean.

Levels of Decision Making

Monitoring of the performance of trade and transport corridors is only one part of the monitoring of the trade performance of a particular country; it should be seen as a part of a more comprehensive monitoring exercise. There are three levels at which indicators of trade performance can be made: strategic and country, corridor, and project.

Strategic and Country Level

Decisions at the strategic level relate to overall national trade strategy on three issues:

- the products traded
- the markets served by those products
- incentives for the production, logistics, marketing, and delivery standards for those products.

The indicators to inform these decisions relate to actual and potential export products. They help identify specific markets that could be competitive. It is at the micro-level that many measures of logistics performance are needed and most beneficial (Hausman, Lee, and Subramanian 2005; Wilson and others 2003; World Bank 2005).

Performance indicators that have been used in the past at the strategic level have tended to be derived from macroeconomic data, with particular reference to the ratio of the cost of logistics to the value of the delivered product. Comparisons are then made based on national trends over time or comparisons at a fixed point in time with similar indexes from other countries. Other measures include the ratio of free on board (FOB) to cost, insurance, and freight (CIF) prices (box 4.1). As the difference between these two costs are related to trade costs (nearly always just maritime costs), the ratio of costs can be considered a measure of corridor performance, a ratio close to 1 being an indicator of better performance than a ratio much greater than 1. But this measure has fallen out of use, as the

CIF versus FOB in West Africa

Some West African countries procure their petroleum supplies on a least FOB cost basis. There are several regional markets where prices for petroleum products are set, with the lowest costs often found in Singapore or London. These markets are far from West Africa, however, so delivery to destinations in the region can involve high transport and insurance costs, particularly if the procurement is for small quantities.

Although maritime freight and insurance costs together typically average only about 5 percent of the delivered cost in most regions, they can amount to closer to 10 percent when petroleum is procured from a distant source. When these higher transport and insurance costs are added to the FOB price from London or Singapore, the delivered cost can be higher than if the procurement had been on a least CIF price basis, which would probably result in procurement from a closer supplier, such as Nigeria.

Source: World Bank 2012.

many difficulties associated with its measurement and application have become apparent.

Other indicators that can be used at the strategic level include the following:

- merchandise trade and exports as a share of total trade and exports
- the proportion of merchandise exports shipped under CIF conditions and the proportion of merchandise imports received under FOB conditions
- typical shipment times to and from major markets
- percentage of delivered costs of domestic industries attributable to logistics (this measure is better than the logistics share of gross domestic product [GDP], which is influenced by the share of manufactured goods in total GDP. A low logistics share of GDP might simply reflect a large services share of GDP and say nothing about the efficiency of the logistics system itself)
- average value of producer and retailer inventories (and 20-foot equivalent units [TEUs] stored in ports and inland container depots)
- full container load/less than container load ratios (and 20- to 40-foot container ratios, where relevant).

However, as no common conceptual framework or method has been used, few international comparisons can be made. Although perhaps helpful in assessing what types of products and in what markets a country could expect to be competitive, the indicators provided at this level are less helpful in identifying problems in specific corridors or supply chains and whether and how the problems are amenable to correction.

Country-level performance indicators can provide a measure of the progress made in introducing various trade and transport reforms. Indicators of such reforms could include the following:

- private participation in the ownership and operation of trade and transport infrastructure
- use of modern customs practices
- availability of financial instruments to support trade transactions
- use of technologies for electronic commerce.

Corridor Level

The corridor level is often the level of decision making at which performance indicators can have the greatest practical impact, as they reveal where in the supply chains of specific products or specific corridors the impediments to logistics efficiency occur. Potential measures to address the impediments can be designed and their potential impact evaluated by analyzing indicators at this level.

Use of indicators at this level of decision making implies that decisions at the strategic level have already been made, implicitly or explicitly. If they have not been made, and there is no intention to provide indicators to indicate the efficacy of current choices of strategy, it must be assumed that those choices are optimal or not open to question. The indicators appropriate for use at this policy level illustrate performance at each principal stage of a supply chain or in a particular corridor.

Trade policy issues at this level include issues related to the demand for specific trade facilitation services. They can best be addressed in the context of supply chains or corridors where impediments to logistics efficiency are most likely to be found and where any new options for addressing such impediments are likely to exist (World Bank 2004, 2006a, 2006b). Indicators at this level can also address whether the relationships between costs and prices in a particular situation are indicative of a market failure or whether the overall price and quality offered by logistics services in a particular supply chain or corridor are likely to make the products using them competitive in the markets they are aimed at.

A tradeoff needs to be made between the level of detail included in the indicators—where more detail indicates a more useful indicator—and the maximum level of detail that is comprehensible by the people expected to act on the interpretation of the indicators. Less detail usually implies easier comprehension and understanding. Indicators used at this level can rarely lead to a definitive policy conclusion. Instead, they provide indications that one policy is likely to be more effective than another.

Project Level

The third level at which indicators can be used is in the assessment of impacts at the level of projects aimed at resolving specific issues identified at the policy level. The indicators can refer either to the intensity of use of physical infrastructure (such as the TEU handled per port berth) or to the quality and efficiency of infrastructure services (such as the turnaround time of container ships at berths). In the same way that use of indicators at the policy level implies prior decision making at the strategic level, the use of indicators at the project level implies prior decision making at the policy level or the making of assumptions that policy choices already made are in some sense optimal or not open to question.

Indicators of the use of physical infrastructure at this level have been in use for some time. However, they have not resulted in values that can be used comparatively, nor have they achieved widespread acceptance. Quality of service indicators frequently used at this level are generally well understood but difficult to measure with any precision. The values or units of measure of both infrastructure and service quality indicators are expected to change significantly over time, although the concepts of the indicators may remain more constant.

The remainder of this module focuses on the performance of corridor-level parameters to assist in decision making at the international corridor level. Resources to assist in measuring performance at the country level are indicated in Module 1. Indicators that help at the project level are so specific to the project being considered that it is not feasible to give advice on what should be measured and how it should be measured.

The performance indicators described in the module are only the basic indicators necessary to assess any international trade corridor. They are aimed at determining whether a corridor is performing well in terms of delivering its traded goods to markets at a competitive price and if not, what aspect of performance provides the greatest potential for improvement. Once these assessments have been made, and the general location of opportunities for improvement found, a more detailed level of indicator is needed to find what opportunities for improvement exist. Some of the common ones are described in the corridor-specific modules in Part II.

As an example, use of the basic indicators might show that containerized goods transported in a particular international trade corridor are not competitive in their destination market and that it is at the port in the transit country where there appears to be the greatest opportunity for improvement (reduction in the level of times or costs or increases in their level of reliability). More detailed port performance indicators are needed to determine where in the port these opportunities are to be found. It would not be worthwhile to measure these more detailed port indicators if the use of the basic indicators shows that the port is performing well and the problems are to be found elsewhere.

Characteristics of Indicators

There are many potential indicators for monitoring the performance of trade corridors. As the monitoring process needs to be relatively simple to be replicable and affordable, only a few of these indicators can be included in the monitoring process. Although a much more inclusive set of indicators might be needed for assessment of a specific corridor, this module suggests a minimum set of indicators that should be measured for all corridors and replicated at frequent intervals. Taken together, the indicators should provide a comprehensive perspective on how well a corridor is performing. To be included in this minimum set, an indicator should satisfy several criteria, set out below.

Measurability

The indicator should be easy to measure and replicate at different points in time and in a wide range of types of corridors. One reason why few if any replications of indicators have been made is that the data to measure indicators have been difficult, time consuming, and expensive to collect.[2] Given that the main purposes of monitoring indicators is that they be easily replicable, this criterion is desirable. If it is not met, the whole monitoring system will fail, as no replication will take place.

Though replicability is desirable it is a less essential condition than ease of measurement. If the data to measure the indicator are being collected anyway, using them for the indicator involves only minimal additional cost. As far as possible, monitoring indicators are based on this principle. Failing this, it is desirable to identify where data can be captured through automated procedures or where industry or government collects information that can be used as proxies for these data. In some situations, it will be necessary to collect data. In this case, the issues of frequency, sample size, and accuracy become major concerns.

Important is the ability to repeat data collection. Many monitoring indicators have been measured only once. Although one-time data collection can be of some use—in the comparison of one corridor with another, for example—it is of little use in seeing how a corridor changes over time or whether measures to improve a corridor's performance have had any impact.

One reason for the lack of repetition is the high cost of making the original measures and the fact that the measurement is made as part of a broader assessment of the performance of a corridor's activity funded by an international institution and undertaken by an international consulting company. Unless this funding and its terms of reference include training for subsequent measurement of the monitoring indicators, there will be no mechanism for even a second application of the monitoring activity, let alone any possibility of regular repetition over a period of time.

As repetition of the monitoring process is one desirable characteristic, the cost of monitoring must be such that it does not rely on funding from an international financial institution or require an international consulting firm. Repetition of the monitoring each year is not necessary and probably not feasible. At the other extreme, repetition every five years is probably too infrequent for important changes in the performance of a corridor to be detected soon enough for remedial action to be taken. It is also too infrequent for knowledge of how to undertake the monitoring process to be retained. Repetition every two or three years is the frequency that optimizes desirability with feasibility. More frequent monitoring can, of course, be undertaken, depending on the objective.

Cost

The indicator should add only marginally to the cost of collecting data. Some potential monitoring indicators are already collected by traders, freight forwarders, and public sector agencies operating in the corridor. Others require extensive and costly special surveys. If the monitoring is to be repeated at acceptable intervals, measurement of the parameters should be technically simple and not too expensive.

Relevance

The indicator should be relevant to making decisions about logistics at the level of corridor activities. In particular, it should be usable by governments, traders, logistics operators, and agencies involved in trade facilitation.

Specificity

An indicator should be capable of reflecting changes in corridor performance, including where in a corridor any excess cost or time is incurred. If only the parameters for the corridor as a whole are available, it is impossible to know where a particular inefficiency is occurring, although the impact on competitiveness of the products traded can be assessed. To fully comply with this condition, indicators need to be very detailed and specific while at the same time complying with the other desirable conditions. There thus needs to be a compromise that provides enough detail to indicate where inefficiencies are occurring and where action needs to be taken without making the data collection too expensive and complicated.

Consistency

The indicator should be consistent and its parameters easily understood. Lack of consistency between definitions used in the collection of data in previous corridor monitoring indicators has made it difficult to compare their results. Consistency is maintained by the precision with which the parameters of the indicators are defined.

It is important to be precise on several aspects to which the indicator applies, including type of products and their packaging, the size of the consignment and the frequency of shipments, whether it is for import and export traffic, the component of the corridor to monitor, as well as the specific origins and destinations of the traffic monitored.

Types of products and packaging. The relevant characteristics of a corridor can be very product specific, but it is possible to categorize products in several ways, depending on the importance of delivery time. Perishable goods whose unit value reduces rapidly over time can be in the highest category and bulk products that have a constant value over time in the lowest category. Related to this is a categorization by unit value, with products having the highest unit value in the highest category and products with the lowest unit value in the lowest category. Products with a high unit value, such as some precious minerals and some pharmaceutical products, are often shipped by air, whereas products with low unit values, such as some bulk minerals, are transported by slow means of transport, so that the cost of transport does not add much to their unit value.

The most useful categorization of products is the way in which they are transported, which is highly correlated with both the urgency of delivery and unit value. Given the many modes of transport available and the many different stages of transit within a corridor, there are multiple possible combinations of modes of transport. Rather than categorizing by mode of transport, it is therefore more usual to categorize by the form of packaging, which tends to stay constant throughout transit through the corridor.

The three main forms of packing for manufactured products are loose as individual packages or consignments (often called break-bulk), containerized freight, and bulk freight.[3] It is possible to break these three categories into many subgroups. For example, refrigerated and chilled products can be subcategories of both break-bulk and containerized freight; dry and liquid can be subcategories of bulk freight. Most liquid bulk products are transported by pipeline or tanker vehicles over land and special tanker vessels at sea. Transfer between the two takes place in specialized ports or port terminals. For these reasons, the focus of corridor monitoring is on containers and dry bulk products. Bagged, palletized, and oversized shipments (such as large machinery) can be subcategories of general freight. However, categorization by the three main packaging types is sufficient to cover most of the needs for corridor performance monitoring.

Consignment size and frequency. The time and cost of transporting products through a corridor is highly dependent on the size of the consignment and the frequency of shipment. In order to ensure consistency between the values for monitoring indicators in the same corridor over a period of time and between corridors at a given point in time, it is important that they relate to the same size and frequency of shipments. For the indicators used in this Toolkit, specifications that apply to most corridors for which comparative monitoring measures are likely to be used could be the following:

- *Break-bulk shipments*: Five truckloads every month for six months, using three-axle trucks with a gross vehicle weight of 24 tonnes that is 25 percent overloaded (that is, it transports a payload of about 16 net tonnes). The assumed value of the freight is about $50 per tonne for exports (high for agricultural products but about average for the semimanufactured products typically transported as break-bulk).
- *Containers*: Five 20-foot containers shipped once every month for a period of six months. The assumed value of the freight is about $25,000 per TEU (about $3,000 per tonne), about average for shipments of manufactured goods typically exported to and imported from developing countries.

- *Dry bulk shipments*: A single consignment of 5,000 tonnes every month for a period of six months. The assumed average value is about $25 per tonne, which can apply to many agricultural and mineral products often transported as dry bulk.

Some corridor diagnostics have been limited to imports, on the assumption that most proposed corridor improvements will apply much more to imports than to exports. Other evaluations have been limited to containerized products, on the assumption that most trade facilitation measures apply more to containerized and general freight than to bulk products.

The selection of the characteristics to be included in the evaluation is related to the objectives of the project and can influence how easy it is to evaluate the project subcomponents. If the project objectives are relatively simple, such as reducing the costs of current trade and transport, then the characteristics to be evaluated can simply be the volume and type of traffic impacts of improvements in time and cost of transport performance of the corridor. But even with these simple measures, some choices have to be made as to what times and costs are to be evaluated. These choices can be related to the selection of subcomponents to be evaluated.

Imports and exports. Monitoring indicators are related to the competitiveness of the products traded in the corridor. If the products are imports, they need to be competitive in the domestic market of the country to which they are imported, where they will compete with domestically produced products as well as goods imported from other countries and via other corridors. If they are exports, they will compete in the markets of the destination country with products made domestically in those countries as well as with imports from other countries or transported via other corridors.

The impact of transport infrastructure, logistics services, and trade facilitation procedures on imports and exports is very different. Starting with maritime transport for imports, the balance of trade between inbound and outbound has an impact on the charges made as well as possibly on the routing of ships and the time taken. For many developing countries, there is a greater volume of inbound loaded containers than outbound, although there are many notable exceptions with a large imbalance in the other direction. Where the imbalance is large, the charge in the direction with less demand can be a small fraction of that with greater demand, as the containers would otherwise have to be transported empty back to their origin. There is an even greater impact for dry bulk ships, where there is rarely any product to transport in the reverse direction. It is difficult to generalize for break-bulk shipments, although there is often a more even balance between inbound and outbound freight.

The difference extends to port activities, where imports generally take several days longer to transit through the port than exports. Customs and other agencies impose strict requirements, to ensure that all duties are paid and all health and industrial regulations met. An exception was created in recent years by the U.S. requirement that containers for export to the United States be scanned before being loaded onto a ship for transport. This requirement imposes costs and possibly delays before the goods are shipped, so it does not affect the time and cost as defined for corridor monitoring. Even beyond the port, the imbalance between import and export flows can have a large impact on trucking costs to the final destination (or from the point of origin for exports). For landlocked countries, there are differences in the time and cost for imports and exports to cross the border with their transit neighbors. For these reasons, it is important that the corridor monitoring indicators differentiate between imports and exports.

Stages of corridor activity to monitor. Some methods of monitoring corridor performance deal with 20 or more specific transport and trade facilitation and storage activities. For some purposes, in particular the identification and evaluation of actions to improve corridor performance, such detail may be useful. But for the three main uses of corridor indicators (assessing overall performance, comparing the performance of a corridor over time, and comparing performance of a corridor with other corridors) such detail is rarely needed. However, it is usually necessary to consider more than just the corridor as a whole if the monitoring indicators are to have any practical use in addition to measuring the impact of the corridor on the competitiveness of the products traded in the corridor in their final markets.

Previous corridor monitoring has broken down activities within a corridor into categories, such as component (road transport, border crossings, ports, and so forth) or location (based on figure P.2). No corridor monitoring methods have included maritime transport, although some have included the time for maritime access to the port of destination (for imports) or origin (for exports).

For the comparison of different trade corridors, it is useful to include at least five stages of a corridor from a coastal country and another two stages for a landlocked country (more can be added for doubly landlocked countries). Figure 4.1 illustrates an example of the stages of a corridor for which monitoring parameters are measured.

FIGURE 4.1 Corridor Monitoring Points

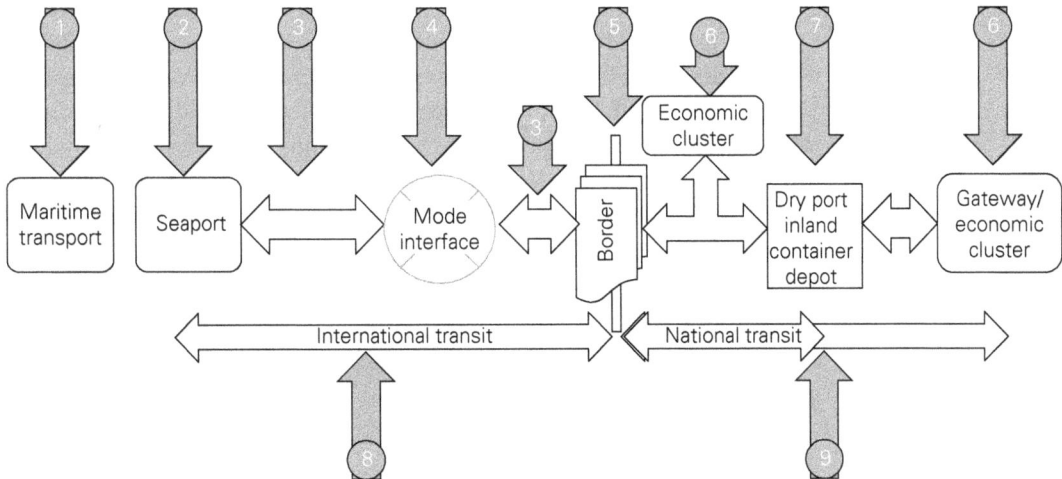

Many activities can be included in these stages. For example, if rail transport is used as the main mode for exports, there will probably be road transport from the exporters' premises to the rail terminal, unloading from the truck, storage at the terminal, and loading onto a rail wagon at the interchange terminal. For monitoring purposes, all of these activities can be included in the first stage of transit, as they are related to moving the product to its main mode of transport. For the same multimodal transport of import products, these activities are included in the fifth stage of transit.

At some border crossings between landlocked and transit countries, it is necessary to offload consignments from the vehicle used for transport in one country and reload them onto another vehicle for transport in the second country. Depending on the country in which the activities take place, such consignments are included in the border crossing into/out of the transit or landlocked country.

There can be an explicit measure of the time and cost of land transport to access the port through its urban area, as such transport can sometimes be a significant cause of delay and additional cost. Land transport is a growing problem, though its solution may lie in urban transport planning. This segment should be monitored, even though doing so may require specific transport surveys and analyses, as transporters and freight forwarders can rarely distinguish this cost in their invoices to their clients.

International origins and destinations. If the indicators are to be used to compare corridors, they need to relate to common origins or destinations. For most products transported in containers there are three major destination markets: the East Coast of the United States, the West Coast of the United States, and Europe. Although South Asia is rapidly increasing in importance as a source for imports to developing countries, most analyses use just one source, East Asia. For each of these markets, maritime transport is an important part of the trade corridor and accounts for a significant share of the cost of the delivered products (and for the delivered cost of imports to developing countries from these three sources).

Parameters to Monitor

Determining what corridor indicators to use as measures of performance has become more complex as supply chains have evolved from support for simple production activities to maintenance of distributed production systems in which intermediate locations that previously might have involved no more than an intermodal transfer are now part of the production process itself. The design of an effective system for monitoring the performance of a corridor requires decisions about four key dimensions:

- the parameters to be monitored
- the locations for which they should be measured
- the types of product and forms of shipment for which they should be measured
- the frequency with which the monitoring should be made.

Five main indicators measure the performance of a corridor:

- the volume of trade passing through a seaport gateway, a border post, or some other important checkpoint and handled by different modes (volumes reflect trade growth and can be used to assess how choices of time, cost, and reliability affect flows along a corridor)[4]
- the time taken to transit the whole corridor and each part of it
- the cost to importers or shippers to move cargo over the length of a corridor or a part of it
- the variation in time and cost for the whole corridor and each part of its components (reliability)
- the security of goods transported in the corridor and the safety of the people involved in that transport.

It is possible to include other indicators, such as capacity of corridor components, but these other indicators can be assessed based on the five primary indicators.[5] For example, facility congestion as a result of lack of capacity or growth in volumes will be reflected in the time indicator.

Volume

One of the obvious indicators of performance of a corridor is the volume of trade moving through it. Volume can be linked to the capacity of different components to determine the limitations on the scale of transport services and potential bottlenecks as a result of limits imposed by physical infrastructure and the productivity of cargo-handling operations. Volume is used to identify opportunities for investment in infrastructure and cargo-handling facilities.

According to classical theory, the volume of trade is a function of the economic size of the partners and inversely related to the disutility of transport and other trade costs between them. It is often modeled using gravity model approaches. Therefore, improvements in corridor performance should be reflected in trade volumes on that corridor. Trade and transport volumes on a corridor can therefore be regarded as a reference indicator, linked to the level of economic development as well as to traffic reassignment in response to corridor performance. For instance, in East Africa, more than 80 percent of Uganda's overseas trade volumes are on the Northern corridor, where costs are lower than on the Central corridor. Thus, traffic assignment in regions that have competing corridors are reflective of the relative performances of the corridors.

Trade volume data must distinguish among three types of trade flows:

- *Volume through corridor*: A distinction should be made between volumes for the coastal country or economic center and transit cargo to inland destinations or landlocked countries.
- *Volume through any border crossing*: Ideally, bilateral trade flows between corridor countries should be distinguished from volumes originating or destined for other countries.
- *Domestic trade, captured through traffic counts or weighing stations*: It is important to capture domestic flows that use sections of a corridor located in one of the countries or regions.

There are three main sources of data on volume: seaports, border posts, and traffic checkpoints along the corridor. Port operators routinely collect data on traffic flows through the port, including bulk and containerized cargo. At border posts, customs also collects data on traffic volumes (figure 4.2),

FIGURE 4.2 Number of Trucks Passing through the Malaba Border Post, in the Northern Corridor of East Africa, July 2010–June 2012

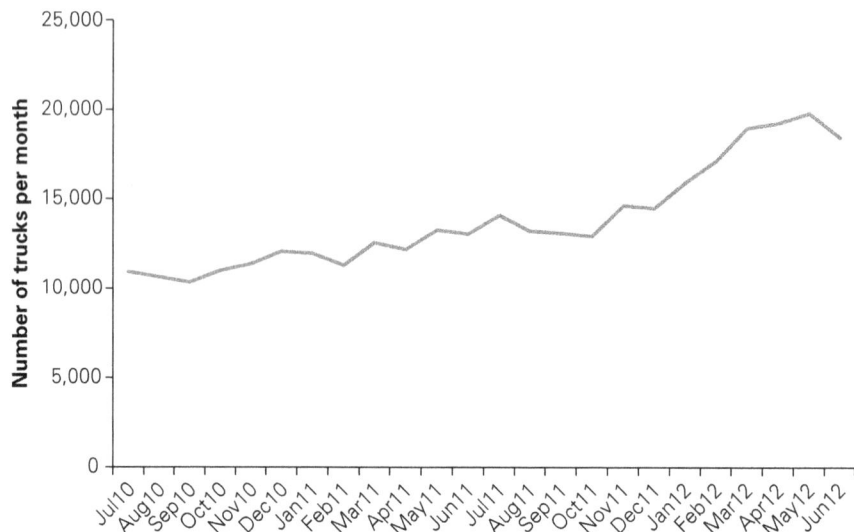

Source: World Bank, based on data from Uganda Revenue Authority.

though the quantities are not always accurate. Often the data mix items based on types of packaging and weight. Road authorities commonly have traffic count stations along major routes, which can be used to obtain data on cargo-carrying trucks. Railways have better systems, which can easily yield volume data.

Additional disaggregation of the data is possible by (a) main cargo type (differentiating containerized goods, general cargo, liquid bulk, and dry bulk) for maritime trade and possibly by inland mode of transport when multimodal options exist and by (b) vehicle for intraregional trade, supplementing the volume information with traffic counts, which are critical for assessing infrastructure or facilities such as dry ports and border crossings. Ideally, the volume data should be captured by type of cargo by direction by country (tonnes, TEU), as well as by inland mode of transport. These data should describe trade in terms of inland transport for each routing option.

Flexibility refers to the combinations of time, cost, and reliability that are available in a particular corridor. It is proportional to the volume and variety of goods traded in the corridor: the greater the volume and the variety, the more options are likely to be available. A combination of both dimensions is used as a proxy for the range of services available in a corridor, because obtaining a direct measure would involve too much investigation for a

Trade and Transport Corridor Management Toolkit

repetitive monitoring process. The measure of total trade in the corridor is the value of each type of product (break-bulk, containerized, and dry bulk) for both exports and imports that passes through the main port of the corridor (for coastal countries) or crosses the land border (for landlocked countries). The measure of variety of goods traded in the corridor is the cumulative number of goods at the standard industrial classification (SIC) two-digit category that make up 85 percent of the goods traded in the corridor.

Time

Time is one of the most important indicators of corridor performance. Both the total time it takes to move cargo from door to door and the time it takes to pass through the various components of a corridor are important. The total time is the sum of the times for each component.

Time is often provided as an average. However, in logistics, there are usually a range of services that offer different combinations of cost, time, and reliability in order to meet the diversity of demand. Shippers of bulk cargoes and low-value commodities are more concerned with minimizing cost than time, whereas shippers of containerized cargoes, especially high-value goods, are more concerned with time and particularly reliability. These tradeoffs have become more complex as production patterns have changed and become more integrated with logistics processes themselves. Just-in-time production is difficult to separate from logistics and places particularly stringent demands on time and reliability. Goods with short shelf lives place high values of time and reliability relative to cost. Although goods with short shelf lives have traditionally been higher-value goods, they now increasingly include medium-value goods, such as manufacturing subassemblies or components and spare parts. Increasingly, producers look to a mix of low-cost slow and high-cost fast shipments. As a result, the range of indicator values is more important than the average, and a production possibility frontier is more relevant than a range. Simple single-value logistics indicators are of less relevance as production patterns evolve.

In most instances, the relevant parameter of time is the least time needed to transit each stage of the corridor and the corridor as a whole. But the least time might involve a high level of uncertainty and risk in the delivery of the product. Many chance events can occur during transit that could add to the time, so that if a trader based transit decisions on the minimum time and only a few of the chance events occurred, there would be a high probability that the consignment could be late. If the product is needed for a just-in-time production process, production could come to a halt or the manufacturer would have to hold sufficient stocks to prevent this from happening, defeating the whole purpose of the just-in-time system. A delay in land access to a port can cause a sailing to be missed, causing delays throughout the supply chain. For perishable exports, there is a high probability that the product will lose value if it is not delivered to the market at the expected time.

Similar but different considerations apply to imports. With decentralized production systems, many imports are in an incomplete state; like exports, their completion for domestic markets or reexport to markets in third countries may be part of a just-in-time process. The consequences of delay are therefore similar. Imports are more likely than exports to be fully manufactured and ready for delivery to their wholesale or retail markets. The distributors will have marketing and delivery plans that are based on the expected delivery time of the consignments. Any delay in transit through the corridor will have an impact on the stocks the importer maintains to ensure regularity of supply.

The monitoring indicator used is the minimum transit time on the assumption that there are no unforeseen delays or interruptions. This measure is close to the minimum time plus an allowance for "normal" delays.

Reliability

As much as possible, the measures of time and cost should provide detail on the distribution around the mean. Some measures use minimum times or costs, whereas others provide averages. Some provide minimum or maximum values but do not indicate the percentage of shipments these values cover. Some that do provide a range of times and costs show a conventional normal distribution (with the same variation above and below the average), whereas most experience shows very skewed distributions, with little variation below the average but large variation above.

The reliability of transport times and costs can often be more important to traders than the actual times and costs. Traders need to be sure that goods arrive as expected. They can build in longer transit times in their production and delivery schedule. In contrast, uncertainties in delivery times require them to maintain additional stocks, which can increase costs.

Not all traders have similar perceptions of the reliability of transit times and the way to deal with lack of certainty. For some, the important characteristic is the probability of the goods arriving at a certain point in the supply chain. For others, it is the cost associated with certainty of arrival at the final destination at the required time.

To monitor corridor performance, a perception is needed that is generally understood by traders and forwarders and reflects the way they deal with uncertainty. For transit times, the measure used is the addition to the "normal" time needed to be 85 percent certain that the goods arrive at their final destination at the promised time.

As with other possible specifications of reliability, this measure has some problems. For example, the time needed to be 85 percent certain of the final delivery time is not the same as the sum of the times that would provide 85 percent probability that each stage of the transit is completed in the expected time, because the probabilities of delay are not cumulative: each stage of transit has its own distribution of expected transit times around the average. The distribution is highly skewed: there is a much higher probability that the time will exceed the minimum than that it will be less than the minimum.

Another problem with this measure is that it does not specifically take into account any costs of stockholding that are needed to cope with the uncertainties of transit time; it relates to the additional transit time allowed to avoid the need to hold these additional stocks. This Toolkit recommends the estimation of additional time rather than additional stockholding cost because it is easier to measure. Time has only one dimension, but stockholding can have several, including the deterioration of the goods while in storage and the actual cost of holding the additional product, which depends on whether the trader owns the storage space or leases it as needed. There is also the interest charge on the value of the additional stock held.

The reliability indicator is particularly valuable in estimating logistics costs for specific trade using a given corridor. Reducing the variation in time can be measured by estimating the additional time required to achieve a certain probability of arriving on or before the scheduled time. The likelihood of a delivery being made at or before an agreed time can be estimated based on the standard deviation of the transit time, which in turn affects the level of inventory held. An improvement in reliability (reduction in uncertainty) affects inventories.

Figure 4.3 shows the probability of a process being accomplished within a defined period of time. For instance, a probability of 95 percent for delivery at or before an agreed time would require that one standard deviation ($\sigma 1$) be added to the average time for delivery. If the variation in transit time is reduced, so that the standard deviation decreases from $\sigma 1$ to $\sigma 2$, then the variation in time will be reduced by a factor of $1 - \sigma 2/\sigma 1$. Panel b of figure 4.3 shows less variation in time performance than panel a.

Price

The cost of transport to the shipper is relatively easier to measure than the time. The way in which the size and frequency of shipments has been

FIGURE 4.3 Impact of Reduction in Uncertainty in Transit Time

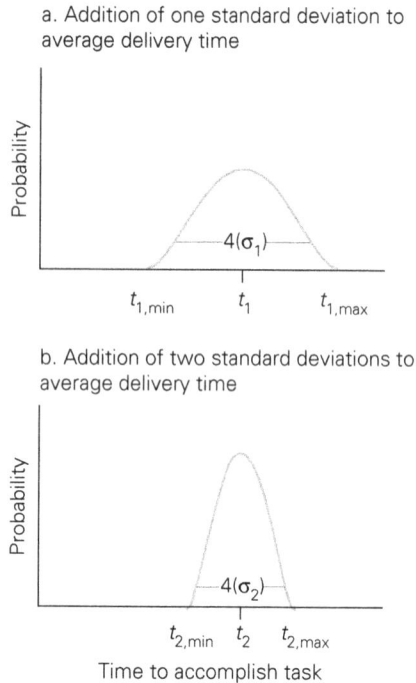

a. Addition of one standard deviation to average delivery time

b. Addition of two standard deviations to average delivery time

Time to accomplish task

Source: Arnold 2007.

specified should be sufficient to remove much of the variation in cost. However, there remains the vexing questions of discounts for large volumes but especially of payment for irregular charges (informal payments) at various stages of transport through the corridor. The level of concern about these payments on the land transport corridors stages has increased, because these payments have become more prevalent and can be as great as the formal costs of transport. For monitoring purposes, informal payments are almost certainly covered in the amount transporters and freight forwarders charge their clients. The reflection of the charges in the tariff is likely to be higher than the actual informal costs incurred, as the transports and forwarders add in an allowance to ensure that they are not out of pocket. The cost of interest for monitoring is the cost actually paid by traders, so the tariff or charge they pay to the transporter or forwarder, including any allowance to cover informal charges, is the appropriate one.

There is also a time penalty associated with informal payments, as payment often involves negotiation. On some road corridors in West Africa, the time involved in negotiation and payment is a greater burden than the amount of the payment (West Africa Trade Hub 2009). The method used by the West Africa Trade Hub to identify the cost and time penalty of informal payments is rather demanding for a regular monitoring exercise in all trade corridors, but it is feasible where a regional or corridor agency can conduct the surveys.[6] Different approaches should be taken depending on the circumstances of the corridor. Where there is an agency that can organize them, driver surveys throughout a corridor are the preferred way of collecting data on informal payments. Where no such agency is available, information from freight forwarders and transport operating companies can be used to estimate such payments.

Safety and Security

Safety and security are two very different concepts. Safety relates to accidental damage to goods in transit. Security relates to the risk goods are exposed to as they pass through a corridor. It reflects intentional actions that may affect the delivery and integrity of goods in transit.

Safety is relatively unimportant for low-value products transported as dry bulk goods. It increases in importance as the value increases for break-bulk and containerized products. A simple measure of the safety of goods is the insurance premium charged to the owner of the goods to avoid the cost of loss through damage or threat. As this cost is included in the total maritime charge if the goods are being transported CIF, no additional amount needs to be added for the safety of the goods on the maritime section of a trade corridor. However, as it is useful to know the insurance component of the CIF charge and the insurance charge for the land transport section of a trade corridor, these data need to be sought separately.

The cost of compliance with international supply chain security is usually incurred before goods are shipped from the producer. If the producer or the forwarder is not an Authorized Economic Operator (AEO), there will be additional time spent at border crossings and in ports while the goods (especially containers) are physically inspected and scanned.[7] This Toolkit assumes that the costs and times monitored are for AEOs and the additional security time and cost are for traders and forwarders that do not have this status.

Many developing countries have not yet implemented systems of AEOs. The advantages to traders of having this status are so great that the number of complying countries and traders is increasing rapidly, however. Where such facilities are not available, the cost of compliance can be measured as the extra informal cost that needs to be paid for goods that have correct documentation to be cleared within 24 hours of arrival at a port or border crossing.

Comparative Analysis of Corridor Performance

The findings of a corridor diagnostic are summarized for the core performance indicators defined in Module 1. Typically, corridor performance measures include time, cost, and reliability. Ideally, the measures should be determined for different types of traffic and units of transport. Although there is increasing emphasis on costs and times per TEU, in some instances it may be more relevant to measure per tonne or per consignment unit.

Analysis is usually conducted for a single corridor. However, when evaluating the competitiveness of the corridor with respect to alternative routes, it may be necessary to examine alternative international connections. The analysis can be limited to a simple comparison of the cost and time of moving goods through the land-link portion of the corridor and the gateway. This type of analysis provides insights into the relative importance of the two components. The analysis becomes more complex if the transport or trade corridor accounts for a significant portion of time and cost for the entire movement. In this case, the analysis would include the time and cost for competing routes. As the time and cost for the international component of the corridor and the competing routes will depend on the foreign origin/ destination, this analysis will have to be conducted for several international components and competing routes.

Performance Mapping

Data from a corridor diagnostic can be mapped to show where bottlenecks to performance occur. The mapping uses the cost and time data provided by shippers, transport and logistics service providers, and terminal operators to develop a flow chart of typical movement through the corridor. This mapping indicates the time and cost of the various activities, as well as any factors contributing to the variation in time to complete the activity. This information is used to identify activities that account for the majority of the time and cost for movement through the corridor.

Identification of bottlenecks uses the data provided by all stakeholders regarding congestion and resulting delays on the links and nodes of the corridor. These bottlenecks are generally caused by insufficient infrastructure, low throughput, or regulatory impediments.

The graphical method used by the United Nations Economic and Social Commission for Asia and the Pacific (UNESCAP 2013) indicating corridor performance is widely used. It shows the interaction between time and distance for a mode of transport (figure 4.4). The model was designed and executed in a spreadsheet and is therefore readily accessible to all users.

FIGURE 4.4 Interaction between Time and Distance Using UNESCAP Methodology

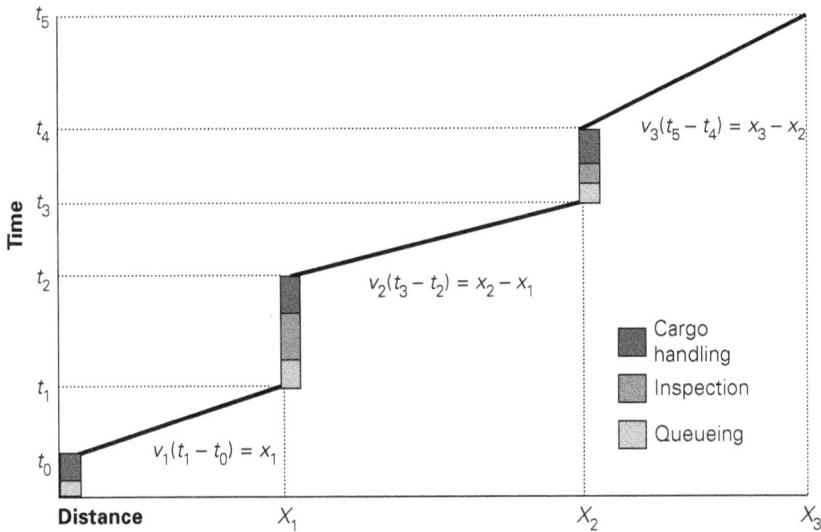

$$v_3(t_5 - t_4) = x_3 - x_2$$

$$v_2(t_3 - t_2) = x_2 - x_1$$

Cargo handling

Inspection

Queueing

$$v_1(t_1 - t_0) = x_1$$

Distance X_1 X_2 X_3

Source: Arnold 2007.

Note: Variables *x, t,* and *v* represent distance, time, and speed, respectively. The diagonal transport line represents progress toward the destination. The flatter the line, the more efficient the mode of transport. Each vertical bar represents the time it takes cargo to pass through a particular node along the corridor. This time reflects queuing, inspections, and cargo processing or handling. The vertical axis can also be used to represent cost instead of time.

The model reveals the activities that consume the most time or money. Generally, the steeper the line, the more inefficient or costly the mode of transport. This model can serve as an entry-level diagnostic summary tool.

Performance Benchmarking

A recent development in corridor assessments that has generated interest in most countries is benchmarking performance. Benchmarking uses the performance data provided by logistics service providers, terminal operators, and regulators to evaluate the efficiency of services at gateways and borders in one corridor and compares it with performance in similar corridors.

Very few attempts have been made to benchmark corridor performance. One approach is FastPath, developed by Nathan Associates for the U.S. Agency for International Development (USAID). FastPath can be used to help identify and evaluate potential solutions in developing countries to port and logistics chain inefficiencies. It identifies and prioritizes specific areas for improvement with credibility and transparency, so that all stakeholders can participate in modifying the analysis and arrive at a mutually acceptable result. FastPath provides a snapshot of how the corridor is performing at a moment in time and what can be done to improve its performance. It can also be used to monitor the impact of intervention measures to improve corridor performance.

FastPath uses a precise specification of the costs, times, and reliability parameters, separating formal and informal costs. The results are provided in the form of tables rather than a graphic, as in the UNESCAP model. The FastPath tabular framework is easily applicable to any corridor and can be incorporated in a database of the indicators of many corridors. It is relatively easy to convert FastPath tables into UNESCAP graphs (in many cases the preferred form of presentation).

The main summary tables are produced from the spreadsheets. It is also possible to construct many analytical and comparative tables to examine how one corridor compares with another as well as how a corridor is performing with respect to a specific parameter. These data facilitate a variety of analyses, including analysis of the following:

- the difference between import and export costs and times
- the difference between minimum and 85 percent time and cost values at different stages
- the share of costs borne in each country in a multinational corridor or by different stages of a corridor
- the relative importance of informal payments (time and cost) to total payments.

Comparison of corridors covers a variety of issues, including the following:

- the difference between total cost and time for each market
- the shares of land, port, and maritime transport costs
- the share of total and land transport costs in the transit country
- the time and cost differences between landlocked countries and their coastal neighbors to each market.

The reports include a comparison with other corridors that have been analyzed using the same method.

Notes

1. Examples include the World Bank scheme established under the Trade and Transport Facilitation in South East Europe project, the Corridor Performance Measurement and Monitoring System of the Central Asia Regional Economic

Cooperation (CAREC), and the Transport Corridor Europe-Caucasus-Asia (TRACECA) Route Attractiveness Index (TRAX).

2. A good example of repeated corridor surveys is the Central Asia Regional Economic Cooperation (CAREC) initiative with the International Road Transport Union (IRU) in Central Asia, which has collected data annually since 2008.

3. Under U.S. law, *break-bulk* means packages that are handled individually, palletized, or unitized for purposes of transportation, as opposed to materials in bulk and containerized freight.

4. Freight volume measured in TEU is one of the World Bank's core sector indicators for roads and highway projects.

5. The indicators employed in TRAX are cost, time, reliability, safety, and security.

6. The hub carries out a survey of truckers at regular intervals each year. It has been doing so for several years.

7. Authorized Economic Operator regimes are described in Module 6.

References

Arnold, J. 2007. "Best Practices in Management of International Trade Corridors." Transport Paper TP-13, World Bank, Washington, DC.

Hausman, Warren, Hau L. Lee, and Uma Subramanian. 2005. "Global Logistics Indicators: Supply Chain Metrics and Bilateral Trade Patterns." Policy Research Working Paper 3773, World Bank, Washington, DC.

UNESCAP (United Nations Economic and Social Commission for Asia and the Pacific). 2013. *Introduction to UNESCAP Time/Cost Distance Methodology.* http://www.unescap.org/ttdw/common/TFS/ImprovingTx/VV1/All/Introduction-Time-Cost.asp.

West Africa Trade Hub. 2009. "Improved Road Transport Governance (IRTG) Initiative on Interstate Trade Corridors." http://www.watradehub.com/sites/default/files/resourcefiles/feb10/8th-irtg-report-2nd-quarter-2009.pdf.

Wilson, John S., Catherine Mann, Yuen Pau Woo, Nizar Assanie, and Inbom Choie. 2003. "Trade Facilitation: A Development Perspective in the Asia Pacific Region." WPS 2988, World Bank, Washington, DC.

World Bank. 2004. "Chad: Trade and Transport Facilitation Audit." World Bank, Poverty Reduction and Economic Management, Washington, DC.

———. 2005. "Logistics Perception Index." World Bank Concept Note, Poverty Reduction and Economic Management, Washington, DC.

———. 2006a. "Argentina: El desafio de reducir los costos logisticos ante el crecimiento del comercio exterior." World Bank, Washington, DC.

———. 2006b. "TTFCA Performance Measurement: Pilot Corridors." World Bank, Washington, DC.

———. 2012. "Measures to Reduce the Economic Impact of High Fuel Prices." Draft report, World Bank, Africa Transport Unit, Washington, DC.

Resources

FastPath. http://www.fastpathlogistics.com.
   See text for description of the FastPath model.

Transport Corridor Europe-Caucasus-Asia (TRACECA) Route Attractiveness Index
   (TRAX). http://www.traceca-org.org/fileadmin/fm-dam/TAREP/58jh
   /TECHNICAL_DOCUMENTS/ROADS_Trax_methodology_ENG_01.pdf.
   TRAX is used to assess the attractiveness of a route based on interviews with
   transport operators and freight forwarders. Five criteria are used: time, cost,
   reliability, safety, and security.

UNESCAP (United Nations Economic and Social Commission for Asia and the
   Pacific) Methodology. http://www.unescap.org/sites/default/files/4.4.Time-cost
   -distance-methodology-ESCAP.pdf.
   The UNESCAP methodology (illustrated in figure 4.4) is a practical and simple
   way of illustrating the time and cost involved in the transport process. It can
   clearly show the most time consuming or costly parts of a shipment.

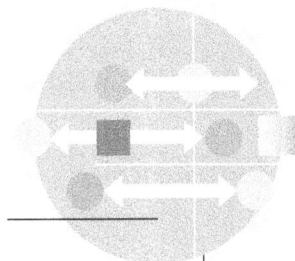

PART II

Improving Corridor Performance

The Toolkit identifies mechanisms for improving the performance of a corridor through interventions by the public and private sectors. These interventions include investments in infrastructure and modification of policies and regulations, especially those related to trade facilitation. It also considers the government's capacity to maintain the infrastructure and regulate the flow of goods along the corridor and the private sector's ability to provide a variety of services. Given the need for interaction between the public and private sectors, the Toolkit argues for the involvement of a variety of stakeholders who are critical to improving the performance of any corridor.

This part of the Toolkit comprises eight modules covering the components that are most commonly part of corridor improvement projects. Each module identifies the main issues faced, the data sources, the analytical approaches and indicators of performance, and potential intervention measures. The modules include examples and direct the reader to sources that provide more detail on technical approaches or illustrate how the issues may have been addressed.

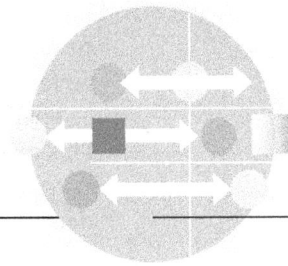

Border Management in a Corridor

The time it takes to clear goods through international borders is one of the major sources of delays to the movement of trade and transport along corridors. The delays derive from the need to comply with the formalities associated with the cross-border movement of trade and transport traffic. These activities relate to the examination, inspection, and approval of documents and shipments by customs, trade, industry, agriculture, health, security, and other agencies. They also include the physical movement of goods by transport and logistics services providers (freight forwarders, customs clearing brokers, and so forth) as well as storage or handling at terminals. Efficient border management requires the reconciliation of the twin goals of enforcing compliance while expediting the movement of cargo across international boundaries.

This module identifies the main issues faced at border-crossing points that affect the movement of goods and the performance of trade corridors. It proposes measures that can be taken to expedite border-clearance formalities to reduce costs and time. It is designed to be applicable at the sites of final clearance of goods for import or export as well as for clearance of goods in transit from landlocked countries (at the border or at an inland location away from the border). Several examples illustrate different aspects of performance diagnostics and performance improvement measures.

There is already detailed material on customs and border management. This module therefore does not go into detail on the intricacies of border management. Instead, it draws attention to those aspects that affect the efficiency of traffic flow through border posts. The main reference materials are two handbooks published by the World Bank: *Customs Modernization Handbook,* edited by De Wulf and Sokol (2005) and *Border Management Modernization,* edited by McLinden, Fanta, Widdowson, and Doyle (2011). Both handbooks cover the changes in the border management agenda and provide detail on various aspects that are touched on only lightly in this module. They provide the theoretical underpinnings and principles for the module and should be referred to for detailed exploration of the issues raised here.

The first volume, *Customs Modernization Handbook,* enunciates principles that should guide customs modernization. It acknowledges that conditions differ greatly across countries and that it is important that each customs administration tailor its modernization efforts to national objectives, implementation capacities, and resource availability. Nevertheless, meeting the modernization objectives requires the adoption of several core principles, including the following:

- adequate use of intelligence and reliance on risk management
- optimal use of information and communications technology (ICT)
- effective partnership with the private sector, including through programs to improve compliance
- increased cooperation with other border control agencies
- transparency, through information on laws, regulations, and administrative guidelines.

Success in customs modernization is tied to the overall trade policy environment. Simple, transparent, and harmonized trade policies reduce administrative complexities, facilitate transparency, and minimize the incentives and opportunities for rent-seeking and corruption. Customs modernization therefore needs to be examined from the broader and complementary perspective of trade policy reform. The broad context for the design of border-specific interventions should therefore be clearly defined and understood.

The second and more recent volume, *Border Management Modernization,* provides a comprehensive treatment of key developments in and principles for improving trade facilitation through better border management, including practical advice on particular issues. It sets a new agenda for border management reform, with an emphasis on areas not covered in traditional approaches. It advocates for a much wider approach that encompasses a "whole of government" perspective. It makes clear that although improving the performance of customs remains a high priority for many countries, customs is only one of many agencies involved in border processing; evidence suggests that customs is often responsible for no more than one-third of regulatory delays. Therefore, in a corridor context, it becomes necessary at most border posts to obtain sound data to be able to pinpoint the real source of delays and costs that affect overall performance.

The World Customs Organization (WCO), the World Trade Organization (WTO), and specialized United Nations (UN) agencies that work on trade facilitation have designed and implemented several important guiding conventions on procedures related to border management. For example, the Revised Kyoto Convention binds countries to implement specific standards at common border crossings. According to it, whenever possible, customs should operate joint controls; where a country intends to establish a new customs office or convert an existing office into a common border crossing, it should coordinate with the customs administrations in neighboring countries. Cooperation by neighboring customs and border management authorities can have a profound effect on the speed of movement of trade and transport through international borders and is central to improving corridor performance.

The module is structured as follows. The first section identifies the main issues concerning the functioning and impact of border management on corridor performance. The second section presents the data and information that is required to understand these issues. It is complemented by an annex that lists the key data and questions that can be asked of stakeholders to obtain both quantitative and qualitative data on border management. The third section identifies measures that can improve border-crossing performance. The last section summarizes these interventions.

Border Issues Affecting Corridor Performance

Types of Controls

Border management can take place at three main locations along a corridor: at a gateway port or airport, at a land border station, or at an inland clearance facility. When there are controls for the same shipment at two or more of these locations, there is need for coordination and even integrated systems and procedures between these locations, without which some processes may be repeated, increasing costs and time.

There are two interrelated sources of delay in the border clearance of goods: the presence and involvement of regulatory agencies at the border and the procedural steps followed by these agencies to clear drivers, vehicles, and goods. Each has to comply with the laws, regulations, and policies of all of the countries through which goods transit. Although customs in most countries is the main front line state agency at the border, their checks constitute only one process that must be completed to move freight across borders. Several other agencies carry out their own checks (table 5.1).

Border Agencies Involved

In most countries, multiple agencies—as many as 40 in a few countries—are involved in border management. It is therefore important to identify which agencies are operating at each border crossing in a corridor and whether they intervene directly in processing and clearing goods. A distinction should be made between the agencies involved in clearing goods at a designated customs clearance facility and those that are physically present at a border station. Some agencies may be involved in clearance but not necessarily physically present at the border station. The roles played by the most important agencies are summarized in table 5.2.

Although border performance is a function of the performance of regulatory agencies, service providers, infrastructure, and the interactions among them, the involvement of numerous agencies in the border-clearance process can result in duplication of paperwork, which in turn can be a source of

TABLE 5.1 Types of Border Checks of Cargo, Vehicles, and Drivers along Roads in a Corridor

Cargo	Vehicles	Drivers
• Customs transit control (for taxation purposes) • Customs control of restricted and prohibited items • Quarantine inspection (phyto-sanitary and veterinary health inspection) • Technical conformity board, food and health, dangerous and perishable goods control, and so forth	• Infrastructure usage fees • Vehicle insurance • Transport authorization • Weights and dimensions • Vehicle technical certificates and roadworthiness • Customs security of loads • Quarantine inspections • Special features for vehicles (for example, equipment and identification marks for refrigerated trucks or vehicle carrying dangerous goods)	• Passport and visa • Customs inspection • Quarantine inspection • Driver's licenses • Special certificates (for example, for the transport of dangerous goods) • Service license • Health/vaccination certificate

Source: UNESCAP 2007.

TABLE 5.2 Roles of Different Agencies in Border Management in a Corridor

Agency	Controls at the border
Customs	Customs officials collect or secure duties. Though the traditional role of customs of collecting duties has waned in high- and middle-income countries, it remains important in low-income countries, which rely heavily on customs revenue.
Quarantine	Quarantine officials ensure the health of people, animals, and plants by preventing infectious diseases and alien pests from entering the country. They disinfect vehicles, monitor health regulations, and check health carnets.
Public health, agriculture	Public health agencies enforce sanitary and phyto-sanitary requirements by obtaining documentary evidence (certificates) or testing and physically inspecting cargo.
Standards	Industrial products may be subject to verification of their conformity with international, regional, and national standards for health, safety, security, and fairness.
Security	Security considerations at most border stations worldwide were strengthened in the wake of the September 11, 2001 terrorist attacks. These considerations created the need for detectors to prevent the entry or exit of radioactive material. Atomic energy control bodies intervene when a suspicious consignment is detected.
Environment	Environmental agencies control hazardous waste, enforce recycling regulations, and regulate trade in endangered species items and protected products, such as timber.
Foreign affairs	In some countries, consular officers can issue visas at the border.
Immigration	Immigration authorities verify the identities of people entering or exiting the country, largely by passport and visa checks. In some countries, customs also handles immigration functions. In some countries, immigration checks are handled by a special department or by police (border police/border guards).
Transport	Transport authorities weigh trucks, collect road taxes, and enforce transport permit and licensing requirements.

delays at borders. This problem may be particularly acute in corridors of low-income countries, where not all agencies may be automated. The requirements of the many agencies provide scope for administrative discretion at the corridor level, which in turn provides incentives for traders to resort to "speed payments" to expedite cargo clearance.

Clearance of Goods

Good practice in the clearance of goods is typically guided by World Customs Organization guidelines. Modern practices are described in McLinden and others (2011). Review and reform of the border-clearance processes can yield benefits in reducing crossing times. Complex procedures are often a result of, as well as a reason for, the involvement of numerous players in the clearance processes. They can also lead to corrupt practices at the border.

It is critical to understand and map the goods clearance process (see annex figure 5A.1 for an example of a process map). The process map can form the basis for proposing simplification and streamlining of the clearance process. The mapping should make a distinction between goods passing through a border in transit and goods for domestic consumption. Different border regimes and procedures apply depending on how the goods and the vehicles that carry them will be handled. Goods in transit should be treated under the general guidance presented in Module 6.

Import for home consumption, also known as final clearance, changes the status of a good from international to domestic cargo. Domestic status could be defined as eligible for free circulation in the domestic market. Clearance requires payment of import duties and domestic taxes as well as compliance with national regulations applicable to the domestic market. Customs and other agencies are involved in the clearance process. For customs, the basic reference document is the commercial invoice, which describes the international sales contract between the seller (often an exporter) and the purchaser (often an importer). In many countries, declarants are limited to the cargo owner and its legally authorized agents.

Clearance of goods imported for home consumption need not necessarily take place at the border; it can occur inland. For inland clearance, inland container depots and dry ports have evolved as a convenient intermediate solution between clearance of cargo at the border (generally the least convenient option for shippers) and clearance on the buyer's premises (the most convenient option for the importer but the least convenient for customs). They are ideal locations for any transshipment or transloading of cargo.

Nontariff Barriers

An increasingly important source of costs and delays faced at the border are nontariff measures (NTMs). A survey of NTMs in East Africa found that clearance from as many as six public regulatory agencies was required to meet food safety, agricultural health, and quality standards in Uganda (World Bank 2011). NTMs refer not only to procedural requirements on the movement of goods but also to restrictions on the delivery of transport services. Unlike tariffs, which are subject to multilateral trade negotiations, NTMs on imports for home consumption are often nontransparent and hence provide scope for administrative discretion. Business surveys reveal that procedural requirements for complying with technical barriers to trade (TBTs) and sanitary and phyto-sanitary (SPS) requirements are important at the corridor level. These measures are likely to become more important in the coming years, given the increasing number of goods subject to them and the media attention given to health and environmental concerns.

Countries often impose TBT and SPS requirements for legitimate reasons. It is the prerogative of countries to impose such requirements—provided the specifications are transparent and scientifically justifiable, less trade restrictive alternatives are not locally applicable, information regarding such specifications is easily available to the trading community, and the requirements are not subject to revisions without notice.

TBT requirements are imposed on manufactured goods to ensure that imported goods conform to specifications (such as size, design, labeling, and packaging). From a trade facilitation perspective, the cost and time associated with meeting and confirming the compliance requirements are important, as these requirements also apply to the inputs imported by domestic export-oriented enterprises (such as the imports of textiles by Bangladesh and Nepal or goods entering into much of the intraregional trade in electrical goods in East Asia). Compliance with these requirements may require certification by a national bureau of standards. The state agencies responsible for enforcing the TBT requirements are typically present at the customs border, not necessarily at the border station (in countries where they are separate). This assignment of responsibility can cause delays, because samples have to be sent to laboratories at some other location.

SPS measures on agricultural goods are imposed to protect public, plant, and animal health. Expediting the border clearance of fresh produce or live animals in particular (fresh fruit, vegetables, and livestock) is crucial as such goods are time sensitive. Increasingly, SPS requirements are imposed on canned and agro-processed goods as well. Complying with SPS requirements can be time consuming, as border clearance of these goods may require certification and physical inspection from state agencies.

Data and Information Sources

An important step in assessing border performance is to collect and analyze data. Both qualitative and quantitative data need to be collected. The main performance indicators for customs and border management include

- time it takes goods to cross the border from the entry gate in one country to the exit gate in the other country, disaggregated by activity
- customs clearance time on each side of the border
- truck transloading time within the customs control area
- cost of truck transloading within the customs control area
- proportion of goods cleared for home consumption at the border
- proportion of goods subject to physical examination at the border
- proportion of cargo with prearrival clearance
- proportion of goods in transit.

Qualitative Data Collection

Qualitative data can be obtained through interviews of key public and private sector stakeholders involved in goods clearance, both at the border and at their headquarters. Customs is an important source of information at the border. The main data cover the following issues:

- principal enforcement responsibilities, process flows, and traffic volumes
- impact of complex regulations on efficiency and effectiveness
- modernization processes
- efforts to coordinate activities among border agencies.

Annex 5B provides a series of questions that can be used to obtain this information.

Quantitative Data Collection

There are two main ways to collect quantitative data: using a multiple border instrument, such as time release studies, or commissioning border-specific surveys. Customs is an obvious starting point, as most administrations have computer systems from which data can be quickly retrieved.

Time release studies. A time release study is a widely used performance assessment tool for measuring the time taken for the release of goods (from their arrival at borders until their release to the importer). Developed by the World Customs Organization (WCO), it has been used extensively in many countries, in some cases with support from development organizations, including the World Bank. Although the time release study was originally developed for analyzing customs performance, it is now increasingly recognized that it is important to account for the time taken for the entire clearance chain, from the arrival of goods at the land border until their release to the importer (as delays may be not just a result of customs but also caused by the actions of other regulatory border agencies). Box 5.1 provides an example of a time release study in Uganda. Annex figure 5A.1 shows an example of a process map for a border post in Zimbabwe. The WCO Time Release Study Guide was revised with a view to strengthening land border management.

The main time markers covered by land border time release study are

- arrival of goods
- unloading of goods
- delivery to customs area, where goods are generally temporarily stored

Using the Results of a Time Release Study on Border Operations in Uganda

Uganda conducted a time release study in 2010 to determine how long it takes to clear goods at the border. Stakeholders (customs brokers, the Ministry of Agriculture, the export promotion board, and transporters) were involved from the outset. The study was conducted at selected border stations; data were collected over seven days, using a questionnaire developed for the purpose. The WCO time release study online software was used to analyze the results.

Although initially there was suspicion among the customs staff and other actors (especially customs brokers), the working committee managed to abate their fears by emphasizing the potential for positive outcomes for all involved in clearing goods. Data collection took longer than expected, because of lack of funding. There were technical problems as a result of a slow network connection to the WCO online software.

The report on the findings provided Uganda customs with baseline information on the time taken to clear goods out of customs and identified potential areas of improvement in the border-clearance process. It resulted in reengineering of customs procedures. Following completion of the study, the following changes were made:

- A joint border management was established at Malaba and Katuna.
- An accreditation process to transporters and clearing agents was initiated.
- Twenty-four-hour-a-day operations were initiated at some customs stations in order to improve service delivery.
- Customs put in place some initiatives to improve the system, but no time release studies have been conducted since then to measure their effect.

Source: World Customs Organization, http://www.wcoomd.org.

- lodgement of goods declaration
- payment of duties and duty discrepancies (can take place after intervention by other agencies)
- acceptance of the declaration
- documentary control
- physical inspection

- intervention by other agencies
- goods released by customs
- removal of goods from the border post premises.

It is advisable to combine the time release study with monitoring of the physical movement of the means of transport.

A time release study achieves the following:

- It yields quantitative data for monitoring the average time between the arrival of the goods and their release into the economy by each intervening agency.
- It identifies the external constraints affecting the border release of goods (such as the granting of authorization or permits, the application of other laws, and inspections by agencies).
- It provides the basis for identifying administrative measures for streamlining the clearance process in border posts at the corridor level.

Dedicated border performance monitoring. Time release studies are useful for most corridor projects. Dedicated monitoring can be more useful to project design. In such cases, one or all corridor border posts are monitored, and detailed data are collected to measure performance and identify bottlenecks. Such monitoring is widely used in Africa; it has also been employed in Southeast Asia.

Performance measurement at border-crossing points

- captures information on import and export commercial traffic movements through border facilities on both sides
- registers the times it takes goods to cross the border, making a distinction between physical movement and the time it takes to process documents while goods are stationary
- notes any irregular events that may affect the time of both of the above. Examples could include processes that are too fast or too slow, including congestion; atypical flows; and improperly completed, incomplete, or missing documents.

Two data sheets are often used, one to track the movement of goods from the moment a truck joins a queue at the border or enters the customs yard to the moment it leaves the customs control area and a second to track the time it takes to complete various stages of the document clearance process. The second data sheet can be attached to any documents, so that each officer involved in processing the documents can record the time he or she starts and completes the assigned task. Where processes are computerized, this information can be retrieved as and when needed. (Module 1 discusses the design of corridor observatories.)

Data capture points may differ, depending on border specificities. Table 5.3 identifies some of the common points.

Surveyors would have to be positioned at locations where they can easily capture the required data, without much intrusion. A distinction should also be made between time taken in document processing (while the vehicle is parked in one location) and the time for physical movement (when the truck has to move to a different location for weighing or scanning, for instance). During data collection, care has to be taken that date and time formats are consistently captured. Cleaning up data can be onerous and introduce more errors. Table 5.4 provides examples of data on physical movement.

The last column can be valuable to interpreting and understanding the observed patterns. For instance, at some border posts, foreign trucks are not allowed to enter the country. In such instances, cargo is transloaded from one truck to another. Transloading can complicate the monitoring process, especially when the number of trucks is different (that is, goods from one large truck are transloaded onto two or more smaller trucks or vice versa).

TABLE 5.3 Data Capture Points at Border Posts

Position	Time to record
Place where truck queues to cross border	• Start of border-crossing process
Place where goods arrive	• Entry of vehicle into country • Initial customs registration
Place where physical examinations take place (physical inspections may or may not take place during transshipments)	• Start of inspection • End of inspection
Place where agencies other than customs processes import documents (if any)	• Start of processing • End of processing
Place where customs signs release note	• Time when release note is signed (and importer is free to move goods inland)
Place where truck exits gate of customs control area	• End of border-clearance process

TABLE 5.4 Examples of Data Collected at Border Post

License plate of truck	Country of registration	Name of importer	Arrival at back of queue (date and time)		Move to examination bay (date and time)		Notes (if any)
987-654Y	Botswana	Alpha Mines	05/11/13	19:20	05/11/13	20:05	
123-456X	Zambia	XYZ Limited	05/10/13	13:40	05/10/13	13:55	

Monitoring the transloading process can be time consuming and require several observers. Where customs declarations can be submitted in advance of the goods' arrival at the border, care must be taken to distinguish between goods arriving under such a regime and goods whose clearance starts only when the goods arrive (box 5.2).

Data Analysis

Border-clearance time is a common indicator in most corridor projects. The focus should be on the average and distribution of border-crossing time, but other measures should also be included, as outlined below.

Time to cross the border. Both time release studies and dedicated border assessments can provide information that helps target border interventions to improve overall corridor performance. The procedural requirements that have to be complied with to clear goods as they move through a corridor can be major sources of delays. Analysis of the data therefore focuses on both the mean time and the distribution around the mean, which is probably more important than average time. Lack of reliability increases logistics costs, because shippers have to carry more inventories, suffer stock-outs and disruptions to operations, or make emergency shipments at higher costs. More important from a logistics costs perspective, the unpredictability of clearance times around the mean can reveal patterns of behavior by both official agencies and importers, including discretionary or corrupt practices. On some corridors, it is necessary to ask questions and collect data on informal payments to speed the clearance process.

Cost to cross the border. Various types of cost are incurred at borders in addition to normal duties. These costs include direct costs, such as user fees (public and private), cost of transloading goods, where required, compliance costs to meet regulatory requirements, parking charges, and various types of insurance (vehicle, bond, goods liability, etc.). During project design, it is important to estimate all costs, as one objective of corridor interventions at the border is to lower them.

On some corridors informal fees must be paid to expedite the clearance of cargo. Informal payments associated with border clearance have traditionally not been captured well in the design of corridor projects. However, they can be significant and are worth assessing. A survey of traders on the India-Bangladesh border found that the majority of exporters made speed money payments of 1–3 percent of the shipment value (World Bank 2013). These informal costs are passed on to shippers,

BOX 5.2

Monitoring Performance on the Border between Zambia and Zimbabwe

The crossing at Chirundu, between Zambia and Zimbabwe, is one of the busiest border posts in Southern Africa. About 400 heavy goods vehicles transit the border in both directions every day.

Monitoring of the Chirundu border posts was carried out over a period of one year. The relatively long time span enabled the authorities to get an accurate picture of the average time spent at the border. The monitoring was conducted by a company that collected data from both primary sources (customs, drivers, and agents) and official records of traffic as it passes on both sides of the border.

Two types of data were collected during the monitoring period: descriptive data on the vehicle and consignment carried and data on the time taken at each stage of the clearing process. Data were collected on traffic flows for both northbound and southbound traffic (there is imbalance in traffic in this corridor). The data were used to calculate the time it took to complete each clearance process at the corridor.

The monitoring was based on a clear sampling design that took into account the traffic volume, day of week, and time of day, as well as the percentage of prearrival and postarrival document submission patterns. The data were recorded on a simple spreadsheet that showed the time spent by drivers with different authorities or agents on both sides of the border and the reasons for the delays in the clearance process. Total and average values for each transit movement were calculated, split into border-clearance and preclearance delays.

Reports from the monitoring identified the average hours taken by trucks for carrying goods to transit the border, both northbound and southbound, and the causes of delays attributed to the various actors in the supply chain; and analyzed the effects of commodities on transit times. The monitoring exercise indicated the magnitude of the problem of border delays at Chirundu, providing the rationale for setting up the one-stop border post by the two countries. The monitoring also provided the baseline data for the introduction of a one-stop border post in 2009.

Source: Curtis 2008.

often with a markup, increasing the costs of using a corridor. The uncertainty of informal payments makes the costs to traders unpredictable.

Other costs include the fixed costs of transport equipment, such as vehicles (trucks, wagons, locomotives) that are idle during the clearance process. At some border posts, these costs alone add up to several million dollars a year. They are increased by the opportunity costs of capital tied up in goods waiting to be cleared. One study estimates that each day of delay is equal to 1 percent of trade or increasing the distance between trading parties by as much as 70 kilometers (Djankov, Freund, and Pham 2006).

Improving Border-Crossing Performance

An efficient border post should facilitate the twin goals of ensuring compliance and expediting cargo clearance processing. An essential feature of efficiency is that there be no traffic delays and that in case of border congestion priority should be given to expediting clearance from the border by exploring the possibilities of establishing control and compliance either before goods reach the border or after they leave. There are several ways this can be done:

- better use of risk management systems
- innovative use of technology
- managing traffic flows
- coordination and information sharing
- information sharing across borders
- one-stop border facilities
- addressing nontariff measures
- clearing cargo away from the border.

No single measure can solve all the problems at a border-crossing point. Several measures should be adopted simultaneously.

Better Use of Risk Management Systems

Border officials in corridors have to reconcile the seemingly contradictory objective of enforcing control with the trade facilitation objective of expediting cargo clearance. Border control agencies in many parts of the world use variants of the principles of risk management to achieve this. Risk management refers to the technique in which customs or other control agencies restrict their physical inspection and checking activities to consignments perceived to be high risk while expediting the release of consignments of traders deemed to be compliant or of less risk. Risk management as a concept is not new; the vast majority of border agencies have in place some form of risk management procedures or guidelines, either formal or informal.

Border agencies increasingly require submission of advance information on goods and passengers entering the country for making a risk-based decision. Prearrival clearance allows traders to submit data to a border agency early in the transport of goods, for advance processing by the border agency and immediate release of the goods once they reach the border.

A system of risk assessments provides the basis for selectivity in physical inspections. Risk criteria typically include the following:

- the origin of the goods
- the importer's track record
- the types of goods
- trade patterns
- incentives for misclassification
- shipment value.

These criteria form the basis for classifying goods as high, medium, or low risk. The border agency typically assigns goods to one of three color-coded channels. Goods assigned to the Red channel are deemed high-risk cargo; they have to undergo both documentary and physical inspection. Goods assigned to the Yellow or Orange channel are deemed medium-risk cargo and are subject only to documentary control. Goods assigned to the Green channel are deemed low-risk cargo; they may be immediately released from the border with no checks, although they might be subject to postclearance document review.

Innovative Use of Technology

Dramatic increases in border traffic and fears of international terrorism have forced governments to design new methods of border control and processing, reducing congestion and waiting times. These new methods, widely adopted in market economy countries, were gradually expanded when security became a major issue worldwide. They include the following:

- moving customs clearance away from the physical border and nearer to where goods are stored or consumed (with an effective internal transit control scheme)

- developing international cooperation to reduce data discrepancies
- introducing accreditation and voluntary compliance schemes for both travelers and importers with expedited formalities for eligible parties.

The objective is to maintain reasonable security without disrupting cross-border movements. The model requires technological solutions (X-ray scanners, other detection equipment, and ICT infrastructure). It also requires major innovations in postrelease control and adequate auditing capacity, along with enforcement, interagency cooperation, and an environment that provides a reliable audit trail. These methods are not available to all countries.

Managing Traffic Flows

Managing space in a border station is often an issue at border posts. Traffic flows may be subject to different inspection and control, based on a risk-based decision. Traffic should be separated as early as possible when approaching the station. Heavy goods vehicles should be taken out of car lanes at some distance from the station and driven or parked on dedicated roads, as width is a problem at many border stations. Separation allows traffic that requires and is ready for formal controls to reach the station without delay. If separation is not feasible, a holding area can be established before the border and traffic released at defined intervals to keep the approach lanes clear.

International transit trucks require much less processing than other trucks and should be provided with special lanes. Empty trucks should be diverted from main commercial lanes. When two border stations are within a short distance of one another and the border crossing is wide enough, traffic requiring clearance to enter the arrival country could be directed to special lanes in the departure country.

The processing of truck drivers can be managed in a similar manner. Separate desks can be established to process drivers away from tourist and general passenger movement. Eventually, it may even be conceivable to process drivers in their vehicles, as advanced economies do.

Coordination and Information Sharing

Collaborative border management is based on the need for agencies and the international community to work together to achieve common aims. The model suggests that border management agencies can increase control while providing a more efficient service and that they can do so while retaining their own organizational mandates and integrity.

Collaborative border management takes advantage of the availability of information at the earliest point in the transport and supply chain at which border management agencies can become involved. This point could be at a factory while goods are being packaged for shipment, at a port at the point of departure, or at any time before the physical destination border is reached. Ensuring compliance at the virtual border reduces clearance time at the physical border, allowing border management agencies to focus on the audit and examination of high-risk items.

Lack of coordination and information sharing by national regulatory agencies is often a source of delays at the border. Countries in recent decades have made systematic efforts to address the problem of lack of coordination and information sharing by national regulatory agencies by creating national single windows. The term *national single window* is used to denote coordinated information exchanges and information sharing by national regulatory agencies. In countries with such systems, traders can submit all import, export, and transit information required by regulatory agencies at one time through a single electronic gateway rather than submit the same information repeatedly to various government entities. In principle, the system allows for the simultaneous processing of information by all national regulatory agencies, thereby avoiding the delays associated with sequential processing.

A broadly conceived single window covers the activities of all trade-processing organizations involved in the front office formalities of trade. It covers customs and government licensing, inspection, and approval agencies, such as the ministries of trade, industry, health, economics, agriculture, defense, and finance. With this scope, a single window must focus on organization, governance, regulation and legislation, project management, process reengineering, funding, and planning. ICT is important for the success of national single windows, but it is subsidiary to many other aspects.

The implementation of a national single window typically requires unprecedented cooperation and collaboration by government ministries agencies and other statutory bodies. The government has to define potential operational models for the national single window in discussions, both internally and with other stakeholders. The operational model should include everything from obtaining and establishing technology and infrastructure platforms to managing, operating, and providing services through the national single window.

International experience suggests success factors for single window systems include commitment by all stakeholders, cooperation by agencies, government support, and information sharing (box 5.3). Ultimately, the system should reflect what works best with a country's local laws and intergovernmental relationships in a given trading environment.

Singapore's Single Window

In the mid-1980s, the Singapore government decided to streamline the processes involved in approving trade permits. Special committees made up of high-powered government officials and business leaders were set up to ensure backing for the use of information technology (IT) to support the improvement of the trade regulatory framework and processes. Starting with a few government agencies in 1989, the Singapore TradeNet System grew to provide the trading community with electronic means of submitting trade documents to all relevant government authorities for processing through a single electronic window. Within 10 minutes of submission of the permit application, traders receive an electronic response, with details on the approval conditions or reasons for rejection.

TradeNet 4.0, the current version, is simpler than previous versions, with fewer fields required to submit a permit application. Other new features include integration with TradeXchange, an electronic platform for information exchange between traders and logistics operators both within Singapore and internationally.

Source: UNECE 2010.

Information Sharing across Borders

One source of border-processing delays is lack of access to information regarding the many requirements of state agencies. Information should be accessible electronically; in developing countries with limited automation, such information should be available to traders at the border in printed form. Transparent guidelines for stopping vehicles at the border reduce the scope for arbitrary administrative discretion at border crossings.

Cross border information sharing has been successfully used to reduce border crossing time in East Africa where delays at border crossings have long been identified as hindering trade. The delays were often due to various factors including inefficient paperwork processes; lack of advance notification of goods, fraudulent declarations; lack of efficient, international information exchange by revenue authorities; and lack of transit and trade statistics. A significant improvement was made by developing a platform for efficient customs and transit data exchange, management, and reporting (box 5.4).

BOX 5.4

Reducing Delays by Sharing Customs Information in East Africa

Traders typically lose a great deal of time because agencies in each country reenter trade-related information in their computer systems for customs and other border-control purposes. Reentering data also makes the process vulnerable to input errors and fraud; border management measures to combat this risk can further delay the clearance process. Starting from a document that has already been verified by one customs authority ensures data integrity and, more important, traceability of the declarations across borders, which is critical for reconciliation and risk management.

Uganda and Kenya have been at the forefront of an initiative to share data in their customs administrations. In 2009, the two countries worked with the U.S. Agency for International Development (USAID) to develop a system to connect their customs systems. The system, the Revenue Authorities Digital Data Exchange (RADDEx), transmits customs transit declaration data in near real time from a point of initial lodging (port, border post) through all relevant transit points to the final destination. This electronic transmission reduces transit delays through provision of advance notification, facilitation of prelodging, elimination of duplicate data entry, and risk analysis.

RADDEx was first developed for use at the Malaba border post between the two countries. It enabled the sharing of data between the border-crossing point and the main transit port of Mombasa in Kenya. The border management requirements of the two countries already shared several data elements. For Uganda transit declarations in Kenya, for example, 38 data elements were already captured in Kenya, with the declarant adding or modifying only 3 elements (including the declarant's name) in Uganda.

RADDEx has led to significant reductions in preparation and processing the declarations by

- avoiding duplicate data entry by declarants at different border posts
- enabling prearrival declaration and data processing
- sending advance notice for document preparation
- facilitating the verification.

Source: USAID 2011.

One-Stop Border Facilities

Although not always warranted, there is a growing trend for government agencies to use border posts as primary locations for the enforcement of border controls. However, the most common and traditional border configuration model does not always allow optimal operations. Typically, two sets of activities are performed at a border post. A user meets the requirements to exit one country and then goes through a process to enter the other country. In the case of trucks, this process can mean inspection of goods twice, including the offloading of trucks or the destuffing of containers. Such an inefficient process increases costs and delays.

To overcome some of these problems, several countries, especially in Africa, have been introducing one-stop border posts. Such posts seek to combine the border-clearance activities of the two countries in a single location. In theory, the posts are either replaced by or made more efficient through the simplification of clearance procedures that increase cooperation and coordination of controls, foster data and intelligence sharing, and improve control over fraud. One-stop border post facilities should yield economies of scale, better cooperation, simplified formalities, improved control over fraud, and informal data and intelligence exchanges.

There are three common configurations (figure 5.1):

- A straddle one-stop border post has a single building over the border, such that officers within the building are actually operating on their own sovereign territory. This model is typically suited to new facilities. An example of a straddle facility is the Nemba-Gasenyi border post on the border between Burundi and Rwanda. A straddle facility requires that inspections and other activities be carried out jointly.
- A common country facility is one in which a single structure is developed in one of the two countries to house officers from both countries. This model requires strong cooperation between the two parties. One country needs the authority to carry out controls in the other; the host country needs a legal framework that allows foreign officers to work on its soil. Examples of common facilities for train clearances are the Malaba border post between Kenya and Uganda and the Cinkansé border post between Burkina Faso and Togo, both of which have been legally defined as international territory.
- The most common variant is juxtaposed facilities, in which agencies of the two countries share facilities. Each facility handles entries into the country in which it is located. This model is generally used where facilities already exist or a natural barrier, such as a river, forms the boundary.

FIGURE 5.1 Types of One-Stop Border Post Configurations

a. Straddle border facility

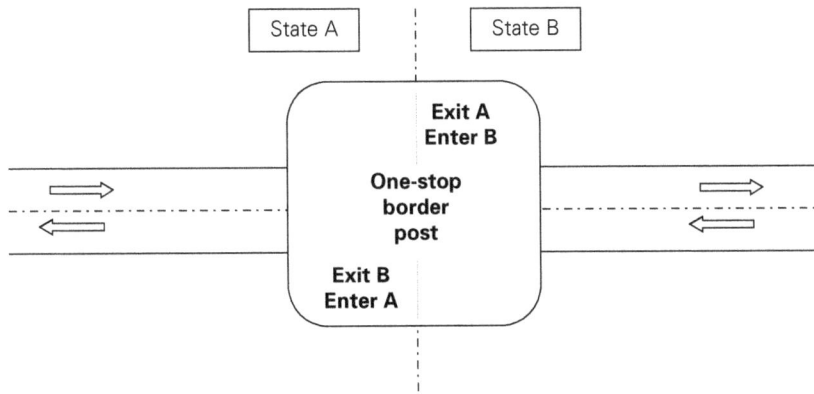

b. Common facility in one country

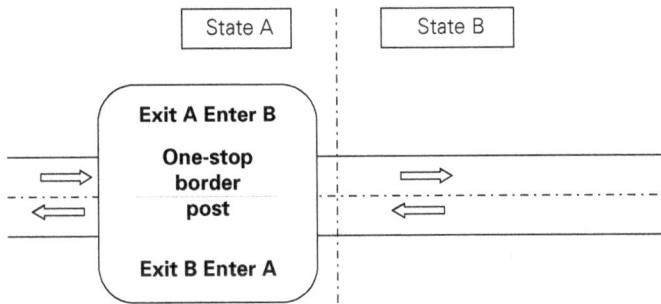

c. Juxtaposed facilities

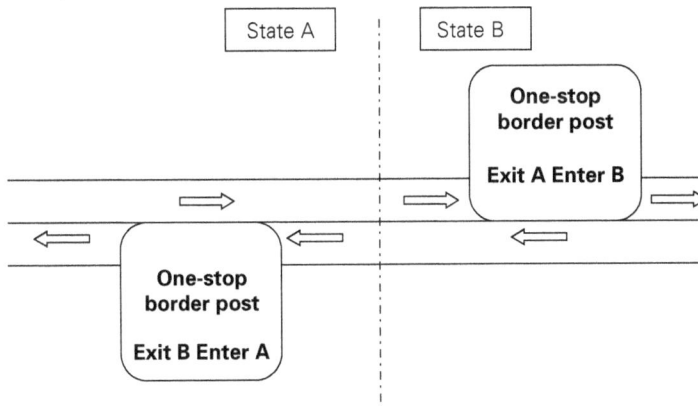

Source: World Bank, based on CDC 2011.

The laws in each country must allow officers to carry out their laws in a common control zone in the adjoining state (extraterritorial jurisdiction) and to host foreign officials. An example is the Chirundu border post between Zambia and Zimbabwe.

A one-stop border post can offer several potential benefits:

- The staff of an authority (such as customs) of both countries is stationed in one set of offices, on one side of the border.
- The driver of the truck, or the traveler, is attended to by an authority representing both countries in one place.
- In the case of customs, the vehicle and its load are inspected by the authorities of both countries, one after the other.
- The documents for the goods, which may be entered on two sets of documents, are processed in one set of offices.
- The truck needs to queue only once, on one side of the border.

However, for the benefits to be fully realized, several conditions must be met:

- Procedures must be harmonized and simplified.
- Information technology must be fully utilized.
- Intelligence must be shared.
- Transparency must be ensured.
- Staff must be trained.
- Effective change management of the border facility must be evident across all stakeholders, including border agencies, transporters, clearing agents, importers and exporters, and the general public.

Ideally, before a one-stop border post is introduced it is important to streamline processes to reduce delays. In general, conditions for success are simple, but experience shows that they are sometimes difficult to fulfill. The main problems relate to architectural design; the clarity of procedures; the streamlining of laws; and the ability to detect fraud, arrest offenders, and prosecute cases without violating either country's laws. Bilateral agreements should be flexible enough to allow for adjustment to local conditions and circumstances.

Addressing Nontariff Measures

Institutional support aimed at strengthening corridor coordination committees is important to tackling some NTMs. These measures are linked to national regulatory structures. Costs and delays at the border are a reflection of the different regulatory procedures followed by countries. Many of the initiatives that reduce delays (such as simultaneous processing of activities at border posts) can be handled effectively by a strong corridor coordination committee consisting of stakeholders, including government agencies and private sector representatives who stand to gain from a well-functioning corridor.

Other measures may also be warranted. For example, most TBT and SPS requirements involve substantial upfront investments. Where corridors straddle many countries, it would be in the interests of the countries to strive for mutual recognition of standards at the corridor or regional levels. The ongoing process for eliminating NTMs in the Association of Southeast Asian Nations (ASEAN) is illustrative of the possibilities for countries with limited financial flexibility. The ASEAN countries' ongoing approach to reducing NTMs involves mutual recognition of standards and regional standards. The approach entails the following features:

- Eliminating NTMs in selected sectors, chosen on the basis of their importance for the region.
- Identifying NTMs in selected sectors of member countries. The ASEAN Secretariat relied on different sources, including country submissions, submissions by chambers of commerce, and the Trade Analysis Information System (TRAINS) database of the United Nations Conference on Trade and Development (UNCTAD). The analysis revealed customs charges and TBT requirements as the most important impediments to trade in the selected sectors.
- Identifying the priority areas for regional harmonization. This identification led to two initiatives: the regional harmonization of SPS measures for poultry products and the regional harmonization of product-specification standards for electrical goods.

The initiatives led to three Mutual Recognition Agreements (in electrical and electronic equipment, telecommunications, and cosmetics). Other regional measures included reducing the scope for government involvement in securing health and safety standards. For example, the directive on cosmetics, which became effective in 2008, replaced the cumbersome presale product-by-product approval system with a risk-based postsale surveillance system.

A national bureau is typically responsible for providing required TBT certification; agriculture, veterinary, or public health authorities are responsible for providing the required SPS certification in most countries. The presence of trained officials at the border helps reduce border delays, especially where border posts are physically separated from the state agency, which may be in the capital.

Clearing Cargo away from the Border

Landlocked countries face a special problem when importing goods. The goods arrive at a port in a neighboring country—or even a neighbor of a neighbor—and need to transit toward the destination country, where full customs clearance must take place. A well-functioning transit system could deal with this problem easily, but transit systems do not function well in low-income countries.

These difficulties could be reduced if the landlocked country were to conduct some or all customs clearance procedures at the first port of call on the foreign territory. This is the practice in Djibouti, where since 1950 Ethiopian customs has been based to facilitate the transit of goods destined for Ethiopia. (Bhutan customs is based in the Port of Kolkata, in India, for the same purpose.) Transit through the territory of Djibouti is unencumbered by the escort services and traffic-sharing obligations that characterize transit trade in some countries. Final clearance then takes place on Ethiopian territory.

In many cases, the clearances required from the state and inspection agencies need not be at the border station but can be in the vicinity, thereby relieving traffic congestion. Physical inspection of goods can be conducted at inland bonded warehouses. Many immediate border checks on freight (such as for quality standards) can be deferred until the consignment reaches its final destination, sometimes even after it has been cleared from the border.

To expedite clearance away from the border, countries must have basic but reliable information on shipments entering the country and the administrative/organizational ability to perform and enforce postrelease control. Goods must arrive in secured trucks or containers whose seals have not been tampered with.

Summary of Possible Interventions for Improving Border Management

Table 5.5 summarizes the most common border management issues and questions found in corridor projects and proposes possible interventions to address them. Actual interventions should be adapted to deal with specific constraints.

TABLE 5.5 Possible Interventions for Improving Border Management

Issue	Questions	Possible interventions
Long border-crossing times	• How long does it take to cross the border? • Do the procedures make a clear distinction between transit and final clearance? • Are disaggregated data available on how long each part of the process takes?	• Simplify cargo clearance procedures. • Separate traffic flows for transit and domestic cargo. • Introduce or improve use of risk-based clearance system. • Use prearrival clearance procedures.
Congestion	• What causes congestion? • Are there separate lanes for different streams of traffic?	• Separate traffic flows for transit and domestic cargo. • Simplify clearance procedures. • Move clearance away from the border. • Introduce better coordination among border agencies. • Increase capacity of facility.
Delays because of repeated data capturing	• Do agencies in the same country share information? • Do agencies of the two countries share information?	• Introduce data sharing among customs agencies. • Coordinate traffic flow on the two sides of the border. • Introduce a single window system. • Introduce one-stop concept.
Nontariff measures (NTMs)	• Are NTMs contributing to clearance times?	• Strengthen corridor management to address NTMs. • Develop a portal with required information.
Drivers delayed in immigration	• Are commercial truck drivers caught in queues for tourist travel?	• Establish separate counters for commercial truck drivers. • Introduce multiple entry visas for drivers. • Process drivers inside their trucks.
Delays as a result of vehicle checks and fees	• Are trucks delayed as a result of transport or other vehicle checks?	• Standardize vehicle load limits and dimensions. • Harmonize cross-border charges between countries. • Simplify vehicle permit requirements. • Introduce a corridor or regional insurance scheme.

Annex 5A Flow Chart for Beitbridge Border Post (Cargo Inward), Zimbabwe

FIGURE 5A.1 Flow Chart for Beitbridge Border Post (Cargo Inward), Zimbabwe

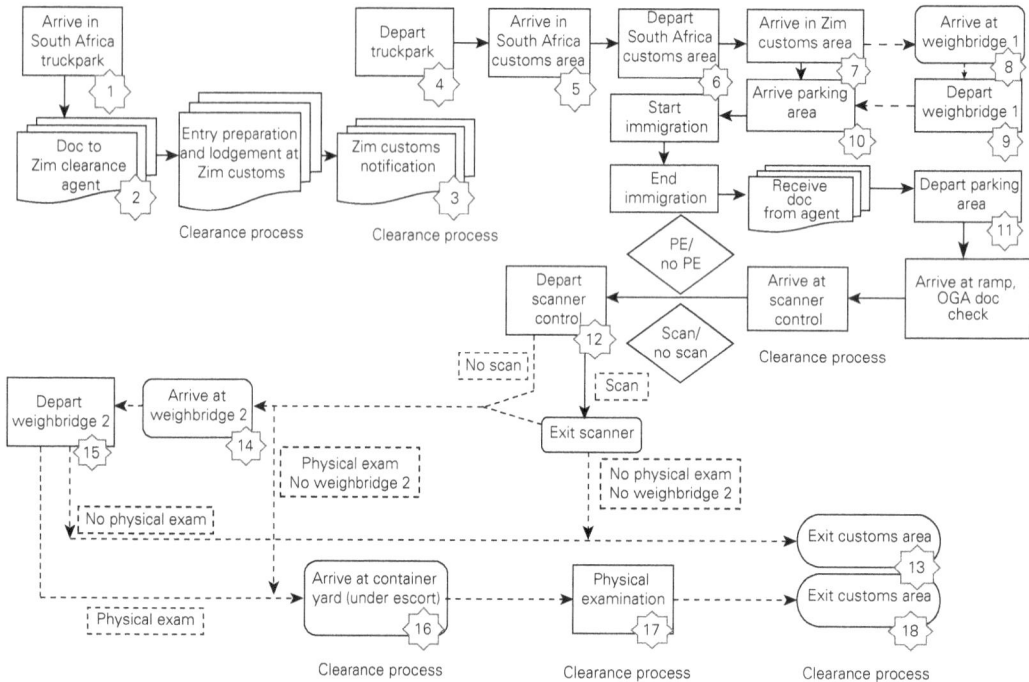

Note: Weighbridges 1 and 2 are alternatives at the option of the driver. Doc = document; OGA = other government agency; PE = physical exam; Zim = Zimbabwe.

Annex 5B Questions for Discussion of Customs

A. General Questions

1. Have the various forms for declaration of imports, exports, goods in transit, and goods under temporary admission been replaced with a standard administrative document?
   - ☐ Yes
   - ☐ No

2. Does the document allow for entries in English, French, or a language common to corridor countries?
   - ☐ Yes
   - ☐ No

3. Is the Harmonized Commodity Coding and Classification System (HS) of the World Customs Organization used to categorize traded goods?
   - ☐ Yes
   - ☐ No

4. How are duties computed?
   - ☐ Based on invoiced value, with additional reference to historical prices
   - ☐ Based on fixed schedule of prices

5. How many different percentages are used to compute duty based on the value of the cargo? _____

6. Can customs declarations be submitted and reviewed before the arrival of the cargo?
   - ☐ Yes
   - ☐ No

7. For which of the following is electronic data processing and communications systems used?
   - ☐ Remote submission of vessel manifest or master airway bill
   - ☐ Remote submission of customs declaration
   - ☐ Remote submission of supporting documents (scanned copies)
   - ☐ Calculation of duties and taxes
   - ☐ Notification of consignee of cargo status
   - ☐ Selection of level of inspection for individual shipments
   - ☐ Monitoring of bonded storage inventory
   - ☐ Notification of other border management agencies of cargo requiring their approval

8. Which customs functions are performed using the Internet?
   - ☐ Submitting declarations
   - ☐ Downloading government forms
   - ☐ Searching government regulations

9. Which of the following does the customs risk management system include?
   ☐ Preshipment inspection system
   ☐ Green and Yellow channels
   ☐ Risk profiles that include more than three parameters
   ☐ Risk profiles for shippers, forwarders, and clearance agents
   ☐ System for tracking shipper behavior and periodically updating risk profiles
   ☐ Central office responsibility for controlling risk assessments
   ☐ Random selection of customs officers for physical inspections
   ☐ Scanners as integrated part of inspection protocol (that is, a Blue channel)

10. Is customs responsible for coordinating activities associated with enforcing health requirements, product standards, and security issues?
    ☐ Yes
    ☐ No

11. Is a licensed customs broker required to clear cargo?
    ☐ Yes
    ☐ No

12. Is the license in the name of the firm or individual?
    ☐ Firm
    ☐ Individual

13. Which of the following requirements must customs brokers meet?
    ☐ Meet minimum educational requirements
    ☐ Renew their license annually
    ☐ Undergo periodic retraining
    ☐ Be certified in the use of customs information technology (IT) systems
    ☐ Maintain a bond of a fixed amount

14. Are electronic signatures used to complete customs-related transactions?
    ☐ Yes
    ☐ No

15. If not, is there a plan to do so?
    ☐ Yes
    ☐ No

16. Which of the following is a major impediment to the introduction of modern procedures?
    ☐ Resistance of customs officers
    ☐ Insufficient technical skills or training
    ☐ Condition of facilities
    ☐ Lack of computerization

17. How is the control of cargo movements across borders managed?
    - ☐ Integrated border management
    - ☐ Customs operating as the lead agency
18. Is customs responsible for coordinating the activities associated with enforcing health requirements, product standards, and security issues?
    - ☐ Yes
    - ☐ No
19. Does customs operate seven days a week?
    - ☐ Yes
    - ☐ No
20. Does it operate 24 hours a day?
    - ☐ Yes
    - ☐ No
21. If not, how many hours a day does it operate? _____
22. Which of the following do customs facilities have?
    - ☐ Reliable electricity
    - ☐ On-line computer systems
    - ☐ Land lines
    - ☐ Air-conditioned offices
    - ☐ Scanners
    - ☐ Offices for customs brokers and forwarders
    - ☐ Parking and offices for transporters
    - ☐ Third-party storage and consolidation
23. Which customs-related activities are performed at the border?
    - ☐ Processing declarations
    - ☐ Clearing cargo
    - ☐ Scanning and physical inspections
    - ☐ Payment of duties
    - ☐ Lab tests and quarantine
24. What percentage of customs declarations are submitted electronically for imports? _____ Exports? _____
25. At which of the following places can import cargo be cleared behind the border?
    - ☐ Inland bonded warehouses
    - ☐ Inland container depots/dry ports
    - ☐ Customs inspection stations in major urban areas
26. What is the average number of loaded trucks that cross the border into the country per day? _____
27. What is the average number of declarations filed per loaded truck?
    _____

28. For loaded trucks entering the country, what percentage carry cargo that is:
    □ Cleared at the border: _____
    □ Cleared inside the country: _____
    □ In transit to third countries: _____

29. What restrictions apply to trucks and containers crossing the border?
    □ Not permitted; back-to-back transfer is required
    □ Permitted, but trucks must have a customs bond
    □ Permitted, but with a quota that limits the number of foreign trucks that can enter the country
    □ Permitted, but with a reciprocity agreement
    □ Permitted, but with a transports internationaux routiers (international road transport, or TIR) or similar guarantee

30. For trucks carrying import cargo waiting to be cleared at the border, what is the average number of trucks in the queue? _____ What is the average time spent in the queue? _____

31. What percentage of trucks carrying import or export cargo transfer it to other trucks at the border? _____ What is the average time required for this transfer? _____

32. Which of the following requirements must trucks transiting through a country meet?
    □ Travel in a convoy or with an escort
    □ Travel along a designated route
    □ Have an electronic seal
    □ Arrive at exit point within a fixed time
    □ Have Global Positioning System (GPS)/Radio Frequency Identification (RFID) monitoring
    □ Have a bond/guarantee
    □ Have a TIR or similar carnet

33. What kind of coordination is there between authorities on both sides of the border?
    □ Harmonized customs declarations
    □ Electronic or manual exchange of declarations
    □ Sharing of intelligence
    □ Joint inspections
    □ No coordination

34. Is there a single window for submission of all documents related to clearing cargo?
    □ Yes
    □ No

35. Is it electronic?
- ☐ Yes
- ☐ No

36. What is the principal source of discrepancies in declarations?
- ☐ Misclassification
- ☐ Undervaluation
- ☐ Contraband or intellectual property violations
- ☐ Goods for temporary admission
- ☐ Prohibited goods

37. What are the principal causes of delay in crossing the border?
- ☐ Congestion in terminal and on access road
- ☐ Transfer of cargo between vehicles
- ☐ Late arrival/presentation of cargo documents
- ☐ Availability of funds for paying duty and taxes
- ☐ Availability of connecting transport
- ☐ Physical inspection, security checks
- ☐ Testing samples
- ☐ Customs office hours and staff efficiency

38. What are current or planned improvements in procedures and infrastructure?
- ☐ New facilities
- ☐ Scanning equipment
- ☐ Relocation of laboratories
- ☐ Upgraded access roads
- ☐ Simplified procedures
- ☐ Increased risk management
- ☐ Greater use of computerization
- ☐ Reorganization of customs service

39. What is the major difficulty in applying customs regulations?
- ☐ Inconsistent interpretation of the rules
- ☐ Allowance for discretionary behavior
- ☐ Irregular enforcement

B. Questions about Ports and Airports

40. What is the average number of shipments processed daily? _____

41. Does customs operate seven days a week?
- ☐ Yes
- ☐ No

42. How many hours a day does it operate? _____

43. What percentage of the following documents is filed electronically?
   Master airway/ships bills _____
   Manifests _____
   Declarations _____
44. What percentage of import declarations is submitted before the cargo arrives? _____
45. What percentage of customs declarations is submitted electronically?
   Imports: _____
   Exports: _____
46. What percentage of shipments is cleared at an inland location? _____
47. What percentage of shipments is cleared in each lane?
   Green (declaration): _____
   Yellow (review of declaration and supporting documentation): _____
   Blue (scanning): _____
   Red (physical inspection): _____
48. What is the average time to clear a shipment (from lodgment to release of cargo) for the following lanes?
   Green: _____
   Yellow: _____
   Blue: _____
   Red: _____
49. What is the average time to clear exports of manufactured goods?
   _____
50. Is customs responsible for coordinating the activities associated with enforcing health requirements, product standards, and security issues?
   ☐ Yes
   ☐ No
51. What are principal sources of delay for clearance of exports?
   ☐ Inspection for contraband or misclassification
   ☐ Documentation for duty drawback and value added tax (VAT) refund
   ☐ Certification of origin, quality standards, health
52. How does the consignee determine the status of the cargo with regard to the various clearance procedures?
   ☐ Customs broker
   ☐ Responsible agency
   ☐ Short message service (SMS) sent automatically by customs
   ☐ Website of shipping line or port/airport or port community platform
   ☐ Computer-generated message sent automatically by customs to customs broker

53. Which of the following is a main source of discrepancies in declarations?
    - ☐ Misclassification
    - ☐ Undervaluation
    - ☐ Contraband or intellectual property violations
    - ☐ Goods for temporary admission
    - ☐ Prohibited goods
54. What are the main causes of delay in crossing the border?
    - ☐ Congestion at terminal or on access road
    - ☐ Late arrival/presentation of cargo documents
    - ☐ Availability of funds for paying duty and taxes
    - ☐ Availability of connecting transport
    - ☐ Physical inspection, security checks
    - ☐ Testing of samples
    - ☐ Customs office hours and staff efficiency
55. What infrastructure constraints delay customs processes?
    - ☐ Limited capacity
    - ☐ Poor layout or condition of facilities
    - ☐ Restrictions on use of infrastructure
    - ☐ Limited access to infrastructure
56. Which of the following is a major difficulty in applying customs regulations?
    - ☐ Inconsistent interpretation of the rules
    - ☐ Allowance for discretionary behavior
    - ☐ Irregular enforcement
57. What are current or planned improvements in procedure and infrastructure?
    - ☐ New facilities
    - ☐ Scanning equipment
    - ☐ Relocation of laboratories
    - ☐ Upgraded access roads
    - ☐ Simplified procedures
    - ☐ Increased risk management
    - ☐ Greater use of computerization
    - ☐ Reorganization of customs service
58. Rate the following:
    - ☐ Importers: ☐ Good ☐ Adequate ☐ Poor
    - ☐ Exporters: ☐ Good ☐ Adequate ☐ Poor
    - ☐ Clearing and forwarding agents: ☐ Good ☐ Adequate ☐ Poor
    - ☐ Port authority: ☐ Good ☐ Adequate ☐ Poor
    - ☐ Port terminal operator: ☐ Good ☐ Adequate ☐ Poor

☐ Airport authority: ☐ Good ☐ Adequate ☐ Poor
☐ Air cargo terminal operator: ☐ Good ☐ Adequate ☐ Poor

59. If poor, what are the reasons? _____

References

CDC (Corridor Development Consultants). 2011. *One Stop Border Post Source Book.* Windhoek, Namibia.

Curtis, B. 2008. "The Chirundu Border Post. Detailed Monitoring of Transit Time." SSATP Working Paper 10, World Bank, Sub-Saharan Africa Transport Policy Program, Washington, DC.

De Wulf, L. and J. B. Sokol, eds. 2005. *Customs Modernization Handbook.* Washington, DC: World Bank. http://siteresources.worldbank.org /INTEXPCOMNET/Resources/customs_Modernization_Handbook.pdf.

Djankov, S., C. Freund, and C. S. Pham. 2006. "Trading on Time." Policy Research Working Paper 3909, World Bank, Washington, DC.

McLinden, G., E. Fanta, D. Widdowson, and T. Doyle, eds. 2011. *Border Management Modernization.* Washington, DC: World Bank. http://www-wds.worldbank.org /external/default/WDSContentServer/WDSP/IB/2011/01/07/000356161_20110 107013015/Rendered/PDF/588450PUB0Bord101publi130BOX353816B.pdf.

UNECE (United Nations Economic Commission for Europe). 2010. "Case Study: Singapore." UNECE, Geneva. http://www.unece.org/fileadmin/DAM/cefact /single_window/sw_cases/Download/Singapore.pdf.

UNESCAP (United Nations Economic and Social Commission for Asia and the Pacific). 2007. "Study on National Coordination Mechanisms for Trade and Transport Facilitation in the UNESCAP Region." UNESCAP, Bangkok.

USAID (U.S. Agency for International Development). 2011. *Revenue Authorities Digital Data Exchange (RADDEx).* USAID, Washington, DC.

World Bank. 2011. *Streamlining NTMs: A Toolkit for Policymakers.* Washington, DC: World Bank.

———. 2013. "Mission Report on Assessment of Bangladesh Land-Customs Stations." South Asia Region, World Bank, Washington, DC.

Resources

COMESA (Common Market for Eastern and Southern Africa), EAC (East African Community), and SADC (Southern Africa Development Community). "The Mechanism for Reporting, Monitoring and Eliminating Non-Tariff Barriers." http://www.tradebarriers.org/about#. Accessed December 23, 2013. The mechanism for reporting, monitoring, and eliminating nontariff barriers provides timelines for the removal of nontariff barriers (NTBs). All three regional economic communities have established monitoring mechanisms to address NTBs.

IRU (International Road Transport Union). 2009. "Reduce Border Waiting Times." IRU Working Paper on Road Border Crossing Improvements, Geneva.

http://www.iru.org/index/cms-filesystem-action?file=mix-publications/Krauss-BWTO.pdf.

The document identifies the main issues and constraints faced at the European Union's external borders with nonmember states and proposes measures to tackle them. It is based on surveys carried out in 2008 of border queuing and waiting times. The surveys were complemented by information submitted by member associations of the IRU. Among the recommendations were those to implement procedural reforms to simplify the border clearance processes as well as some physical interventions to segregate and improve the flow of traffic through border posts.

UNECE (United Nations Economic Commission for Europe). 2013. "Single Window Repository." UNECE, Geneva. http://www.unece.org/cefact/single_window/welcome.html.

The Single Window Repository is an online compilation of countries' single-window experiences. Several cases are available on the United Nations Centre for Trade Facilitation and Electronic Business (UN/CEFACT) website, including case studies of Finland, Germany, Ghana, Guatemala, Hong Kong SAR, China, Japan, the Republic of Korea, the Republic of Macedonia, Malaysia, Mauritius, Senegal, Singapore, Sweden, and the United States. According to UN/CEFACT, 30 single windows are in operation worldwide; the repository intends to cover all of them. Following UN/CEFACT Recommendation 33, the repository has a standardized approach in which all national experiences in the repository provide information on the introduction of the single window, its establishment, services, operational model, business model, technology, promotion and communication, judicial aspects, standards, lessons learned, future plans, and contact information.

UNECE (United Nations Economic Commission for Europe). 2009. "Transport Review: Transport without Borders." Geneva. http://www.unece.org/fileadmin/DAM/trans/doc/reviews/UNECE-Transport-Review-2009-2.pdf.

This report is a compendium of experiences with border facilitation initiatives across the world. It contains several case studies, including studies of Africa, Central Asia, and Europe. It addresses various topics, such as the use of information technology, single window systems, border design, and development of master plans.

World Bank. 2011. *Streamlining NTMs: A Toolkit for Policymakers*. Washington, DC: World Bank. http://hdl.handle.net/10986/6019.

This toolkit provides practical tools for analyzing the cost implications of complying with nontarrif measures (NTMs). It contains questionnaires and guidelines to evaluate the underlying issues NTMs are trying to address and provides recommendations based on international best-practice examples.

WCO (World Customs Organization). (undated) "Guidelines on the Development and Use of a National Valuation Database as a Risk Assessment Tool." Brussels. http://www.wcoomd.org/en/topics/valuation/instruments-and-tools/guidelines.aspx.

The guidelines address various aspects of the development and use of a national valuation database as part of a risk management system. They can be used by a customs administration along with other risk tools to assess potential risk regarding the truth or accuracy of the declared customs value for imported goods.

WTO (World Trade Organization). 2013. "The Trade Policy Review Mechanism." Geneva. http://www.wto.org/english/tratop_e/tpr_e/tprm_e.htm.
The WTO's surveillance of trade policies under the Trade Policy Review Mechanism (TPRM) provides information on the policy-induced NTMs of each member country on exports, imports, and measures affecting trade. These reviews provide information only on goods, not on transport services. The reviews of NTMs are based on member country government notifications, not on reverse notifications (that is, the TPRMs do not provide information on the NTMs of the member country from the perspective of the importing country).

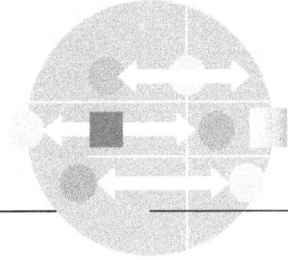

Customs Transit Regimes

In the context of a trade and transport corridor, *transit regime* is used to describe (a) the part of international transport during which a goods-carrying vehicle physically crosses the territory of a country en route to its destination, without loading or unloading goods or (b) a formal arrangement providing for streamlined and simplified procedures in the movement of goods along a corridor between two customs control points either within or between countries. Facilitation of transit is paramount to any country's trade. It is particularly important for landlocked countries, because all their trade must transit through their neighbors' territories.

Goods are moved along a corridor based on transport and transit rights granted to operators by corridor countries. In several regions, the transit regimes are deeply flawed, incomplete, or nonexistent, which can increase costs. Analysis of transport and transit rights is therefore important and should be conducted at very early stages of any corridor performance assessment. Few other elements have such importance for the circulation of goods.

Customs transit regimes include laws, institutions, mechanisms, and procedures that facilitate the movement of goods. They allow for the temporary suspension of duties, taxes, and commercial policy measures that are normally applicable to import goods, thereby allowing customs clearance formalities to take place at the destination rather than at the point of entry into the customs territory. Customs transit regimes are intended to facilitate the international movement of goods while protecting the revenues of the country through which goods are moving (the transit country) by preventing their illegal diversion for consumption in the domestic market.

When properly designed and implemented, customs transit regimes can be used for the movements of all goods crossing a border. Their contribution to the development of trade can be the greatest of all trade and transport facilitation measures. Reforms may be the most difficult to put in place however, especially where the economy is informal, or governance is poor. Strong and long-term commitment and years of preparation are necessary before positive effects can be realized.

An efficient customs transit regime is a keystone of corridor management and can serve an array of corridors in a region. Though the concept is relatively new, most of the core principles are centuries old. Reform should be based on established benchmarks; it should not tamper with core mechanisms or omit key features of an existing, well-functioning regime, as some misguided innovations have done.

The first section of this module is an overview of customs transit regimes. The second section identifies the main issues concerning the functioning and impact of transit regimes on corridor performance. The third section presents the data and information that are required to understand these issues. The fourth section identifies measures that can improve border-crossing performance. The last section summarizes these interventions.

Overview of Customs Transit Regimes

Transit usually refers to land (road and rail) transportation. In assessing transit arrangements, it is useful to distinguish between international and national transit. International transit procedures are used when national borders are crossed. National transit is used when goods are transferred within national borders, from the point of first entry into a country to another location in the same country where customs procedures are conducted (dry ports are an example) or between two customs regimes within a country (for example, to or from a free trade zone). Both types of transit can be combined, as they often are in landlocked countries, where imported goods arrive at national borders from other countries and are then shipped under national transit to the main economic centers.

Customs transit is not a clearance or series of clearances; it is a transport operation under customs control. It is not conceptually different from international shipping. In most cases the agent for a transit operation is the carrier or freight forwarder, not the owner of the goods. The agent provides the guarantee and lodges the transit declaration (manifest) with customs. This agent is normally (but not always) different from the party making the final declaration.

In successful customs transit regimes, efficiency results largely from the fact that goods travel internationally between their departure and destination points without any interference of customs at borders. In this kind of door-to-door transit system, only one procedure covers international and national transit for all the countries on a trade corridor.

There are essential conceptual and operational differences between transiting goods through the transit country and securing final clearance of the goods in the destination country. These differences are not always recognized, including by government decision makers. As a result, the design and implementation of transit systems in developing countries often depart from good practice.

A transit regime is, in essence, a public-private partnership by which customs grants access to simplified transit procedures to authorized operators who comply with a set of criteria, including professional, moral, and financial guarantees. For transit traffic, the due diligence expected from customs en route is limited to checking seals and verifying the guarantee instrument. As a general rule, no inspection of the goods is required. Other border agencies, such as those responsible for standards or quarantine, are not parties to transit operations.

The key requirements for a well-functioning transit system were developed over centuries. They include the following:

- *Secure load compartment*: Customs should make sure the cargo is secure and the load compartment (closed trailers or containers) cannot be tampered with once sealed.
- *Guarantee*: The principal of the transit operation (the owner of the goods or, more often, his agent [a freight forwarder or trucker]), should act as surety by depositing a guarantee (or a bond) covering the value of taxes and duties at risk in the transit country or countries. The amount of the guarantee may depend on the fiscal risk of the operation: some products (such as alcohol or electronic goods) are considered high risk. The guarantee may be flexible and reflect the transit operator's status (trustworthiness); in some modes (such as railways), it may even

be waived. Proof of the guarantee can take various forms; for example in the TIR[1] system, the proof of the guarantee is a carnet.

- *Controlled access to the regime*: Regulation of transit operators is needed from both a customs and a transport perspective; the transit operator must be trustworthy and qualified for the service it provides.
- *Mutual trust*: Customs controls performed at the departure office and certified by the seal should be recognized by all customs offices en route. The customs seal should remain intact until the cargo reaches the destination office, as long as there is no suspicion or evidence of fraud.
- *Monitoring mechanisms*: Customs should properly manage the information on goods in transit and reconcile information on entries into and exits out of the customs territory (or during clearance, in the case of national transit), in order to identify violations and potential leakages.

The typical transit procedure is implemented as follows:

- At the initiation of transit (departure), customs verifies the transit manifest and affixes the seals against a guarantee provided by the principal or agent.
- At the termination of transit (destination), customs checks the seals and manifest and discharges the guarantee after reconciling information on entries into and exits out of the customs territory (inbound and outbound manifest information).
- Between these two points (initiation and termination), customs should do nothing more than check that the seal is intact and the guarantee is valid.

Although it is not good practice for a well-functioning transit regime, it is still common practice to oblige carriers to travel in a convoy escorted by customs officers when the cargo transported is high risk or when not enough security is offered by the seals and the guarantee. It is common and acceptable practice to impose (reasonable) specified routes and impose a maximum delay for the transit.

Associated with the physical movement of goods are information flows (the manifest) and financial flows (the guarantee). A functional transit regime ensures that the physical, information, and financial flows are synchronous. If they are not, a delay in the information associated with manifests may postpone the discharge of bonds and increase costs.

Bonds and guarantees are basic financial products available from local banking and insurance industries. Under community transit within the European Union (EU) or common transit between the EU and the countries of the European Free Trade Association (EFTA) (Iceland, Liechtenstein, Norway, and Switzerland), regular transit operators have a comprehensive guarantee, equivalent to a standing line of credit, which, among other benefits, should make the guarantee available at the time the transit declaration is introduced. Pricing may vary, but fundamentally the cost of the guarantee is proportional to the value of goods and the time between initiation and discharge. Inefficient information exchange and delayed discharge can entail significant costs.

Transit Issues in Developing Countries

Successful implementation of a customs transit regime depends on the way customs balances its role as facilitator and revenue collector. The facilitation challenges can be understood by looking at the impact of deviations from core transit principles. Common deviations are identified below.

Poor Guarantee Management

Unlike final clearance, which happens in one place, transit requires the exchange of information between at least three places: the transit initiation, the transit termination, and the location of the guarantor (to validate and discharge the bonds). The management and tracing of the manifest is not always properly and rigorously implemented; in many cases it is not automated, causing major errors and delays (in the discharge of bonds, for example). The tracing and reconciliation of manifests can be imperfect even if there is no fraud. According to the International Road Transport Union (IRU), 95 percent of reported TIR-related customs claims arise from the loss of carnet pages in customs systems, not from fraudulent behavior (Arvis and others 2011).

Lengthy Initiation

Along virtually all developing country corridors, the time to initiate transit in a port is similar to the time to clear goods for local consumption in a coastal country. In some instances, it can take even longer: in 2008, for instance, it took four weeks to clear goods out of the Port of Dar es Salam, in Tanzania. In many cases, customs does not clearly separate clearance from transit procedures, applying the same process to both. Transit goods should not be subject to the same risk management and control as goods cleared for home consumption.

The transit manifest relates to the container or trailer, which may be hauled by various vehicles between origin and destination (there may be a change of tractor, or transport may be multimodal, such as by ship or rail and then road). The transit declaration should be a simplified document, which should be processed in an entirely distinct way from clearance at the border. The transit manifest and final declaration are separate documents serving separate purposes. For instance, a transit manifest might not carry information about the Harmonized System (HS) classification of the cargo. Customs does not need to value the goods for each vessel precisely—it needs only to be sure that a proper guarantee is issued by the transit operator for all its goods currently in transit. Document checking, classification, and valuation should not be sticking points for transit goods. In theory, transit can be initiated in a port using the information already available in the shipping manifest.

Clearance at the Port of Entry

Clearance at the port of entry in the gateway country has been attempted for some landlocked countries. Beyond the obvious issues of territorial jurisdiction, the main problem with this idea is that to prevent fraud or fiscal loss, the transit country still needs a system to make sure that goods will be released only for consumption in the destination country. At best, there can be preclearance, with the risk of adding a layer of procedures. Preclearance is feasible only in rare instances—where the transit corridor is very short, for example, or transit trade dominates domestic trade at the port of entry.

Lax Regulation

Lax regulations encourage the development of low-quality services—services that cannot cover the full transit supply chain and undermine the development of good, comprehensive services. Hence, particular importance should be given to regulations allowing transit operators (truckers and freight forwarders) and customs brokers to be part of the transit system. Better services may be encouraged by creating thresholds for the operators authorized to participate in transit operations, such as thresholds for company size (number of trucks, ownership); professional requirements; and deposits (for brokerage operations). Customs transit regimes are facilitation tools; access to them should not be seen as a right but as a privilege.

In most Commonwealth countries, liberal regulations make customs brokers de jure or de facto mandatory intermediaries for customs operations, resulting in an overly intermediated supply chain. For example, moving cargo from Durban, South Africa to clearance in Blantyre, Malawi required eight brokers (World Bank 2010). In addition, different domestic banks covered the transit in each of the four countries on the corridor (Malawi, Mozambique, South Africa, Zimbabwe).

Controls and Convoys

Customs authorities are often reluctant to allow simplified procedures for transit, out of fear of losing their control powers. During transit they may resort to the use of convoys, in which the vehicles in transit are escorted by police and customs officials.

Convoys need time to be formed (up to four days in some countries) and are slow. They impose additional delays—and costs—on the principal and do not eliminate all risk of fraud and corruption. Moreover—and against any logic—convoys do not exempt principals from the need for guarantees. Though convoys tend to be less prevalent than they once were, they still exist, notably in West and East Africa and Western Asia. Other means, such as control points and checkpoints (roadblocks), can be used to exert control en route.

Misuse of Information Technology Systems

Automation and information technology (IT) can significantly improve processes (including customs transit). But they are not always and everywhere welcome. In some cases, they are not fully exploited in order to protect jobs or opportunities for informal earnings. In other cases, automation cannot yield the desired benefits because the level of IT development is not the same along the corridor or the equipment or systems are not interconnected or interoperable.

Transit goods can be traced through the automation of carnets or transit manifests. Tracking, in contrast, involves localizing the merchandise. The prices of Global Positioning System (GPS) tracking devices are falling, and they are ever more popular with large trucking firms that want to know where their vehicles are at all times, so they can alert consignees about delivery time. Drivers who have breakdowns also want their companies to know where to find them. GPS devices have become important management tools for logistics operators.

Suppliers often recommend electronic devices to customs authorities and products such as electronic seals (e-seals) with GPS tracking have appeal. However, real-time tracking is not a precondition for a transit system to work.

There are serious disadvantages of real-time tracking, including the reinforcement of the control mentality (with the potential for abuse) instead of a partnership approach with incentives for compliant operators offering guarantees. In addition, there is no established best practice or clear guidance for how customs can use tracking information; no developed country has yet implemented such a system. Tracking is not a facilitation objective but an IT solution for intrusive controls; it should not necessarily be considered a component of a corridor facilitation project. Recent experience suggests that the eventual contribution of e-seals and tracking may be less for improving procedures than for helping rebuild confidence between customs and transit operators when used in an environment of lack of trust and potential corruption.

Data and Information Sources

Data for assessing the operation of a transit regime and possible improvement interventions are collected from customs officials, clearing and forwarding agents, banks, and major shippers. Both qualitative and quantitative data are needed, collected largely through interviews. From a corridor perspective, the main indicators of performance of a transit regime include

- time and cost to initiate transit, form any convoys, acquit transit declarations, release transit bonds, and so forth
- type of declaration used and whether a single administrative document is used
- number of times transit is reinitiated and terminated within the corridor
- extent of transit fraud, proportion of goods lost or damaged in shipment
- number of documents required to initiate transit
- differences in transit requirements by road and rail
- types of controls for transit operations (use of convoy under customs escorts, electronic seals, time limits for transiting the country, use of technology such as GPS for tracking, bonds/guarantees, TIR, or a similar carnet).

Improving Customs Transit Regimes

Various global and regional initiatives have sought to improve transit regimes, mainly because of the virtuous circle formed by regional transit regimes and other regional agreements on trade or transport: the success of one depends on the proper implementation of the others. There is a very strong case for improvements of customs transit regimes, which are important components of full corridor logistics. A well-functioning transit regime allows for the smooth transit of goods along the corridor, with fast initiation of transit, limited interventions at the borders, no intrusive control en route, and an integrated guarantee and documentation tracing system between the countries on the corridor. A sensible transit regime is based on regulation of entry (access to the system) and incentives for compliance (for example, waivers of guarantees).

Establishing a transit regime can be part of a package of service reforms, notably of trucking and brokerage services. For efficient corridor operations, policy makers need to adopt a comprehensive approach to transit-related policies beyond the customs transit regime: associated transport policies, infrastructure policies, and corridor cooperation policies, reviewed in other modules in this Toolkit.

Transit regimes are based on three universal principles: bonds, transit declaration/manifests, and trustworthy operators. Inefficiency can be traced to the failure to respect one or more of these principles.

Linking transit regimes across borders into door-to-door carnet systems—such as TIR or common transit in Europe—has obvious advantages. Although regional agreement posits the existence of carnet systems, no working examples exist other than the two schemes in Europe and Central America described below.

A transit regime does not need heavy IT infrastructure or infrastructure that is distinct from that of customs IT. Transit requires the tracing of manifests and carnets, for which real-time technologies—such as e-seals using GPS—are neither essential nor always desirable.

Two main strategies can be used to improve transit performance. If they do not lead to significant improvements, a reengineering should be considered. Both strategies are described below.

Introducing International Customs Transit Regimes

Over the years, general transit provisions have been codified by a number of international conventions. The most important are the articles on transit in the General Agreement on Tariffs and Trade (1994), the World Customs Organization's revised International Convention on the Simplification and Harmonization of Customs Procedures (1999), and the International Convention on the Harmonization of Frontier Controls of Goods (1982).

The TIR international customs transit regime—initially known as *transports internationaux routiers* (international road transports) and now referred to in documentation and legal texts simply as TIR—is the only global customs transit system. It was established by the Customs Convention on the International Transport of Goods under Cover of TIR Carnets (TIR Convention) under the United Nations Economic Commission for Europe (UNECE). The TIR Convention currently has 68 parties, primarily in Europe and Central Asia, the Middle East, and North Africa. It is the main instrument for trade from Europe to distant trading partners in Eastern Europe, Central Asia, North Africa, and the Middle East. It has not yet been widely implemented in the Americas or East Asia, where TIR membership is spotty. Widely seen as the best practice for international transit regimes, the TIR system allows for significant cost and time savings and is a model for other regional transit frameworks.

The main features of TIR are explained in UNECE's *TIR Handbook* (2010). Its five main pillars of TIR include

1. secure load compartments, with standards defined in the convention
2. international guarantees valid throughout transit: wherever the transport operator cannot (or does not wish to) pay the customs duties and taxes due, the international guarantee system ensures that the amounts (up to a determined amount) rightly claimed are paid to customs
3. control by national associations of transport operators of members' access to the TIR regime, issuance of guarantee documents, and management of the guarantee system at the national level in partnership with customs
4. TIR carnets, proof of valid guarantee, accepted and recognized by all the countries implementing the TIR system
5. international and mutual recognition of customs controls performed by customs at departure.

The sequence of a typical TIR operation is shown in figure 6.1.

The players in the TIR system include the following:

- the government of the contracting party (usually the customs authorities)
- the UN TIR bodies (the TIR administrative committee, the intergovernmental working party on customs questions affecting transport, the TIR Executive Board, and the UNECE TIR Secretariat)
- an international organization (currently the International Road Transport Union [IRU])
- the national issuing and guaranteeing association
- the authorized transport operator (the TIR carnet holder).

The roles and responsibilities of TIR players are described in detail in the TIR Convention, which is binding on all of them. Customs is responsible for

- applying the TIR Convention at the national level, designating TIR customs offices, and training customs officials,

FIGURE 6.1 Sequence of TIR Operation

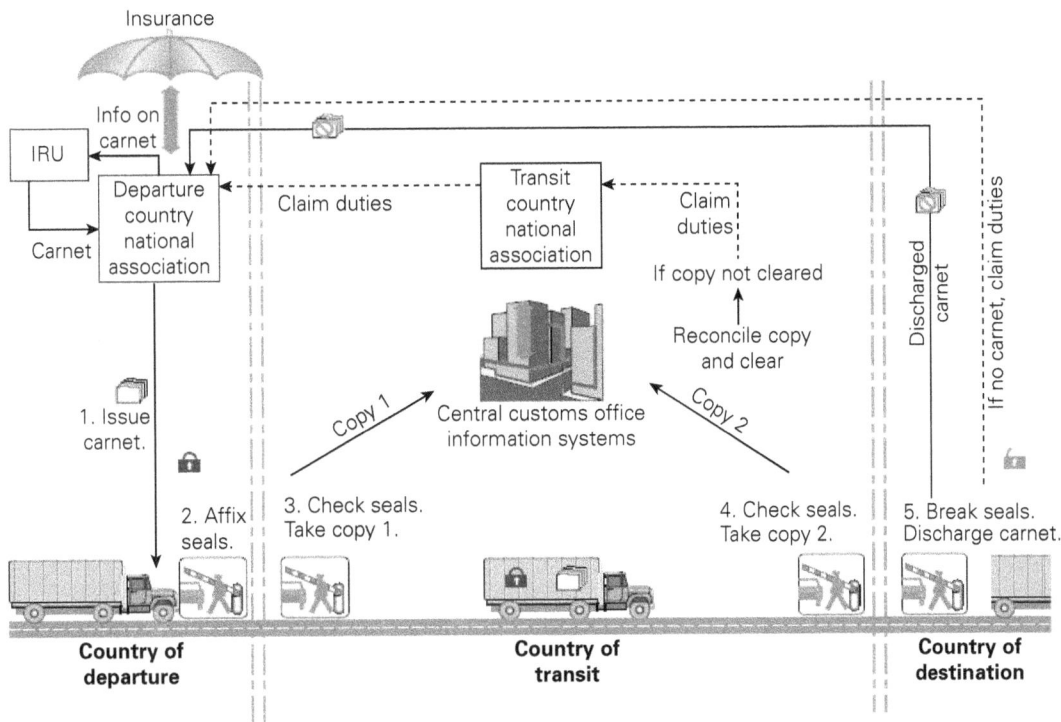

Source: Arvis and others 2011.

Note: info = information; IRU = International Road Transport Union.

- controlling access to the TIR system; authorizing the national association and establishing a "guarantee" agreement between customs and the national association; authorizing transport operators to become TIR carnet holders
- issuing the certificate of approval for vehicles by establishing or designating a national authority for the inspection and approval of road vehicles and containers.

The UN TIR bodies (with the exception of the Secretariat) are composed of representatives of governments. The main responsibilities of these bodies are related to administering and implementing the TIR Convention, including mandating an international organization to organize the functioning of the TIR chain of guarantee and the centralized printing of TIR carnets.

An international organization (currently the IRU) is the main international private stakeholder in the TIR system. Its main responsibilities include the centralized printing and distribution of TIR carnets and the effective organization and functioning of an international guarantee system. To fulfill these duties, the IRU establishes agreements (Deeds of Engagement) with the national associations on the functioning of the international "guarantee" system and monitors and audits the national associations in order to make sure they comply with the rules and regulations of the TIR Convention.

The national association is the main private TIR stakeholder at the national level. It is responsible for

- concluding with customs the guarantee agreement, which allows the association to act as guarantor for TIR carnet holders
- concluding with the IRU agreements on the functioning of the guarantee system (Deeds of Engagement)
- concluding agreements with TIR carnet holders (Declarations of Engagement)
- guaranteeing TIR operations on their national territory for both national and foreign holders
- cooperating with customs in the management of TIR activities.

Transport operators (TIR carnet holders) are the first beneficiaries of the facilitation measures resulting from the implementation of TIR customs transit. Their main responsibilities in the chain include the following:

- concluding an agreement (Declaration of Engagement) with the national association
- obtaining authorization by customs authorities
- obtaining certificates of approval for road vehicles and keeping them up to date
- filling in the TIR carnet in line with the commercial documents and ensuring accuracy of data
- applying risk management measures in the operation of TIR transports.

In essence, TIR operations can be carried out in participating countries by an authorized truck operator (the TIR carnet holder), with the network of national associations acting as guarantor. Both the national associations and the IRU, which prints and distributes the carnets, are private. In countries using the TIR system, the national guaranteeing association is recognized by the country's customs authorities.

In most cases, the association, representing transporters, guarantees payment within the country of up to €50,000 (in selected countries, up to €60,000) in duties and taxes that may become due because of any irregularity in the course of the TIR transport operation. Because the national guaranteeing association is not a financial organization, its obligations are usually backed by insurance policies provided by the market. The IRU arranges for a large international financial institution (an insurance holding) to back up the surety provided by the guarantee chain to customs.

The TIR carnet is a physical document with a set number of pages and one copy for each page, including vouchers (*volets*) and counterfoils (*souches*). A different page serves for each border operation (exit or entry). At each border, the original voucher is detached and kept by customs. A copy is left in the carnet.

Regional Integration of Transit Systems

There are obvious advantages to integrating transit across borders in a region or along a trade corridor, eventually linking countries or even regions. There is no doubt that a unified international regime is superior to a chain of national procedures. However, the only fully developed regional systems are TIR and the European Community and Common Transit Systems implemented in the EU and EFTA. Each represents a logical solution to the bond and manifest problem at a different degree of regional integration.

The many attempts to copy the TIR and the Common Transit System in developing regions have not succeeded (Arvis and others 2011). International transit calls for the harmonization of country-specific procedures and documentation, and it requires an internationally accepted guarantee system. A major development in transit systems is the proof of valid guarantee (for example, the carnet), which allows for a single transit procedure throughout several territories. Operators gain greatly from the elimination of duplicated or repeated procedures (documentation, seals, guarantees) at borders and reductions in complexity and in administrative costs.

Authorities in each customs territory along a trade corridor are ultimately responsible for transit in that territory, and they can set their own rules. However, large gains are possible from cross-border cooperation and the creation of a framework to integrate transit across territories into a single seamless procedure. A key element of the framework is a single document (for example, the TIR carnet) that accompanies the shipment along the transit chain and allows officials to verify the shipment's compliance with the transit regime.

A regional transit/single-procedure regime should include the following ingredients to ensure cross-border compatibility and an effective chaining of transit procedures in each country:

- harmonized documentation
- common standards for transit operators

- common enforcement standards
- a regionally integrated system to ensure interoperability in bonds across countries and consistency in manifest reconciliation (to discharge or call guarantees consistently, customs in country B should be able to call a bond issued by a guarantor in country A)
- interconnected data exchange systems.

Both the European Community and the Common Transit Systems streamlined the main features of the TIR in the 1980s, taking advantage of greater economic and financial integration within EU and EFTA countries. For a group of countries, the Common Transit System is now conceptually very similar to the national transit system (box 6.1).

The TIR was designed to help connect national transit systems without the preconditions of harmonization and integration. In contrast, the European Community and Common Transit Systems require a very high degree of customs and financial integration—and trust—within the region in which they are implemented. The most binding requirement is that a bank in one country must be willing to routinely issue bonds that another country's customs can confidently call. Meeting this requirement demands a high degree of integration, but it may be possible within small or very homogeneous groups of developing countries. Transit regimes must be preceded by harmonized transport policies, standards for access of transport operators to the system, and other aspects, such as insurance and banking.

Improving Transit Management

Regional transit systems have not been successful outside Europe and its immediate neighbors (Central Asia and North Africa). The value of integrating the transit systems and regime over a trade and transport corridor, or even a subregion covering several corridors, has long been recognized, as has the fact that TIR and the European Community and Common Transit Systems are the natural references for transit at the regional level. However, no other regions have succeeded in moving beyond harmonization, with the possible exception of the Tránsito Aduanero Internacional de Mercancías (TIM) in Central America, which has implemented, to a very large extent, the principles of Common Transit System.

Transit facilitation relies on four categories of components linked to broader reforms and capacity enhancement in border management:

1. building national capacities by
   - elaborating and implementing good legislation that enables customs to function like a real national transit system, with the provision for

BOX 6.1

The European Community and Common Transit Systems

The Common Transit System is the procedure used for the movement of goods between the 28 EU member states and the EFTA countries. The European Community Transit System is a procedure used for customs transit operations by the EU member states (and Andorra and San Marino). It is in general applicable to the movement of non-Community goods for which customs duties and other charges at import are at stake. The two systems function according to the same rules. Imports are subject to duties in the destination country, in accordance with the EU's common external tariff, and to value added tax (VAT), in accordance with national tax rates.

Guarantees can be of three kinds: a cash deposit, guarantee by a guarantor (who vouches for the trader), or a guarantee voucher (a multiple of the standard €7,000), valid for up to one year. For a regular procedure, the guarantee must apply specifically to an individual trip. Authorized (trustworthy) transporters (and other principals) may present comprehensive guarantees valid for multiple trips and longer periods, but these guarantees cover only the total duty expected to be at risk in an average week (the so-called reference amount).

In general, the calculation of a transit guarantee is based on the highest rates of duties and other charges applicable to the goods. It depends on the customs classification of the goods. The amount covered by the comprehensive guarantee is 100 percent of the reference amount. If the principal complies with a certain criterion of reliability, the amount of the guarantee to be specified to the guarantors may be reduced by customs to 50 percent or 30 percent of the reference amount. For high-risk goods, customs can be allowed to calculate the guarantee at a percentage related to the risk of nonclearance.

The European Community and Common Transit Systems represent very streamlined evolutions of the regional carnet-based system. The systems are now fully computerized, do not require the soft infrastructure of TIR (the IRU and national associations), and allow for competition in providing guarantees. In essence, the systems function like a national transit system but apply to an economically integrated region. The New Computerized Transit System has made the European transit systems even friendlier.

a transit manifest different in form and substance from the customs clearance declaration
- creating a service specialized in transit
- training customs officers in border posts accredited for transit

2. improving the information system, by implementing a rigorous paper- or IT–based documentation cycle that reconciles entry and exit documents
3. regulating access to the system for operators involved in transit
4. establishing international cooperation, through the harmonization of documentation, the mutual recognition of controls and guarantees, and the exchange of information.

Some specific actions can be taken, including

- *Creating incentives for compliant operators*: Transit regimes should provide incentives for compliant transit operators offering the best services with minimal fiscal risk. The European Community and Common Transit Systems rely largely on the concept of Authorized Economic Operators (AEOs) with specific incentives—such as reductions or even waivers of the comprehensive guarantee—for their operations.[2] On most corridors in developing countries, the same principle of incentives (lower guarantees, fast track) could be applied, provided transit regimes are preceded by measures that reform and reinforce the trucking and logistics sectors to promote quality services to traders by professional and trustworthy operators.
- *Improving the documentation flow*: To control the start and completion of a transit procedure, a system for monitoring the movement of goods is needed. This system could be based on paper documentation shipped from the customs post upon exit from the transit country (after validation of the valid transit transaction) and issued by the customs post that controls the origin of the transit shipment. Increasingly, however, such documents are sent electronically. When copies of the documents match, the transit operation is completed and the guarantee released. When they do not match, the transit procedure is not completed satisfactorily, and import duties, taxes, and other charges are increased by a stipulated fine.
- *Using information technology (IT)*: Customs agencies need to properly manage the information on transit manifests or carnets, in order to trace the goods entering and exiting the country, with adequate management of transit manifests or carnets; discharge the bonds; and communicate with other participants or an overseeing body (such as the IRU) in the case of a carnet system.

IT can be of great practical help. Within customs in the transit country, the system electronically tells the exit post to expect the arrival of a shipment operation within a plausible timeframe. When completing the operation, the transit information is input and the guarantee automatically released.

Automation of customs documentation is widespread. Several applications have modules for national transit, including the United Nations Conference on Trade and Development's (UNCTAD) Automated System for Customs Data (ASYCUDA)++ and ASYCUDA World. However, widespread interconnection of national customs has not yet been achieved. It remains highly desirable and indispensable for a truly regionally integrated system, such as the New Computerized Transit System in Europe, which allows for a seamless exchange of information on a transit manifest or the initiation and termination of a bond. This system is currently the only fully computerized functional application for regional transit.

- *Requiring guarantees*: The guarantees acceptable by customs are defined by the regulations of the transit country. Within the open options of financial securities, the choice of which type of guarantee is the exclusive responsibility of the principal. A guarantee can be provided as a bond by a bank or as a form of insurance by a guarantor, which can be reinsured internationally by well-known and reliable insurance companies (as is the case with TIR). Nonguarantee forms of security, such as deposits or reference to title to a vehicle, which is in place in some countries, cannot be recommended. At times, the principal is also the guarantor—a common practice for rail transport, which grants customs access to more direct recourse mechanisms.
- *Establishing border infrastructure*: Transit per se does not require heavy border infrastructure. As the process at the border should be limited to fairly simple diligence (checking the manifest and the seals, without inspecting the goods), there is no need for heavy infrastructure. Border posts should accommodate fast lanes for vehicles under a transit regime so that they do not have to stop at the border and can be distinguished from trucks needing to be cleared at the border.

Reengineering Transit Regimes

In most regions out of the areas where TIR and the European Community and Common Transit Systems are operational, the design of transit is likely to depart radically from these transit benchmarks (Arvis and others 2011). The existence of a number of design or implementation flaws may make gradual improvement of existing concepts and procedures an ineffective option. In most cases, radical redesign or reengineering should be considered, typically within existing regional agreements but with a different implementation focus.

Two transit regimes have been reengineered. One is TIM, which was implemented with the support of the Inter-American Development Bank (IDB) and the other is the attempt by the Economic and Monetary Community of Central Africa (CEMAC, covering Cameroon, the Central African Republic, and Chad) with support from the World Bank, to improve transit on the Douala corridor along the same principles. A number of steps have been taken under both, but new regimes are not yet fully operational.

The two experiences and the knowledge of current arrangements in most subregions suggest that a reengineering of the transit regime is likely to be a complex and long project, as a result of the following factors:

- Stakeholders who benefit from the fragmentation of the supply chains (for example, border-related activities) may resist change.
- Countries may not be enthusiastic about working together or entering into the kind of data-sharing agreement essential for the functioning of any transit regime.
- Cooperation is needed among stakeholders in several countries who may not have an existing structured dialogue on which the project can build.
- Parallel capacity building of customs systems may be necessary.
- Prior substantial transport industry reforms may be needed to improve the market structure and quality of service needed to regulate operators' access to the profession and market based on quality and compliance.
- The very concept of a regional transit regime may push some parties to reconsider short-sighted options (such as GPS tracking) to organize rather than truly simplify transit within corridors.
- The project could be sidetracked into negotiation of new cross-border agreements, with a focus on the legal framework, and the approval process could be complex.

Summary of Possible Interventions for Improving Transit Regimes

Table 6.1 summarizes the most common transit issues and questions found in corridor projects and proposes possible interventions to address them. Actual interventions should be adapted to deal with specific constraints.

TABLE 6.1 Possible Interventions for Improving Transit Regimes

Issue	Questions	Possible interventions
Transport and transit rights	• Are some countries limiting access to the corridor (through permits or quotas)? • If so, why are they doing so?	• Harmonize differences. • Review and revise existing bilateral or multilateral agreements.
Management and arrangements for transit	• How integrated are the transit regimes in the corridor? • How many times is transit reinitiated and terminated in the corridor? • Who is likely to lose or gain from integration of the transit regime? • What are the requirements for initiating transit, and how different are they from the procedural requirements in terms of information and risk management for local clearance?	• Introduce a chain transit regime across corridor countries, based on international best practice. • Introduce a common customs code to replace any existing nominal transit regime. (The current degree of regional financial, trucking, and customs integration will essentially determine the implementation options.) • Involve all stakeholders in the reform process.
Compatibility with the regional regime	• How compatible are current transit-related projects with a potential regional transit regime?	• Harmonize current projects and plans with regional integration of transit regimes.
Financial integration	• To what extent are bonds interoperable across countries? • Is interoperability possible in other areas, such as cross-border insurances?	• Introduce reforms in other areas, especially finance, to integrate transit regimes between countries.
Management of bonds	• How are bonds submitted by the principal of the transit operation? • How is the value of bonds assessed (vouchers, comprehensive guarantees, or valuation on a case-by-case basis)? • What institutions (public, private) are involved in issuing and discharging transit bonds? • How are transit operations tracked and discharged? • How are transit documents reconciled, within countries and along the corridor? • Is a convoy system used? What physical, document, and other checks are employed? • What are the costs of the convoy system? • Is GPS tracking used?	• Increase the use of IT to manage bonds. • Integrate transit-related IT systems across borders to allow data sharing and reduce need, cost, and time to initiate numerous bonds. • Minimize and subsequently abolish intrusive practices in transit operations such as convoys, checkpoints, inspections en route, and GPS tracking.
Initiation of transit	• How long does it take to initiate transit? • Are the requirements separate and distinct from those for local clearance?	• Distinguish requirements for local clearance from requirements for transit, including risk management. • Introduce data sharing across agencies.

(table continues on next page)

TABLE 6.1 *continued*

Issue	Questions	Possible interventions
Fraud	• What is the extent of fraud in transit?	• Obtain hard evidence of fraud and its magnitude. • Identify reasons and patterns for fraud (commodities, routes, types of operators).
Border posts	• Does the layout of border posts and the interventions of customs and other border agencies accommodate separate lanes for fast transit, with minimal delays imposed by other traffic?	• Improve border traffic flows to facilitate speedy transit operations. • Create special lanes for vehicles carrying goods under a transit regime.
Regulation of entry into transit operations	• Who can be a transit principal? • Can trucking operators be the principal of transit operations across the region? • What types of trucks, cargo, and seals are allowed? • Are there incentives for compliant operators?	• Strengthen regulation for access to the system (transit-authorized operators). • Build national capacity in corridor countries in customs code for transit, operators, and so forth.

Note: GPS = Global Positioning System; IT = information technology.

Notes

1. TIR stands for *transports internationaux routiers* and is the acronym for a customs transit system that was established by the Customs Convention on the International Transport of Goods under Cover of TIR Carnets (TIR Convention).
2. An Authorized Economic Operator (AEO) is an accredited transit operator with a sound and verifiable record of compliance with regulatory requirements over a period of time. Accreditation can be extended by customs to importers, exporters, transporters, and brokers with the most declarations, the highest customs value, and greatest revenue contribution; the degree of compliance is a way of identifying actors that could operate bonded facilities. The World Customs Organization provides a list of AEO guidelines that can be used to guide this process.

References

Arvis, J.-F., R. Carruthers, G. Smith, and C. Willoughby. 2011. *Connecting Landlocked Countries to Markets: Trade Corridors in the 21st Century*. Washington, DC: World Bank.

UNECE (United Nations Economic Commission for Europe). 1982. International Convention on the Harmonization of Frontier Controls of Goods. Document ECE/TRANS/55/Rev.1, Inland Transport Committee, Geneva.

———. 2002. *TIR Handbook: Customs Convention on the International Transport of Goods under Cover of TIR Carnets (TIR Convention, 1975)*. Document ECE

/TRANS/TIR/6. Geneva: UNECE. http://www.unece.org/tir/handbook/english
/newtirhand/10.pdf.

———. 2010. *TIR Handbook*. Geneva: UNECE. http://www.unece.org/tir/tir-hb
.html.

WCO (World Customs Organization). 1999. International Convention on the
Simplification and Harmonization of Customs Procedures (as Amended).
Brussels.

World Bank. 2010. "Malawi Country Economic Memorandum: Seizing
Opportunities for Growth through Regional Integration and Trade." Report
47969-MW, Washington DC.

WTO (World Trade Organization). 1994. General Agreement on Tariffs and Trade
1994. Geneva. http://www.wto.org/english/docs_e/legal_e/06-gatt.pdf.

Resources

IDB (Inter-American Development Bank). *Tránsito Aduanero Internacional de
Mercancía (TIM)*. http://www.iadb.org/en/indes/transito-internacional-de
-mercancias-tim,8124.html.

This website provides information on a training course run by the IDB on the
TIM system. The training is intended to increase knowledge of customs and
quarantine administrations on the use of automated tools for TIM to monitor
and improve the control of transit operations, maintain appropriate indicators
of performance of the system for risk analysis purposes, and identify ways to
improve the system.

IRU (International Road Transport Union). *TIR System*. http://www.iru.org
/en_iru_about_tir.

This website describes the foundations of the TIR system, its geographic
coverage, and the way it works. It provides information on the carnet system
and guidance on completing a TIR carnet. Information is provided in Arabic,
English, French, and Russian.

UNECE (United Nations Economic Commission for Europe). *TIR Home*. http://
www.unece.org/trans/bcf/tir/.

This website provides information on the TIR system, including a description
of the system and its administration, statistics on usage of the system, training
materials, and other documents. It is a ready reference source for contemporary
discussions of the evolution of the system.

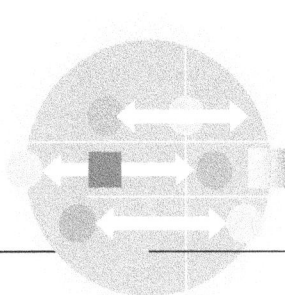

Road Freight Transport

In most regions, road transport (trucking) is the dominant transport mode for moving freight along corridors.[1] In fact, more than 80 percent of overland trade traffic is by road, and nearly all trade freight is carried by road at some point. Efficient delivery of road transport services is hence essential for the unimpeded movement of freight and people along corridors.

Trade performance depends on efficient road services everywhere in the world. It is particularly important for developing countries, especially landlocked ones, because roads provide the main connectivity links to the sea. For many of these countries, road transport is often the only available mode for moving freight. Even in landlocked countries that have rail or waterway connections, the volumes of freight using rail or waterways is rarely sufficient to make them financially sustainable.

Road infrastructure is one of the most important factors that can affect the performance of trade and transport corridors. It often is a top priority among investments of developing countries, partly based on the assumption that investments in road infrastructure alone will significantly reduce transport prices.

However, with a few exceptions, inadequate road infrastructure is no longer the main binding constraint to cross-border trade at any corridor level. Although investments have improved roads, facilitating road transport and reducing the transport costs for trucks, end-users of transport services have not benefited much from these improvements in some regions.

Transport cost and prices (rates) are two other important factors influencing the choice of a route or a mode. Transport costs can be perceived as the fixed and variable input costs of providing road transport services. Transport prices are a function of transport costs and any margins added by operators. The margins are in turn a function of market structure and political economy factors in the market. It is not unusual for transport prices to be different on domestic and international corridors, reflecting the dynamic interaction of these various factors.

Transport and transit rights granted by countries along a corridor to other countries' transport operators are also paramount for the success of the corridor, as they translate into mutual market access rights.

Market access for road transport operators can be regulated at both the national and international levels, based on criteria that are qualitative, quantitative, or a combination of the two. For example, the qualitative criteria of the European Union (EU) stipulate that all EU truckers can carry goods in the European Union as long as they meet the requirements for access to the profession of road transport operator. Currently, operators must fulfill four criteria to access the profession:

- Have a good reputation.
- Have capital assets every annual accounting year of at least €9,000 for the first vehicle and €5,000 for each additional vehicle.
- Have professional competence, as measured by an obligatory exam with common arrangements, grading, and certificates.
- Have an effective and stable establishment in a member state.

The best known example of explicit quantitative criteria for access to the national market comes from Greece, where historically, the privilege to carry goods belonged to the state, which passed it on to truckers by selling a limited number of licenses every year. In 1970, the government decided that the 33,000 licenses on the market were sufficient and stopped issuing additional licenses. For 40 years, commercial road transport became a closed profession until 2010.

The combination of qualitative and quantitative criteria is very common in international agreements (both bilateral and multilateral), where parties grant each other traffic rights through a specific number of permits issued to truckers who comply with defined qualitative criteria.

This module identifies operational practices and policies that affect road transport efficiency and measures to reduce road transport costs. It is structured as follows. The first section identifies the main issues faced concerning the functioning and impact of road transport on corridor performance. The second section presents the data and information that is required to understand these issues. This section is complemented by an annex that lists the key data and questions that can be asked of stakeholders to obtain both quantitative and qualitative data on road transport. The third section identifies possible solutions to the most common issues. The last section summarizes these interventions.

Important Considerations along Corridors

Several recent studies on road transport shed light on the structure and operating practices of the industry in different regions and countries. One influential study, *Transport Prices and Costs in Africa: A Review of the Main International Corridors* (Teravaninthorn and Raballand 2009), argues for the collection of country-level data in order to better target interventions to decrease transport costs for end-users and for a sharp focus on market liberalization beyond the predominant focus on infrastructure.

Raballand and Macchi (2009) conducted trucking surveys in 13 African countries. They found that transport costs are not much higher there than elsewhere but that prices are. The higher prices are a result of market access factors and operating practices, as elaborated on by Londoño-Kent (2009). The causes of high transport prices on a corridor can include the following:

- the structure of the trucking industries in developing countries
- the ways the transport services are regulated and operate
- the poor quality of infrastructure and the high level of variable costs, especially the costs of maintenance, tires, and fuel
- delays at border-crossing points, especially caused by procedures
- delays at gateways (such as congested access to ports).

Structure of the Trucking Industry

Road freight industries in many developing countries are highly fragmented, partly because of lack of or poor enforcement of regulations. In such environments, many small operators are allowed to provide road transport services without much, if any, quality or compliance control, often leading to an oversupply of road transport services in relation to demand.

The structure of trucking industries in developing countries can be divided into at least two categories.[2] The first category consists of a plethora of small operators, either individually or family-owned enterprises with one or a few vehicles. These transport operators usually provide low-cost basic trucking services that meet a substantial share of demand.

The second category consists of small, medium-size, and, to a limited extent, large enterprises, which typically combine trucking with integrated logistics (freight forwarding, storage, and distribution) services. Large trucking operators have a clear advantage over smaller operators in terms of the quality of service they can offer. They can provide reliable, high-quality operations, and they have the physical and managerial capacity to enter into long-term contracts with traders. Moreover, they are better able to secure cargo for the return trip, which reduces the number of empty backhauls and thus enhances the trucking companies' profitability and competitiveness. However, despite their operating efficiency, they tend to have higher unit costs than small operators and hence cater to a different market, namely, medium-size and large traders who need reliable transport and logistics suppliers.

In markets where there are many small operators and not enough demand for road transport services, operators may engage in collusive behavior to share the limited loads. They form oligopolies or cartels or put in place queuing systems (*tour de rôle*) to make sure each operator gets a load. When there is an excess of trucks, trucks can queue for very long periods for their next load. The cost and time to the trader/shipper is increased when queuing rules mandate giving preference to trucks registered in the city, province, or country where the queue is formed. A common outcome of this arrangement is that trucks return empty to their origin location rather than endure the long waiting time for a return load. Queuing systems are inherently inefficient.

Box 7.1 shows an estimate of the cost of cartels in the trucking sector in Nepal. Having to wait in line is the most obvious cost, although a greater ill is the barrier that prevents the freight owner and the trucker from negotiating directly. Despite the recognized negative impact on transport efficiency, queuing systems remain widely prevalent; they have been abolished in only a few cases.

Weaknesses in regulation are still common in several regions. Research suggests that transport prices vary widely across corridors in different regions of the world, as well as within the same region. Transport prices along corridors in Africa are on average higher than in South Asia or Brazil. For instance, transport prices on the Douala–N'Djamena route (linking Cameroon and Chad) were $0.11 per tonne-kilometer—three times higher than in Brazil ($0.035) and more than five times higher than in Pakistan ($0.02). Delivery time—the time from cargo arrival at the port to delivery to the inland destination—is also an indicator of the quality of road service.

BOX 7.1

Cost of Monopoly in Trucking: Evidence from Nepal

The trucking markets in Nepal are controlled regionally by transport entrepreneurs associations (TEAs). There are 24 such associations across the country. The TEAs' stated aims are to equally distribute benefits among members and to self-regulate the industry. The role of the associations is most visible during the times of the year when demand is low and there is an oversupply of trucks. The TEAs intervene to share the available loads across their members, thereby diminishing market competition and keeping prices high. Some associations operate their own weighbridges to prevent vehicle overloading precisely for this reason.

A 2011 study by the U.S. Agency for International Development (USAID) estimates the costs to Nepal's economy of the practices of the TEAs. According to it, the deadweight losses from the TEAs' practices of queuing, other systems of rotation, and use of odd-even loading systems for trucks could be as high as $65 million a year. The findings are consistent with evidence from elsewhere. In Central Africa, for example, similar practices were found to reduce vehicle utilization and raise prices (Teravaninthorn and Raballand 2009).

The review by USAID provides evidence that the authorities lack the capacity to regulate the trucking industry. Actions are therefore needed to

- implement existing rules and regulations in order to organize the sector (issues can be addressed through the existing framework if properly implemented)
- review existing acts and policies, and propose necessary changes
- create a social security mechanism for the players in the industry by working with insurance companies to provide some sort of collective insurance policy in addition to the legal requirement that extends only to a minimal amount of accidental insurance, in order to diminish the dependence of truck operators on TEAs
- create awareness among new and existing stakeholders about market conditions, in order to reduce the oversupply of trucks.

The authorities are modernizing the legal framework for trucking while pursuing reform within the context of a regional corridor project, with a focus on the main trade corridor between Nepal and India. USAID and the World Bank are supporting these efforts. The truck cartels in Nepal are very strong, however. A comprehensive trucking industry reform package must also be sensitive to the political economy aspects.

The ADB (2008) found that the shortest delivery times were in Central and West Africa; delivery times in Southern Africa were comparable to those in other regions of the world.

Cross-Border Issues

In regions that are not integrated, notably in developing countries, three main systems are used to regulate whether trucks can cross international borders. The reasons for using each system are different and depend on the various national authorities represented at borders, including ministries of transport, customs, and others.

In the first system, vehicles are not allowed to cross from one country to the other. All loads must be transferred from a vehicle registered in one county to a vehicle registered in the other. This system is the least efficient and can result in penalties measured in hundreds of dollars per truck load and several days of lost time. In a variation of this system, the vehicles of each country can travel a defined maximum distance to a location where the freight can be transferred from one truck to the other. In some instances, the nationality of the driver who can take the truck this maximum distance is also regulated. In rare instances, two drivers may be needed, either to change roles at the border or for a driver of one nationality to drive the vehicle to the border and a driver of the other nationality to drive it back to the original country.

The second system may allow vehicles to cross the border with a temporary importation license, provided they comply with the technical standards set by each country along the corridor. The types of trucks that are allowed may be determined by regional standards that relate to vehicle dimensions and axle loads. This system would not work where there is no harmonization of vehicle standards by adjoining countries, such as in East Africa, where the standards of new members of the East African Community (Burundi and Rwanda) are different from standards of the older members (Kenya, Tanzania, and Uganda).

In the third system, trucks from one country can enter the other if they provide their registration and insurance certificates, using a simple carnet. This relatively simple process provides the best-practice benchmark, to which the inefficiencies of the other two systems can be compared.

Quantitative Restrictions

Queuing systems are more common in domestic sharing of cargo, though freight allocation schemes are still typical for international transport in some parts of the world, including in several countries in West Africa.

Trade and Transport Corridor Management Toolkit

Such schemes prevent free competition in road freight services and interfere with contracting arrangements between shippers/traders and transport providers. These schemes are based on bilateral agreements that set the number of permits (quota) for access to each country's market and the conditions under which the permits can be used. In general, the number of permits exchanged is not based on any supply–demand analysis. Instead, the system can be used as an instrument for protecting national transport operators. Because the number of permits is usually renegotiated annually, it is possible, from one year to the next, to reconsider any "excessive" benefits that may have been granted to the other country and freeze any increase of the quota. An example is the quota system in the corridors between Ghana and Burkina Faso. The quota or freight allocation system by the Burkina Shippers Council ensures that at least two-thirds of the road freight between the two countries must be transported in trucks registered in Burkina Faso.

Kunaka and others (2013) review more than 70 bilateral road transport agreements. They find several characteristics that hamper efficient road freight operations:

- There is little consistency in the content of bilateral agreements. Operations on a corridor are often governed by a chain of bilateral agreements. There may therefore be benefits to reforming the regulatory regimes for road transport services.
- At times, there is unequal treatment of operators depending on their country of registration. Although the agreements may provide for reciprocity, some countries interpret the rules more strictly than others.
- Some bilateral agreements are dated, and information on what they regulate may not be readily accessible. Others lack modern provisions, such as provisions on protection of the environment, road safety, or security. If the corridor project aims to enhance the quality of services, it may be necessary to review the content of the agreements.
- Some agreements set technical and environmental standards that restrict market access for noncompliant transport operators. An example is Austria, which in the mid-2000s concluded bilateral road transport agreements with its Central and Eastern European neighbors that promoted more environmentally friendly modes of transport. The strict environmental standards in these bilateral agreements resulted in a very limited number of transit permits being issued across Austria.
- Restrictions embedded in some agreements can introduce market distortions and increase costs. If one party has larger trade volumes or more efficient operators, it may capture a larger share of the market than countries where the supply response is weaker.

These characteristics manifest themselves in operational constraints that affect corridor operations. The lack of restrictive bilateral agreements can be an obstacle to efficient road transport operations within a corridor. Fragmented requirements can also encourage and sustain rent-seeking tendencies that make seamless operations difficult if not impossible.

Kunaka and others (2013) identify 11 factors that affect the openness of bilateral agreements to facilitating international road transport operations:

- limitations on the scope of the agreement
- transport authorization requirements and complexities/restrictions of transport permit management
- list of types of traffic exempted from permit requirements
- list of types of traffic exempted from quota requirements
- cabotage traffic limitations
- transit quota limitations
- third-country traffic limitations
- prescribed routes and border-crossing points
- taxation-related limitations
- facilitation measures (driver, vehicle, cargo) in place
- transparency requirements.

It is recommended that countries negotiating agreements establish provisions dealing with and clarifying these factors.

Ideally, the criteria for access to markets should be qualitative; however, moving only to quality controls is not necessarily a low-hanging fruit, because liberalization must be preceded by reforms of the trucking sector that lead to its formalization and professionalization. In countries where such reforms have been successfully undertaken, accompanying compensatory measures were necessary, because the social implications were significant. A good example of a quota system that combines qualitative and quantitative criteria for access to international markets was put in place by the European Conference of Ministers of Transport (ECMT; see box 7.2).

The ECMT system represents a successful attempt to prevent what was seen as unfair competition between low- and high-cost road freight companies in different countries in Europe. It also serves as an example of the practical difficulty of eliminating the quota system once it has been long established. For instance, although the fundamental aim of the ECMT system is to gradually liberalize international markets at a high level of quality, in recent years the ability of the system to achieve that aim has been reduced by several geopolitical and economic factors. There is currently little political support for liberalization measures. Some countries have

BOX 7.2

The European Conference of Ministers of Transport Multilateral Quota System

The European Conference of Ministers of Transport (ECMT) was established in 1953 by 19 countries to provide a mechanism for coordinating the rebuilding of war-damaged transport infrastructure in Europe. Increased trade flows and prosperity led the ECMT to enlarge its areas of focus, which includes transport services, safety, security, and environmental protection.

The Multilateral Quota System, estimated to be used for 5–9 percent of all international road freight in Europe, was introduced on January 1, 1974, by the ECMT Council of Ministers. It has the following strategic aims:

- reduce empty running, optimizing the use of vehicles
- gradually liberalize road freight transport
- harmonize the conditions of competition
- promote the use of environmentally friendly and safe vehicles (since 1991).

ECMT permits are multilateral licenses for the international carriage of goods by road for hire or reward (not for own-account carriage) by transport undertakings established in an ECMT member country on the basis of a quota system. They can also be used for transport operations performed between ECMT member countries and in transit through the territory of one or several ECMT member countries by vehicles registered in an ECMT member country.

If goods are transported via an ECMT country where the use of ECMT permits is restricted or via a nonmember country, the countries may be transited with a bilateral permit or some other means of transport (for example, rolling road [truck-on-train]).

An ECMT permit may be used by only one vehicle at a time. It does not authorize cabotage or exempt the carrier from requirements relating to any other authorizations for the carriage of exceptional loads in terms of size or weight or for specific categories of goods (for example, dangerous goods).

Forty-three ECMT member countries participate in the quota system. The quota is determined every year by the Council of Ministers based on agreement within the Group on Road Transport. Countries receive their

(box continues on next page)

BOX 7.2 *continued*

share based on a methodology that takes into account the size and technical standards of the fleet, among other factors.

With European integration progressing and globalization posing challenges of a new magnitude for the transport sector, ECMT Ministers decided in May 2006 to evolve into the International Transport Forum, an intergovernmental organization with 54 member countries. This forum acts as a strategic think tank for transport policy. It also manages the Multilateral Quota System.

become more protectionist, an attitude undoubtedly reinforced by the ongoing European financial crisis (Kunaka and others 2013).

Generally, borders provide a good location to obtain information on the supply and patterns of road services. Authorities at the border verify that vehicles crossing have the necessary permits, which normally should not take long and need not be a barrier to the smooth movement along the corridor. However, border-crossing procedures, especially for trucks carrying freight in transit, add costs and create delays along trade and transport corridors. Expeditious crossing of borders is an important indicator of a corridor's performance. Efficient procedures that allow the vehicle, its load, and its driver to cross as easily as possible are crucial for trade.

In addition to quantitative restrictions (permits, quotas), the main aspects that affect border-crossing time and costs include the following:

- customs and other fees, taxes, guarantees, and duties on vehicles and freight
- insurance
- weights and dimensions
- registration and worthiness certificates.

It is general practice for countries to exempt foreign vehicles that are temporarily admitted on their territories (for tourism or through transit) from customs duties and taxes, based on recognition of the fact that their owners have paid such duties and taxes in their home countries. Bilateral agreements also usually exempt from duties and taxes fuel in factory built–in tanks, which is an integral part of the engine fuel supply systems; lubricants necessary for the journey; and spare parts and tools for repair of the vehicle. However, in some developing countries, it remains common practice to impose charges at the entry border (guarantee bonds, cash deposits through local agents, or payment of a one-time charge on entry).

Concerning vehicles, the solution to such problems lies in harmonization based on international multilateral legal instruments. It is important to verify that corridor countries have acceded to relevant international conventions relating to temporary importation of road vehicles. The use of unified (sub)regional agreements is not the most convenient solution for carriers, but it does help avoid cash or bond deposits or charges at each border crossing and expedite travel through several countries. Relevant legal instruments are the International Convention on the Harmonization of Frontier Controls of Goods (1982), the Customs Convention on the Temporary Importation of Private Road Vehicles (1954), the Customs Convention on the Temporary Importation of Commercial Road Vehicles (1956), and the Revised Convention on the Simplification and Harmonization of Customs Procedures (Kyoto 1973, as amended). Concerning goods, the best way to avoid bonds, guarantees, and other charges at borders is to put in place transit systems along corridors (see Module 6).

Unless roads are tolled, it is also common practice to require foreign trucks to pay infrastructure usage fees on crossing the border. For example, the Common Market for Eastern and Southern Africa (COMESA) adopted a standard and simple fee of $10 per 100 kilometers for all member countries. Such standardization is particularly important if the tariffs are very high (increasing transport cost) or benefit domestic operators over foreign registered fleets (reducing competition).

Many developing countries are parties to the General Agreement on Tariffs and Trade (GATT) and members of the World Trade Organization (WTO). They are obliged to ban any discriminatory practices.

Insurance

A general problem in trading across borders is liability in the event that a vehicle causes injury or death or the cargo is lost or damaged. This issue is addressed at the national level by requiring transport operators/shippers to purchase insurance. For efficient movement of trucks along a trade corridor, it is important to put in place international/regional insurance schemes that cover the transport units and their cargo as well as the driver while transiting the corridor. The oldest and best known international third-party liability insurance scheme is the green card system (box 7.3).

Many regional organizations have established similar schemes of third-party insurance for vehicles undertaking international road transport (with greater or less success). Table 7.1 lists some examples, often distinguished by use of different color schemes but intended to function in similar ways.

BOX 7.3

The Green Card Insurance System

Compulsory third-party motor insurance was gradually introduced in most European countries between the world wars. But financial protection remained available only to victims of resident drivers in their countries, not for victims of visiting drivers from other countries. This problem was taken up in 1947 by the UN Economic Commission for Europe (UNECE) with the following question to governments: "Could the legislation of their countries contemplate an agreement by which insurers or a bureau of insurers in their countries undertakes to reimburse an insurance company or bureau of insurers in another country, amounts paid by the latter to victims of road accidents?" The reactions were positive, and the System of the International Certificate of Motor Insurance (the green card system) was established on January 25, 1949, with significant advice and assistance from insurance experts. Secretariat services were initially entrusted to the Motor Insurers' Bureau (United Kingdom); in 1991, the Secretariat was established as an independent entity.

Implementation of the green card system started on January 1, 1953. The managing organization of the system is the Council of Bureaux, under the aegis of UNECE.

The objectives of the system are to ensure that victims of road traffic accidents do not suffer from the fact that injuries or damage sustained by them were caused by a visiting driver rather than a driver resident in the country in which the accident occurred and to obviate the need for drivers to obtain insurance cover at each of the frontiers of the countries they visit. These objectives are achieved through the activities of the green card bureaus, established by law or regulation in each of the 46 countries participating in the system. All green card bureaus operate with the recognition and approval of their governments.

Each bureau has two functions. First, as a "bureau of the country of the accident," it has responsibility in accordance with national legal provisions for compulsory third-party motor insurance for the handling and settlement of claims arising from accidents caused by visiting motorists. Second, as a "guaranteeing bureau," it guarantees certificates of motor insurance (green cards), which are issued by its member insurance companies to their policy holders. National bureaus cooperate on the basis of the internal regulations signed bilaterally.

BOX 7.3 *continued*

The green card is equivalent to the national motor insurance certificates of each and all of the countries a motorist visits. As such, it is accepted without any obstacle or cost by the authorities of all countries for which the individual green card is valid. The green card certifies that the visiting motorist has at least the minimum compulsory third-party insurance cover required by the laws of the countries visited.

The green card system remains primarily a European system, including most European countries and some of their neighbors, in most cases bordering the Mediterranean Sea. The position of the Council of Bureaux is that the green card system could be joined by the countries "west of the Urals and the Caspian Sea and countries bordering the Mediterranean Sea."

Source: Council of Bureaux, http://www.cobx.org.

TABLE 7.1 Regional Third-Party Insurance Schemes

Card color	Participants
Blue	Brunei, Cambodia, Indonesia, Lao PDR, Malaysia, Myanmar, the Philippines, Thailand, Vietnam
Brown	Benin, Burkina Faso, Côte d'Ivoire, The Gambia, Ghana, Guinea, Guinea-Bissau, Liberia, Mali, Niger, Nigeria, Senegal, Sierra Leone, Togo
Orange	Algeria, Bahrain, Arab Republic of Egypt, Iraq, Jordan, Kuwait, Lebanon, Libya, Mauritania, Morocco (green card member), Oman, Qatar, Saudi Arabia, Somalia, Sudan, Syrian Arab Republic, Tunisia (green card member), United Arab Emirates, Republic of Yemen
Pink	Cameroon, Central African Republic, Chad, Republic of Congo, Equatorial Guinea, Gabon
White	As of 2013, a proposal was being considered to establish a white card system for members of the Economic Cooperation Organization (ECO) if the territorial scope of the green card system could not be expanded to include all members. Participants are Afghanistan, Azerbaijan (green card candidate), Islamic Republic of Iran (green card member), Kazakhstan (a green card candidate), Kyrgyz Republic, Pakistan, Tajikistan, Turkey (green card member), Turkmenistan, and Uzbekistan.
Yellow	Burundi, Democratic Republic of Congo, Eritrea, Ethiopia, Kenya, Malawi, Rwanda, Tanzania, Uganda, Zambia, Zimbabwe

It is important for all trade players that the liability of the carrier in the event of damage or loss to the cargo be clearly defined. The Convention on the Contract for the International Carriage of Goods by Road (1956) (CMR) facilitates international road transport by providing a common transport contract, including a common consignment note and harmonized liability limits. It establishes the conditions governing the contract for the international carriage of goods by road between the carrier and the forwarder as well as the conditions of liability of the carrier in case of total or partial loss of goods. The CMR belongs to private law and has no direct implications for governments. However, in order for transport operators to implement it, governments must ratify the convention and include it in national legislation.

In countries with well-established financial systems (including insurance and banking), the aspects related to insurance of the vehicle, driver, and cargo are dealt with following a holistic approach.

Vehicle Weights and Dimensions

Differences in national technical standards for vehicle weights and dimensions can be a major impediment to the smooth movement of trucks along corridors. The modalities of taxation for overloaded vehicles can also differ across countries along the corridor, creating confusion and opportunities for arbitrary enforcement and corrupt practices.

Overloading is most common in markets lacking predictability and stability (fewer runs for higher profits) and in environments with weak enforcement of regulations. Vehicle weighing is an important operation, as overloading impedes competition, puts road safety at risk, and damages road infrastructure. At the same time, successive and abusive weighing may slow traffic flow and add to transport inefficiencies.

For all these reasons, overloading of trucks needs to be prevented. It is common practice to fine drivers for failure to comply with weight standards and to impose user charges proportional to the damage produced to infrastructure. This practice does not solve the problem, however.

Across the world, there are numerous examples of effective axle-load limit controls for trucks. The Sub-Saharan Africa Transport Policy Program (SSATP) has documented good practices in East and Southern Africa, including a system at the border between Botswana and South Africa where the weighbridge is linked to customs. Customs authorities can use information on the weight of trucks to verify loads. In fact, it is routine practice for trucks engaged in international transport to be weighed at border-crossing points. If they are not, a border or port weight certificate (or certificate issued at initiation of the journey) should be used to avoid intermediate en-route checks.

For such a system to work, authorities along the corridor have to have confidence in the integrity of the systems in place elsewhere for vehicle checks. On corridors where standards are harmonized and the level of enforcement is good, successive weighing operations could be avoided by introducing a unified weighing certificate, mutually recognized, as recommended in Appendix 2 to Annex 8 to the International Convention on the Harmonization of Frontier Controls of Goods of 1982. In South Africa, the authorities have introduced self-regulation for approved operators. Trucks belonging to such operators do not have to stop at all weighbridges; instead, they are subject to random checks.

It is also possible to deploy new technologies, including weigh-in-motion devices, to screen trucks without bringing them to a complete stop. The SSATP has documented the importance of countries implementing holistic vehicle overload control programs and has developed guidelines for the cross-border management of vehicle overload controls (Pinard 2010).

International standards for the weights and dimensions of vehicles have been defined in connection with the standards for road infrastructure or in various other forums, such as UNECE. Best practices of harmonization exist at regional levels, notably in highly integrated regions (the European Union).

Vehicle Registration and Worthiness

Countries typically use bilateral or multilateral agreements to mutually recognize vehicle registration and inspection certificates. However, the use of characters of national languages in registration certificates and number plates is still common in many countries. The practice causes difficulties for traffic police and authorities at border crossings when clearing documentation and carrying out procedures. It creates new difficulties when electronic clearance systems are implemented. For mutual recognition of vehicle registration certificates, standardized distinguishing signs of the states of registration, detailed requirements of technical conditions, and periodic inspections of vehicles as well as standardized registration number plates of vehicles need to be used.

As in many other areas, harmonization based on international legal instruments represents the most appropriate solution. The best-known sources on vehicle registration and technical inspection are the Vienna Convention on Road Traffic (1968) and Appendix 1 to Annex 8 to the International Convention on the Harmonization of Frontier Controls of

Goods (1982), which introduced a unified technical inspection certificate that is mutually recognized along the corridor.

Restrictions on Truck Drivers

The ability of truck drivers to cross international borders is critical to corridor logistics. Border-crossing systems for the movement of truck drivers can be almost as imposing as systems for vehicles across trade and transport corridors. The typical requirements for drivers at a border-crossing checkpoint include driving and service licenses and visas (passports or mutually recognized photo identification). Most bilateral agreements adopt mutual recognition of valid driving permits or international driving permits. Certifications from the immigration authorities are required to verify the identity of individuals entering or leaving the country.

In most cases, procedures require that drivers have a passport and usually a visa to enter the second country. Unlike seafarers and aircrew, professional road vehicle drivers do not enjoy special global arrangements for issuance of visas or temporary entry for them to undertake international transport operations. There is no visa category for vehicle drivers in many countries; normally, they are considered visitors or sometimes foreign workers. Visa issuance relies on bilateral consular arrangements. Drivers from most countries experience difficulties in obtaining entry visas, which causes delays in the delivery of goods and the change of vehicles at the corridor level. This costly and time-consuming procedure adds little if anything to national security or employment protection that could not be achieved with a multiple-entry visa system.

En Route Checkpoints

Trucks operating on corridors are subject to various other checks and controls that affect their utilization and costs. One of the controls, dealt with in Module 6, is making sure that transit trucks actually leave the country without diverting their load for internal consumption. The conventional solution to ensuring that trucks exit the country was to form them into convoys (made up of hundreds of trucks), escorted by customs or even army vehicles. The convoys are intended to safeguard against the possibility of transit goods being released for sale in the transiting country. The convoys can be several kilometers in length; they are often required to move at night in order to minimize congestion on main roads. Traders bear the cost of forming convoys. Trucks can be forced to wait a long time for convoys to depart, with the delay exacerbated by delays at the customs checkpoints of the next country resulting from the arrival of hundreds of trucks at the same time.

"Informal" checkpoints, which are prevalent in some regions, are another potential source of delays and costs. A study in West Africa for the U.S. Agency for International Development (USAID) (UEMOA 2013) estimates that informal trade barriers add about $20 per tonne to road freight transported between Ghana and Burkina Faso. It is important to estimate the significance of the checkpoints on costs and time. Indications in West Africa are that the time lost is often more important than the cost impact.

Informal checkpoints are set by various official and quasi-official agencies. Traffic police, for example, often establish checkpoints—ostensibly to check for compliance with vehicle standards but actually to solicit bribes. Customs and immigration agencies are also frequent operators of informal checkpoints.

In West Africa, regular surveys and dissemination of data on the impact of the checkpoints have been used to reduce their number. Uniformed services have set up hotlines that drivers can call to report road harassment. Complaints are one important way drivers can help the uniformed services weed out officers who use their positions for personal gain.

Truck Access to Ports

Congested access to ports is a major issue on many transport and trade corridors. When ports are located in or close to downtown areas, truck access to the port or its container terminal can be difficult and result in congestion for other road users. This problem is particularly severe where truck queues are allowed to form across or along urban streets and there are no separate staging areas for trucks to reduce the traffic blockages. The problem is exacerbated where urban and port planning activities are conducted separately and not integrated. This issue has become critical to the efficiency of road transport operations on most corridors. It is dealt with in Module 11.

Data and Information Sources

The main indicators of road transport services include the following:

- percentage of corridor road infrastructure in good, adequate, and bad condition
- transport prices for using corridor

- disaggregated transport time for using corridor by segment
- customs guarantees or similar requirements (for vehicle)
- customs guarantees or similar requirements (for cargo)
- insurance (for vehicle, driver, and cargo) compulsory at border
- user charges or toll fees (for road infrastructure)
- number of trucks in each direction
- cargo volume carried by road (for each direction)
- weight limits (gross, per axle)
- number of crashes, fatalities.

Data on transport infrastructure and services along a corridor are collected through interviews with the responsible government entities, as well as with private sector players, such as trucking firms, major shippers, and clearing and forwarding agents. Some information can be obtained from secondary sources.

Data collection activities are divided into two main parts. The first is a checklist regarding the physical characteristics of infrastructure and the supervision of the condition and use of this infrastructure. The collection of data on corridor road infrastructure is described in Module 1. The second is quantitative and qualitative data on trucking services along the corridor. Annex 7A presents the main interview questions.

Detailed data on the performance of trucking services can also be obtained from surveys of truck operators. Questionnaires for trucking surveys should be designed to cover a wide spectrum of issues considered critical to understanding the structure of the industry and the manner in which transport services are provided, as well as to understand how the enterprises perceive the environment in which they operate. The questionnaire should be divided into different sections, which may be administered to different levels of interviewees.

In East Africa, the SSATP used a questionnaire with nine sections, covering the nature of trucking activities, company relations, fleet characteristics, labor, trucking operations, marketing, regulations, support services, and productivity. In Southeast Asia, the World Bank used two questionnaires, one administered to senior managers at firms, to get insights on strategic issues affecting the trucking industry, and the other administered to operations managers, to obtain detailed information on costs and operational issues.

A critical consideration is the construction of a survey sampling frame. The sampling frame is usually created by obtaining information from the regulatory authorities on trucking firms or permit populations in the country. Permits can be very useful, as they can help identify operators on specific corridors. The sample can be designed to target certain types of operators and to distinguish between firms of different sizes of fleets, types of trucks, temporary and renewed permits, and so forth. Not all countries maintain functional permit management systems. Where such systems are not reliable, the sample has to be based on estimates of the populations or information from trucking associations. Associations are in any case critical to the success of a trucking survey.

The results of a trucking survey are compiled into a report on the supply and demand for road transport services along the corridor. The report identifies the major bottlenecks and opportunities for improvement in road transport services.

Improving Trucking Services within a Corridor

Several measures can be taken to improve the availability and quality of trucking services within a corridor. Chief among them are measures to improve regulation of the market and liberalization of market access.

Improving the Quality of Regulation

The term *regulation* encompasses the legislation, institutions, and practices that govern an activity or sector. Regulatory constraints play a significant role in determining transport prices along a corridor and are indispensable in establishing well-functioning markets. When properly conceived and enforced, regulations help create an enabling environment for the private sector to provide good-quality services and earn profits.

Recent research in Sub-Saharan Africa and South Asia suggest that end-users of road services face higher transport prices in trade and transport corridors with limited competition. The road freight industry in many developing countries is often supported by a regulatory framework that seeks to protect specific categories, such as individual- and family-owned trucks, against competition from large enterprises. These restrictions, enforced through queuing and quota systems, can prevent competition and delay the creation of healthy markets. A balance has to be struck between a properly regulated environment and one that remains competitive. In some markets, a laissez-faire approach may result in very low prices but yield poor-quality services (figure 7.1)

Transport prices and the quality of service provided by suppliers of road services depend in part on regulatory regimes. For freight transport,

FIGURE 7.1 Transport Prices in Selected Countries, 2008

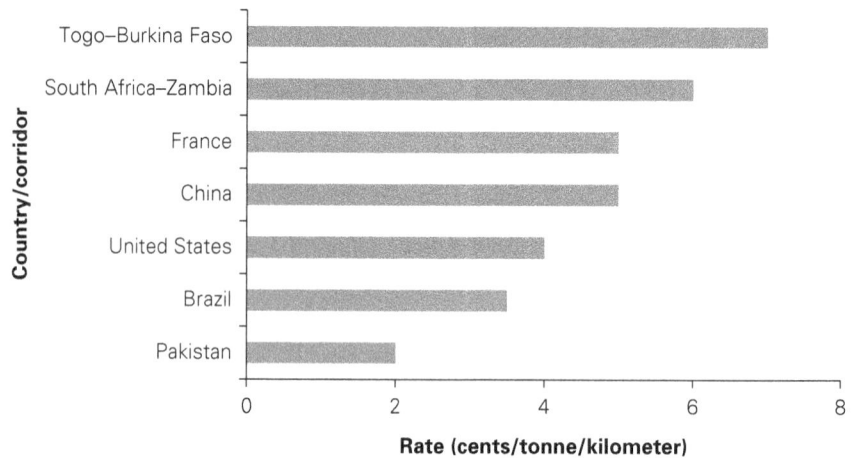

Source: World Bank, based on data from Teravaninthorn and Raballand 2009.

minimizing onerous regulation means replacing anticompetitive quantity licensing with less economically distorting quality licensing. Under a system of quality licensing, trucking licenses are provided to enterprises that meet specified minimum professional standards. Unlike the quantity-based freight allocation quota system, the quality-based system does not set limits on the number of operators. Instead, by demanding higher standards, it raises the professionalism of the industry.

To obtain a quality license, an operator must meet minimum safety, security, and environmental standards and demonstrate technical skills and financial capacity. Freedom of entry results in an increase in efficiency, with fewer trucks operating more hours and longer distances. End-users of transport services benefit, in the form of lower transport prices across transport and trade corridors.

One objective of a quality licensing system is to facilitate the creation of small and medium-size trucking companies that can better serve the needs of international traders than can individual truck owners. The qualities that are controlled through the licensing system are the financial, legal, and ethical status of the companies; the quality of the trucks they operate; and the skill and training of their drivers. Incentives and technical assistance are needed for new companies to reach the minimum acceptable standards on these three measures of quality (box 7.4).

Trade and Transport Corridor Management Toolkit

Modernizing Trucking in Pakistan

Pakistan has some of the lowest trucking rates in the world, partly as a result of the structure of the industry. The majority of trucks are owner operated and run as informal businesses. In 2007, there were as many as 209,000 registered trucks, most of which were old and highly fuel inefficient. Most operated on the national corridor linking Karachi and the industrial heartland to the north, which generates most of Pakistan's gross domestic product. The low rates reflect poor maintenance and overloading (about 40 percent of trucks are overloaded).

In 2007, the government drafted a comprehensive trucking policy to modernize the sector. The policy contains several progressive provisions, which, if realized, would improve the quality of trucking services. Some of the key provisions of the policy include the following:

- *Enhancing access to vehicle financing*: The policy designates the sector as an "industry," which under Pakistani law enables firms to borrow from banks at lower than commercial rates. Limited access to finance was an impediment to modernizing and replacing the fleet. Replacement trucks must be no more than four years old and at least Euro III compliant. The policy is already having an impact, as a few firms now have fleets of at least 50 trucks and have carved out a new, higher-class market segment.
- *Testing and certifying vehicle worthiness*: The policy mandates regular tests of fitness of vehicles and their road worthiness certification. It provides for the training and capacity building of staff involved in the tests.
- *Centralizing the registration of motor vehicles*: The registration of motor vehicles in Pakistan is handled by the provinces. As a result, it is usually difficult to obtain current information on the vehicle fleet. The policy proposes a central depository for motor vehicle registration for nationwide maintenance of data.

Other complementary measures are also being pursued, including driver licensing, provision of rest areas and stops for trucks, and improved standards for the manufacture and registration of trucks.

Liberalization of Market Access

Over the past few decades, many countries introduced substantial reforms to their trucking industry by liberalizing market access, thereby introducing competition. These reforms helped drive down prices. Shippers and traders also benefited from the freedom to contract directly with trucking companies of their choice (box 7.5) (World Bank 2009). Deregulating the trucking industry can take a long time and require skillful negotiations with current transport operators, who may fear that they will lose out.

BOX 7.5

Deregulating the Trucking Industry: Lessons from Mexico and Eastern Europe

Regulatory reforms in trucking can have profound impacts on market operations and transport prices, as the examples below show

Mexico

Until 1989, the trucking industry in Mexico was highly regulated, as regulation was deemed essential for promoting fair pricing, preventing dangerous cost-cutting competition, and providing quality trucking services to traders. In practice, regulation restricted competition in the trucking industry.

The industry was deregulated gradually in the late 1980s, just before the signing of the North American Free Trade Agreement (NAFTA). Deregulation enabled shippers and traders to contract directly with trucking service providers. Significant outcomes of the deregulation include the following:

- Many truck operators entered the market. Within a few months of deregulation, some 30,000 permits had been issued for new entrants.
- Within five years, transport prices to end-users had dropped by 23 percent in real terms.
- The frequency, access, and speed of delivery of road services improved.
- More flexible pricing of trucking services helped reduce overall transport costs of the trucking industry.

BOX 7.5 *continued*

Czech Republic, Hungary, and Poland

Road freight transport was one of the first sectors to be liberalized in Central and Eastern Europe in the wake of the breakup of the Soviet Union. The Czech Republic, Hungary, and Poland passed laws granting free entry to the trucking market in the late 1980s. Since then, market forces have freely determined transport prices. Liberalization coupled with privatization (which included reforms such as elimination of rate and route controls) led to the entry of many new trucking operators with competitive prices and better-quality service. Trucking companies set up several innovative logistics services, resulting in faster delivery times and less breakage or spoilage of cargo. Most of the significant service innovations were started by the larger, internationally connected trucking companies.

Source: Teravaninthorn and Raballand 2009.

Promoting Cross-Border Integration of Trucking Services

The problems of regulation of trucking are most apparent where international services are concerned. Kunaka and others (2013) identify the main regulatory issues at the international level as the lack of consistency in regulatory frameworks across countries, leaving operators to deal with a spaghetti bowl of regulations should they choose to operate across international borders; the discriminatory treatment of operators depending on their country of registration; and the lack of regulations on some contemporary issues, such as protection of the environment, road safety, security, and the abuse of technical and environmental standards to restrict market access for some operators. Fragmented requirements can also encourage and sustain rent-seeking tendencies that make seamless operations difficult if not impossible. Taken together these and other constraints distort markets and increase costs for both operators and users. In Southeast Asia, the Lao People's Democratic Republic and Thailand showed that removing restrictions on market access to international trucking services can have significant impacts on prices.

Based on the bilateral agreement between Lao PDR and Thailand, beginning in 2001, trucks registered in either country have been allowed into the other's territory to drop off and pick up cargo. The move was intended to reduce damage to and theft of cargo that occurs during transshipment, eliminate the need for customs checks for properly sealed cargo, and reduce unofficial payments. In 2004, the authorities agreed to liberalize market access even further by removing the quantity controls. The change had an immediate impact on transport supply, with the number of operators from Thailand jumping from 2 to 123 (figure 7.2). In 2011, 111 Thai firms were operating between the two countries. The supply response in Lao PDR was much smaller, because of the limited capacity of its trucking industry. However, even though the market remains dominated by a very few Thai firms, prices fell 20 percent.

Clearly, therefore, a reform agenda for the road trucking sector needs to be multipronged, covering regulatory, social, and economic issues. It has to include the types of vehicles that can be operated, how they are licensed and financed, training for drivers and their qualifications, institutional arrangements for oversight of the sector, consumption of infrastructure and cost recovery measures, safety and environmental protection, and other measures.

Facilitating the Movement of Truck Drivers

One way of facilitating visa issuance is for the national authorities for international road transport to act as intermediaries. They could prepare a list of professional drivers that they exchange with the counterpart authorities of other countries. The authorities of other countries would then submit the list to their ministries of foreign affairs for forwarding to embassies or consulates. Embassies or consulates would expedite the issuance of visas for drivers on the list. However, this can still be cumbersome and prone to corruption.

For countries that are members of a regional regime, the use of a "driver carnet" would be more efficient than multiple entry visas. A best-practice

FIGURE 7.2 Number of Trucking Companies with Licenses to Operate between Thailand and Lao PDR, 2000–11

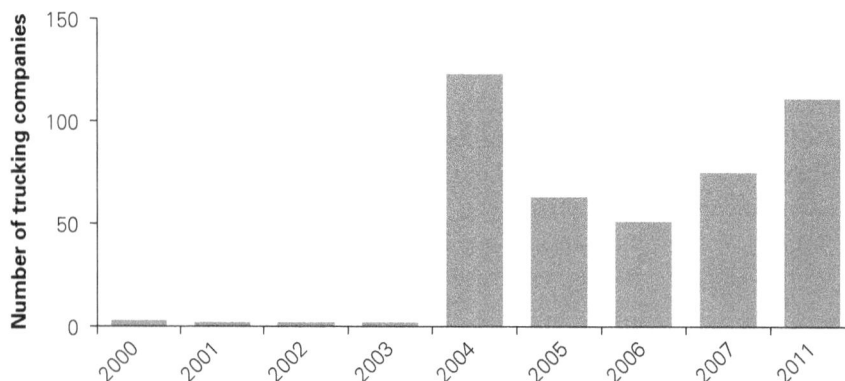

Source: World Bank 2013.

solution can be found in the League of Arab States, where private and commercial drivers who are resident in any of the member countries can easily cross into other countries upon presentation of a carnet on which is recorded the date and place of each entry and exit. In Southern Africa the Southern Africa Development Community (SADC) member states have adopted common curricula for the training of drivers and have also adopted a common design for drivers licences. The licences are easily recongizable and accepted across all the 14 member countries of the regional block.

Summary of Possible Interventions for Improving Trucking Services

Table 7.2 summarizes the most common trucking issues and questions found in corridor projects and proposes possible interventions to address them. Actual interventions should be adapted to deal with specific constraints.

TABLE 7.2 Possible Interventions for Improving Trucking Services

Issue	Questions	Possible interventions
Structure of industry	• How are the trucking industries in the corridor countries structured? • How old are the fleets? • Are there financing schemes for fleet renewal? • Are there national trucking professional associations? • Is there a regional trucking association? • Are there trucking industry oligopolies or cartels?	• Formalize and professionalize the trucking industry as a precondition for gradual liberalization of access to the profession and market. • Provide a financing scheme for trucking fleet renewal. • Harmonize regulation of the trucking industry across corridor countries.
Market access regulation (for domestic and international transport)	• What are the requirements for access to the profession of transport operator and to the market? • Are the conditions different by type of transport (own account, commercial, exclusively domestic carriage, international carriage)?	• Strengthen regulation of quality and relax or remove quantity controls.
Regulation of international road transport services	• Are vehicle technical standards of different countries harmonized within the corridor? • Are there agreements (bilateral, multilateral) on road transport within the corridor?	• Harmonize vehicle standards along the corridor.

(table continues on next page)

TABLE 7.2 *continued*

Issue	Questions	Possible interventions
	• What are the transport permit requirements to provide services? • Is cabotage allowed? Are any types of traffic exempted from permit or quota requirements? • Are there transit limitations? • Are there third-country traffic limitations? • Are routes and border-crossing points prescribed? • Are there taxation-related constraints? • Are facilitation measures (driver, vehicle, cargo) in place? • Are such measures publicized?	• Conclude a comprehensive road transport agreement among corridor countries based on fundamental elements. • Adopt a phased market integration approach for corridor and neighboring countries.
Transit management	• What is the impact of transit-related requirements (such as guarantees) on transport operations?	• Modernize transit regime management, based on recommendations in Module 6.
Movement of drivers	• Are visas required for truck drivers? • How long are they valid? • Is there mutual recognition of driver's licenses? • Must professional drivers have a permit or license?	• Adopt multiple-entry or visa-free entry for truck drivers. • Introduce harmonized training and testing for drivers. • Standardize vehicle licenses, including professional driver's permits.

Annex 7A Questions for Discussion of Road Transport

A. Questions for Public Works or Highway Department Officials

1. Which of the following features does the corridor road network have?

   ☐ Multilane dual carriageways
   Share of corridor: _____ percent

   ☐ Restricted access
   Share of corridor : _____ percent

   ☐ Tolled sections of road
   Share of corridor : _____ percent

   ☐ Designated rest stops
   Average interval between stops: _____ kilometers

   ☐ Additional right of way for expansion
   Average width of undeveloped right of way: _____ meters

   ☐ Uniform speed limit
   Speed limit: _____ kilometers per hour

   ☐ Planned maintenance based on road roughness

   ☐ Designated truck terminals near urban centers

   ☐ Special police responsible for regulating traffic

   ☐ Blackspot program for improving safety on the corridor

   ☐ Road funds earmarked for maintenance of the corridor

   ☐ Limited access ring roads ringing major cities along the corridor

   ☐ Partial truck bans on trucks operating within major cities for portions of the day

B. Questions for Operations Managers of Large Trucking Companies

2. About how many companies operate commercial truck fleets of 50 or more vehicles? _____

3. About what percentage of foreign trade is carried by articulated trucks (8- to 14-wheel trucks with a separate tractor and trailer connected at a mounting point)? _____

4. About what percentage of the commercial truck fleet (six wheels and above) is modern trucks (10 years old or less)? _____

5. Check the statements that are true of your company:

   ☐ Domestic, not marine, containers, are used for the inland movement of goods.

   ☐ Import duties for trucks are limited to the lowest two tariff bands.

   ☐ Trucks are used as collateral in commercial loans or trucks.

- ☐ GPS or a similar tracking systems is used to manage larger fleets.
- ☐ There is queuing for loads at selected gateways.
- ☐ There are national or local centers for booking return cargoes.
- ☐ The centers are Internet based.
- ☐ Standard contracts are used for carriage of goods transported in commercial trucks that stipulate liabilities for losses.

C. Questions for the Trucking Regulatory Authority—General Regulation

6. What are the applicable axle load limits for different types of trucks (single and tandem axles and gross vehicle weight)? _____
7. What are the limits on vehicle length and height? _____
8. How many weigh stations are there in the corridor for enforcement of axle-load limits? _____
9. How many are operated? _____
10. What percentage of the time are they operational? _____
11. What is maximum age of imported vehicles? _____
12. What is maximum age of vehicles that can be operated on national routes? _____
13. Which of the following statements is true in this corridor?
    - ☐ Trucks must meet emission standards, such as Euro III.
    - ☐ Restrictions are placed on the quality of trucks for interstate transport of certain goods.
    - ☐ Trucks carrying interstate cargo must maintain logbooks.
    - ☐ Road worthiness certificates are based on an annual inspection.
    - ☐ Road worthiness requirements are strictly enforced.
    - ☐ All trucks are inspected annually for emissions.
    - ☐ Emissions standards are strictly enforced.
    - ☐ Liability insurance is mandatory.
    - ☐ Vehicle insurance is mandatory.
    - ☐ Interstate driver's licenses and vehicle registrations allow trucks to operate throughout the county without restrictions on crossing state/provincial boundaries.
    - ☐ No tax is imposed on trucks carrying goods across a state or provincial border.
    - ☐ Uniform regulations govern the transporting of goods along the corridor.
    - ☐ The government regulates the price of fuel.
    - ☐ There is a uniform speed limit throughout the corridor.

D. Questions for the Transport Regulatory Authority—Cross-Border Transportation

14. Which of the following statements is true in this corridor?
    - ☐ Regional vehicle insurance provides coverage in more than one country.
    - ☐ A regional driver's license or certification allows truckers to transport goods across borders.
    - ☐ Multientry visas are granted to drivers who regularly operate across national borders.
15. For which of the following are regulations harmonized on both sides of the border?
    - ☐ Axle-load limits
    - ☐ Gross vehicle weight
    - ☐ Vehicle length
16. Which of following international road transport conventions has the country signed?
    - ☐ International Transport of Goods (TIR)
    - ☐ Temporary Importation of Road Vehicles
    - ☐ Temporary Admission for Containers
    - ☐ Harmonization of Frontier Control of Goods
    - ☐ Kyoto Convention for Harmonization

E. Questions for the Authority of Individual Road Sections

17. Provide the following statistics on major road sections along the corridor:
    - ☐ Length of section: _____ kilometers
    - ☐ Number of lanes in each direction: _____
    - ☐ Lane width: _____ meters
    - ☐ Maximum (gross vehicle weight): _____ metric tonnes
    - ☐ Axle-load limit: _____ (metric tonnes)
    - ☐ Divided carriageway: _____ percent of total length
    - ☐ Limited access: _____ percent of total length
    - ☐ Toll road: _____ percent of total length
    - ☐ Average speed during peak hour: _____ kilometers per hour
    - ☐ Average speed during off peak: _____ kilometers per hour
    - ☐ Traffic levels on principal links of corridor: _____ passenger car units
    - ☐ Proportion of vehicular traffic accounted for by multiaxle trucks: _____ percent
    - ☐ Condition of road: _____ road roughness index
18. Provide the following information on major links along the corridor:
    - ☐ Traffic volume and peaks: _____ (annual average daily traffic)
    - ☐ Average velocity: _____ kilometers per hour

☐ Average speed limit: _____ kilometers per hour
☐ Capacity: _____ (annual average daily traffic)
☐ Condition of road: _____ road roughness index

19. In which of the following activities is there private sector involvement?
☐ Construction
☐ Maintenance
☐ Tolling

20. What are the major chokepoints along the corridor? _____

21. What investments are planned through
☐ Investment: _____
☐ Maintenance: _____
☐ Improved traffic control: _____

F. Questions for Trucking Company Officials

22. What is your principal business?
☐ Transport for own account
☐ Contract haulage
☐ Handle less than truckload shipments (grouppage)

23. How are most of your transport services contracted?
☐ Individual shipments
☐ For certain period of time, during which prices are set
☐ For a specific quantity service
☐ Storage and distribution

24. What are the major routes served that use the corridor? _____

25. For most of your company's shipments, what type of cargo do you carry?
☐ Liquid or dry bulk
☐ Loose cargo in bags or cartons
☐ Cargo in international or domestic containers
☐ Construction materials and other project cargo

26. Which of the following specialized services does your company offer?
☐ Movement of cargo in transit under customs bond within the country
☐ Movement of cargo in transit through neighboring countries
☐ Courier and express delivery
☐ Container handling
☐ Inventory management
☐ Cold chains
☐ Oversize project cargo

27. Who are your major clients?
☐ Manufacturers
☐ Producers
☐ Wholesalers/retailers

    ☐ International shipping lines or forwarders
    ☐ Traders
    ☐ Construction firms
28. Who arranges for shipments?
    ☐ Shipper
    ☐ Forwarder
    ☐ Broker
    ☐ Consignee
29. How does your company arrange for return cargoes?
    ☐ Back-to-back contracts
    ☐ Driver locates cargo
    ☐ Queries to current and former clients
30. How do your customers rank the following features?
    (Rank between 1 and 6, 1 being the highest and 6 being the lowest)
    ☐ Minimizing cost
    ☐ Minimizing transit time
    ☐ Ensuring safety of goods in transit
    ☐ Ensuring reliability and scheduled movements
    ☐ Providing specialized equipment
    ☐ Providing value-added services
31. Does your company offer a range of service quality based on increasing the cost to reduce the transit time or increase reliability?
    ☐ Yes
    ☐ No
32. What is the size of your truck fleet? _____
33. How many trucks in your fleet are of the following types?
    ☐ Flatbed: _____
    ☐ Open side: _____
    ☐ Closed van: _____
    ☐ Container chassis: _____
    ☐ Refrigerated: _____
34. What are the sizes and capacities of the trucks used for long-haul shipments? _____
35. Are these trucks fixed axle or articulated?
    ☐ Fixed axle
    ☐ Articulated
36. Provide the following information on shipments that use the corridor:
    ☐ Annual volume transported: _____ tonnes and 20-foot equivalent units (TEUs)
    ☐ Typical distance door-to-door: _____ kilometers
    ☐ Portion of this distance on the corridor: _____ percent

☐ Share of trips with empty backhauls: _____ percent
☐ Average distance traveled on corridor per trip: _____ kilometers
☐ Average time to travel this distance: _____ minutes
☐ Variance of time: _____ minutes
☐ Average speed: _____ kilometers per hour
☐ Average vehicle operating cost per kilometer for the largest trucks: _____

37. What are the principal causes of delay on the corridor?
☐ Congestion
☐ Authorized and unauthorized checkpoints
☐ Accidents
☐ Weather

38. Of the total fleet operating cost, what percentage is accounted for by the following?
☐ Fuel and lube: _____
☐ Drivers and their assistants: _____
☐ Maintenance and repairs: _____
☐ Taxes and fees: _____

39. How is the price for haulage set?
☐ Per tonne-kilometer
☐ Per tonne for specific origin-destinations
☐ Per truck kilometer

40. Is there real-time monitoring of truck movement using any of the following?
☐ Global Positioning System (GPS)
☐ Cell phones

41. Is it necessary to obtain specific licenses or approvals to provide contract haulage (common carrier, third-party carriage)?
☐ Yes
☐ No

42. If so, do these licenses or approvals place any constraints on the services offered in terms of the following?
☐ Types of goods carried
☐ Types of vehicles operated
☐ Routes served

43. If so, do they place any limitations on the following?
☐ Capitalization
☐ Extent of foreign ownership
☐ Level of insurance required

44. Who enforces the limits on axle loads and gross vehicle weights? _____

45. How are these limits enforced? _____
46. Are there restrictions on which routes you can operate?
    - ☐ Yes
    - ☐ No
47. If so, how are they enforced? _____
48. What is the average amount of overloading for long-haul shipments?
    _____ tonnes
49. What documents are used for the carriage of goods?
    - ☐ Standard consignment note or waybill
    - ☐ Informal delivery note
50. If a standard document is used, who designed it?
    - ☐ Government
    - ☐ Transporters association
    - ☐ Other (specify) _____
51. What is the average percentage of goods lost or damaged in shipment?
    _____
52. When does loss or damage primarily occur?
    - ☐ During transit
    - ☐ During cargo handling
53. How is the liability for loss or damage allocated between the shipper, truck operator, and consignee? _____
54. Which, if any, of the following provide cargo insurance?
    - ☐ Shipper
    - ☐ Truck operator
    - ☐ Consignee
55. For which of the following activities does your company use computerized systems?
    - ☐ Processing orders
    - ☐ Managing procurement
    - ☐ Controlling costs
    - ☐ Managing the fleet
    - ☐ Locating backhaul cargo
    - ☐ Negotiating rates
    - ☐ Billing for services
    - ☐ Confirming delivery
    - ☐ Tracking shipments
    - ☐ Managing inventory
56. Does your company use electronic data interchange for confirming orders or exchanging shipping documents?
    - ☐ Yes
    - ☐ No

57. Does your company use Internet banking or electronic transfers to pay for supplies and receive payment for services rendered?
    ☐ Yes
    ☐ No
58. Does your company transport cargo outside the country?
    ☐ Yes
    ☐ No
59. Are vehicles with acceptable characteristics and insurance allowed to cross the border with a temporary import license?
    ☐ Yes
    ☐ No
60. If not, do bilateral or regional agreements restrict the movement of vehicles across the border?
    ☐ Yes
    ☐ No
61. Do they specify quotas or other restrictions on the types of vehicles that can cross the border or is it in a complete prohibition thereby requiring transfer of cargo between vehicles?
    ☐ Quotas or other restrictions are specified.
    ☐ Crossing the border is prohibited (cargo is transferred to other vehicles).
62. If quotas are used, which of the following applies?
    ☐ The number of trips that can be made by vehicles registered in the countries on either side of the border is similar.
    ☐ There are limitations on which companies can participate, with vehicles rather than the number of trips authorized.
63. What are the principal difficulties crossing the border?
    ☐ Customs
    ☐ Immigration
    ☐ Transport regulation
    ☐ Phyto-sanitary and other inspections
64. What documents are required for cross-border movement? _____
    ☐ Permit
    ☐ Insurance
    ☐ Weight certificate
    ☐ Commercial invoice
    ☐ Manifest
    ☐ Other
65. What requirements govern the transporting of goods through neighboring countries?
    ☐ Specific routes must be followed.

☐ The vehicle must be escorted by a customs official.

☐ The vehicle must move as part of a convoy.

☐ The company must post a performance bond or other guarantee.

☐ Other (specify) _____

66. What type of seal is required? _____

67. For the guarantees, what amount is required? _____

68. Who issues this guarantee? _____

69. Is there any use of a TIR or other regional carnet?

☐ Yes

☐ No

70. What are the major constraints to improving efficiency of your operations?

☐ Demand (imbalanced flows, emphasis on cost rather than quality)

☐ Supply (finance, taxes, excess capacity, overloading, security, congestion)

☐ Regulation (restriction of operations or services, checkpoints)

☐ Border crossings and transit movements (delays and cargo handling)

☐ Informal costs, other corrupt practices

71. Is your company introducing any of the following solutions?

☐ Service contracts with liability clearly defined

☐ Fleet rationalization

☐ Improved fleet management and minimization of empty backhauls

☐ Consolidation of shipments

☐ Large truck/logistics terminals at strategic locations

☐ Tighter integration with other supply chain activities

72. What types of checkpoints exist on the corridor?

☐ Toll collection

☐ Tax collection

☐ Police inspection

☐ Customs inspection

73. How do these checkpoints affect the time and cost of traveling on the corridor?

☐ Add to delays

☐ Increase costs

☐ Both

74. What are the principal infrastructure problems affecting the road transport industry?

☐ Insufficient capacity

☐ Poor maintenance

☐ Problems with traffic safety

☐ Shortage of truck terminals and roadside amenities

- ☐ Insufficient access to urban areas
- ☐ Lack of urban bypass roads

75. Are these problems expected to get worse as demand increases?
    - ☐ Yes
    - ☐ No

76. What are the effects of inadequate infrastructure?
    - ☐ Congestion
    - ☐ Lower average speed
    - ☐ Higher operating costs
    - ☐ Delays, as a result of restricted access
    - ☐ Uncertain transit times

77. Are there efforts underway to address these problems?
    - ☐ Planned investment in new road capacity
    - ☐ Increased funding or better contracting for maintenance services
    - ☐ Changes in policies restricting access to certain roads
    - ☐ No plans

78. Are these efforts expected to have a significant impact in terms of savings in time and cost?
    - ☐ Yes
    - ☐ No

79. What are the principal constraints to expanding your business?
    - ☐ Inadequate access to finance
    - ☐ Intense competition and low returns
    - ☐ Difficulties obtaining licenses or certification

80. Which of the following, if any, is the government doing to improve the situation ?
    - ☐ Reducing taxes
    - ☐ Improving access to finance
    - ☐ Simplifying regulations
    - ☐ Renegotiating bilateral agreements
    - ☐ Restricting or eliminating check points
    - ☐ Better enforcement of regulations on vehicle roadworthiness

81. Rate the following:
    - ☐ Highway department: ☐ Good ☐ Adequate ☐ Poor
    - ☐ Policy: ☐ Good ☐ Adequate ☐ Poor
    - ☐ Customs: ☐ Good ☐ Adequate ☐ Poor
    - ☐ Port terminal operator: ☐ Good ☐ Adequate ☐ Poor
    - ☐ Air cargo terminal operator: ☐ Good ☐ Adequate ☐ Poor

82. If poor, what are the reasons? _____
    _____

Notes

1. Only 15 of the 35 less developed landlocked developing countries have a rail link to a port in a transit neighbor, 2 have a river-to-sea or lake connection, and 7 have both. Six have neither, relying exclusively on roads for all international transport.
2. Although there is a rich body of anecdotal evidence, there are few reliable statistics on the structure of trucking industries in most low-income countries.

References

ADB (Asian Development Bank). 2008. "Central Asia Regional Economic Cooperation Transport Sector Strategy Study." Manila. http://www.carecinstitute.org/uploads/corridors.

Kunaka, C., V. Tanase, P. Latrille, and P. Krausz. 2013. *Quantitative Analysis of Road Transport Agreements (QuARTA)*. Washington, DC: World Bank.

Londoño-Kent, P. 2009. Background paper for *Freight Transport for Development Toolkit*. World Bank, Energy, Water and Transport Department, Washington, DC.

Pinard, M. 2010. "Guidelines on Vehicle Overload Control in Eastern and Southern Africa." SSATP Working Paper 90, World Bank, Sub-Saharan Africa Transport Policy Program, Washington, DC.

Raballand, G., and P. Macchi. 2009. "Transport Prices and Costs: The Need to Revisit Donors' Policies in Transport in Africa." World Bank, Washington, DC.

Teravaninthorn, S., and G. Raballand. 2009. *Transport Prices and Costs in Africa: A Review of the Main International Corridors*. Washington, DC: World Bank. http://imagebank.worldbank.org/servlet/WDSContentServer/IW3P/IB/2008/10/22/000333038_20081022063438/Rendered/PDF/461810PUB0Box3101OFFICIAL0USE0ONLY1.pdf.

UEMOA (West African Economic and Monetary Union). 2013. "23rd Road Governance Report: Survey Results for the First Quarter of 2013." Lomé, Togo.

UNECE (United Nations Economic Commission for Europe). 1982. International Convention on the Harmonization of Frontier Controls of Goods. Document ECE/TRANS/55/Rev. 1, Inland Transport Committee, Geneva.

USAID (U.S. Agency for International Development). 2011. "Study on Impact of Transportation Monopoly: Report on the Road Goods Transport Industry in Nepal." Washington, DC.

World Bank. 2009. *Freight Transport Development Toolkit: Road Freight*. Washington, DC: World Bank, Energy, Water and Transport Department.

———. 2013. "Draft Lao Trade and Transport Facilitation Assessment Report." Washington, DC.

WTO (World Trade Organization). 1994. General Agreement on Tariffs and Trade 1994. Geneva. http://www.wto.org/english/docs_e/legal_e/06-gatt.pdf.

Resources

Borderless Alliance. *Removing Trade Barriers in West Africa*. http://www.borderlesswa.com/.

The Borderless Alliance was launched in 2012 with support of several partners, especially the U.S. Agency for International Development (USAID) West Africa Trade Hub. It provides a platform for the private sector to propose solutions to impediments to the movement of goods and transport in West Africa. It is a repository for data collected on irregular practices, mainly checkpoints, along the main corridors in the region.

Federal Highway Administration. 2007. "Chapter 6: Harmonization Approaches." *Commercial Motor Vehicle Size and Weight Enforcement in Europe*, 57–60. Washington, DC: U.S. Department of Transportation, Office of International Programs. http://international.fhwa.dot.gov/pubs/pl07002/vsw_eu07_06 .cfm.

This chapter distinguished between the approaches to harmonization of the European Union and the United States. In the European Union, a goal is consistency within the union while maintaining each country's economic interests. In the United States, individual states operate independently, with less regard for harmonization with bordering states or countries.

Nathan Associates. 2007. "Toward a Roadmap for Integration of the ASEAN Logistics Sector: Rapid Assessment and Concept Paper." Paper prepared for USAID, Washington, DC. http://pdf.usaid.gov/pdf_docs/PNADI778.pdf.

This document presents the status and performance of the logistics system of the Association of Southeast Asian Nations (ASEAN) region. The analysis was based on consultations with various stakeholders. It analyzes several corridors within ASEAN, proposes guiding principles, and makes recommendations for realizing the proposed ASEAN logistics connectivity roadmap.

Report to the Land Transportation Standards Subcommittee. 1997. *Harmonization of Vehicle Weight and Dimension Regulations within the NAFTA Partnership Report*. http://www.comt.ca/english/programs/trucking/NAFTA%20Side %20by%20Sde%20Oct%2097.pdf.

This document analyses the differences in axle-load limits within regions of North American Free Trade Agreement (NAFTA) countries, making the case for an international approach to standardization of such limits. The document identifies the dilemma that is common with measures to achieve standardization, namely, the fact that standardized limits that are lower than already permissible in some regions would very likely be unacceptable, as they introduce inefficiencies for some shippers and carriers, while limits that are higher than currently permitted may not be politically or practically acceptable in regions with more restrictive policies.

UNECE (United Nations Economic Commission for Europe). 2009. *Transport Review: Transport without Borders*. Geneva. http://www.unece.org/fileadmin /DAM/trans/doc/reviews/UNECE-Transport-Review-2009-2.pdf.

This report is a compendium of experiences with border-facilitation initiatives across the world. It contains several case studies, including studies of Africa, Central Asia, and Europe. It addresses various topics, such as the use of information technology, single window systems, border design, and development of master plans.

World Bank. 2011. "Performance of Transport Corridors in Central and South Asia." Report 66943, Washington, DC. http://www-wds.worldbank.org/external/default /WDSContentServer/WDSP/IB/2012/02/21/000356161_20120221230013 /Rendered/PDF/669430BR0Draft0official0use0only090.pdf.
The paper presents the results of corridor monitoring in Central Asia. The analysis finds that informal barriers are high in Central Asia and delays by border agencies other than customs can be very high. Reduction of delays needs careful assessment; measures need the support of governments and international organizations. The analysis was based on a data collection mechanism that is one of the rich sources of data on road corridors in particular.

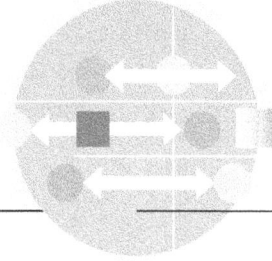

Rail Transport

Rail transport can have an advantage over road transport on long-distance or high-volume corridors. It offers potential benefits in the form of lower transport costs and shorter transit times, resulting from potentially higher speeds, shorter border-crossing times, and fewer en route delays. For developing countries, which export mainly high-volume, low-value bulk goods (such as minerals and agricultural products), freight along corridors can be served by well-run railways at lower cost than road transport.

Rail is in principle ideal for landlocked countries with long distances to the sea. It is an especially appealing possibility where domestic rail freight is in decline, leaving railroad capacity underused (which means marginal operating costs are low). Freight railways can also deliver external community benefits that are increasingly valued by policy makers, particularly in the areas of safety and the environment, given their lower greenhouse gas emissions.

Efficient rail services within corridors also benefit transport users. On the main international corridors, an absent or dysfunctional rail service provides opportunities for the road trucking industries to inflate transport charges for moving freight, as railways (and inland waterways) are an alternate surface mode to road transport along some trade corridors. Because of potentially higher capacity, rail transport can play an important role in moving freight, especially bulk and containerized cargoes. In addition, because rail is more secure, it is preferred on some corridors for moving goods in transit.

This module explores the importance of rail transport in trade and transport corridors. It is structured as follows. The first section identifies the main issues faced concerning the functioning and impact of railway transport on corridor performance. The second section presents the data and information that are required to understand the issues. This section is complemented by an annex that lists the key data and questions that can be asked of stakeholders to obtain both quantitative and qualitative data on railway transport. The third section identifies possible solutions to the most common issues. The last section summarizes these interventions.

Rail Freight Issues in a Trade Corridor

At least seven issues related to railways may need to be considered in the context of a trade corridor:

- international interconnectivity
- comparative advantage of railways
- management and operation of railways
- international border crossings
- availability of backhaul loads
- ownership of containers.

International Interconnectivity

The interconnectivity of railway tracks across boundaries is fundamental to the seamless movement of trains across international borders (box 8.1). The same gauge must be used along the corridor or technical solutions provided to effect efficient interchanges.

Even where trains can physically cross borders, delays may be experienced as a result of several operational practices, including the following:

- the transfer of cargo or wagons at the border
- the carrying out of inspections on both sides of the border
- the poor synchronization of the movement of freight trains, which leads to congestion at border stations
- the breaking up of shipments to accommodate differences in power of locomotives used by different railway administrations.

BOX 8.1
Breaking up and Coordinating Railways in Central Asia

Rail transport has long dominated passenger and freight transport in the former Soviet Union, where long distances between centers and the movement of predominantly bulk commodities make railway a competitive and preferred mode. Given their large railway stock, countries in the region also continue to favor railway transport as a matter of strategic preference.

The railways were developed as an integrated system during the Soviet era. That system was disbanded in 1992, succeeded by 19 nationally autonomous railway administrations, making coordination much more difficult. With new international borders, trains now have to stop at the border to change crews and equipment. Rail rates also increased significantly.

Following the breakup of the Soviet Union, traffic volumes changed. Although output was already falling at the time of the breakup, it accelerated for some of the newly fragmented railway systems (box figure B8.1.1 shows changes in traffic volume in tonne-kilometers [tkm]).

BOX FIGURE B8.1.1 Railway Traffic Volumes in the Soviet Union and Successor Countries, 1981–2007

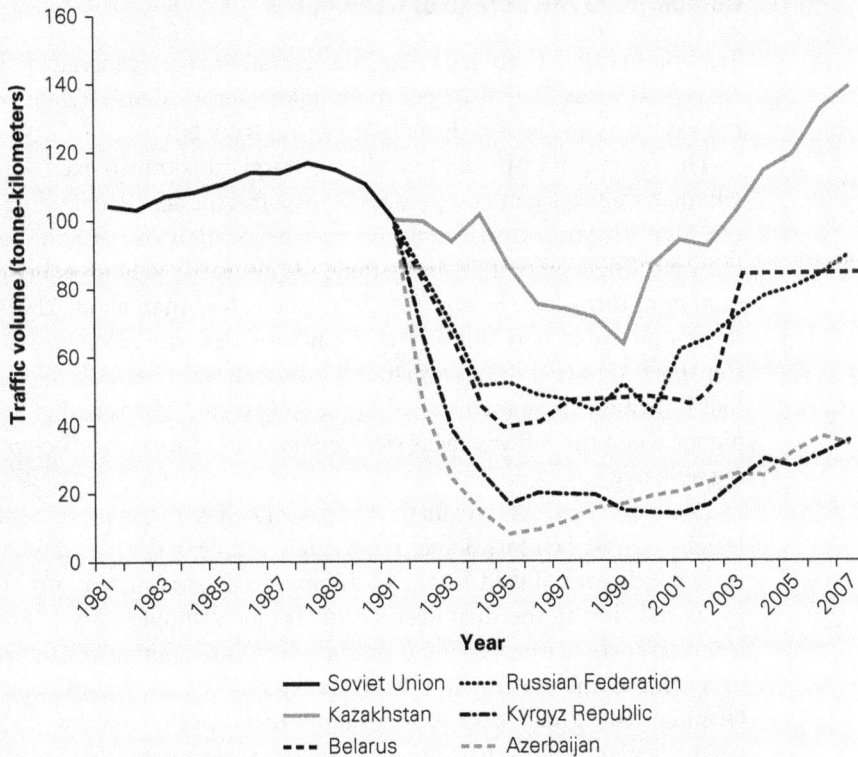

(box continues on next page)

BOX 8.1 *continued*

The railways of Belarus, Kazakhstan, and the Russian Federation rebounded quickly, but their output took several years to return to 1992 levels. In the other countries, notably Azerbaijan and the Kyrgyz Republic, volumes recovered much more slowly; they are currently less than half what they were before the breakup.

The experience of the former Soviet Union points to the importance of cross-border coordination in railway operations. In 1992, a Railway Transport Council was established to coordinate across the new separate administrations, but it was not effective. Traffic volumes across the network reflect a reorientation of trade flows, and therefore corridors, across the region. Whereas in the past, the bulk of rail traffic went to or through Moscow, the major flows are now east-west, between China and the European Union. Hence, some countries, such as Kazakhstan, now serve as land bridges. Almaty in particular has become an important node in the continental system of railways.

Source: Based on World Bank 2012.

Comparative Advantage of Railways

Transport costs for moving bulk goods by railways are generally low. Rates are typically less than $0.03 per tonne-kilometer; on dense freight-oriented railways, they can be less than $0.02 (World Bank 2011).

The volume of traffic and the distance freight is transported determine whether railways can compete with road freight across corridors. Given the high proportion of fixed and low proportion of variable costs for railways, financial sustainability depends on traffic volume being above a minimum threshold. Where freight traffic is less than about 250,000 net tonnes per year, it is unlikely that rail services can compete with road transport. Where traffic is less than 1 million tonnes per year, it is unlikely that railways can be maintained in the long term.[1] The thresholds will be higher when the railway faces strong competition from an efficient trucking industry.

There are also high terminal costs associated with the movement of rail freight across corridors. Except in the few places in the world where railways are directly linked from the shipment's origin (such as a mine or an industrial site) to the final destination, traders/shippers have to bear the terminal costs of transferring freight from rails to another transport mode to reach the final destination. Road transport does not have an equivalent terminal cost. Thus, there is a minimum distance threshold that railways need to satisfy before their lower en route costs can compensate for these additional terminal costs. The minimum viable distance for railways to compete with trucks for freight transport has been estimated at 400–800 kilometers (Bullock 2009). With few exceptions, the distance to a deep water port for landlocked countries is greater than this. For these countries, railways are therefore preferable to roads.

The line haul rate, excluding local consolidation and delivery, is only one factor taken into consideration by traders/shippers when they have a choice. The costs of pick-up and delivery also need to be considered, as do service-level factors, such as transit time, reliability, and service frequency.

Management and Operations of Railways

Until the 1980s, railway companies in most countries were government departments or publicly owned corporations with varying degrees of financial management and management autonomy. The public sector still operates some railway systems, particularly in the East Asia and Pacific region and the Middle East and North Africa. In contrast, in Latin America and the Caribbean and Sub-Saharan Africa, most railways are now run by the private sector under long-term concessions.

The terms of railway concessions vary across countries. A typical approach followed in many countries is for the state to continue to own some or all railway assets (typically infrastructure) and transfer other assets (normally the rolling stock) as well as responsibility for operating and maintaining the railway to a concessionaire under the terms and conditions stipulated in a concession agreement. The concessionaire operates the railway as a business activity at its risk and cost.

Growing evidence indicates that concessions in developing countries attract a limited pool of mainly foreign private operators. These operators fall into two categories: operators that favor vertical integration of the transport distribution chain through the acquisition of dominant positions in specific productive and transport sectors and operators that specialize in a single transport activity.

In the first category, it would appear that operators are willing to earn low rates of return from one or several of the distribution chain activities they operate as long as their control of a significant part of the distribution chain yields sufficient overall benefits. The second category of operators is characterized by an investment focus on rail operations only, suggesting that operations need to be sufficiently profitable to attract nonvertically integrated enterprises.

Although the performance of railway concessions across the world shows mixed results, there are some common conclusions:

- The traffic volume carried by railways increased following the concession in many countries. Railways performed more efficiently following the concession, and there was little evidence of monopolistic behavior. The threat of transport mode substitution (that is, from rail to road) limited the railway operators' ability to charge abusive tariffs, regardless of their market share.
- Increasing rail competitiveness appears to benefit transport users primarily through lower road rather than lower rail transport costs.
- Until recently, participation in railway concessions appears to have been driven more by the desire of firms to control logistical distribution chains than by the desire to earn substantial direct returns on their investment. Concessionaires are reluctant to spend more on infrastructure than is required for day-to-day maintenance. Thus, the funding of long-term asset renewal and upgrading remains an issue for the railway network in many countries.

Railways still offer the most economical solution to transporting non-time-sensitive bulk freight on distances of at least 400 kilometers. As such, their revival through concessioning is warranted where business fundamentals are sound. At the same time, better solutions must be found to ensure that host governments continue to benefit from substantial economic rates of return from these concessions and private operators' financial returns are high enough to entice broader and more competitive investor participation.

International Border Crossings

Railways usually have shorter border delays than trucks, for four reasons. First, railway border stations are usually located at major railway stations/ junctions and marshalling yards, not necessarily on the border. They therefore facilitate processing without the space constraints often found at border-crossing points. Second, rail traffic at border stations is usually cleared or inspected during scheduled stopping times, when other needed technical operations (such as locomotive changes, shunting, maintenance, and gauge changes) take place. If border control fits in with the train's scheduled stopping time, there need be no additional time-consuming delays. Third, rail transport avoids the informal checkpoints that hinder and add to the cost of road freight. Fourth, rail has lighter and faster transit arrangements, as there is often greater security during transit, with few opportunities for cargo to be tampered with in movement.[2]

However, cross border railway services can still experience delays. Documentation and other border-crossing requirements for international rail freight movements may be complicated and costly. Rail border crossings can entail operational procedures that typically include inspections, break-of-gauge operations (as at the China/Kazakhstan border), marshalling (the classification and separation of railcars and the transfer and acceptance of railway documents on the rolling stock and the freight), checks by customs agencies (railway bills of lading against wagon lists and cargo documents), and physical inspections on plant and animal controls. A broken seal or documentation problem could delay a whole trainload of consignments, compared with just the truckload for road freight. As a result, although rail freight delays are less frequent, incidents can be more costly.

Unnecessary or incompatible train inspections may be a source of border delays. Receiving railways usually carry out mechanical inspections of trains. The objective of such inspections is to reject wagons in poor conditions that might cause safety problems or require repairs. If a wagon is rejected, it must be shunted out of the train and the train must be remarshaled. Where inspections are inconsistent, a wagon authorized to proceed in one country may be rejected in another country. High variability in border-processing times combined with variations in train running performance can result in bunched trains and longer waits at borders for processing. These problems can be self-amplifying: unpredictable processing time at borders may itself be a major cause of service disruptions.

Importance of Backhaul Loads

Backhaul loads make any transport mode financially more sustainable. The ability to transport backhauls depends on a certain level of compatibility between the products being transported. Many of the constraints that once made products incompatible for backhaul have been overcome. For example, for transporting exports of grain, fertilizer was once deemed infeasible as a backhaul product because of its contamination of the bulk wagons. But contamination can now be avoided by using collapsible polypropylene liners, making bulk fertilizer a possible backhaul product in grain wagons.

Compatibility between containers and bulk products is more difficult to address. However, as containers must be backhauled anyway, it may be operationally feasible and financially viable to load grain and minerals into them, at least for rail transport to the deepwater port.

Zambia provides an example. Copper ingots exported from Zambia are loaded into what would otherwise be empty backhaul containers. In addition to saving on transport costs, this practice provides increased security for an otherwise high-risk product. Even chilled or refrigerated products can make use of regular backhaul container wagons through the use of clip-on refrigeration units (box 8.2).

Ownership of Containers

Despite efforts to increase compatibility between forward and backhaul loads, the high volume of imports compared with exports for most land-locked developing countries imposes another type of cost across corridors: demurrage charges for overdue containers. The international shipping lines that own many of the containers in circulation impose time limits, enforced by financial penalties, on how long a container may remain inland before being returned to the port. The limit is often as little as 15 days, and the daily penalty often increases with the number of over-limit days incurred. To avoid long delays, it is often less expensive for the importer to incur the cost of returning the container to the port empty than to incur the penalties associated with waiting for a return load.

Use of block trains (trains in which all wagons start from and end at the same point) and multiparty negotiations among the railways of countries along a trade corridor, customs and border police of the transit country, and the shipping lines that own the containers can help ensure that containers are returned to the port within the deadline. For single-wagon railway

---

BOX 8.2

Mali's Mango Exports

Adoption of a multimodal transport system has allowed landlocked Mali to export perishable products to distant markets. As a result of the new system, the transit time from Sikasso to Northern Europe was cut from about 25–30 days to about 12–15 days.

Mangoes are loaded onto refrigerated containers that are then loaded onto trucks. The trucks transport the mangoes across the Malian/Ivorian border to the town of Ferkessedougou. At Ferkessedougou, the containers are transferred from the truck to the rail platform. They are then shipped directly to Abidjan via railway and loaded onto ships bound for the European destination points. The refrigerated containers are equipped with distributed generator units, which ensure the continuity of the cold chain and allow the fresh fruit to be kept at a controlled temperature.

Source: World Bank 2010.

consignments and road freight, such negotiations are more difficult; as a result, these forms of transport are more likely to incur high demurrage charges.

Data and Information Sources

The main indicators of performance of rail services in a corridor include the following:

- corridor rail track condition (proportion subject to temporary speed restrictions)
- track capacity
- cargo volumes in each direction
- average haul length in corridor
- travel time
- time to exchange wagons
- border-crossing time
- price for transporting a 20-foot equivalent unit (TEU) or tonne
- number of times wagons are exchanged.

Data on rail operations are collected from train operators, regulatory authorities, port operators, customs officials, and major shippers. The main questions for discussion are outlined in annex 8A.

Potential Improvement Measures

Interconnection and Interoperability across Borders

Different regions have experimented with ways to provide seamless cross-border railway services. Several railway corridors have been defined in Southern Africa; arrangements are also in place in Europe and Central Asia.

The Southern Africa Railway Association cites the following as some of the advantages the coordination of cross-border railway service offers:

- single-train interchange points and inspections and therefore reduced operating costs for operators
- enhanced equipment utilization arising from reduced turnaround time for wagons and locomotives
- cross-border working of locomotives and crews
- international train timetables and joint planning and marketing
- avoidance of need to break up train loads
- matching of motive power to load offered

- communication among corridor railways on movement of international trains
- priority given to international trains in allocation of resources such as locomotives and wagons
- through billing and payment at one point for international shipments.

Although the approach is beneficial, it suffers from weaknesses in some of the railways whose infrastructure and systems cannot match the operations in the more advanced economies. For instance, some railway administrations are not able to track movement of cargo, compromising the integrity of the overall system. Therefore, while individual railways may know what is moving on each corridor, the data are not regularly shared with cooperating railway administrations. Still, the formation of corridor groups for railways show the potential in coordinating train operations internationally in a seamless manner. Kenya and Uganda extended this model further and obtained even tighter integration of their railway services (box 8.3).

Integration with Other Modes of Transport

Because of their limited reach, railways are almost always dependent on other modes, normally roads, to consolidate or distribute traffic. The most

---

BOX 8.3

Joint Concessioning of Railways in East Africa

The Northern corridor in East Africa connecting landlocked eastern Democratic Republic of Congo, Burundi, Rwanda, Uganda, and Kenya to the Port of Mombasa, in Kenya, comprises a road, railway, lake, and pipeline system. The rail system, which operates within Kenya and Uganda, has a narrow gauge (1,000 millimeters). It used to be part of a regional system with Tanzania. In fact, until the 1970s, the three were operated as one system, called East Africa Railways and Harbours Corporation (EARHC). The same corporation also operated ferries on Lake Victoria, providing a flexible intermodal transport service linking Kenya, Tanzania, and Uganda, predominantly along two corridors, the Northern corridor and the Central corridor between the landlocked countries and the Port of Dar es Salaam, in Tanzania. However, following the breakup of EARHC, the individual railways continued to deteriorate. By the early 2000s, they were in a bad state, with traffic volumes just a fraction of capacity.

BOX 8.3 *continued*

In 2005, operation of the railways in Kenya and Uganda was given in a concession to a private operator, Rift Valley Railways (RVR). The concession was a joint one, in recognition of the two systems' interdependence. The governments recognized the importance of an operational railway and adopted a joint approach to the management of the interconnected system. The joint concession enabled the system to exceed the minimum potential traffic thresholds for viability and made the investment attractive to the private sector.

The concession agreement granted exclusive rights to RVR for the provision of freight services in both Kenya and Uganda. However, rehabilitation of the network was slow, and traffic volumes remained small. In 2012, the system carried about 1.5 metric tonnes per annum (mpta), down from 2 mtpa in 2005/06, though volumes have since risen.

Despite the low volumes, the railways retain an advantage when it comes to pricing and have great potential. Rail tariffs are less than two-thirds those of road transport, though transit times are much longer and less reliable. Service from Mombasa to Nairobi takes 19–24 hours; service from Nairobi to Kampala takes three to six days. Still, the railway system offers landlocked Uganda a cheaper alternative to road transport.

The problems faced following the breakup of the railways in East Africa have been experienced elsewhere in Africa when parts of the integrated networks are concessioned in one country without the involvement of neighboring countries. Following concession in Southern Africa, there was reduced cooperation by railways, a decline in overall performance, distortions in traffic routing patterns, and deterioration in infrastructure. As a result of the reduced capacity, some traditional rail traffic moved to the road, causing immense damage to road pavements. To avoid similar problems, the Kenya-Uganda case has attempted to deal with the coordination aspects.

efficient railways offer lower unit prices, as shown in the example of South Africa's system (figure 8.1). Less efficient systems can have unit rates that are higher than road transport. Where this is the case, they can lose traffic to road transport.

The interfacing of railways and other modes of transport in a corridor takes place at intermodal facilities, such as inland container depots (ICDs). There are several considerations in deploying ICDs or dry ports as part of

FIGURE 8.1 Road and Rail Freight Tariffs in Southern Africa, 2010

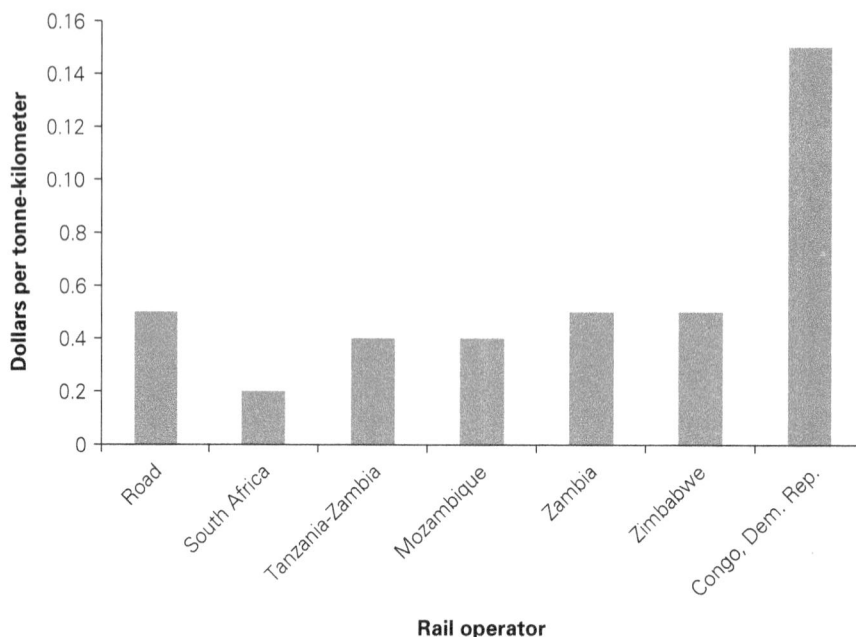

corridor infrastructure. ICDs are typically located on the outskirts of a hub city, where the price of land is lower, arterial highways and railways provide good access, and freight does not interfere with urban traffic or traffic at a rail head. ICDs are found along most corridors in all regions of the world. In Africa, several landlocked countries have or are planning ICDs with road and/or rail connectivity (table 8.1). When inland facilities are located near the final destination or an economic center, they serve as cargo consolidation and distribution centers. The role and attributes of inland facilities should be assessed to the same extent as other components of the corridor.

Several ICDs in Africa are transfer nodes between road and rail transport. ICDs can be managed by either the public or the private sector. Where such facilities handle international cargo, customs and other border-management services should be on site. In general, the rationale for an intermediate platform without multimodal connection or some other valid reason to interfere with the smooth flow of traffic is questionable, as the case of Nepal suggests (box 8.4).

TABLE 8.1 Examples of Rail/Road Interface Inland Container Depots in Sub-Saharan Africa

Country	Location	Corridor
Botswana	Gaborone	Trans-Kalahari
Burkina Faso	Ouagadougou, Bobo-Dioulasso	Tema-Ougadougou, Abidjan-Ougadougou
Cameroon	Ngaoundere	Douala-Bangui
Congo, Dem. Rep.	Beni, Mwene Ditu (Kasai)	North-South, Dar es Salaam
Côte d'Ivoire	Bouaké, Ferké	Abidjan-Ougadougou
Ethiopia	Mojo, Semera	Ethio-Djibouti
Kenya	Nairobi, Mombasa	Northern
Mozambique	Moatize	North-South
Namibia	Walvis Bay	Trans-Kalahari, Trans-Caprivi
South Africa	Johannesburg City Deep	North-South
Tanzania	Isaka, Mbeya	Dar es Salaam
Uganda	Tororo, Malaba, Kizarewe	Northern
Zimbabwe	Harare	North-South

BOX 8.4

Inland Container Depots in Nepal

Nepal is a landlocked country that has access to seaports via transit routes across India. In the early 2000s, Nepal, with support from the World Bank, constructed three inland container depots (ICDs) at the major border-crossing points with India. The largest is at a railhead, connected to the railway network of India. Trade traffic coming or going through Indian ports is moved by rail between the port and the ICD, where it is transferred to road transport. Shippers prefer the railway because it is cheaper than road transport; the Indian authorities prefer it because they can implement a more secure transit regime than they can with road transport.

The railway now handles more than 60 percent of Nepal's container-ized third-country trade traffic, but operations are hampered by the requirement to run Nepali trade only on block trains. The current practice for Nepal and India is to operate Nepal-only trains between the dry port and the Port of Kolkata. Because cargo volumes are limited, the headway between trains is long. In addition, India Railways gives priority to passenger trains, neutralizing the potential network effects that could be derived from Nepal trade traffic riding on the back of the denser Indian trade traffic flows. As a result, freight deliveries and transit times for Nepal are characterized by a high degree of uncertainty.

Exploiting Superior Customs and Border-Management Arrangements

Seamless international rail freight movement requires harmonization and agreement at the regional and bilateral level. Such measures are particularly important for developing countries with contiguous rail lines (in countries like India, Russia, and the United States, the ratio of international trade and transit trade through rails to domestic trade is low).

Railway networks built within national borders provide scope for multiple barriers for international rail freight services. Such barriers may have been acceptable before globalization, but modern demands based on globally integrated supply chains require cooperation and the physical integration of systems. The role of governments in facilitating international rail integration is important in many regions.

However, some improvements in performance can be gained through operational procedures, for example when locomotives and drivers change at the border. In principle, the process need not be time consuming and can be done alongside other needed technical operations. But to be efficient, the locomotive and crew that take over must be in place on time. Efficient exchange of information between the two railway systems is required. Such communication is difficult to achieve at many borders. In some corridors, the solution has been to fully integrate the two railway systems (examples include Kenya and Uganda, Burkina Faso and Côte d'Ivoire, and Argentina and Paraguay).

Studies conducted under the auspices of the Transport Corridor Europe-Caucasus-Asia (TRACECA) (2003) show that border-crossing procedures can be simplified and standardized if the railway company organizes its traffic in the form of block trains operating on a timetable between the seaport and the main destination in the landlocked country. If the traffic is largely containerized, control procedures can be kept to a minimum. TRACECA also recommends railway border-performance indicators to establish common standards.

Summary of Possible Interventions for Improving Rail Transport

Table 8.2 summarizes the most common rail transport issues and questions found in corridor projects and proposes possible interventions to address them. Actual interventions should be adapted to deal with specific constraints.

TABLE 8.2 Possible Interventions for Improving Rail Transport

Issue	Questions	Possible interventions
Performance of rail system	• What commodities and what quantities are moved by rail? • What is the capacity of the system? • What is potential traffic with improvements? • What are the cost, time, and reliability of the system? • What are the current and potential backhaul cargos? • Can the system move refrigerated containers? • Who owns and operates the system?	• Identify commodities for which rail has a distinct advantage, especially bulk or large volumes of containers. • Explore revival of the railway through concessioning to improve performance, when warranted by business fundamentals. • Concession corridor railways in different countries to the same operator.
Network interconnectivity	• What is the current degree of interconnection of railway services in the corridor? • Why and where are trains broken up? • What priority is given to freight versus passenger trains?	• Conclude bilateral and multilateral agreements for seamless international rail freight movement. • Operate rail services on a corridor basis for seamless movement, and run block trains. • Encourage joint operator marketing of services and through billing for services. • Facilitate fast interchange of wagons and exchange of locomotives where cross-border operations are not possible.
Competition and complementarity between road and rail services	• What are the strengths of rail over other modes? • What is the relative cost, time performance, and reliability of rail? • What is the minimum threshold for traffic flows for the short-run viability and long-term financial sustainability of rail?	• Improve railway performance, especially reliability and service frequency.
Customs and border management	• Are there separate procedures for clearance of railborne cargo? • Where does clearance take place? • Is railborne cargo subject to transit controls?	• Arrange with customs for light and fast transit procedures for rail traffic. • Provide customs and other border controls at the same locations as train servicing and interchanges rather than at the border.
Management of containers	• What are the time limits for the return of empty containers to shipping lines? • Is the system connected to an inland container depot or dry port for container consolidation and deconsolidation?	• Operate block trains to the extent possible, with fast turnaround times. Use block trains to ensure that containers are returned to the port consistently within the deadline.

Annex 8A Questions for Discussion of Rail Transport

A. Questions about the Rail Network and Services on the Corridor

1. What percentage of the track is single gauge? _____
2. What percentage of the track is double gauge? _____
3. What gauge is the rest of the track? Gauge _____ Percent of total _____
4. What percentage of the track has separate freight tracks? _____
5. What percentage of the track has electrified lines? _____
6. Which of the following statements about the system are true?
   - ☐ Advanced train control systems monitor train movements using train identification and automatic route setting.
   - ☐ Most freight wagons have double-axle bogies.
   - ☐ Heavy load wagons carry 70 tonnes or more.
   - ☐ Trains have more than 50 wagons.
   - ☐ The system has 24-hour freight terminal operations.
   - ☐ Privately owned rail wagons account for a significant part of the rolling stock for freight, other than tanker and hopper wagons.
   - ☐ Rail wagons are allowed to cross the border.
   - ☐ Bilateral quotas limit the number of wagons that can cross the border.
   - ☐ Maintenance of the track in the corridor is performed by the private sector.
   - ☐ A significant portion of the locomotives are less than 15 years old. Percent: _____
7. For which of the following are rail operations harmonized on both sides of the border?
   - ☐ Maximum train lengths
   - ☐ Maximum wagon capacity
   - ☐ Braking operations
8. Provide the following statistics on the system:
   Length of track on corridor: _____ kilometers
   Share of double track on corridor: _____ percent
   Type of train control: ☐ Dynamic ☐ Fixed block
   Average train speed: _____ kilometers per hour
   Maximum train density (number of daily trains on most dense corridor): _____
   Average annual distance per locomotive: _____ kilometers
   Kilometers of track per employee: _____
   Average tonne-kilometers per freight wagon: _____
   Maximum size of locomotives (brake horsepower): _____

B. Questions about Railway Operators

9. What is the annual traffic?
   Freight tonnes: _____
   Freight tonne-kilometers: _____
   Container 20-foot equivalent units (TEUs): _____

10. For rail freight, what is the percentage share of tonnes (or tonne-kilometers) for each cargo type?
    Liquid bulk: _____
    Dry bulk: _____
    Bagged or loose: _____
    Container: _____
    Construction material and project cargo: _____

11. What percentage of the traffic is generated from the following sites?
    Seaports: _____
    Cross-border traffic: _____
    Mines, refineries, and similar facilities: _____
    Manufacturing centers: _____
    Agricultural centers: _____

12. Who are the major shippers?
    ☐ Producers of raw materials and energy products
    ☐ Manufacturers and producers
    ☐ Agricultural processors
    ☐ International shipping lines or forwarders
    ☐ Traders
    ☐ Construction firms

13. What percentage of shipments are arranged by the following parties?
    Shipper: _____
    Consignee: _____
    Forwarder: _____

14. Does the railroad operate unit freight trains?
    ☐ Yes
    ☐ No

15. What percentage of these unit train operations carries bulk cargo?
    _____ Containers? _____

16. What proportion of track capacity is accounted for by:
    Passenger trains: _____
    Unit freight trains: _____
    Mixed-use trains: _____

17. Is priority given to passenger or freight traffic?
    ☐ Passenger traffic
    ☐ Freight traffic

18. What is the railroad's share of freight transport in the corridor? _____
19. Do most freight trains operate on a fixed schedule?
    ☐ Yes
    ☐ No
20. If not, does the schedule depend on when the train has sufficient cargo?
    ☐ Yes
    ☐ No
21. How does the uncertainty of departure and arrival times affect the competitiveness of rail relative to road transport? _____
22. What is the percentage share of private sector involvement in rail operations?
    Ownership of rail wagons: _____
    Organization of unit train operations: _____
    Dedicated services for high-volume cargo generators: _____
23. What type of multimodal terminals does the railroad have?
    ☐ Freight yards with warehousing
    ☐ Inland container depots
    ☐ On-dock or off-dock port container yards
24. What is the size of the fleet of freight wagons? _____
25. Does the rolling stock fleet include specialized wagons?
    ☐ Yes, single- or double-stack container wagons
    ☐ Yes, refrigerated wagons
    ☐ No
26. What are the maximum values for the following?
    Axle load: _____
    Wagon load: _____
    Train length: _____
27. What is the average annual level of utilization of the rail wagons in terms of the following measures?
    Tonne-kilometers: _____
    Loaded kilometers: _____
    Average trip length: _____
28. What percentage of railway services are freight-only services in the corridor? _____
29. What is the average number of train movements per day on the corridor in each direction? _____
30. What percentage of trains are freight trains? _____
31. What is the average number of wagons per train on this route? _____
32. For freight trains operating on the corridor, what are the average values for the following?
    Distance traveled: _____ kilometers

Number of freight wagons: _____

Amount of freight carried per loaded wagon: _____ tonnes

Percent empty wagons: _____

Travel speed and variation: _____ kilometers per hour

Time spent at stops or other delays: _____ minutes

Transit time and variation: _____ minutes

33. What is the average turnaround time for a freight train at the following places?

Gateway port: _____

Inland container depot: _____

Freight terminal: _____

34. What is a typical freight rate in the following units?

Per TEU-kilometer: _____

Wagon-kilometer: _____

Tonne-kilometer: _____

35. What are the major factors affecting train turnaround time?

☐ Rail yard productivity

☐ Availability of cargo

☐ Availability of locomotive rolling stock

☐ Railyard operating hours

36. Is information and communications technology used extensively in managing the railway?

☐ Yes

☐ No

37. What functions are performed by computerized systems?

☐ Accounting and cost control

☐ Booking transport and billing for services

☐ Calculating rates

☐ Fleet management

☐ Tracking shipments

☐ Planning/coordination with shipper

☐ Integrating sequential services and transactions

38. For which of the following is electronic data interchange used?

☐ Confirming orders

☐ Exchanging shipping documents

39. For which of the following are payments made using Internet banking or electronic transfers?

☐ Supplies

☐ Transport services

C. Questions about Cross-Border Movements

40. Are there rail connections to the networks in neighboring countries?
    - ☐ Yes
    - ☐ No
41. Do the tracks have the same gauge?
    - ☐ Yes
    - ☐ No
42. How are cross-border movements handled?
    - ☐ Exchange of locomotives at the border
    - ☐ Transloading near the border
43. What is the average time for crossing the border, including any transloading, and how does it vary? _____

D. Questions about Regulations

44. What is the axle-load limit? _____ What is the wagon load limit? _____

45. What documents are used for the carriage of goods on the railway?
    - ☐ Standard railway bill
    - ☐ Ocean bill of lading for dry port
    - ☐ Freight forwarders multimodal bill of lading
46. How are rail rates determined?
    - ☐ Regulated
    - ☐ Negotiated
    - ☐ Based on tonne-kilometers
    - ☐ Based on type of cargo

E. Questions about Impediments to Service

47. Which of the follow reduces the quality of service?
    - ☐ Condition of track and equipment
    - ☐ Maintenance standards and budgets
    - ☐ Track capacity
48. What is the principal constraint on the efficiency of freight train service in the corridor?
    - ☐ Rail line capacity as a result of
        - ☐ Train control system including signaling
        - ☐ Mix of passenger and freight
    - ☐ Condition of the track as a result of
        - ☐ Budgets for maintenance
        - ☐ Monitoring of track condition
        - ☐ Age of track and roadbed
        - ☐ Drainage
    - ☐ Terrain
        - ☐ Mountains

☐ Bridges
☐ Prioritization of passenger traffic
☐ Restrictions on commercial operations and pricing
☐ Market information

49. What will be the principal benefit of removing this bottleneck?
☐ Reduce transit time
☐ Reduce cost of service
☐ Increase reliability of delivery time
☐ Better connection with downstream activities

50. What are the principal disadvantages of freight trains relative to road transport?
☐ Longer travel time
☐ Uncertain delays in railyards
☐ Inadequate availability and condition of equipment
☐ Unbalanced flows
☐ Limited train slots
☐ Longer door-to-door movements

51. What is the major constraint to improving the competitive position of rail transport?
☐ Difficulty in managing unit train operations
☐ Conflicts with passenger operations
☐ Inability to provide scheduled movement
☐ Inability to provide daily movements
☐ Lack of coordination with cargo movements at seaports and border crossings

52. What efforts are being made to improve the competitiveness of rail system?
☐ Reorganization to create separate freight, container, and unit train operations
☐ Improvements in fleet management through better information and schedule maintenance
☐ Capital investment in rolling stock
☐ Increased private sector participation
☐ Improved cargo tracking systems
☐ Organization of intermodal services
☐ Improvements in signaling and information systems

53. Rate the following:
☐ Train operators: ☐ Good ☐ Adequate ☐ Poor
☐ Clearing and forwarding agents: ☐ Good ☐ Adequate ☐ Poor
☐ Customs: ☐ Good ☐ Adequate ☐ Poor

54. If poor, what are the reasons? _____

Notes

1. Railways achieve financial sustainability when they have sufficient long-term financial resources to cover operational costs, invest, and meet debt service and other financing requirements (World Bank 2011).
2. Two or three containers can be loaded onto a single rail flatcar with no space between in such a way that the doors of one container are right up against the doors of the next, making it impossible to open them en route.

References

Bullock, R. 2009. "Off Track: Sub-Saharan African Railways, Africa Infrastructure Country Diagnostic." Background Paper 17, World Bank, Washington DC.

TRACECA (Transport Corridor Europe-Caucasus-Asia). 2003. *Harmonization of Border Crossing Procedures: Recommendations of Border Harmonization Evaluation Workshop.* Baku, Azerbaijan.

World Bank. 2010. *Growing Mali's Mango Exports: Linking Farmers to Markets through Innovations in the Value Chain.* Washington, DC: World Bank.

———. 2011. *Railway Reform: Toolkit for Improving Rail Sector Performance.* Washington, DC: World Bank.

———. 2012. *Eurasian Cities: New Realities along the Silk Road.* Washington, DC: World Bank.

Resources

Citadel Capital. 2008. *How to (Re)Build a Better Railroad.* Citadel Capital, Cairo. http://citadelcapital.com/wp-content/files_mf/1323170077CCHowToRVR.pdf. This brochure outlines the business, political, and financial case for the investment by Citadel Capital in the joint Kenya-Uganda Railway system.

UNECE (United Nations Economic Commission for Europe). 2010. *Euro Asia Transport Links: Inland versus Maritime Transport Comparison Study.* Geneva. http://www.unece.org/fileadmin/DAM/trans/doc/2010/wp5/ECE-TRANS-WP5-GE2-05-Draft%20EATL%20Comparison%20Study-id2.pdf. This report presents the findings of a comparative assessment of Euro-Asian maritime and rail links. It is based on a survey of logistics firms. As the response rate to the questionnaire was just 14 percent, the report draws on various other sources of information as well.

World Bank. 2011. *Railway Reform: Toolkit for Improving Rail Sector Performance.* Washington, DC. http://www.ppiaf.org/sites/ppiaf.org/files/documents/toolkits/railways_toolkit/index.html. The railway toolkit provides a comprehensive and detailed exposition of rail sector issues (including railway economics and pricing, financial sustainability of railways, private sector participation in railways, and creating an enabling environment for commercial railway structures) in both developed and developing countries. It includes detailed case studies of railway reforms in Australia, China, India, Lithuania, Morocco, Poland, and Camrail in West Africa.

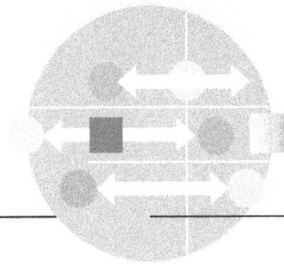

Shipping and Maritime Transport

The quality and efficiency of maritime services depends in part on the efficiency of hinterland connections through overland corridors. Volumes of traffic depend in turn on the ports' physical infrastructure and capacity as well as the services provided at the port by port terminal operators, customs and other border agencies, customs brokers, freight forwarders, land transport operators, and banks. Most analyses and projects look at ports that serve an inland corridor, with the objective of improving the efficiency of land transport corridor in order to deliver exports at a competitive price to overseas destinations or reduce the cost of importing from overseas origins. With this broader perspective, this module considers the maritime links between the ports of land corridors and the overseas ports at the other ends of those links.

Maritime services provide the link between land corridors and the overseas countries that are the destination of exports and the origin of imports. The first issue a trader needs to address is whether there are maritime services to and from the port to the overseas countries and if so, whether the products can be shipped at a cost and time that make it profitable to do so. The main considerations relate to maritime tariffs, service frequency and reliability, and the scope of destinations served. There is therefore a link between traffic volumes and port connectivity to other ports across

FIGURE 9.1 Vicious Circle of Port Volumes and Port Attractiveness

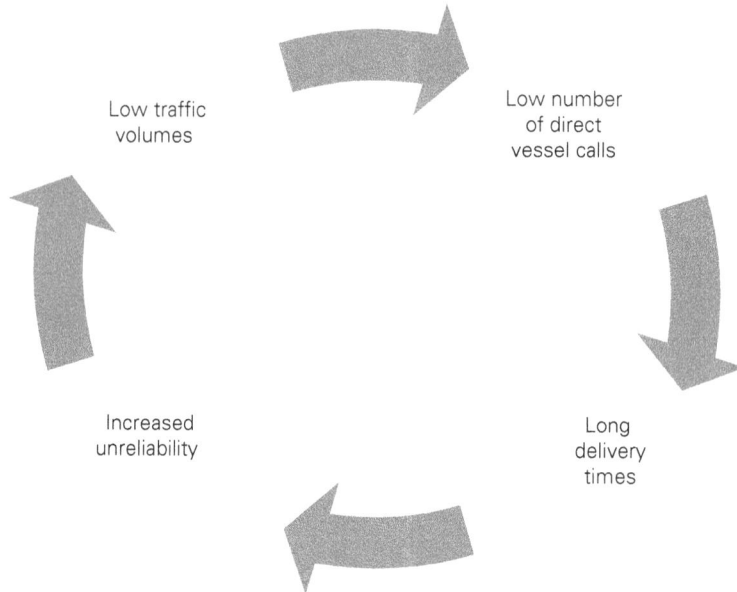

the world. This link can create a vicious cycle, which can become virtuous if corridor volumes increase in tandem with port attractiveness (figure 9.1).

This module is structured as follows. The first section identifies the main issues faced concerning the functioning and impact of shipping and maritime transport on corridor performance. The second section presents the data and information that are required to understand the issues. This section is complemented by an annex that lists the key data and questions that can be asked of stakeholders to obtain both quantitative and qualitative data on shipping and maritime transport. The third section identifies possible solutions to the most common issues. The last section summarizes these solutions.

Types of Container Services

There are three basic types of container services: hub-to-hub services supported by feeder services to and from the hubs, "pendulum services," and feeder services. The main factor that affects the cost and quality of a maritime service between any two ports is the level of demand. If demand for either the origin or destination port is high, the port may serve as a hub for at least one shipping line. If demand is not high, the port probably serves as a feeder to a larger port.

Hub-to-Hub Services

Hub-to-hub services were developed in the 1980s and 1990s, with most services operating along the major global trade lanes between East Asia and the North American West Coast, East Asia and Europe through the Suez Canal, and Europe and the North American East Coast. These routing patterns became particularly pronounced with the introduction of post-Panamax container vessels, which were too large to pass through the Panama Canal. The large vessels had unit operating costs (costs per 20-foot equivalent unit [TEU]) about 25 percent lower than Panamax vessels (vessels that could pass through the Panama Canal). The most common type of service is now a hybrid, with pendulum services along the main routes supported by feeder services to other ports in the world.

If the level of demand from the hinterland of a port increases enough, it can encourage some shipping lines to provide direct trunk services, giving the port hub status, at least for that shipping line. Some hub ports depend almost exclusively on transshipment facilities between trunk and feeder services or in some cases between two or more trunk services themselves.

Many considerations influence where shipping lines decide to transship oceanbound cargo:

- *Handling capacity and port fees.* Typically, the fees for transshipped cargo are about a quarter of the fees of destination cargo. Shipping lines put pressure on ports to get low fees.
- *Location of major shipping routes.* Limiting the deviation from the optimal path between an origin and destination saves shipping lines money. Transshipment is discretionary and can be moved anywhere along a shipping route. Relay-type transshipment is used when two or more mainline services intersect and can be used to connect cargo between origin and destination. Shipping lines use this strategy to optimize and rationalize their vessel fleets and networks. They seek to minimize their system costs.
- *Deep harbor and entrance channel to accommodate large vessels.* Transshipment locations make sense when they are located in places with good geographical and natural conditions.
- *High productivity in the transshipment port.* Shipping lines seek to apply a supermarket approach in which they handle high volumes at low prices and high levels of efficiency.

Although some ports specialize in cargo transshipment, local demand usually forms the foundation for transshipment operations. For this reason, transshipping typically takes place at a transport hub. Where such ports have excess capacity, the transshipment cargo can be handled at marginal cost, leading to the low rates mentioned above.

Transshipment ports operate in a very competitive market with very low profit margins for shipping lines. If another hub port offers lower tariffs, better facilities, or even a chance for a trunk shipping line to play a role in the management of the port (providing the opportunity for preferential treatment for its services over those of other shipping lines), there is a good chance that the shipping line will shift its hub operations there. In 2000, for example, Maersk moved from Singapore to Tanjung Palapas, just 57 nautical miles away, because it offered lower charges, better service, and a chance to invest. It also moved most of its Mediterranean hub services from Gioia Tauro (Italy) to Suez East (the Arab Republic of Egypt), where it has an equity share in the container terminal. (For a discussion of the pressures on shipping lines to change the patterns of their services, see Ducruet and Notteboom 2012b.)

Pendulum Services

Pendulum services involve a set of port calls within a region (such as East Asia, Europe, the U.S. East Coast, or the U.S. West Coast), followed by a transoceanic transit and then by a set of port calls in another region, structured as a continuous loop. Their schedules are based on balancing the number of port calls with the frequency of service. Pendulum service between Asia and Europe might have on average 8–10 ships and involve 8–12 port calls. Most trans-Atlantic pendulum services have slightly fewer ships and make fewer port calls. In fact, Ducruet and Notteboom (2012a) argue that pendulum services are one example of an extreme form of shipping line bundling.

Rodrigue, Comtois, and Slack (2009) distinguish three types of pendulum services. In symmetrical services, the number of port calls in the origin region is about the same as in the destination region. In asymmetrical services, the number of calls in the origin and destination zones are very different. The number can differ because of differences in competition, demand patterns, and the frequency and quality of feeder services in the two regions.

A third type of pendulum services are interhub services, with calls at a small number of ports in both regions. This kind of service depends more on feeder services than the other types of pendulum service. It directly connects major hubs or gateways. The advantages of interhub services are high capacity, low unit costs, high frequency, and lower cycle time. They tend to be operated by the largest containerships.

A pendulum service is flexible in terms of the selection of port calls, particularly where the ports have nearby and competing ports (as is the case in East Africa, the East Coast of the United States, and Western Europe). The operator may opt to bypass one port and call at another in the same group if one port's efficiency is not satisfactory and its hinterland access is problematic, as often happens in the Mediterranean and Middle East. The pattern of port calls adapts to reflect changes in market demand and port efficiency, with important consequences for the frequency and range of maritime services available to serve a land corridor.

Feeder Services

Feeder services operate between hub ports and smaller ports. These services can be arranged on a direct hub port to feeder port basis, or the same ship can call at several feeder ports. Feeder services typically serve several ports smaller than hub ports that are either in the same country as the hub port but too far from it to be served effectively by land transfer of containers or in a neighboring or nearby country that does not support a hub port. The size of ships operating on feeder services and shipping rates vary significantly, depending on the type of feeder service provided. Reaching one port from another usually requires at least one transshipment. Although the per unit charges for the hub-to-hub service that the feeder services link do not vary much, as high levels of demand justify the use of large ships, the differences in unit tariffs between a pair of hub ports and a pair of feeder ports can be substantial.

Shipping services to feeder ports can be more costly on a TEU per kilometer basis, because they include the cost of transshipment in the hub port and the higher unit cost of the feeder service in smaller vessels. Hub-to-hub services have the lowest per unit tariffs and the highest frequency and reliability. Every time a container is transshipped from a hub-to-hub or pendulum service can increase the tariff by up to $300 per container (the size of the container does not seem to have much impact, as the cost is incurred in transferring the container from ship to shore and back again rather than in landside transfers or storage).

Each transshipment from a feeder to a trunk service can add several days to transit time, depending on the scheduling of the feeder services and the arrangements between the shipping companies for the feeder service and the trunk service (hub-to-hub or pendulum). As a result, transit time per kilometer is longer, because there is a loss of time in transshipment (up to several days if service to the feeder port is infrequent and does not coincide with pendulum service to the hub port). Although the time taken for these intermediate port calls is small in relation to the total transit time between the origin and destination ports (perhaps 2 days in a total transit of 22 days), it can affect the competitiveness of trade between neighboring countries where one is at the start of a feeder route and the other is at the end of the route. In such a case, one of the countries gains on its imports and the other gains on its exports.

Reliability of service from a hub port is also greater than from a feeder port, as there is no risk of a missed connection and there are fewer opportunities for the container to be lost, mishandled, or interfered with.

The higher unit cost and longer transit times have negative competitive consequences for land corridors that lead to feeder rather than hub ports.

Data and Information Sources

The main indicators of port performance in a corridor context include the following:

- the Liner Shipping Connectivity Index (LSCI)
- the number of vessel calls at the corridor port
- the shipping rates to and from main destinations
- the sailing time to main destinations
- the number of cargo transshipments between the port and main origins
- the average number of containers loaded/offloaded per vessel
- the transit time from port to inland facility (if any)
- the time limits for containers to be returned to port
- the deposit required for containers removed from port.

Annex 9A identifies issues for discussion with shipping lines.

Liner Shipping Connectivity Index

The Liner Shipping Connectivity Index (LSCI), published by the United Nations Conference on Trade and Development (UNCTAD), reveals how well a country is integrated into global liner shipping networks. Based on a weighted average of capacity and utilization data, it can be considered a proxy for the accessibility to global trade. The higher the index, the easier it is to access a high-capacity, high-frequency global maritime freight transport system and thus effectively participate in international trade. The LSCI can be considered as a measure of connectivity to maritime shipping and trade facilitation. It is particularly useful in determining global connectivity, which can have a significant impact on corridor performance, given the importance of maritime transport to trading costs and transit times.

The LSCI is measured each year for about 160 countries. It is based on the following components:

- *Number of ships calling.* Calls can involve imports, exports, or transshipments. Where the share of transshipment calls is high, the number of ship calls can be somewhat misleading, because calls are not related to the connectivity of the country to the global trade system but rather to the presence of a transshipment hub. Still, maritime services remain available for importers and exporters. This figure is normalized per capita, as countries with larger populations are likely to get more calls than countries with smaller populations.
- *Container-carrying capacity.* The higher the capacity, the greater the potential to trade on global markets. However, capacity may not be available for imports or exports; some of it might be taken up by transshipment. This figure is normalized per capita.
- *Number of shipping companies, liner services, and vessels per company.*
- *Average and maximum vessel size.* This measure is a proxy for economies of scale, as larger ships have lower shipping costs per TEU.

Economies with the highest LSCI values are actively involved in trade. They include the export-oriented economies of China and Hong Kong SAR, China, which ranked first in 2013, and the transshipment hub of Singapore, which ranks third (UNCTAD 2013). Large traders such as the United Kingdom (6th), Germany (8th), the United States (9th), and Japan (15th) also rank among the top 15. Countries such as Malaysia (10th), Spain (11th), the United Arab Emirates (16th), Egypt (17th), and Oman (19th) rank high because of the transshipment functions their ports perform.

Shippers are more likely to connect to a port or country that has a higher level of global shipping line connectivity than to one with poor connections, consistent with the model of preferential attachment developed by Barabasi and Albert (1999).[1] Using this logic, the LSCI can be a useful indicator for estimating likely trade flows on a corridor that has competing corridors connecting to different ports or countries. Connectivity explains in part why some landlocked countries make greater use of corridors to more distant ports than corridors connecting to nearer ports with less connectivity. An example is Zambia, where flows on the North-South corridor to Durban in South Africa are heavier than on the Dar es Salaam corridor to Tanzania, in part because Durban has greater connectivity than Dar es Salaam.

The LSCI is a good general indicator of shipping connectivity, but it provides values only at the country level (sufficient for trade corridors in many developing countries that only have one port) and only to all destinations taken together. Other sources are needed to assess connectivity between individual ports in a country and corridor and the origin and destination countries.

Surveys of Shipping Lines

A relatively simple but laborious way to obtain detailed information on shipping is through an Internet search of the websites of the container lines serving the corridor port. For each pair of ports, most websites can provide information on the following:

- range of services, including intermediate ports of call
- transit times between origin and destination ports
- frequency of each service (a pair of ports may have more than one service from each shipping line).

With a little ingenuity in logging into the website as a potential client, it is also possible to get an idea of the tariffs between ports. Other sources are needed for information about the quality or reliability of services. Commercial databases (by Drewry and INTTRA, for example) provide information on liner reliability on major trading routes. The INTTRA database tracks more than 18 percent of seaborne containers. For most developing countries, an Internet search and compilation of data other than tariffs can be completed within a few days. Finding tariff data can be much more time consuming.

Information on the quality and reliability of the services can be obtained from interviews with traders and shipping agents in the port that serves the corridor. These interviews are often carried out as part of a Trade and Transport Facilitation Assessment (TTFA). If the timing of the TTFA is convenient for the corridor study or project, data can be collected on the quality and reliability of maritime services. For instance, commercial traders can provide information on typical rates between ports. Commercial traders are usually able to negotiate better rates than spot market rates. However, even then, a comparison of the U.S. Army Universal Services Contract rates with rates paid by specific traders indicates that traders pay up to 25 percent more per TEU. Spot rates are, however, indicative of changes in negotiated rates over time.

Container rates vary widely in all shipping markets. Therefore, when comparing tariffs at pairs of ports, care is necessary to make sure that the rates are for the same time period. One way to do so is to use an index, such as the Shanghai Containerized Freight Index, a weighted average of the rates between Shanghai and 14 destination markets.

Trade publications

For more general data, *Lloyd's List*, the leading daily newspaper for the maritime industry, and the *Journal of Commerce* provide indicative container tariffs between main trading regions. The *Journal of Commerce* also provides an index of rates from Shanghai to the U.S. West Coast and East Coast and time series of rates over the previous year (table 9.1). *Containerisation International* provides occasional summaries of tariffs between major global regions.

U.S. Army Universal Services Contract

The Universal Services Contract of the U.S. Army provides tariffs for movements of 20-foot, 40-foot, and refrigerated containers between regions of the United States and ports around the world, for both inbound and outbound containers. Some of the tariffs are for specific overseas ports, others are for all ports within a region.

Adapting to Changes in Maritime Shipping

One reason why maritime transport is often excluded from trade corridors is that few policy or investment options can influence what services are provided. The cost, frequency, and quality of service are all driven by market considerations. The main consideration is therefore how ports and corridors that connect them to their hinterland adapt to changes in maritime shipping services.

TABLE 9.1 Container Spot Rates from Shanghai to Selected Ports, 2009–12

(Dollars per TEU)

| Date | Shanghai to | | | |
	Northern Europe	**Mediterranean**	**U.S. West Coast**	**U.S. East Coast**
October 2009	1,232	1,279	1,431	2,439
May 2011	830	980	1,850	3,200
May 2012	1,818	1,872	2,330	3,490

Source: Journal of Commerce, https://www.joc.com/search/site/spot%20rates?page=1.

Note: TEU = 20-foot equivalent unit.

Several recent developments are likely to have significant—but so far unknown—impacts on the pattern of shipping services, and therefore ports and their corridors:

- the widening of the Panama Canal
- the increase in vessel sizes
- the rise in fuel prices
- the threat of piracy
- the amalgamation of container shipping lines
- the introduction of specialized vessels.

Expansion of the Panama Canal

The expansion of the Panama Canal, expected to open for business in 2015, will have a huge impact on some pendulum services across the world. It will become possible for larger vessels (up to 12,500 TEU) to cross from the Pacific to the Atlantic Ocean through the Canal. These changes can in turn affect the pattern of feeder services. There is little that can be done about any of these changes, other than to encourage port authorities and container terminal operators to provide the services larger ships will need (see Module 10).

Widening of the Panama Canal will allow Post-Panamax ships from East Asia to transit the Panama Canal and serve ports on the East Coast of the United States. Pendulum services that currently operate from East Asia to the U.S. West Coast will thus have new options. Implementation of these options could change the pattern of feeder services in the Caribbean and along the west coast of South America. The new pendulum services could also reach Europe, possibly restarting round-the-world routes.

Increase in Vessel Sizes

The introduction of very large container ships on the major trade routes is resulting in a cascading of larger vessels to some feeder routes. The increase in ship size is likely to reduce the frequency of service. In the late 1990s, feeder vessels of only 500 TEU were most common. A few years later, 800 TEU vessels entered service. Feeder ships of 2,000 TEU are now operating, though on most routes ships are typically 500–1,500 TEU. The main reasons for the increase in size is the cascading of smaller size ships as larger vessels enter service on the hub-to-hub routes, increasing demand for containers to feeder ports, and the concentration of

TABLE 9.2 Types of Feeder Vessel

Feature	Small (500 TEU)	Medium (850 TEU)	Medium-large (1,700 TEU)
Dimensions (meters)	100 x 18 x 6.5	135 x 21.3 x 8	176 x 24 x 9
Maximum capacity (TEU)	500 (372 at 14 tonnes)	840 (526 at 14 tonnes)	1,700 (1,050 at 14 tonnes)
Deadweight tonnage	5,250	9,000	16,250
Gross tonnage	4,000	7,600	11,250
Speed (knots)	15.5	19.0	21.0
Type of holds	Covered	Open top (center) and covered (front)	Open top
Type of ship	Geared or gearless vessels	Usually gearless, with two large open-top holds	Usually gearless, sometimes twin-engined to improve maneuverability

Source: Containership-Info, http://www.containership-info.com.

Note: TEU = 20-foot equivalent unit.

hub-to-hub services on routes with higher demand. The use of larger feeder vessels increases demand for better facilities at feeder ports, especially length of berths and terminal handling infrastructure. (Table 9.2 gives the characteristics of common sizes of feeder vessels.)

The type and size of feeder vessels depend on the demand for containers at the feeder port (it is more important to maintain frequency with a small ship than to reduce unit operating costs with a larger vessel). The type of ship depends on the facilities available at the feeder port. If the port does not have gantry cranes, the ship needs to have an on-board crane.

Rise in Fuel Prices

The rise in fuel prices in recent years has had profound effects on shipping line operating practices and pricing. Shipping lines have resorted to slow steaming to conserve fuel, leading to longer sea voyage times. Pressure to reduce overland transit times therefore has to be seen within the context of trends in deep sea shipping services. The increase in fuel costs has also led shipping lines to add a variable bunker adjustment factor to their rates, which has caused prices to rise on some routes. It is important to explore the total prices per TEU on the main routes linking a corridor port to the global economy relative to competing ports.

Impact of Piracy

The threat of piracy, especially in the Horn of Africa, has affected the routing of some services from East Asia to Europe. Some shipping lines have changed their routes to avoid the Suez Canal and instead now go around the Cape of Good Hope. This change has affected not only the routing of pendulum services between East Asia and Europe but also the pattern of feeder services throughout the Middle East, East and West Africa, and the Mediterranean. Ports in West Africa have seen an increase in services, while there has been a reduction, albeit small and possibly temporary, in services to ports in East Africa.

Amalgamation of Shipping Lines

The number of container shipping lines fell dramatically in the last decade, through both mergers and financial failures. The impact was exacerbated by the establishment of commercial arrangements among the remaining shipping lines in which they purchase capacity on one another's ships. Amalgamation of shipping lines reduces the frequency of service to many midrange and smaller ports. It is important to establish trends in shipping line competition dynamics in the services connecting to ports within the corridor.

Introduction of Specialized Vessels

For regions in which ports have been slow to invest to become hub ports, shipping lines have developed special ships to make best use of available port capacity while still operating feeder services. An example is West Africa, where many ports are trying to achieve hub status but until recently none of them had invested enough in additional facilities to become hubs.

At least one shipping line (Maersk) designed a new class of container ship (WEMAX) to continue providing low-cost services to multiple ports without the need for transshipment. The new 4,500-TEU vessels are purpose-built to provide direct links from Asian to West African ports without the need to pass through a hub port. The ships are 265 meters long with a draught of 13.5 meters.

Summary of Possible Interventions for Improving Maritime Transport Services

Table 9.3 summarizes the most common shipping and maritime transport issues and questions found in corridor projects and proposes possible interventions to address them. Actual interventions should be adapted to deal with specific constraints.

TABLE 9.3 Possible Interventions for Improving Maritime Services

Issue	Questions	Possible interventions
Port connectivity	• Do maritime services serve the main overseas destinations of the export products transported through the land part of the corridor? • What is the type, frequency, and reliability of services? • Do maritime services allow imported products to arrive at a cost that makes them competitive in their destination markets? • Are the shipping lanes leading to the port at risk of piracy?	• Explore potential for consolidation of cargo to increase vessel calls.
Port performance	• What is the level of performance of the port? • How does it compare with that of other ports in the corridor and competing corridors?	• Improve port performance. • Assess the relative performance of competing ports.
Hinterland connections	• Is the port linked to container freight stations or dry ports? • What is the capacity of linked facilities, including the transport connection? • Do shipping lines provide through bills of lading?	• Determine the capacity of linked facilities and the efficiency of the connecting transport system. • Encourage shipping lines to provide through bills of lading. • Improve the transit system between the port and inland facilities.
Port infrastructure	• Are maritime services limited by the facilities available in the corridor ports? If so, to what extent do those limitations affect the competitiveness of exports or the affordability of imports? • Is infrastructure a constraint?	• Improve port facilities, depending on cargo potential.
Shipping lines	• What are planned changes in vessel size? • What are the likely impacts of any port development plans, including the plans of shipping lines?	• Assess the likely impact of change in vessel size on port connectivity. For example, introduction of larger vessels may reduce both tariffs and frequency, with different implications for different products traded.

Annex 9A Questions for Discussion of Shipping and Maritime Transport

A. Port Authority

1. Which of these statements is true about container services at the origin or destination port?
   - ☐ Mainline carriers make frequent scheduled calls at the port.
   - ☐ Mainline services call at the port as part of a string for a particular service (each string includes different combinations of ports but common starting and end points).
   - ☐ Larger regional services with vessels larger than 1,200 20-foot equivalent units (TEUs) call at the port.
   - ☐ Shuttle feeders provide pendulum services connecting to a regional transshipment port.
   - ☐ Most of the container services calling at the port have weekly or biweekly service on a fixed day of the week schedule.
   - ☐ Larger vessels can enter without pilots (with certified masters) or tugs (with bow and stern thrusters).
   - ☐ The gateway port operates as a landlord leasing out facilities that the private sector operates _____ percent of throughput by private operators.
   - ☐ The container terminal operates under concession agreements with private terminal operators.
   - ☐ The container terminal has Panamax or Post-Panamax gantry cranes.
   - ☐ The container and other cargo terminals have on-dock rail services at the back of the terminal, allowing for direct transfer to rail wagons.
   - ☐ Private off-dock container yards are used for storage of loaded import containers.
   - ☐ A distribution park located within or next to the port provides bonded storage for cargo that is reexported or locally distributed.
   - ☐ The port has full truck scanners for checking containers being loaded onto a vessel.
   - ☐ Some containers are equipped with radio frequency identification (RFID) tags for tracking. Percentage with RFID: _____
   - ☐ The port community has a computerized information system that allows the port and its users to exchange information on the status of cargo moving through the port and on regulatory procedures
   - ☐ The port accepts payment for port charges through automatic account debiting on local banks.
2. What are the maximum draft and length of vessels entering the port?

Maximum draft of vessels entering port: _____ meters

Maximum length of vessels entering port: _____ meters

3. Provide the following statistics about containers:

Number of container terminal operators in the port: _____

Maximum size container vessel calling at the port: _____ TEU

Length of container berths: _____ meters

Range of draft at these berths: _____ meters

Annual number of container vessels calling at the port: _____

Current volume of container traffic: _____ TEU

Average annual rate of growth in container traffic (last five years): _____ percent

Average dwell time for loaded containers: _____ days

4. Provide the following statistics about dry bulk:

Number of terminals in the port: _____

Length of cargo berths: _____ meters

Range of draft at these berths: _____ meters

Annual number of bulkers calling at the port: _____

Average time at berth: _____ hours

Average berth waiting time: _____ hours

Current volume of traffic: _____ metric tonnes

Average annual rate of growth in traffic (last five years): _____ percent

5. Provide the following statistics about liquid bulk:

Number of terminals in the port: _____

Length of cargo berths: _____ meters

Range of draft at these berths. _____ meters

Annual number of tankers calling at the port: _____

Average berth waiting time: _____ hours

Current volume of traffic: _____ metric tonnes

Average annual rate of growth in traffic (last five years): _____ percent

B. Container Shipping Line

6. What routes do your vessels serve? _____

7. What is the range in the size of the vessels (TEU) for each route? _____

8. What kind of vessels are they?
   ☐ Feeder vessels
   ☐ Vessels making direct calls

9. If feeder calls, what are the main transshipment hubs? _____

10. What is the frequency of vessel calls for each of the routes?
    ☐ Several times per week

☐ Weekly service
☐ Fortnightly service
☐ Monthly service
☐ Less frequently than once a month
11. Are vessel calls
☐ On fixed day of the week
☐ At fixed intervals
☐ Variable
12. What was the volume of inbound and outbound traffic last year?
_____ TEU
13. What percentage of boxes is shipped?
Container yard to container yard: _____
Under through bill of lading: _____
14. What complementary services are provided?
☐ Pickup/delivery on a through bill of lading
☐ Stuffing/destuffing
☐ Off-dock or on-dock storage
☐ Consolidation and warehousing (through an affiliate)
15. What are the average, minimum, and maximum times for the following?
Waiting for a berth: Average _____ Minimum _____ Maximum _____

Berth turnaround: Average _____ Minimum _____ Maximum _____

Container dwell time: Average _____ Minimum _____ Maximum _____
16. What is the typical and maximum berth throughput? _____ boxes per vessel hour
17. What is the average terminal handling charge per TEU?
To the shipper for exports: _____
To the consignee for imports: _____
18. Are ship manifests submitted electronically?
☐ To the port
☐ To customs
19. Are computer systems used to
☐ Report the status of the container as it moves through the ports. If so, to whom? _____
☐ Coordinate the activities of the shipping line, terminal operator, and customs for moving containers through the port
☐ Coordinate the payments by consignees of duties and taxes, port services, and shipping services

20. What is the average time to clear import containers?
    Without physical inspection: _____
    With physical inspection, including moving the box to the inspection area: _____
21. Are there significant delays as a result of any of the following?
    ☐ Availability and time required for pilotage
    ☐ Port state control
    ☐ Scanning
22. What are the major impediments to improvements in efficiency of port operations?
    ☐ Berth capacity
    ☐ Storage area
    ☐ Waterside access, depth
    ☐ Landside access, congestion
    ☐ Availability of storage
    ☐ Port charges
    ☐ Coordination between port users and port management
    ☐ Coordination between port and regulatory agencies
23. What current or planned improvements in the port are expected to increase the amount and quality of shipping services in the port?
    ☐ Increase in draft
    ☐ Expansion of terminal facilities
    ☐ Better integration of cargo handling and cargo clearance
    ☐ Improvements in landside access to the port
    ☐ Changes in the port management structure
    ☐ Revisions of port pricing structures and policies
24. Rate the following:
    Port authority: ☐ Good ☐ Adequate ☐ Poor
    Terminal operator: ☐ Good ☐ Adequate ☐ Poor
    Truck operators: ☐ Good ☐ Adequate ☐ Poor
    Rail operators: ☐ Good ☐ Adequate ☐ Poor
    Port terminal operator: ☐ Good ☐ Adequate ☐ Poor
    Clearing and forwarding agents: ☐ Good ☐ Adequate ☐ Poor
    Customs: ☐ Good ☐ Adequate ☐ Poor
25. If poor, what are the reasons? _____

Note

1. In the Barbasi-Albert model, a network grows as each new node attaches itself stochastically to another, with a bias toward better-connected nodes.

References

Barabasi, A., and R. Albert. 1999. "Emergence of Scaling in Random Networks." *Science* 286 (5439): 509–12.

Ducruet, C., and T. Notteboom. 2012a. "Developing Liner Service Networks in Container Shipping." In *Maritime Logistics: A Complete Guide to Effective Shipping and Port Management*, edited by D.W. Song and P. Panayides, 77–100. London: Kogan Page.

———. 2012b. "The Worldwide Maritime Network of Container Shipping: Spatial Structure and Regional Dynamics." *Global Networks* 12 (3): 395–423.

Journal of Commerce, https://www.joc.com/search/site/spot%20rates?page=1.

Rodrigue, Jean-Paul, Claude Comtois, and Brian Slack. 2009. *The Geography of Transport Systems*, 2nd ed. New York: Routledge. http://people.hofstra.edu /geotrans/index.html.

UNCTAD (United Nations Conference on Trade and Development). 2013. *Review of Maritime Transport*. Geneva: UNCTAD. http://unctad.org/en /PublicationsLibrary/rmt2013_en.pdf.

Resources

Fink, Carsten, Aaditya Mattoo, and Ileana Cristina Neagu. 2001. "Trade in International Maritime Services: How Much Does Policy Matter?" *World Bank Economic Review* 16 (1): 81–108. http://citeseerx.ist.psu.edu/viewdoc/download ?doi=10.1.1.12.6888&rep=rep1&type=pdf.
Maritime transport costs impede international trade. The authors examine why these costs are so high in some countries and quantify the importance of two explanations: restrictive trade policies and private anticompetitive practices. Both matter, they find, but private anticompetitive practices have greater impact. Trade liberalization, and the breakup of private carrier agreements, would lead to a reduction in average liner transport prices of a third and cost savings of up to $3 billion on goods carried to the United States alone. The policy implications are clear: not only should government policy be further liberalized, there should be stronger international disciplines on restrictive business practices. The authors propose developing such disciplines in the current round of services negotiations at the World Trade Organization.

Hall, P., R. J. McCalla, and B. Slack, eds. 2011. *Integrating Seaports and Trade Corridors*. Farnham, United Kingdom: Ashgate Publishing Ltd.
This book has 3 parts and 16 chapters, each by a different author. The first part examines global economic change and its implications for ports, trade corridors, and supply chains. The second part deals with measuring and improving gateway and corridor performance. The third part presents six international case studies. The case study of West Africa provides a complex benchmarking system applied to 13 port/corridor combinations. The text is more conceptual than practical, but it provides a framework for considering the main issues affecting trade corridors and ports.

Rodrigue, Jean-Paul, Claude Comtois, and Brian Slack. 2009. *The Geography of Transport Systems*, 2nd ed. New York: Routledge. http://people.hofstra.edu/geotrans/index.html.

This volume provides basic but detailed information on transport systems. It covers both conceptual and methodological approaches. It is not specifically concerned with trade corridors, but the topics it covers, including of sea ports, are of direct relevance to corridor analysis. The book examines globalization, supply chain management, energy, and the environment, among other topics. One of its nine chapters is allocated to international trade and freight distribution; most of the other chapters relate to maritime transport.

UNCTAD (United Nations Conference on Trade and Development). 1985. *Port Development: A Handbook for Planners in Developing Countries*, 2nd ed. Geneva: UNCTAD. http://r0.unctad.org/ttl/docs-un/td-b-c4-175-rev-1/TD.B.C.4.175.REV.1.PDF.

Although now dated, this handbook provides a guide to the many issues involved in port planning and practical advice on how to address them. Many of the parameters of design of port components are still applicable, as ship dimensions are included in the design parameters.

———. 2013. *Review of Maritime Transport*. Geneva: UNCTAD. http://unctad.org/en/PublicationsLibrary/rmt2013_en.pdf.

This annual publication is the most comprehensive review readily available of developments in maritime transport over the year prior. The 2013 version has six chapters and five annexes, covering:

- developments in international seaborne trade
- structure, ownership, and registration of the world fleet
- price of vessels and freight rates
- port and multimodal developments
- legal issues and regulatory developments
- developing countries' participation in maritime businesses.

One of the annexes has the latest scores and rankings of the Liner Shipping Connectivity Index.

———. UNCTAD Liner Shipping Connectivity Index. http://archive.unctad.org/templates/page.asp?intItemID=2618&lang=1.

UNCTAD's Liner Shipping Connectivity Index (LSCI) aims at capturing a country's level of integration into the liner shipping network. It can be considered a proxy for accessibility to global trade. The higher the index, the easier it is to access a high-capacity, high-frequency global maritime freight transport system (and thus effectively participate in international trade). Countries with high LSCI values are actively involved in trade. The LSCI can be considered as both a measure of connectivity to maritime shipping and a measure of trade facilitation. It reflects the strategies of container shipping lines seeking to maximize revenue through market coverage.

Wang, J., D. Olivier, T. Notteboom, and B. Slack. 2007. *Ports, Cities and Global Supply Chains*. Farnham, United Kingdom: Ashgate Publishing Ltd.

This book has four parts, covering the conceptualization of port cities and global supply chains, shipping networks and port development, insertion of port cities into global supply chains, and corporate perspectives on the insertion of ports in global supply chains. The text focuses on ports and supply chains. As supply chains are closely related to trade corridors, it provides useful guidance on trade corridors and their relation to ports and maritime services. It also provides some useful statistics not readily available elsewhere, such as the number of containers per person for a sample of about 40 countries. The data are now rather old, however. A new edition of the book is overdue.

World Bank. 2007. "Module 2: The Evolution of Ports in a Competitive World." In *Port Reform Toolkit*, 2nd. ed. Washington, DC: World Bank. http://www.ppiaf .org/sites/ppiaf.org/files/documents/toolkits/Portoolkit/Toolkit/pdf/modules /02_TOOLKIT_Module2.pdf.

The *Port Reform Toolkit* provides guidance on port reform, not port design or the specifics of port operational efficiency. Although useful in providing a context in which the role of a port in a corridor context might change, it does not provide guidance on whether the exiting physical layout and design of a port (or more specifically a container terminal) are adequate for the roles of feeder or hub port.

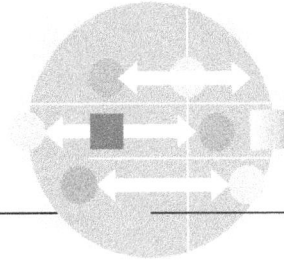

Port Operations

Ports play a fundamental role as gateways to a large proportion of international trade. They also provide a wide range of support services, both regulatory and operational, especially in handling the transfer of goods between land and sea transport systems. Ports play an intermediate role between the land and maritime parts of a trade corridor.

Perhaps not surprisingly, ports are also one of the major sources of cost, delays, and uncertainty in the transportation of goods, especially in low-income regions. Most corridor projects have or should have a port component, either to tackle infrastructure and operation constraints or to reduce procedural delays and costs.

Traditionally, ports were owned and operated by governments (national, regional, or local). Starting in the second half of the 20th century, the regimes of operating ports changed, as the inefficiencies of full public ownership and operation became apparent. New institutional arrangements were developed, of which the most effective was the landlord port model. A Toolkit by the World Bank (2007) tackles the institutional arrangements for ports and advocates the separation of port ownership and operation. In this model, the government continues to own the land at the port, but the superstructure facilities and operations are contracted or concessioned to private operators.

These new arrangements led to closer relationships between port operators and users (including shipping lines), to their mutual advantage.

Simultaneously with these reforms, but particularly over the last two decades, a new pattern of international trade emerged, in which products are not manufactured in one country and consumed in another but rather manufactured in several countries. In these globalized supply chains, the role of ports has expanded to include many of the value-adding services that are part of modern supply chains. These services can range from simple repackaging and labeling to significant steps in the manufacturing process. In order to be competitive in these activities, a port has to provide producers with high levels of performance, in terms of cost and time, as well as become a preferred location.

This module identifies the major issues and possible solutions faced in ports in a corridor context. It is structured as follows. The first section identifies the main issues concerning the functioning and impact of port operations on corridor performance. The second section presents the data and information that are required to understand these issues. This section is complemented by an annex that lists the key data and questions that can be asked of stakeholders to obtain both quantitative and qualitative data on port operations. The third section identifies possible solutions to the most common issues. The last section summarizes these solutions.

Main Issues Relating to Ports and Corridor Performance

Four main parameters affect the ability of a port to fulfill its current and future roles:

- *Physical characteristics of the port*. After the volume of trade through the port, the physical characteristics of the port have the greatest impact on whether a shipping line will provide frequent service to the port and perhaps consider it a hub. These characteristics have as great an impact on exports as on imports.
- *Efficiency of port operations*. Efficiency refers to the rate of loading and unloading containers, the land space available, and the container berth space available.
- *Dwell time of import and export cargo*. Dwell time affects the cost of importing or exporting freight through the port. It is susceptible to improvement with institutional and regulatory measures.
- *Port organization*. Port organization refers to the support services to maritime international trade, including services provided by shipping

agents, freight forwarders, logistics service providers, and transport operators.

Physical Characteristics

Four physical characteristics affect the capacity of the port and its ability to handle ships of a given size:

- the dimensions (depth, width, and radius of curves) of the access channels
- the length and depth alongside the berths
- the dimensions of the turning circle for ships
- the space available for storing cargo and handling related services, such as truck parking, rail access, and customs and other regulatory and control functions.

The depth and width of the access channels and the port berths determine the size of ships that can use the port; the size of ships affects their unit operating costs and therefore the maritime tariffs that are charged and the competitiveness of the trade corridor served by the port. The design of container ships takes account of the number of ports that can accommodate them. As argued in Module 9, as larger ships enter service on the highest-demand routes, larger vessels are cascaded to routes with less demand. Smaller ports have to adapt to be able to accommodate the larger entrants. Doing so may entail deepening entrance channels and berths, hence the preponderance of channel depths of 25–35 meters (figure 10.1).

FIGURE 10.1 Channel Depths of Ports Worldwide, 2009

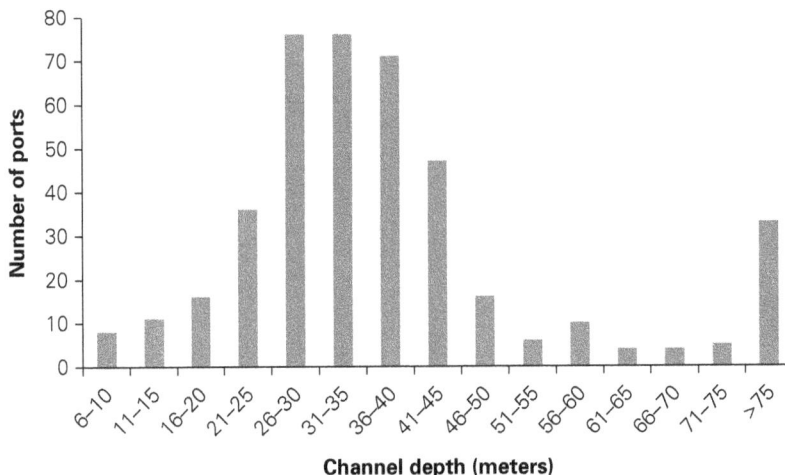

Source: Rodrigue, Comtois, and Slack 2009.

Each new generation of container ships needs deeper and wider access channels and larger minimum radii of their curves (if they have any). The first generation of container ships had a draft of about 9 meters and needed channel depths of about 11 meters. Fourth-generation ships (Post-Panamax) have a draft of about 11 meters and need a channel and berth depth of about 13 meters. The largest Suezmax container ships have a draft of almost 16 meters and need channel depths of almost 18 meters (table 10.1).

The access channels to some upstream ports have a natural depth of only about 10–13 meters, enough for the second-generation feeder ships with a capacity of up to about 2,000 20-foot equivalent unit (TEU). Most have access channels adequate for Panamax vessels of up to 4,000 TEU, and a few have the 14 meters necessary for Post-Panamax vessels of up to 8,000 TEU per channel (table 10.2).

TABLE 10.1 Dimensions and Capacity of Different Generations of Vessels

Period	Vessel type	Length (meters)	Draft (meters)	Capacity (TEU)
1956–70	Converted cargo, converted tanker	135–200	< 9	500–800
1970–80	Cellular container ship	215	10	1,000–2,500
1980–88	Panamax	250–290	11–12	3,000–4,000
1988–2000	Post-Panamax	275–305	11–13	4,000–5,000
2000–05	Post-Panamax Plus	335	13–14	5,000–8,000
2005–11	New Panamax	397	15.5	11,000–14,000
2011–	Maersk Triple E class	400	14.5	Up to 18,000

Sources: Rodrigue, Comtois, and Slack 2006, http://www.maersk.com.

Note: TEU = 20-foot equivalent unit.

TABLE 10.2 Area and Depth of Access Channel of Selected Medium-Size Ports, 2013

Port	Container capacity (TEU)	Area (hectares)	TEU/hectare	Depth of access channel (meters)
Douala	200,000	14	14,286	8.5
Aden	300,000	35	8,571	15
Dar es Salaam	350,000	12	29,167	11
Djibouti	400,000	22	18,182	18
Bahrain	400,000	90	4,444	12.8
Alexandria	420,000	16	26,250	14
Abidjan	530,000	27	19,630	14
Mombasa	620,000	17	36,471	10

Trade and Transport Corridor Management Toolkit

TABLE 10.2 *continued*

Port	Container capacity (TEU)	Area (hectares)	TEU/hectare	Depth of access channel (meters)
Rio Grande	630,000	60	10,500	13.0
Montevideo	650,000	10	65,000	9.5
Puerto Limon	800,000	21	38,095	19.0
Buenos Aires	1,100,000	13	84,615	9.8
Standard for medium-size ports (100,000–1,000,000 TEU)			15,000	
Standard for large ports (more than 1 million TEU)			30,000	
Total	4,300,000	314	13,694	

Sources: World Ports (http://www.worldportsource.com/index.php) and port websites.

Note: TEU = 20-foot equivalent unit.

As larger container vessels cascade down to lower-demand routes, ports with shallower channel depths have to dredge the existing channels or build new ports with deeper access channels.

Although there is a high correlation between container ship capacity and required draft, the correlation is far from perfect, particularly for vessels of up to about 4,000 TEU capacity, which are often built for particular ports or routes (Palsson 1998). As an example, the new West African Maximum (WAFMAX) ships entering service with Safmarine are designed specifically for the East Asia to West Africa route, a route on which the major ports can accept only ships with a draft of 13.5 meters or less. The 22 new ships of this type have a capacity each of 4,500 TEU. Many of them will be geared, as many of smaller ports in the region do not have gantry cranes.

Channel width. A standard parameter for the width of an access channel is that it should be at least equal to the length of the largest ship using the channel. This parameter worked for ship sizes of up to about Panamax size; later generations of ships changed the relationship between beam and length, with a larger increase in length than beam. It is now better to use the beam of the ship as the basic parameter for channel width.

Most channels allow ships to pass in both directions at the same time, so the channel width (at which full depth needs to be maintained) is roughly four times the beam of the widest ship. This formula allows a margin of safety between the channels for each direction and between the channels and the shore. A complication can arise where there are curves in the access channel. The minimum radius of curvature of the channel is determined by both the length and beam of the maximum vessel.

Turning basin. The original standard design parameter for the width and length of a turning basin was that it should be at least five times the beam of the largest vessel expected to use the port or terminal when there are berths opposite each other. For example, the largest ships that can use the Suez Canal (Suezmax vessels) have a beam of 56 meters, so the minimum dimensions of a turning basin to handle them would be 280 meters. Turning vessels this size in this space would allow little margin for error, given that the turning maneuver requires at least two very large and powerful tugs that themselves have an overall length of about 30–35 meters. If, as would be usual, the tug had to push vertically when it is in the basin centerline, there would be only about 20 meters to spare. A greater allowance than the five times beam parameter would be needed to account for the effects of wind, currents, possible loss of power of the tug, and human error. Even increasing the factor to six would add little additional margin for error.

The dimensions of the turning basin may well be a constraint on further increases in vessel size. Often an increase in the dimensions of the turning basin comes at the cost of less container storage space. There is thus a trade-off between reducing the risk of an accident and losing container storage space.[1]

Where the turning basin is away from the berths, slightly different considerations apply. The critical vessel dimension is its length not its beam. For unfavorable maneuvering conditions, a turning basin diameter of four times the length of the largest planned vessel is required; in favorable conditions with modern navigation systems, a diameter of three times the length could be sufficient. Instead of a circle, maneuvering requirements may be satisfied by an ellipse with three times and two times the ship length as the axes, the main axis being lengthwise of the vessel's course.

Berth length. Berth length is determined by the method of docking ships, the location of the berths, and the number of berths needed. Alongside berthing requires a quay length equal to the length of the vessel plus 30–40 meters, or 1.2 times the length. For roll-on–roll-off (Ro-Ro) stern (or bow-to-shore) berthing, the required quay length is about 1.2–1.5 its beam. The minimum depth at the quay is determined by the design vessel's maximum draft. A safety factor for this value in the region of 1–2 meters should be added to cover any heaving motion as a result of wave disturbance.

The results of applying the dimensions of the expected maximum ship size to these formulas for berth and quay depth can then be compared with the dimensions of the port that serves the corridor to give an indication of whether the corridor port will need significant investment if it is to continue its current function or become a hub.

Cargo Dwell Time

The dwell time of containers in a port is one of the most studied and analyzed parameters of container terminal operation (figure 10.2). Analysis of port cargo dwell time serves several purposes (table 10.3). Long dwell times are disadvantageous to importers, who incur high additional costs, and to container terminal operators, whose scarce storage space is used up. In extreme cases, long dwell times can result in the port container yard becoming so congested that additional storage space is needed away from the port terminal.

There are so many parameters that can affect dwell time that few benchmark values have been produced that are reliable. Most studies start by comparing the dwell time of the port or terminal under consideration with the dwell time of comparable or competitive ports or terminals. These studies later use one of these times (or an average) as a benchmark or target that the proposed measures are expected to achieve.

FIGURE 10.2 Container Dwell Times at Selected Ports and Selected Economies, 2010

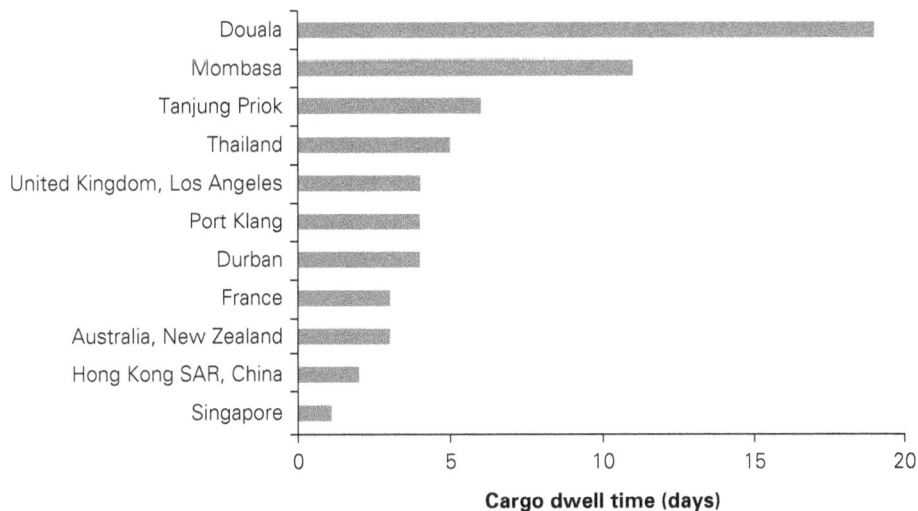

Sources: Raballand and others 2012; Arnold 2011; World Bank 2011.

TABLE 10.3 Uses of Port Cargo Dwell Time Analysis

Use	Methodology	Data input
Port comparator	Statistical analysis	Time distribution by flow
Infrastructure planning	Algebraic occupancy models	Time distribution and storage density
Logistics competitiveness	Supply chain models	Inventory cost, transit time
Port pricing	Elasticity models	Storage charges, duties
Bottleneck analysis	Probabilistic models	Time distribution by activity, likelihood of delay, queue length

Source: Nathan Associates 2010.

It is not the average dwell time that is most important to importers (they can manage their marketing, production, and other activities to take account of long dwell times) but rather the variation and uncertainty of dwell times. Uncertainty makes marketing and production more difficult and results in the need to hold larger stocks of the goods being imported.

Port cargo dwell time is a product of many actors: port operators, customs and other border agencies, and importers of goods. Through the actions of these parties, dwell time varies widely. In most ports, consolidated container loads typically take several days longer than full container loads.

Risk management systems generally establish three channels: green, which does not require any inspections; orange, which requires inspection of documents only; and red, which requires both document and physical inspection of the goods (see Module 5). Imports through the green channel can sometimes be cleared with a short period (hours in a few ports). Orange channels typically take several days longer, and red channels even longer in developing countries.

The World Bank (2011) used a logistics costs model to estimate the cost impact of cargo dwell time in the Port of Tanjung Priok, in Indonesia (the model is described in Module 13). It estimated the cost of the inventory needed to hedge the uncertainty of time using an acceptable probability of stock-out, dependent on the commodity or industry. In addition to the green, yellow, and red channels in Tanjung, there are three other categories of treatment by customs: a priority channel for precleared containers, a channel for traders and agents with impeccable records and secure finances (a subcategory of the green channel called MITA), and a channel for containers that have to be moved to an inland container depot (a subcategory of the red channel) (table 10.4).

TABLE 10.4 Cost Equivalent Impact of Cargo Dwell Time at the Port of Tanjung Priok, Indonesia

Channel	Share (percent)	Average dwell time (days)	Scale parameter (τ)	Equivalent inventory (days)	Logistics costs (percent)
Red	5	10	6.0	42	4.2
Yellow	5	7	5.5	36	3.6
Green	10	6	5.0	32	3.2
MITA nonpriority	40	6	5.0	32	3.2
MITA priority	40	4	4.0	25	2.5

Source: World Bank 2011.

Data and Information Sources

The key performance indicators for port operations in a corridor context include the following:

- average time from ship readiness to unload to gate out
- port container handling capacity
- volume of cargo
- port charges
- truck turnaround time in port
- port productivity, number and length of berths
- proportion of cargo removals by rail, road, and inland waterway.

Data on port operations are collected mainly from port terminal operators, regulatory authorities, shippers, shipping lines, and customs and other government agencies present in a port. Quantitative data should be collected from terminal operators, who normally keep such data as part of their normal business practices. Data of a more qualitative and process-oriented nature can be obtained through surveys of the various actors. The main interview questions are outlined in annex 10.A.

Container Terminal Operational Efficiency

There are three generally accepted measures of the efficiency of operation of a container port and some less widely accepted performance indicators for general and bulk freight. For containers, the three accepted measures are TEU per crane per year, TEU per hectare per year, and TEU per meter of berth per year. These measures are only indicators, as the performance of a container terminal against any one of them can be influenced by factors other than operational efficiency. The number of TEUs per crane, for example, can be influenced by the proportion of 20- to 40-foot containers, the proportion of 20- to 40-foot container spreaders, the level of automation of the port, and even the layout of the terminal.

For two of the three indicators, a higher value is not always desirable. If TEU per square meter of berth space becomes too high, it can be an indication of congestion in the port. If the TEU per hectare becomes too high, it can increase the time it takes off-loaded containers to find a storage space, which can slow the rate at which other containers can be off-loaded. The one indicator for which a higher value is better than a lower value is TEU per crane per year.

For the three indicators to be useful, they need to be measured using common definitions. There are many ways of measuring TEU per crane per year. Some include all hours of the year, others include only the hours the crane is in operation, yet others discount any time that the crane is under maintenance. The area used in the TEU per hectare per year indicator can include the entire terminal area (including roads and railways) or only the area available for storage of containers. The length of berths could include only dedicated container berths or all berths ever used by container ships.

In June 2010, Drewry Shipping Consultants Ltd conducted a survey of about 500 terminals around the world with throughput of at least 100,000 TEU per year in the period 2007–09. It arrived at three operational efficiency indicators for two sizes of container terminal (table 10.5).

Many of the ports serving trade corridors in developing countries are far from the benchmarks standards applicable to ports handling more than 1 million TEU per year. Of the sample of 12 medium-size ports that serve trade corridors in developing countries in the Drewry survey only 3 had TEU per hectare per year values lower than the efficiency indicator value. Still, the values for a terminal might not explain fully why it has a value different from the average; which may have nothing to do with operational efficiency but rather reflect space and equipment constraints. However, for each of indicator, it is possible to estimate what the operational efficiency could be given the characteristics of a terminal.

As an example, we provide a formula for estimating the storage area that would be appropriate for a terminal with a given pattern of demand, specific container stacking equipment, and dwell time for containers in the port. Applying the formula to a particular terminal can reveal whether the storage

TABLE 10.5 Port Operational Efficiency Indicators

Terminal size	TEU per meter of berth per year	TEU per crane per year	TEU per terminal hectare per year
Large (more than 1 million TEU per year)	1,350	130,000	< 30,000
Medium-size (less than 1 million TEU per)	550	80,000	< 15,500

Source: Drewry Shipping Consultants Ltd 2010.

Note: TEU = 20-foot equivalent unit.

area is sufficient for current demand and how much demand could increase before storage became inadequate. The formula can also be used to show the impact of changing any of the demand parameters, the container stacking equipment, or the container dwell time. When all feasible combinations of these changes are included in the formula, it can be used to assess how much storage area would be needed to satisfy a given level of projected future demand:

$$Area = \left(\frac{annual\ TEU\ volume * average\ dwell\ time}{3,560} \right)$$
$$* \frac{area\ per\ TEU\ (m^2)}{f} * \left(1 + \frac{p}{100} \right)$$

where area = storage area in hectares; m^2 = square meter; p = peak factor, as a multiple of the average area; and f = ratio of average to maximum stack height.

This formula takes account some of the container terminal–specific features that affect the area needed for container storage. A long average dwell time of containers in the port increases the need for storage space, as a high ratio of the actual to maximum stacking height reduces the space needed. This ratio is itself influenced by the ratio of loaded to empty containers, as empty containers can be stacked up to six or seven high whereas the maximum for full containers is four or perhaps five if the container yard is built on land rather than piles. The average space per TEU depends on the layout of the container yard and the equipment available (for example, maximum stacking height depends on the type of equipment available, with gantry cranes able to stack higher than straddle carriers). The peak factor is important, as a higher peak to average percentage requires more short-term storage space than a lower ratio.

Reach stackers take up much space between rows of stored containers and can stack containers only four high. They are therefore a constraint on the container storage area. Using the above formula, it is possible to determine the storage area needed in a port when using different types of cranes (table 10.6).

TABLE 10.6 Suggested Gross Container Storage Areas for Different Types of Cranes

Stacking method	Container height (number of containers)	Storage area (square meters/TEU)
Trailer	1	65.0
Straddle carrier	3	10.0
	4	7.5
Gantry crane	3	10.0
	4	7.5
	5	6.0

(table continues on next page)

TABLE 10.6 *continued*

Stacking method	Container height (number of containers)	Storage area (square meters/TEU)
Forklifts, side loaders	2	19.0
	3	13.0

Source: Memos 2004.

Note: TEU = 20-foot equivalent unit.

Similar formulas are available in standard port planning manuals to assess the needs for additional berth lengths and container cranes (or a change of type of crane, for example, from a high-profile [height] to a low-profile [height] crane).

Potential Solutions to Ports Issues

Improving Port Design

Channels, berths, and turning circles. If the current dimensions of the access channels and berths are insufficient for the projected future role of the port, the main option is to enlarge them. An alternative that may be necessary if the quantity of dredged material is very large or contaminated is to move the container terminal to another location that does not use the same access channels.

Land area. If the land area available for container storage is insufficient for projected demand, four options can be considered:

- Expand the land area of the existing terminal.
- Add storage space away from the port container yard.
- Make better use of existing storage space, by using stacking equipment that allows higher stacks or requires less space between rows of stacks or by encouraging importers to move their containers out of the terminal yard more quickly.
- Move the container terminal to another location.

Increasing Port Efficiency

One option for improving the efficiency of the container terminal is to concession it to a private operator.

Container cranes. Options for improving the efficiency of container cranes include the following:

- Replace existing equipment with equipment that has a higher operating capacity.
- Review ways of increasing use of existing cranes, such as operating additional shifts or days of the week.
- Add more cranes per berth, so that the overall loading and unloading rates can be increased. This measure may be necessary as ship sizes increase.

Berths. Options for improving the efficiency of berths include the following:

- Create incentives for ships to arrive at staggered intervals, by requiring advance notice of impending arrival at the port.
- Add new berths.
- Redesignate underutilized berths used for other cargo types (such as general cargo) as container berths.
- Redesign the port layout so that ships spend less time maneuvering into and out of berths.

Dwell time. There is increasingly better coordination among service providers operating in the supply chain. Most ports now have scheduled services, which make it easier to plan and strategize the clearance of cargo. Previously, ports were unable to guarantee consistent vessel turnaround times, and shipping lines could not operate on a fixed voyage schedule. With the introduction of day-of-the-week sailing for feeder vessels, connection times of one to two days are common. The predictability of the arrival of containers allows importers to plan the activities required to clear their cargo, reducing dwell time by one to three days.

Based on work in Africa, Raballand and others (2012) identify interventions that are relevant to most ports in the developing world:

- Identify appropriate indicators, and benchmark the performance of ports.
- Provide incentives for importers to initiate clearance before the arrival of cargo.
- Introduce performance contracts and incentives for customs brokers and customs officials, port operators, and shippers.
- Sensitize all port stakeholders about the importance of minimizing dwell time.

- Assess the way the private sector operates before investing in port infrastructure.
- Optimize the use of space by targeting long-stay containers or cargo and encouraging fast clearance through price incentives.
- Increase capacity only as a last resort. Infrastructure is often an easy response; it is not always the most important determinant of performance, however.

Creating Communities of Port Users

Port efficiency increasingly depends on the integration of the components of the transport chain. This integration extends beyond the traditional environs of port operations and activities into how the port interfaces with the logistics services connected to it. It is not unusual for the handshake between the port and rail and road services to cause problems in port operations and to delay cargo removal. For this reason, efficient interfaces between road and rail transport are critical to overall port efficiency, meaning there is need for close integration of stevedore, road, rail, freight forwarding and clearing, and other port operations.

Whether a particular issue is viewed as a problem depends on the perspective of the observer: what might be a pressing issue for an exporter (for example, the queuing time to enter a port, which might jeopardize the chances of a consignment meeting its shipping schedule) might be only a minor inconvenience for an importer.

One of the most productive sources for getting a balanced perspective on the relative importance of different access issues is a port users council (PUC) or equivalent forum in which all port users and agencies are represented. Such forums exist for nearly all ports in developed countries and for most ports in developing countries. Land access issues are only one area of interest of a PUC. Creation of a PUC is beneficial to a port's operations, including better understanding of land access issues (box 10.1).

Improving the Use of Inland Cargo Facilities

In recent years, off-dock container yards (ODCY) have been developed in major ports, especially in Sub-Saharan Africa, to deal with excess demand for storage in port yards. Just before the global financial crisis, demand at the ports of Mombasa and Dar es Salaam was far outstripping capacity. ODCYs or container freight stations were introduced near the ports. The decision on whether to transfer containers to the ODCY is made by the shipping lines,

Using a Community of Users to Address Operational Challenges at a Port in Sydney

For larger ports, especially ports with significant container movements, it is sometimes useful to create specialized users groups to deal with specific issues. In Sydney, Australia, for example, a logistics taskforce advises the minister of ports on the land transport of containers from the port; a port users consultative group advises on port infrastructure and road, rail, and intermodal issues; and a port cargo facilitation committee looks at land access, particularly the repositioning of empty containers. The Port Botany Logistics Taskforce was established in 2006 to advise the minister for ports and waterways on options for addressing inefficiencies in the transport of containers to and from Port Botany. The Sydney Ports Users Consultative Group meets on a regular basis to advise the Sydney Ports Corporation on the development of port infrastructure, road transport issues, and rail and intermodal terminal operations and infrastructure. The Sydney Ports Cargo Facilitation Committee meets monthly to discuss matters such as the operations of stevedore container terminals, landside transport performance, and the repositioning of surplus empty containers.

in consultation with the ODCY license holder. Introduction of ODCYs increased storage capacity, reducing some of the bottlenecks associated with congestion.

At other ports, cargo is transferred to inland container depots (ICDs). The best ICDs are linked to the port by a high-capacity and efficient railway system. Theoretically, an ICD should perform the same tasks and services as a seaport, without the vessel-related operations and services. An ICD should provide some basic customs and border management functions, regardless of whether it is located in a costal or a landlocked country. Typically, an ICD makes it possible to exploit the advantages of using containers as much as possible. The container is therefore the dominant reference transport unit for cargo moving through ICDs and dry ports. Most ICDs and dry ports handle containers only, although some also handle noncontainerized or decontainerized cargo.

To have a significant impact in small freight markets, ICDs should be multiuser facilities. An ICD can be owned by either the public or private sectors or by a state-owned entity, usually the railways. In all instances, an important factor is the governance of the facility. An essential role of ICDs is the capacity to perform the whole clearing process by customs authorities and other border agencies. Such capacity is a prerequisite for a dry port to be accepted as an end delivery point for imports for shipping lines direct bills of ladings. Such a function is important for import cargo.

To maximize the potential to reduce overall logistics costs, a dry port should also encourage as much two-way flow of cargo as possible. However, on most corridors, balanced traffic in both directions is not always feasible, as countries have large imbalances between import and export volumes.

Reducing procedural requirements is critical to improving the attractiveness of an ICD. One way the requirements can be minimized is by sharing information between the first point of entry (vessel notice and cargo manifest in the case of overseas imports) up to the ICD/dry port (import declaration documents). Streamlining information requirements requires optimization and nonduplication of processes between the seaport and the ICD/dry port. In the case of some landlocked countries, it may be necessary to have appropriate legal instruments in place on covering the set of agreed upon procedures and the transit regime in the transit country for the mutual recognition of information, documents, norms, and controls for an ICD/dry port. Under these circumstances, data interchange between border agencies, especially customs, is critical to prepare and expedite border formalities. Current transit regimes would seem well suited to exploiting the benefits of an ICD/dry port.

Summary of Possible Interventions for Improving Port Operations

Table 10.7 summarizes the most common port operations issues and questions found in corridor projects and proposes possible interventions to address them. Actual interventions should be adapted to deal with specific constraints.

TABLE 10.7 Possible Interventions for Improving Port Operations

Issue	Questions	Possible interventions
Port performance	• What is the port productivity per crane, hectare, and berth?	• Improve port systems and enhance productivity.
Cargo dwell time	• What is the dwell time of cargo in the port and on the waterside and landside? • What factors add to dwell time?	• Adopt a holistic approach to reducing dwell time. • Adopt a participatory approach to reducing dwell time.
Port infrastructure	• Does the port infrastructure limit port capacity, vessel access, and size? • What are the proposed port development plans?	• Expand port capacity. • Deepen access and berths.
Port management	• Are all port users consulted on port management and performance? • Are upstream issues considered in port developments?	• Support port users forums. • Introduce a port community system and integrated information technology (IT) systems.
Container freight station and dry ports	• Is the port complemented by container freight stations and dry ports? • What were the main reasons for developing the container freight stations and dry ports?	• Integrate container freight stations and dry ports into port processes to reduce overall logistics costs. • Coordinate road and rail operations connected to the port.

Annex 10A Questions for Discussion of Port Operations

A. Port Operations and Management

1. Provide the following statistics:

   Principal trade routes served by vessels calling at the terminal: _____

   Number of vessel calls by route: _____

   Number of vessel calls in previous year of different types: _____

   Cellular vessels: _____

   Self-sustaining vessels: _____

   Other: _____

   Container volume: _____ TEU total _____ TEU loaded

   Average berth waiting time: _____ minutes

   Average berth throughput: _____ boxes per vessel hour

   Berth productivity (boxes transferred per day and variance): _____

   Number of container gantry cranes that are operational at any one time: _____

   Peak berth capacity throughput: _____ boxes per vessel hour

   Average and peak berth occupancy: _____

   Average and peak berth waiting time: _____ minutes

   Average and minimum dwell time: _____

   Percent inbound boxes transferred to inland container depot: _____

   Percent inbound boxes transferred to off-dock container yard: _____

   What is the percentage of empties? _____

   What is the percentage of 40-foot containers? _____

2. What is the allocation of responsibilities between the public and private sectors?

Activity	Public sector	Private sector
Capital investment and maintenance		
Source of funding		
Infrastructure		
Wharf equipment		
Intermodal connections		
Ground handling operations		
Pricing		
Collection of charges		
Security		
Coordination with customs and other regulatory activities		

3. What are the major impediments to efficient operations?
   ☐ Planning, budgeting, and funding

☐ Dispersed responsibility for operations
☐ Insufficient facilities
☐ Customs and other regulatory procedures

4. Which of the following is being considered to improve operations?
   ☐ Investment in new facilities
   ☐ Coordination of information systems
   ☐ Revision of port fees
   ☐ Improvements in terms of concessions

5. How large are the largest vessels calling at the terminal?
   _____ 20-tonne equivalent unit (TEU)

6. What portion of these vessels
   Operate on a fixed schedule: _____
   Call on a specific day of the week: _____
   Are feeder vessels: _____

7. What are the principal transshipment ports serving the feeder vessels?
   _____

8. How many berths are there, and what is the range in length and alongside depth? _____

9. How many wharf container cranes are there? _____

10. Are they mobile?
    ☐ Yes
    ☐ No

11. Are fixed cranes Post-Panamax?
    ☐ Yes
    ☐ No

12. How is the terminal operated?
    ☐ Concession
    ☐ Lease agreement
    ☐ Port authority

13. For which of the following is the operator responsible for procurement and maintenance?
    ☐ Berths
    ☐ Storage area
    ☐ Wharf equipment
    ☐ On-dock rail facilities
    ☐ Off-dock truck parking area
    ☐ Off-dock storage area
    ☐ Customs inspection area

14. For which of the following is the operator responsible?
    ☐ Security
    ☐ Inland movement of containers

15. What is the peak berth throughput? _____ boxes per vessel hour
16. What is the average and minimum time that a loaded import container spends in the terminal? Average: _____ minutes Minimum: _____ minutes
17. What is the occupancy of the terminal storage yard? _____ percent

B. Hinterland Connectivity

18. What percentage of inbound boxes are
    Transported inland by road: _____
    Transferred to inland container depots: _____
    Transferred to off-dock container yards: _____
19. What percentage of containers moving in and out of the terminal use road transport? _____
20. Provide the average values for the following:
    Number of trucks entering and exiting the terminal in a typical day: _____

    Time the truck spends waiting to enter the terminal: _____ minutes
    Time for trucks to turn around in the terminal (average and variance): _____ minutes
    Time for truck with loaded containers to complete procedures: _____ minutes at entry gate: _____ minutes at exit gate: _____
21. Are there regular railroad services for moving containers to and from the port?
    ☐ Yes
    ☐ No
22. What is the average number of trains arriving per day? _____

C. Port Information Series

23. Does the terminal have a computerized yard management system?
    ☐ Yes
    ☐ No
24. What percentage of vessels submits manifests electronically?
    _____ percent
25. Can the information on the system be accessed by the shipping lines and shippers?
    ☐ Yes
    ☐ No
26. What type of information does the terminal operator make available to port users via the Internet?
    ☐ Status of containers in the yards
    ☐ Handling and storage charges accumulated

27. Does the terminal operator use electronic data interchange with the following?
   ☐ Shipping line
   ☐ Shippers
   ☐ Consignees
   ☐ Customs
28. How do the terminal operator and customs authority coordinate their activities?
   ☐ Electronic exchange of data on container status and movements
   ☐ Daily planning of container movements to and from the inspection area

D. Port Development Priorities
29. What restrictions on the role of the terminal operator are included in the operating agreement? _____
30. What mechanism is used to monitor or regulate the terminal handling charges? _____
31. What is the major infrastructure constraint at the terminal?
   ☐ Berths
   ☐ Container handling equipment
   ☐ On-terminal storage space
   ☐ Off-terminal storage space
   ☐ Scanners
32. What are the major impediments to more efficient terminal operations?
   ☐ Time for vessel access and egress to port
   ☐ Condition and size of vessels
   ☐ System for queuing vessels and allocating berths
   ☐ Lack of prearrival information on ship loading plan
   ☐ Lack of prearrival information on export containers
   ☐ Labor productivity or disruptions
   ☐ Cargo dwell time
   ☐ Coordination with customs and other regulatory activities
   ☐ Availability of land transport
   ☐ Pricing of services
33. What are current plans to improve performance?
   ☐ Deepening or widening the access
   ☐ Investing in infrastructure and equipment
   ☐ Improving ship and storage yard planning and control
   ☐ Improving monitoring of the container status
   ☐ Simplifying container inspection procedures

    ☐ Improving the exchange of information between terminal operator and customs

    ☐ Automating billing and collection activities

    ☐ Revising port fees or terminal charges

34. Rate the following:

    Port authority: ☐ Good ☐ Adequate ☐ Poor

    Shipping services: ☐ Good ☐ Adequate ☐ Poor

    Truck operators: ☐ Good ☐ Adequate ☐ Poor

    Rail operators: ☐ Good ☐ Adequate ☐ Poor

    Clearing and forwarding agents: ☐ Good ☐ Adequate ☐ Poor

    Customs: ☐ Good ☐ Adequate ☐ Poor

    Road department: ☐ Good ☐ Adequate ☐ Poor

35. If poor, what were the reasons? _____

Note

1. A study of increasing the dimension of the turning basin in the Port of Damietta in the Arab Republic of Egypt showed that an increase from 240 meters to 320 meters would reduce storage space by about 1.5 hectares (USAID 2008).

References

Arnold, J. 2011. "Dar es Salaam Cargo Dwell Time Analysis." Note for the World Bank, Washington, DC.

Drewry Shipping Consultants Ltd. 2010. *Container Terminal Capacity and Performance Benchmarks*. London: Drewry Shipping Consultants Ltd.

Memos, C. D. 2004. *"Port Planning."* In *Port Engineering: Planning, Construction, Maintenance and Security*, edited by G. P. Tsinker, 7–64. Hoboken, NJ: John Wiley and Sons.

Nathan Associates. 2010. *Port Cargo Dwell Time Analysis*. Washington, DC.

Palsson, G. 1998. "Multiple Ports of Call versus Hub-and-Spoke Containerized Maritime Trade between West Africa and Europe." SSATP Working Paper 31, World Bank, Sub-Saharan Africa Transport Policy Program, Washington, DC.

Raballand, R., S. Refas, M. Beuran, and G. Isik. 2012. *Why Does Cargo Spend Weeks in Sub-Saharan African Ports? Lessons from Six Countries*. Washington, DC: World Bank.

Rodrigue, J.-P., C. Comtois, and B. Slack. 2009. *The Geography of Transport Systems*. Abingdon, United Kingdom: Routledge.

USAID (U.S. Agency for International Development). 2008. "Port of Damietta Operational Efficiency: Evaluation and Recommendations." April. Washington, DC.

World Bank, 2007. *Port Reform Toolkit*, 2nd ed. Washington, DC: World Bank.

———. 2011. *Report on Port Cargo Dwell Time Analysis for Tanjung Priok*. Washington, DC.

Resources

Hall, P., R. J. McCalla, and B. Slack, eds. 2011. *Integrating Seaports and Trade Corridors*, Farnham, United Kingdom: Ashgate Publishing Ltd.
This book has 3 parts and 16 chapters, each by a different author. The first part examines global economic change and its implications for ports, trade corridors, and supply chains. The second part deals with measuring and improving port gateways and corridor performance. The third part presents six international case studies. The case study of West Africa provides a complex benchmarking system applied to 13 port/corridor combinations. The text is more conceptual than practical, but it provides a framework for considering the main issues affecting trade corridors and ports.

Inter-Ministerial Group, Secretariat for the Committee on Infrastructure. 2007. "Reducing Dwell Time of Cargo at Ports." Government of India, Planning Commission, New Delhi. http://infrafin.in/pdf/FinalCargo.pdf.
This report provides data on the operational efficiency of India's most important container and general cargo ports and compares their performance with the performance of benchmark ports, such as Rotterdam and Singapore. It makes key recommendations for reducing container dwell time through the following measures:

- optimizing cargo handling systems and equipment
- improving maintenance scheduling
- operating ports 24/7
- augmenting capacities at ports
- creating additional testing facilities
- improving labor productivity
- strengthening roads to and within ports
- creating exclusive cargo freight corridors
- implementing electronic data interchange and port community system
- establishing a single window environment for port users
- simplifying documents.

Kgare, T., G. Raballand and H. W. Ittmann. 2011. "Cargo Dwell Time in Durban: Lessons for Sub-Saharan Africa Ports." Policy Research Working Paper 5794, World Bank, Washington, DC. http://hdl.handle.net/10986/3558.
This paper compares dwell times at several Sub-Saharan African ports, using the Port of Durban as a benchmark. Based on quantitative and qualitative data, it identifies the main reasons why cargo dwell time at the Port of Durban declined dramatically in the past decade, to an average of three to four days: major customs reform; changes in port storage tariffs, coupled with strict enforcement; massive investments in infrastructure and equipment; and changing customer behavior through contracting between the port operator and shipping lines or between customs, importers, and brokers. Cargo dwell time is mainly a function of the characteristics of the private sector, but it is the onus of public sector players, such as customs and the port authority, to put pressure on the private sector to make more efficient use of the port and reduce cargo dwell time.

Le-Griffin, Hanh Dam, and Melissa Murphy. 2006. "Container Terminal Productivity: Experiences at the Ports of Los Angeles and Long Beach." Department of Civil Engineering, University of Southern California, Los Angeles. www.metrans.org/nuf/documents/Le-Murphy.pdf.

The objective of this study was to assess the productivity of the Los Angeles and Long Beach ports and compare it with the productivity of other major container ports in the world. Productivity is evaluated in terms of indicators commonly used by the shipping industry, which provide the basis for a broader discussion of why productivity varies so significantly across ports. The analysis takes into consideration whether maximizing the value of these productivity indicators is the most appropriate goal for terminal operators, given the unique operating environment of their port. The answers to these questions highlight bottlenecks that impede productivity and help identify appropriate improvement strategies.

Memos, C. D. 2004. "Port Planning." In *Port Engineering: Planning, Construction, Maintenance and Security*, edited by G. P. Tsinker, 7–64. Hoboken, NJ: John Wiley and Sons. http://media.wiley.com/product_data/excerpt/40/04714127/0471412740.pdf.

This chapter provides planning parameters for ports and container terminals, with useful indictors for access channels, berths, and turning basins. In addition to the formula used in this module, it provides other bases for estimating vessel queuing time, the time for servicing vessels at berths, the number of berths needed, the storage area needed for general cargo and bulk solid cargoes, and the area of inland container terminals.

Ministry of Transport. 2007. *Container Crane Productivity in New Zealand Ports*. Wellington, New Zealand. http://www.transport.govt.nz/ourwork/sea/containerproductivitynzports/.

This report compares container productivity data from six ports in New Zealand with productivity results from Australian and other international ports. It uses three measures of crane productivity:

- the crane rate (the number of containers a crane lifts on and off a container ship in an hour)
- the ship rate (the number of containers moved on and off a container ship in an hour)
- the vessel rate (the number of containers moved on and off a container ship in an hour of labor).

In measuring these parameters, it recognizes that there are different ways of measuring container productivity. It uses the definitions of the Bureau of Infrastructure, Transport and Regional Economics (BITRE) in Australia. With these definitions, the crane rate is a measure of the average productivity of container cranes at a port after allowing for operational and nonoperational delays in using cranes. As the crane rate does not reflect the productivity of a port's container terminal operation, which may use two or more cranes to load and unload containers from a ship, the ship and vessel rates help give a better overall perspective of container productivity at a port.

Raballand, R., S. Refas, M. Beuran, and G. Isik. 2012. *Why Does Cargo Spend Weeks in Sub-Saharan African Ports? Lessons from Six Countries*. Washington, DC: World Bank. http://hdl.handle.net/10986/13535.

This book brings together the experiences reported in various World Bank policy research working papers. It offers recommendations for reducing dwell times based on wide experience.

Refas, S., and T. Cantens. 2011. "Why Does Cargo Spend Weeks in African Ports? The Case of Douala, Cameroon." Policy Research Working Paper 5565, World Bank, Washington, DC. http://hdl.handle.net/10986/3332.

This paper investigates the main factors explaining long container dwell times in African ports. Using original and extensive data on container imports in the Port of Douala (Cameroon), it seeks to provide a basic understanding of why containers stay on average more than two weeks in gateway ports in Africa. It demonstrates the interrelationships between the logistics performance of consignees, the operational performance of port operators, and the efficiency of customs clearance operations. Shipment-level analysis is used to identify the main determinants of cargo dwell times and the impact of shipment characteristics such as the fiscal regime, the density of value, the bulking and packaging type, the last port of call, and the region of origin or commodity group. External factors, such as the performance of clearing and forwarding agents and shipper and shipping line strategies, also affect dwell times. The distribution of cargo dwell time has many specificities, including a broad tail, high variance, and right censoring, which requires in-depth statistical analysis before policy recommendations are made.

Tanzania Ports Authority, and Tanzania International Container Terminal Services. 2009. *Optimizing Port Capacity in Dar es Salaam: Improving Dwell Times, Update*. Dar es Salaam.

In 2007, the Port of Dar es Salaam experienced exceptionally long dwell times for containers and even longer wait times for ships to enter the port because of the slow rate of off-loading containers. The problem was caused by the lack of storage area, which resulted from the increase in the throughput of containers, compounded by much longer than anticipated dwell times. A series of workshops was held, attended by all stakeholders. A long list of measures (205 in total) was agreed to. This report is an update on progress on implementing those measures. It provides insight into the problems in reducing dwell time and gives an indication of which measures are likely to have the greatest and fastest impact.

UNCTAD (United Nations Conference on Trade and Development). 1985. *Port Development: A Handbook for Planners in Developing Countries*, 2nd ed. Geneva: UNCTAD.

Although dated, this handbook provides a guide to the many issues involved in port planning and practical advice on how to address them. Many of the parameters of design of port components are still applicable, as ship dimensions are included in the design parameters.

USAID (U.S. Agency for International Development). 2008. "Port of Damietta Operational Efficiency: Evaluation and Recommendations." Washington, DC. http://pdf.usaid.gov/pdf_docs/Pnadx143.pdf.

This report evaluates the proposed development of the Port of Damietta, one of five ports on the Arab Republic of Egypt's Mediterranean coast. It provides guidance on assessing the needs for access channels, turning basins, berths, and container storage space.

World Bank. 2007. *Port Reform Toolkit*, 2nd ed. Washington, DC: World Bank.
The *Port Reform Toolkit* provides guidance on port reform, not port design or the specifics of port operational efficiency. Although useful in providing a context in which the role of a port in a corridor context might change, it does not provide guidance on whether the exiting physical layout and design of a port (or more specifically a container terminal) are adequate for the roles of feeder or hub port.

———. 2011. "Import Container Dwell Time Study and Recommendations for Tanjung Priok." November, Washington, DC. http://www-wds.worldbank.org /external/default/WDSContentServer/WDSP/IB/2013/09/04/000333037_2013 0904115439/Rendered/PDF/808710WP0logis0Box0379822B00PUBLIC0.pdf. This report provides a good guide on how to measure and assess dwell time. It examines the impact of some of the usual remedies to long dwell times in the Port of Tanjung Priok, in Indonesia. The methods it describes for measuring and dealing with dwell times are applicable to most container terminals in developing countries.

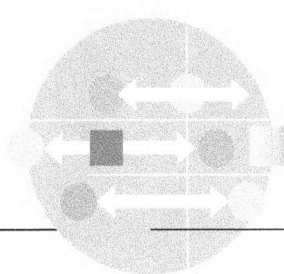

MODULE 11

Land Access to Ports

Most ports are surrounded by large urban centers, as a result of historical reasons and necessity, as some industries require easy access to ports. However, the symbiotic relationship between the two is increasingly creating problems of access to ports. There are often difficulties in allowing new road capacity in heavily built up areas. Several port cities (including Chittagong, Hanoi, and Manila) have resorted to daytime bans on truck movements to ports as a first measure to combat congestion (AAPA 2008). Although they reduce congestion, the bans add to the cost and time of shipping goods through the port.

There are no benchmark standards of land access to a port, partly because all port–urban interfaces differ. Port city authorities in several countries have recognized the urban development and growth benefits of merging land use policy with port development strategies. They take maximum advantage of the value of the port as part the global economy while at the same time maximizing its contribution to the livability of the city (ECMT 2000). However, outside a few developed countries, there has been little integration of port planning with urban planning, at least while the port is still in operation (UNCTAD 2004). It is only after ports are no longer operational that there is consensus on their heritage value and redevelopment as residential, tourist, and cultural and commercial centers. Wharves, docks, and equipment that would once have been demolished can become symbols of local heritage and instruments of urban renewal. However, for purposes of corridor development, the focus has to be on the impact of cities on ports and vice versa. In the United States, AAPA (2008) estimated that more than 13 million jobs are dependent on port activity. It examined four categories of port-related employment: direct, indirect, induced, and port related. Direct employment includes jobs at the port as well as the many supporting services that are the basis for the financial structure of a port city. These services include trade finance and insurance, maritime services (including ship brokering), freight forwarding, and land transport services. All these services and their employment are at risk if a port loses competitiveness.

Module 1 made the argument that the land access part of a corridor accounts for a very large share of the corridor costs. If the arguments for including the maritime sector in the definition of the corridor are accepted, the land transport cost and time for a corridor to a landlocked country account for an average of about 35 percent of the corridor cost and about 27 percent of the corridor time. If the maritime sector is excluded, these shares increase to 78 percent and 69 percent, respectively.

The share of these costs and times that is taken up in crossing the urban area varies by corridor and by how far the origin or destination of the freight is from the port. For freight that originates or is destined for locations in the urban area, the share is close to 100 percent, whereas for locations several hundred kilometers away from the port, the shares are about 1–5 percent.

But it is not always the actual urban transit costs and times that affect corridor costs, but the uncertainty they introduce, particularly in the time to cross the urban area, as argued above. If the distance to the port through the urban area is about 40 kilometers (typical for a port city of about 2 million people and a port in the downtown area), the time to cross the area can range from about one hour when the streets are uncongested to five hours or more when there is severe congestion.

Ports are pivotal nodes and platforms in integrated multimodal supply chains. Much attention has been given to the efficiency of the ports themselves. Much less attention has been given to how easy it is for traded goods to get to or from the port to their origin or destination within the port city or via a transport corridor to a more inland origin or destination. Improving urban access to ports that are in cities that suffer congestion can be significant in reducing the total cost, time, and uncertainty of land access in the corridors leading to the port.

This module addresses the issues and approaches to landside access to ports through the surrounding urban areas. Access to ports through the national road and rail networks is addressed in the road freight and railways modules (Modules 7 and 8). One reason this module is necessary is that there is little practical available information on how best to address the interactions between ports and their cities.

The module is structured as follows. The first section identifies the main issues concerning the functioning and impact of land access to ports on corridor performance. The second section presents the data and information that are required to understand these issues. The third section identifies possible solutions to the most common issues. The last section summarizes these interventions.

Impact of Urban Access on the Functioning of the Port

There is little data about the share of trade corridor time spent accessing a port through its surrounding urban area. What little information is available suggests that it can take up to a day for a truck from an inland destination to cross an urban area to reach the city's port. For trucks coming from or going to the interior of a country or from or to a landlocked neighboring country, this time does not increase the transit time and cost greatly, but the uncertainty of how long such urban transit may take can be a significant issue. For trucks traveling just in the urban area, the lengthy transit time can result in only one return trip being made in a day. Better urban access could result in two trips a day and a reduction of up to 50 percent in the cost per trip.

Need for Extra Storage to Cover Uncertainties Introduced by Urban Transit Time

Exporters need their products to arrive at the port in time to meet the sailing schedule of their contracted ship. Products need to leave the exporter's premises with sufficient time to cover the variability in transit time. Because the manufacturing schedule puts constraints on when goods can be available for loading onto the truck for transport to the port, a larger allowance for urban transit time can impose either changes in production schedules or higher stockholding costs, to provide buffers between manufacturing and transport or in the port as a buffer between land and maritime transport. In extreme cases of urban traffic congestion (as in Jakarta) or daytime truck bans (as in Cairo), trucks need to leave their urban location for the port at least one day sooner and leave the container in the port overnight. The port therefore needs to provide storage space.

Participation in Global Production Networks

To remain or become competitive, ports need to do more than just act as a convenient location for the transfer of freight between maritime and land transport. Modern logistics requirements are increasingly a decisive factor in determining whether a port becomes the center for value-adding activities, including processing.

It is not enough for a port to be closest to an inland destination for it to be competitive with other ports. The port procedures for processing transit freight, the time it takes for the transit freight to reach its final destination, and the variability of that time are even more important than distance. A large part of the time uncertainty can come from crossing the urban area in which the port is located.

For value-adding processing of temporary imports, traders' choice of port is not just a function of geographic accessibility, the time and distance from places of production and consumption, or even how quickly, reliably, and inexpensively goods move these distances. It also depends on how well the port complex can facilitate the transformation of products in response to made-to-order, just-in-time, best-priced, and door-to-door requests.

Such activities once related only to repackaging and labeling; they now include partial assembly of electronic goods and final assembly of garments. These activities often use locally produced inputs that need reliable, timely, and low-cost access to the port just as much as exports and imports do.

In some cities, there is a perception that port traffic is a major cause of congestion. Many cities have attempted to deal with this problem by banning port traffic from city streets during the daytime. In cities where congestion is a particularly serious problem (such as Cairo and Hanoi), not only port traffic but all trucks are banned from operating during the daytime.[1] Such bans may diminish the attractiveness of the port as a center for sub- or final assembly in global production networks.

Congestion resulting from port traffic is a more serious problem than simple figures might indicate. A typical container berth handling 300,000 containers per year will generate about 2,000 truck movements per day, assuming that trucks have to make two trips for each container, one in and one out. But to this must be added the other traffic generated by the terminal—the journey to and from work for the terminal operating staff, customs agents, other public agency staff, and other logistics and service providers. This additional traffic can more than double the traffic associated with moving freight in and out of the port. City traffic can also cause delays to trucks trying to reach the port, reducing port operational efficiency.

Although truck bans can alleviate congestion, they reduce port accessibility and can result in long queues of trucks waiting at the city boundary for the ban to end. They also make operation of ports in downtown areas less efficient, as freight can be taken out of or brought into the port only at nighttime. Trucks can typically make only one port trip during this time. In addition, the port needs larger storage areas, particularly for containers but also for bulk products and general freight, as they must have space for all the freight unloaded during the day in addition to space for cargo left in the terminal on previous days. This problem is particularly important in container terminals, where the average dwell in the port terminal can be more than 10 days.

Data and Information Sources

The main indicators of performance of the port-land transport access system include the following:

- proportion of cargo carried by road, rail, and inland waterway
- maximum length of train that can enter the port
- number of gates at port
- number of trucks in and out of port
- turnaround time for trucks from gate in to gate out
- travel time for trucks from city outskirts to port gate.

Data on the port–land access interface system are collected from port operators, city authorities, and trucking and railways services operators. The main topics for discussion are outlined in annex 11A.

Options for Improving Land Access to Ports

There are three sets of possible solutions to the land access problems of city ports. Two strategies attempt to improve land access to existing downtown ports. The third option involves moving the port outside the urban area.

Improving Land Access to Existing Facilities

Access can be improved through infrastructure enhancements as well as noninfrastructure measures. The main infrastructure measures are of four types:

- Improving road infrastructure, including through additional traffic lanes and improved intersections.

- Improving rail infrastructure, including through new rail links or grade separation of existing links in and out of the port (as in the Alameda Corridor in Los Angeles[2]). The design and planning of rail links is more difficult than it is for roads, because the space and turning area requirements are difficult to accommodate in the restricted areas available in downtown ports.
- Linking ports to inland container depots, including additional storage capacity and the moving of land-based functions out of the port area (or if they are rail linked, moving road traffic off the existing road network to relieve congestion. Road congestion can also be relieved by building new access roads).
- Building additional gates to reduce queues or relocating existing gates to fit better with the road network.

Noninfrastructure measures to improve access can include traffic management and institutional arrangements that improve coordination between agencies involved in port operation and local authorities responsible for management of local traffic. One effective traffic management approach is to introduce an appointment system for trucks accessing the port (box 11.1).

Relocating the Port

Where ports suffer from space or access constraints as a result of the surrounding urban area, port relocation or the development of dry ports or container freight stations linked to the port may be considered. General freight facilities are usually located close to the downtown area, with dry bulk and liquid bulk terminals often located in deeper water and in locations with more storage space and often rail access. As containers replace most general freight, container facilities have to relocate, for deeper water, more land area, and better land access.

Although there is no standard benchmark for how much land is needed for storage of off-loaded containers, one reliable source suggests 1 hectare for every 30,000 20-foot equivalent unit (TEU) in terminals with more than 1 million TEU per year and half that number of containers per hectare in smaller ports (Drewry Maritime Research 2010). A typical downtown container terminal with about 500,000 TEU per year will need at least 33 hectares of storage space—more than many of them can accommodate. Only Rio Grande has adequate storage area (table 10.2). Many other ports (such as Mombasa and Dar es Salaam) now supplement the port storage area with nearby inland container terminals. Most ports in downtown

Improving Productivity at the Port of Aqaba by Improving the Queuing System

In order to diversify the economy of the city of Aqaba, in Jordan, away from total dependence on its port, city planners had to eliminate the long queues of trucks in the downtown area that resulted from the queuing system. To do so, in 2008, they replaced the queuing system with a technologically simple advanced notification system. Under the system, only approved and licensed truck operators can operate out of the port's container terminal. Trucks are not allowed to enter the town until they are notified that the container they have come to collect has cleared all its entry requirements and is ready for pickup. Truckers are further mandated to use predetermined routes provided to the driver by the notification system. Since introduction of the new system, traders contract directly with the transport companies for transporting their containers, rather than having to use the next truck in the queue that is waiting at the container terminal (for imports) or in the free trade zone (for exports).

The impact of this advanced notification system on the trucking industry has been dramatic. The productivity of trucks serving the port increased by a factor of about three. As a result, they now travel about 100,000 kilometers per year instead of the 30,000 kilometers per year they averaged before the change. The volume of container traffic handled at the port rose by 30 percent following the change, with a much reduced truck fleet. Importers obtain reliable and timely transport of their containers, with no increase in the transport price. These outcomes were achieved by taking advantage of a broad community of interests, including the city administration, the ministries of transport and environment, the operator of the container terminal, and the trucking industry.

Source: Arvis and others 2011.

areas are under great pressure to relocate, given the high opportunity cost of the value of the land they occupy.

Other activities competing for downtown land space are often able to pay much higher prices than the port could if it had to rebid for the land it is using or bid for more land. Where the port operator has become a landlord port rather than just an agency of the municipal government, it could well determine that its best interests are served by selling the land and relocating to another location outside the urban area.

Two other factors may affect the decision to relocate a port. The first is problems in navigational access. The need for increased depths of access channels to accommodate larger vessels requires dredging that can be subject to an increasingly complex process for managing the disposal of dredged material, which is often contaminated from discharges of pollutants from urban industrial activity. The second is that a constituency of interests may oppose port operation, based on concerns arising from increasing port-city tensions, particularly social and environmental conflicts (quality of life issues).

Increasing navigational access. Each new generation of container ships needs deeper access channels and berths and additional landside space for the storage of unloaded containers. Larger ships make fewer voyages for the same number of containers, so each voyage has more containers to load and unload. They need more space. Fourth-generation container ships (Post-Panamax) need about 11 meters of depth. The latest generation needs even more depth (Maersk's Triple E series of vessels need at least 14.5 meters).

Very few upstream ports have the natural depth for fourth-generation container ships, which are serving typical downtown ports on feeder services. For example, Shanghai's original container port had only about 8 meters natural depth, Montevideo about 9 meters, and Mombasa about 10 meters. In addition to greater depth, the larger and longer vessels need wider access channels and larger turning circles in the port. Except in the few ports that have enough natural depth and channel width, these features call for significant dredging.

The large amounts of dredged material, contaminated and uncontaminated, require disposal. Historically, a synergy has been exploited, with dredged material used to create reclaimed land for port development. Growing environmental awareness is making this less feasible, however, in many instances leading to a protracted dredging approval process, higher costs, and longer implementation time.

Dealing with constituencies of interest. In port cities, there are constituencies of interest that both support and oppose downtown port development. The major interests in favor of such expansion include labor interests, whose members do not want to move or commute long distances to a potential new port location, and shipping agents and other service providers, which have well-established commercial relationships in the current port location. Interests opposed to downtown port expansion include adjacent landowners and occupants whose property values and life styles will be detrimentally affected by the expansion of an unwanted neighbor. These constituencies can make port expansion and access improvements difficult to achieve, especially on a schedule that does not threaten the port's competitive position.

Many urban ports have been relocated, but the location has not always been chosen to improve land access. In some countries, maritime access has also been a reason. The desire to redevelop the port area to create a new downtown residential or commercial center has also been a motive.

Though poor land access itself is rarely a sufficient justification for a port to be relocated away from a downtown location, it is one of the more important components of a complex of issues that can lead to this result. Relocation can improve access, because road and rail (and possibly inland waterway) access to the port can be planned without the constraints of having to pass through built-up areas. Access can be designed for the specific needs of the port rather than being adaptations of an already existing road and rail network (box 11.2).

BOX 11.2

Relocating the Port of Bangkok

A typical example of relocation of port facilities is that of Bangkok. The original up-river port in the center of Bangkok was becoming inefficient, for a variety of reasons: land access was becoming time consuming and unreliable, port traffic was a major contributor to city traffic congestion, landside space was inadequate for the increasing needs for container storage and expansion would be prohibitively expensive and socially unacceptable, and river navigation could not be improved to accommodate the new generation of container ships. The three main constraints on growth were poor land access because of city traffic congestion, lack of space for expansion, and the limited depth of the access channels (8 meters), which limited container ship size to about 1,500 TEU.

A new port, Laem Chabang, was built about 120 kilometers southeast of the city. Opened for service in 1991, it now handles about 5 million TEU per year. The original port was not closed, but its container capacity was restricted to 1 million TEU per year (in practice, it operates close to its physical capacity of about 1.5 million TEU). In addition to road and rail links between Bangkok and Laem Chabang, there is a barge shuttle service for containers.

Summary of Possible Interventions for Improving Land Access to Ports

Table 11.1 summarizes the most common land access to ports issues and questions found in corridor projects and proposes possible interventions to address them. Actual interventions should be adapted to deal with specific constraints.

TABLE 11.1 Possible Intervention Measures for Improving Land Access to Ports

Issue	Questions	Possible interventions
Access to cities, ports	• Are there time restrictions on when trucks can be allowed into the city or port?	• Address infrastructure constraints to alleviate congestion.
	• Is there a port access management system?	• Introduce management system to facilitate smoother traffic flows.
	• What is the turnaround time for trucks entering a port?	
	• Is there congestion in the port environs?	• Engage with local urban authorities to ascertain development plans, especially industrial location and traffic network.
	• Are there urban planning proposals that will affect port access?	
	• Is there land for future expansion of the port?	• Establish port development plans and land requirements.
	• What are the shares of each type of port traffic (container, general, bulk solid, bulk liquid) on the road, rail, and waterway access modes?	• Maximize the capacity of the most appropriate mode for each type of traffic.
	• What is peak-period capacity for port-related traffic on the main access corridors?	• Add road or rail capacity.
	• Does port traffic cause or add to congestion on the main access links?	• Develop rail-linked inland container depots.
	• Are there allocated traffic lanes for port traffic on the main access links?	
	• Is there adequate off-road parking for traffic waiting to enter the port?	• Add more port gates and parking spaces.
Rail access	• Is there a link from the national rail network into the port?	• Build a rail link
	• Is any part of the access to the port shared with passenger trains?	• Develop rail-linked inland container depots.
		• Negotiate for daytime train paths.
	• What is the maximum length of trains accessing the port? Are there height or axle-load constraints on port trains that are stricter than on the rest of the rail network?	• Increase train length and the number of paths.
	• Are the rail crossings on the local road and port access roads at grade or grade separated?	• Introduce grade separation or preallocation of crossing times.

TABLE 11.1 *continued*

Issue	Questions	Possible interventions
	• If there is a rail link, does it serve container berths or bulk and general freight berths? • Are the in-port rail terminals in a convenient location that minimizes train marshalling?	• Redesign rail access links and in-port rail locations. • Separate trains for each port terminal. • Use push-pull train operation to reduce locomotive shunting. • Carry out final train formation for remote destinations away from port.
Port traffic	• Is there a prebooking or appointment system for trucks entering the port or port terminals? • Does the layout of the port road network minimize traffic conflicts?	• Introduce appointment system for trucks. • Redesign turning movements after gate entry to reduce conflicts with local traffic.
Empty containers	• Are empty containers stored in the port container terminal? • Are there any port activities that result in traffic queues within the port (such as waiting for trucks to be scanned and weighed)? • Are there other city locations for storage of empty containers?	• Store empty containers outside the port. • If space is available, increase to meet benchmarks. • Provide separate lanes for traffic requiring scanning and other inspections, which often create long queues within the port. • Create empty storage capacity closer to demand for export containers (at inland container depots, for example).
Port gates	• Are there enough port gates for the volume of traffic? • Are gate and within-port inspections of drivers and cargo carried out in a logical and time-minimizing way? • Is there a preferential gate system for accredited trucking companies? • Do the port gates lead directly onto the city road network?	• Tailor the number of gates to different types of movements, volume of traffic, and processing and inspection requirements. • Carry out vehicle inspections away from gates. • Introduce a preferential system for preapproved truck operators and logistics service providers. • Relocate port gates to lead onto dedicated access links.

Annex 11A Questions for Discussion of Land Access to Ports

A. Questions for Port Authority or Port Operator

1. Who owns the land in the port?
   - ☐ Government
   - ☐ Local authority
   - ☐ Port authority
   - ☐ Private sector
   - ☐ Other (specify) _____

2. How much land is set aside or reserved for the port? _____

3. Is there a port development master plan for the current site?
   - ☐ Yes. When was it prepared or last updated? _____
   - ☐ No

4. Are alternative sites being considered?
   - ☐ Yes. Location: _____
   - ☐ No

5. Who owns the land at the alternative sites?
   - ☐ Government
   - ☐ Local authority
   - ☐ Port authority
   - ☐ Private sector
   - ☐ Other (specify): _____

6. Is the port connected to an inland container depot?
   - ☐ Yes. Location: _____
   - ☐ No

7. What is the total area of the inland container depots? _____ hectares

8. How is the port connected to the inland container depots?
   - ☐ Road
   - ☐ Rail
   - ☐ Inland waterway

9. Is the port connected to an off-dock container yard?
   - ☐ Yes. Location: _____ Total area: _____ hectares
   - ☐ No

10. How much traffic of each type is moved in and out of the port by each mode of transport?

Mode	Import (tonnes)	Export (tonnes)
Road		
Rail		
Inland waterway		
Short-sea shipping		
Coastal shipping		

11. What are the terminal sizes and volumes for the following types of traffic?

Terminal	Size (hectares)	Annual volume (tonnes, except where otherwise indicated)
Container yard		
Roll-on–roll-off (Ro-Ro) (number)		
Bulk cargo		
General cargo		

12. What proportion of vessels arrives on schedule? _____ percent

13. Indicate the number of hours from the moment each mode of transport enters and exists the port (gate in to gate out):

Mode	Minimum	Maximum	Average
Truck			
Train			
Inland water vessel			
Short-sea shipping vessel			
Coastal shipping vessel			

14. How many containers are carried each year by each mode?

Mode	Loaded	Empty
Road		
Rail		
Inland waterway		
Short-sea shipping		
Coastal shipping		

15. Are there segregated roads linking to the port?
   ☐ Yes
   ☐ No

16. Are there segregated lanes linking to the port?
    □ Yes
    □ No
17. What is the annual average daily traffic on roads linking to the port gates? _____
18. What is the capacity of each road? _____ (annual average daily traffic)
19. Is there a railway line into the port?
    □ Yes
    □ No
20. If so, which of the following describes it?
    □ Single track
    □ Double track
    □ Electrified
21. Does the line connect to an international railway network?
    □ Yes
    □ No
22. What is the annual capacity of the railway? _____ 20-foot equivalent unit (TEU)
23. What is the annual capacity utilization? _____ percent
24. What is the length of the track inside the port? _____ kilometers
25. How long a train can the tracks accommodate? _____ wagons
26. Is the track grade separated from the surrounding road network?
    □ Yes
    □ No
27. Which terminals in the port are adjacent to the track?
    □ Container
    □ Ro-Ro
    □ Break bulk
    □ General cargo
    □ Liquid
28. Is there inland waterway connectivity to the port?
    □ Yes
    □ No
29. If so, does the system have any obstructions?
    □ Yes. Specify: _____
    □ No
30. What is the annual capacity of the system? _____ TEU or tonnes
31. What is the current capacity utilization of the system? _____ percent
32. Does the port have facilities to accommodate the following short-sea shipping services?

□ Ro-Ro ramps

□ Handling equipment

33. What is the annual volume of traffic moved by short-sea shipping services? _____ TEU or tonnes

34. What is the annual capacity utilization? _____ percent

35. What are the most important changes that could be introduced to improve performance of traffic flow in and out and around the port?

□ Infrastructure: _____

□ Operations: _____

□ Regulation: _____

B. Questions for Truck Operators

36. How many trucks are registered to enter the port? _____

37. What proportion of the trucks are internationally registered? _____ percent

38. Are there time restrictions on truck access to the port?

□ Yes

□ No

39. If there are restrictions, during which hours are trucks banned? _____

40. Which days of the week are restrictions in effect?

□ Every day

□ Sunday

□ Monday

□ Tuesday

□ Wednesday

□ Thursday

□ Friday

□ Saturday

41. What is the normal average queuing time to reach the port gate? _____ minutes

42. What is the average time to reach a destination within the port city in free-flowing traffic? _____ minutes

43. When are the roads to the port most congested?

□ Sunday

□ Monday

□ Tuesday

□ Wednesday

□ Thursday

□ Friday

□ Saturday

☐ 6–9 am
☐ 9–12 pm
☐ 12–3 pm
☐ 3–6 pm
☐ 6–9 pm
☐ 9 pm–6 am

44. Is there a prebooking system for trucks to enter port?
☐ Yes
☐ No

45. How is information transmitted?
☐ Mobile phone
☐ Runner
☐ Computerized system

46. How many gates can be used to enter the port? _____

47. How many gates can be used to exit the port? _____

Notes

1. Since 2008, a daytime ban on large trucks in Cairo has been extended to all trucks over 2 tonnes payload. In Hanoi, trucks with loading capacities above 2.5 tonnes are not allowed to enter the city through the Sai Gon Bridge or the streets of other districts from 6 a.m. to 12 p.m. Trucks with loading capacities below 2.5 tonnes are also banned on these roads from 6–8 a.m. and 4–8 p.m.

2. The 32-kilometer long Alameda corridor is now operated by its own transportation authority. The corridor connects the ports of Los Angeles and Long Beach to rail terminals near downtown Los Angeles. Its core is a 16-kilometer, below-grade, three-track section that replaced more than 20 at-grade crossings. It charges transit fees (currently about $20 per loaded TEU) to cover its $2.4 billion capital and operating costs. In December 2011, 40 trains a day were transporting more than 11,000 TEU that would otherwise have used road transport (Alameda Corridor Transportation Authority).

References

AAPA (American Association of Port Authorities). 2008. The *Local and Regional Economic Impacts of the US Deepwater Ports System*. Lancaster, PA.

Alameda Corridor Transportation Authority. Carson, CA. http://www.acta.org /index.asp.

Arvis, J.-F., R. Carruthers, G. Smith, and C. Willoughby. 2011. *Connecting Landlocked Countries to Markets: Trade Corridors in the 21st Century*. Washington, DC: World Bank.

Drewry Maritime Research. 2010. *Container Terminal Capacity and Performance Benchmarks*. London: Drewry Shipping Consultants Ltd.

ECMT (European Conference of Ministers of Transport). 2000. *Land Access to Ports*. Report of the 113th Round Table on Transport Economics, held in Paris, December 10–11, 1998. ECMT Economic Research Center, Paris. http://www .internationaltransportforum.org/IntOrg/ecmt/pubpdf/01RT113.pdf.

UNCTAD (United Nations Conference on Trade and Development). 2004. "Assessment of a Seaport Land Interface: An Analytical Framework." Geneva. http://www.unctad.org/en/docs/sdtetlbmisc20043_en.pdf.

Resources

AIVP (Association Internationale Villes et Ports). "The Worldwide Network of Port Cities." http://www.aivp.org.

One of the few comprehensive sources on port cities is the Association Internationale Villes et Ports (AIVP). Its website provides news on ports and cities as well as 11 case studies of port-city interfaces (all completed since 2008). It also provides an electronic version of port city innovations. This publication (in French with an English summary) includes detailed descriptions of 70 recent port-city development initiatives. Most relate to French ports, but several examples are from other countries (most of them developed countries).

Of particular relevance to the land access issues of ports are the examples of expanding ports and the ways in which land access development has been incorporated into a broader urban development framework. Presentation of the innovative practices is based on 20 types of activity. Four relationships are examined:

- economics: ways of integrating outward-looking port rationale into the local economy
- environment: compatibilities and synergies between economic and environmental goals
- town planning: spatial relationships between port/economy areas and cities
- governance: types of collaboration between local government, economic players, and residents.

OECD (Organisation for Economic Co-operation and Development). "OECD Port-Cities Programme." http://www.oecd.org/regional/oecdport -citiesprogramme.htm.

This website provides links to case studies on various port cities. The case studies benchmark the performance of the ports examined, analyze the impact of the ports, and assess policy and governance challenges.

Port of Rijeka Authority. http://www.portauthority.hr/en/development_projects /rijeka_gateway_project.

The overall objective of the Rijeka Gateway Project is to increase Croatia's trade competitiveness by improving the international transport chain through the Rijeka gateway for both freight and passenger traffic by modernizing the port and road network connections and privatizing port operations. Specific objectives included the following:

- increasing efficiency and improving financial, social, and environmental conditions at Rijeka Port

- rehabilitating infrastructure and replacing equipment
- preparing to redevelop part of Rijeka Port for urban purposes
- improving international road connections linked to the Rijeka gateway and the administration of the road sector.

The project includes three components: port restructuring and modernization, port-city interface redevelopment, and international road improvements.

Port Webpages. The webpages of individual ports provide information on the impacts of cities and their traffic on ports. Among the more comprehensive descriptions are those of Sydney (http://www.sydneyports.com.au/), Rotterdam (http://www.portofrotterdam.com/en/Pages/default.aspx), and Los Angeles (http://www.portoflosangeles.org/).

Rafferty, L. 2002. "East Asia Ports in Their Urban Context, East Asia and Pacific Transport Division." World Bank, Washington, DC. http://hdl.handle .net/10986/17395.

This paper identifies the main issues and challenges faced by port cities in Asia. It includes detailed case studies of five port cities: Shanghai; Hong Kong SAR, China; Singapore; Haiphong; and Sihanoukville. It describes strategies port cities can adopt to maintain their competitiveness while remaining good neighbors to the communities that surround them.

UNCTAD (United Nations Conference on Trade and Development). 2004. "Assessment of a Seaport Land Interface: An Analytical Framework." Geneva. http://www.unctad.org/en/docs/sdtetlbmisc20043_en.pdf.

This study analyzes ports' potential to develop landside connections and facilities and integrate the land interface of the trade, logistics, and supply chain system. It examines the main operational and management practices in international shipping services versus those of land transport systems and proposes a framework for port's landside integration, with particular emphasis on appropriate tools of assessment and analysis. A number of policy initiatives, such as organizational reform and technological developments, are put forward, with a view to ensuring successful landside integration and management, particularly for ports in developing countries.

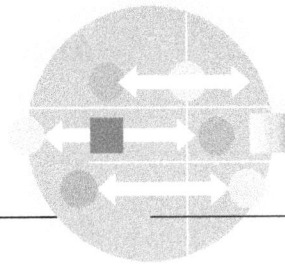

Airfreight

Air cargo often represents an unexploited opportunity in the developing world, with great potential to increase exports, particularly of land-locked countries. Where air services exist, they are not always fully utilized, partly because air transport is one of the most expensive ways of shipping and is not well suited to the types of commodities that low-income countries tend to produce. It therefore needs to be justified as a transport mode within a corridor. The option should be seen as a specific solution to a specific logistics problem, not as a mode to develop for its own sake.

The module is organized as follows. The first section identifies the main issues concerning the functioning and impact of airfreight operations on corridor performance. The second section presents the data and information that is required to understand these issues. It is complemented by an annex that lists the key data and questions that can be asked of stakeholders to obtain both quantitative and qualitative data on border management. The third section identifies measures that can improve border-crossing performance. The last section summarizes these interventions.

Airfreight Issues in Corridor Operations

The key economic drivers for choosing air transport over other modes are the value of time and the lack of availability of other modes. In the first case, the good is nearly always perishable or of high value. The second potential driver for air transport is remote origins or destinations where other modes are not available. In some cases, air transport is the most direct way of shipping.

Air transport can play an important role in the development of a corridor for a variety of reasons:

- In the developing world, many new industries take advantages of climate to produce a perishable good that cannot be produced in other parts of the world during the same season.
- Entire industries have developed through the smart application and use of air transport infrastructure and freight capacity.
- For landlocked countries, air transport may be the only way to quickly receive or ship goods.
- In countries with very poor transport infrastructure, especially the lack of roads, air transport may be the only way to bring exports to market. One example is postconflict Democratic Republic of Congo, where ores are often flown directly from the mine using adjacent air strips.

Airfreight is a private sector issue in terms of demand and service provision. The public sector is responsible for providing the right infrastructure, legal framework, and safety oversight.[1] From a development perspective, the question should be "what is holding back the provision of adequate air-freight capacity?" rather than "how can we bring airfreight capacity into the country or corridor?"

It is important to recognize the role that airfreight plays in a corridor. It may be part of a mix of modes used by an exporter. For example, airfreight may be used to supplement shipments in unexpected cases of higher market demand. A good may be shipped in quantity via containership; as new orders are placed, a small quantity of the order may be sent ahead to meet demand via air while the remainder of the shipment continues in less costly modes.

Market Potential and Volumes of Traffic

The largest intercontinental cargo flows move from east to west. Trade connecting North America to the rest of the world accounts for up to two-thirds of volume (Air Cargo World 2010). The major trade corridor runs through the mostly middle-income countries of East Asia to the consuming countries in the West. The other important trade flow from a development perspective is from south to north. This route connects the low- and middle-income countries of Africa to Europe and the developing countries of Latin America to the United States and Canada.

Air cargo flows are highly cyclical. During the global economic slowdown of 2007–09, volume declined by as much as 20 percent (Air Cargo World 2010). It rebounded in 2010 (Boeing 2010).

The highest growth rates in terms of revenue tonne-kilometers is in the Middle East (figure 12.1). The largest volumes are generated in Asia. When looking at cargo flows and potential, distance is important, because other modes can compete effectively on shorter distances and fuel consumption of aircraft is highest on takeoff and flying at low altitudes. Longer distances distribute this cost over a larger number of kilometers, lowering the overall per kilometer cost.

If a country's development objective is to produce perishable or high-value, time-sensitive exports, the capacity for bringing the product to market must be made available (a "push" development objective). Capacity is provided in the hope that an industry springs up and succeeds. This approach is a high-risk strategy. More is needed than just the provision of air cargo capacity and infrastructure to bring about most development goals.

Established air carriers are more likely to be attracted by "pull" opportunities. For example, freight carriers often enter a market when enough freight

FIGURE 12.1 Airfreight Volumes in Selected Markets, 2001–11

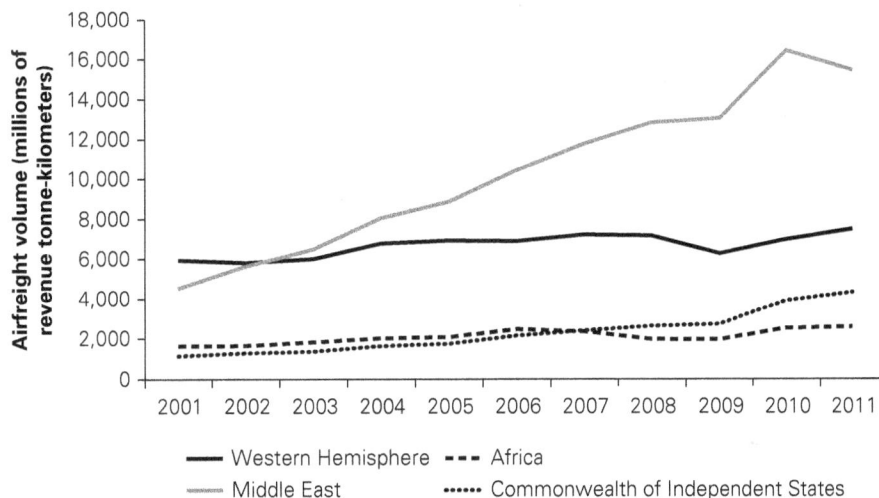

Source: Based on data from Boeing 2012.

forwarders show solid demand. As much as 90 percent of a capacity for a given carrier is booked six months ahead of time, in informal meetings between airline executives and forwarders. The risk for filling the capacity is left with the forwarder.

A country that may already have a product and an export market may have limited ability to bring the product to market because it spoils on the way to the airport or air cargo capacity is constrained. Direct intervention through long-term capacity investments (improvement in airport infrastructure such as aircraft parking and runways, for example) and infrastructure for cold storage could be effective and relatively low-risk options.

For most developing countries, capacity asymmetries exist. Flights arrive with full bellies and leave empty, imposing a cost burden on the arriving shipments. Overcapacity opportunities could present new export opportunities, although evidence is anecdotal. In less dense markets, especially in the developing world, the most likely source of capacity will be from passenger bellies and dedicated charter operations. The garment industry in Mauritius exploited the excess belly capacity of Air France airliners departing Mauritius; the emerging electronics industry in South America is riding on the back of extensive air cargo infrastructure in some countries.

Dedicated scheduled operations generally depend on predictable and known demand. Freight forwarders play an important role. Companies such as Kühne and Nagel reduce the risk a cargo carrier faces by buying vast quantities of cargo capacity many months in advance and then consolidating their clients' shipments in a way that makes efficient use of the purchased capacity. Some dedicated scheduled carriers will not enter a new market without the established presence of freight forwarders, whom they view as a measure of demand.

In Southeast Asia, the electronics industry considers air cargo an essential element in the production supply chain. The economic use and justification of the use of airfreight on a larger scale is related not only to the weight/value ratio of the product being shipped but also the cycle time (that is, the actual timing of the delivery). In effect, the notion of "perishable" is related to just-in-time delivery in the production process.

Types of Air Cargo Services

When looking at trade corridors, it is important to consider the applicability of air cargo for specific markets. Data on air cargo are difficult to obtain, so the analysis initially has to come from the demand side.

In order to determine demand for (and even perhaps supply of) air cargo services, one needs to consult with shippers and importers.

This case-by-case analysis depends very much on the industry and environment. For example, demand for the type and nature of air cargo services at the Democratic Republic of Congo's mining operations, where there are virtually no road networks, is very different from demand by the electronics industry in Malaysia or flower exporters in Kenya.

There are five main types of providers:

- *Dedicated air cargo service providers flying on a schedule.* These providers include cargo-only carriers, such as CargoLux, and dedicated cargo services by carriers that also have passenger services, such as Lufthansa Cargo.
- *Dedicated charter operators.* These operators include one- or two-airplane outfits, as well as companies with larger fleets. The advantage of these flights is that they provide control over the timing and capacity of the flight. The disadvantage is that the aircraft usually arrive empty; the costs of the empty flight have to be factored into overall shipping costs. The cost of dedicated charter capacity is dependent on the symmetry of the routes (that is, if a country only exports but does not import for local consumption, the aircraft would arrive empty, and would have to charge more for the trip carrying the exports).
- *Passenger airlines selling belly space.* Roughly 40 percent of all cargo flies in the bellies of passenger aircraft. Relying on passenger planes can constrain trade, for two reasons. First, capacity could be restricted because passenger services are not as liberalized as cargo services, limiting the number of flights and connections. Second, single-aisle passenger jets, such as the Boeing 737, do not have as much excess belly capacity as larger planes.
- *Integrated express carriers.* Most advanced logistics operators, such as UPS, FedEx, and DHL, fall in this category.
- *Highly specialized and niche services.* Examples include humanitarian aid (United Nations World Food Programme) and high value components and spares.

Airport Infrastructure

The infrastructure at an airport can determine the types of services available. For example, expansion of the Nairobi airport in Kenya is part of a wider project to improve the performance of the Northern corridor linking landlocked Uganda and Rwanda to Nairobi and the Port of Mombasa. It includes improvements to both taxiways and parking. Generally, runway dimensions have to be suited to the services to an airport. For example, a runway that can accommodate a vintage Boeing 727 or DC-8 cannot accept a recently converted Boeing 767, which is quieter and more fuel efficient but larger, therefore requiring a longer runway.

The existence and size of a dedicated cargo apron is also important. In many cases, the inadequate size or lack of a cargo apron is the single most important impediment for airfreight at an airport. In some cases, cold storage and other facilities may be important, though a demand analysis is needed before making investments in such facilities. In some cases, the producer/exporter would rather keep the goods under its own control in refrigerated trucks and deliver just as the exporting aircraft is landing rather than give up control over the product through an airport-run storage facility.

Access to Airport

Airfreight is multimodal, as accessibility of the airport to the hinterland depends on roads.[2] Some pertinent questions to ask include the following:

- Can a potential exporter get the product to the airport in a timely and efficient manner? In Uganda, for instance, fresh produce exporters have to live within 40 kilometers of the airport at Entebbe to be able to export by air.
- If the timing between the arrival of the good at the airport and the actual wait time before departure of the cargo aircraft cannot be well coordinated, are there appropriate storage facilities, such as cold storage, to extend the shelf life of the export?
- Is airport access sufficient to get imports out of the airport and to the final destination efficiently?
- Does the airport meet international standards allowing aircraft to arrive from, or depart to, the corridor partner?

In countries where the main goal is to promote new industries such as horticulture, access from the growing fields to the airport is vital. For this reason, fields are developed along existing roads. In some cases, just one well-routed road in good condition may be all that is needed. However, express services, such as FedEx, UPS, and DHL, depend on a wide road network to pick up and deliver packages for speedy transfer. This form of airfreight, though important, especially as an economy expands and becomes more sophisticated, is not going to appear much in a development context.

Safety

Safety oversight is important not only for the protection of lives but also because Europe and the United States place restrictions on who can fly in from where based on safety criteria. International standards for safety oversight are set by the International Civil Aviation Organization (ICAO), headquartered in Montreal. It issues Standards and Recommended Practices (SARPs) that should be adopted by every contracting country's authority for aviation safety (generally the civil aviation authority). The ICAO audits countries on a regular cycle for compliance with SARPs through its Universal Safety Oversight Audit Programme (USOAP). The results of these audits are tabularized and compared with world averages. A high correlation between these results and actual accident statistics has been found. The world averages themselves are not the goal for a country's audit results, because world averages show a level of overall implementation of SARPs far below what ICOA considers inadequate and because the average is affected by the results of the country's audit.

Regulatory Environment

After air safety, the single most important regulatory item that can hinder airfreight is air services agreements between countries. These agreements may limit the number of flights between two or more countries, or they may restrict a carrier from hopping from country to country while making most efficient use of its capacity. In general, air cargo is usually several steps ahead of air passenger transport in liberalization. However, as a large portion of air cargo travels in the bellies of passenger airliners, the lack of liberalization can still severely restrict cargo capacity.

Data and Information Sources

The main performance indicators for transport in a corridor context include the following:

- Air Connectivity Index
- international air cargo capacity
- air cargo volume
- catchment area of the airport
- travel time to main destinations
- clearance time for cargo.

The airfreight market is highly competitive. Because dedicated cargo carriers with extensive investments in cargo-only aircraft can often be outbid by a passenger airlines with extra belly capacity sold for a marginal profit, they tend to be secretive about data and routes. This means there is no publicly available central repository for data. Research thus requires putting together bits of information from different sources.

The Air Connectivity Index (World Bank 2011) was developed by the World Bank to capture a country's relative importance in the global air transport network. It takes account of the number and extent of a country's connections to other countries, weighing bilateral connections based on the importance of the countries concerned (see Module 1).

It is straightforward to calculate the index using new data on bilateral capacity (number of seats) and frequency (number of flights) from the Schedule Reference Service (SRS) database of global air services. The World Bank proposes to update the index annually. Moreover, the methodology could easily be applied in other important areas, such as maritime transport.

Quantitative data can be obtained from airport and civil aviation authorities in corridor countries. There are also numerous databases on air transport operations, some of which are commercial. The need for detailed information should be dictated by the importance of airfreight within the corridor. Qualitative and process-related information should be gathered through interviews with all major players, including shippers. The main discussion points are outlined in annex 12A.

Improving Airfreight in a Corridor

Several actions can be taken to improve land and air transport integration within a corridor. Interventions should be based on the most pressing constraints or opportunities that exist. For instance, if opportunities lie in enhancing access to markets such as Europe, where there are stringent safety standards, then safety oversight could be the main focus of the intervention. If the main constraint is lack of competition, liberalization could be the main emphasis. The most common potential interventions are identified below, in no particular order.

Safety Oversight

Improving air safety oversight and complying with international conventions are critical preconditions for openness to global air transport services. Countries that are not able to guarantee minimum levels of safety can be excluded from some networks, especially the markets of the rich countries. For instance, the United States does not allow any flights by a foreign carrier directly from that carrier's country into the United States unless the Federal Aviation Administration [FAA]) is convinced, through its own audit (the International Aviation Safety Assessment [IASA]) that safety oversight meets international standards. The European Union (EU) bans airlines it considers unsafe from flying to any EU member country.

The airline industry is globally represented by the International Air Transport Association (IATA), which has its own safety oversight mechanism, the IATA Operational Safety Audit (IOSA). All airlines must undergo the audit annually in order to be an IATA member and be listed on the IATA registry.

Regulation

Countries generally agree to allow flights between them through bilateral or multilateral air service agreements. These agreements usually follow some conventions adopted at the international level under the United Nations. These agreements determine factors such as which foreign airlines are allowed to serve a given country, whether the airline is allowed to service other countries on the same flight, how often flights operate and at which capacity, and which airports in the guest countries are allowed to be served. Key to the routing permitted are the Freedoms of the Air.[3] The most liberalized agreements allow Fifth Freedom and beyond services, without any capacity or frequency constraints, which would largely open the market to regional and international services. Cabotage (the practice of allowing a foreign airline to service a domestic route in a given country, such as Air France servicing traffic between Chicago and New York) is almost never allowed in passenger services.

When exploring possibilities for using air cargo as a solution for corridor logistics, a basic understanding of the existing air service agreements between the countries involved may be of use. In many cases, restrictions applied on specific routes are not found in the main text of the agreements but in attached, often confidential memorandums of understanding. In some cases, the air services agreements may not reflect what is actually happening in the marketplace, as governments have been known to weakly enforce capacity constraints if a violation of an agreement clause caused by one party is followed up with a permissive reaction for the same violation by the other party.

Knowledge of other regulations, governing noise and nighttime operations, for example, is also important. Much cargo, especially perishables in tropical areas, is loaded and unloaded at night, when temperatures are lower. Nighttime restrictions at the departing or arriving airport can therefore have a real and direct impact. In the recent past, noise limitations in Europe forced the older aircraft servicing Mwanza, in Tanzania, to use hush kits, which increase fuel consumption. In 2012, Lufthansa stated that it might liquidate most of its dedicated cargo fleet if Frankfurt placed nighttime restrictions on aircraft operations. Such restrictions will become effective in 2015. It remains to be seen how Lufthansa will respond.

Customs and Security

The most important aspect of airfreight in most cases is quick passage through the airport, at departure and arrival. A delay of six hours or more in clearing imports is considered a problem, as modern technologies enable much more rapid clearance (World Bank 2009). The World Trade Organization (WTO) provides guidelines for the expedited clearance of small shipment in particular. The adoption and introduction of the recommended procedures is a possible solution to the problem.

Though several attempts by the United States to pass laws requiring all cargo to be screened before being loaded onto aircraft have failed, pressure persists to increase screening. In addition, some countries have mandatory antiexplosives "cool-down" laws, which require shipments to remain in storage for a period of time (24 hours in India) before being released. Security concerns can create significant bottlenecks in both departure and arrival processes.

The customs process can be a hindrance to rapid delivery, especially in developing countries. In efficient markets, information on shipments is sent electronically to the arrival customs office at the time of shipping, allowing for quick passage. In poorer countries, where such mechanisms have not yet been implemented, paperwork and physical inspections may take longer than expected.

Infrastructure

Infrastructure is important to airfreight, often in ways that do not seem apparent on first glance. Airports, air traffic control, and air traffic navigation systems are essential parts of an air transport system. Beyond them, the single most important element needed for airfreight is good road access to the departure and destination airport. Airfreight is part of a logistics chain (box 12.1). The airport is not the point of origin or the final destination.

BOX 12.1

The Land and Air Transport Nexus in Flower Exports

Cut flowers present one of the most visible and rapidly growing industries in the developing world. In addition to established exporters, such as Colombia and Kenya, many other countries, including China, Ethiopia, Malawi, and Uganda, are exploring or developing the industry. Prime resources needed for production, beyond inexpensive labor, are location relative to the equator (allowing for a longer growing season), fresh water, fertile soil, and a temperate climate. Colombia is one of the largest suppliers to the U.S. market. Kenya is the largest single supplier to Europe.

A key element in export of flowers is the logistics of bringing the product to market. This industry could not exist without air transport. Cut flowers have a short and predictable shelf life. Their economic value declines rapidly with time (figure B12.1.1). The entire logistics chain, from the instant the flower is cut to the point it reaches the consumer, has strong time constraints, moisture requirements, and temperature control necessities. Rapid transit to the point of sale is therefore vital. Air transport plays a key role in flower exports from tropical regions.

FIGURE B12.1.1 Value of a Rose as Function of Time after Being Cut

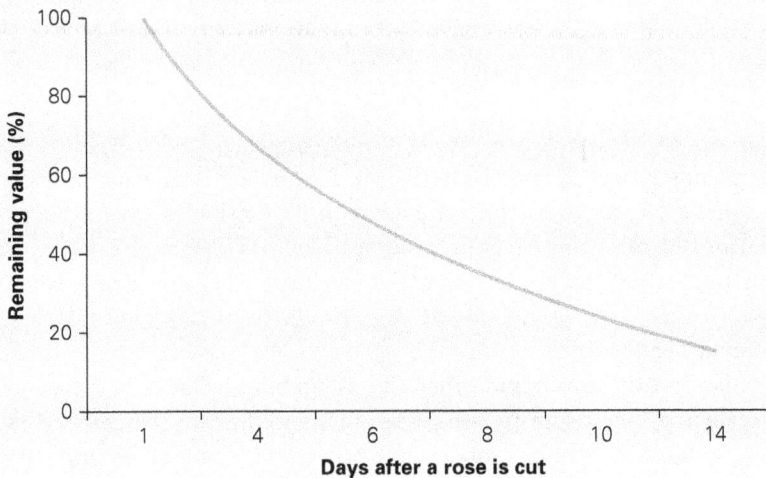

Source: Based on Bofinger 2010.

(box continues on next page)

BOX 12.1 *continued*

Although both Ethiopia and Kenya are major air transport hubs in East Africa, their prospects in flower exports are different. Ethiopia is trying to expand its flower production. The challenge lies in bringing flowers from the greenhouses to the international airport in Addis Ababa—long distances, rough roads, and open trucks carrying the flowers bring a high spoilage rate.

Kenya has exploited its superior domestic logistics system. A good road network connects growing centers with Nairobi's Jomo Kenyatta International Airport over distances of 80–100 kilometers. Two main export routes are Nairobi-Amsterdam and Nairobi–United Kingdom. Of exports from Kenya to the United Kingdom, more than 90 percent reportedly arrive via Kenyan Airways. The airline does not have any dedicated freighters, so the flowers are shipped as freight in passenger aircraft to both the United Kingdom and Amsterdam. Other carriers, such as Lufthansa Cargo and Cargolux, provide dedicated cargo space from Nairobi to Frankfurt and Maastricht. As sales to Dutch wholesalers are resold outside the Netherlands, it is reasonable to assume that part of the shipments' final retail destination may be over other modes of transport.

Given that demand for cut flowers in Europe seems to be holding strong (in contrast to the United States), it would seem reasonable that new entrants are keen to enter the market. Rwanda and particularly Uganda, with its rich and fertile soil, its cargo capacity, and the airport in Entebbe, are well poised to succeed in this market.

At airports themselves, the most basic and important pieces of infrastructure include spaces to organize airfreight for loading. Many larger airports have dedicated cargo terminals. They can be of simple construction or sophisticated structures with cold storage facilities, depending on the type of airfreight services. For example, if a producer of a perishable wishes to retain control of the product being shipped, the needed infrastructure may be limited (box 12.2).

As beyond the apron and other cargo-handling facilities the needs are generally the same as for passenger airports and the infrastructure costs of runways, taxiways, control towers, and other safety- and efficiency-related installations are high, nearly all cargo facilities are located within passenger airports. There are very few cases of cargo-only airports, which are generally not cost-effective.

Exporting West Nile Perch from Tanzania

Tanzania exports West Nile perch. The fish are caught in Lake Victoria by indigenous fishermen; delivered to one of several fish factories; and then cut, cleaned, and processed. They are exported frozen or deeply chilled (and therefore considered fresh) to Europe and North America.

For fresh fish, one factory has the buyer arrange for a dedicated air cargo aircraft to arrive at a predetermined time at the Mwanza airport. The fish are loaded into refrigerated trucks at the factory and driven to the airport once the aircraft is there. Pallets are loaded outside the aircraft, directly from the truck, with the pallets then loaded onto the aircraft. Loading usually occurs at night, when temperatures are lower. When asked if cold storage facilities or a larger cargo terminal would increase the quality of the logistics involved, a factory manager explained that the factory prefers to keep the fish under its control in its own refrigerated trucks until loaded on the aircraft. Therefore the infrastructure needed to better facilitate shipment is adequate apron space.

The length of runway a specific aircraft requires is a function of the size (weight) of the aircraft, the altitude of the runway, and weather (wind and temperature). The airport in Mwanza can support only smaller aircraft, such as the older Boeing 727 or the older DC-8. These aircraft are expensive to fly, so many operators switch to larger but more fuel-efficient aircraft, such as the Boeing 767, as they leave passenger service. The Boeing 767 cannot operate at Mwanza's airport, because of inadequate runway length. The short runway suppresses exports of West Nile perch.

Summary of Possible Interventions for Improving Airfreight

Table 12.1 summarizes the most common airfreight issues and questions found in corridor projects and proposes possible interventions to address them. Actual interventions should be adapted to deal with specific constraints.

TABLE 12.1 Possible Intervention Measures for Improving Airfreight

Issue	Questions	Possible interventions
Airport access	• Can airports be accessed from surrounding areas without hindrance? • What level of coordination is there between cargo and passenger flight arrival times? • Are there time restrictions on when cargo can be delivered to and from an airport?	• Provide hinterland access to airport, especially roads. • Provide storage facilities in case there are restrictions during certain times of the day.
Cargo potential	• What commodities flowing through the corridor require air transport? • What capacity is available, in dedicated cargo flights and in bellies of passenger aircrafts? • How many direct flights per week are available to and from corridor airports?	• Determine which types of cargo in corridor require air transport to key markets. • Consult all air transport users on main issues affecting use of air transport.
Infrastructure	• What are the largest aircraft that can access corridor airports? • Are there dedicated cargo aprons? • What storage facilities are available for cargo?	• Provide sufficient space and systems for cargo processing and handling. • Provide adequate approaches. • Improve systems for customs clearance and border management.
Safety	• Are there aviation safety concerns that affect direct access to some markets? • What are the main safety regulatory issues that affect the availability of air connections?	• Strengthen the safety oversight regime in corridor countries.

Annex 12A Questions for Discussion of Airfreight

1. Which of the following is true about the international airports located on the corridor?
   - ☐ A significant portion of airfreight is carried in freighters rather than as belly cargo on passenger aircraft. Percent carried in freighters:

     _____

   - ☐ The main airport is a regional hub for transshipment of cargo between intercontinental routes and regional routes.
   - ☐ Air cargo agents are allowed to offer storage within the airport and have direct access to the aircraft loading area.
   - ☐ Competing ground handling services are available for aircraft.
   - ☐ If only one ground handling service is available, the contract for these services is competitively bid out.
   - ☐ The cargo terminal is near the parking area for passenger aircraft to allow for quick transfer of belly cargo.
   - ☐ The airport has a separate cargo village providing warehousing and office space for freight operations.
   - ☐ There are cold storage facilities for perishable cargoes located on the airport property.
   - ☐ The airport or the airlines have scanners that can be used with airline palettes.
   - ☐ The airport allows export cargo to be cleared in six hours or less. Percent of cargo cleared in this time: _____
   - ☐ Customs electronic data interchange is used to submit master airway bills.
2. Provide the following statistics on the international airport:
   Number of active runways: _____
   Length of longest runway: _____ meters
   Instrument landing system category: _____
   Number of peak hour aircraft movements: _____
   Annual volume of airfreight (exclusive of mail): _____ metric tonnes
   Annual volume of international airfreight: _____ metric tonnes
   Percent of total freight in belly cargo: _____ Scheduled freighter: _____ Cargo charter: _____
   Annual number of landings by international airfreighters: _____
   Number of aircraft movements: _____
   Maximum size of aircraft: _____

Maximum frequency of movements: _____

Static cargo terminal capacity: _____ tonnes

Annual cargo throughput: _____ tonnes

Number of cargo storage facilities located at the airport: _____

What is the typical time required to clear import cargo, and how does it vary? _____

What is the typical time to clear export cargo, and how does it vary?

_____

What is the average and minimum time for storage of inbound cargo?

_____

What is the average occupancy of a normal storage area? _____

3. How is responsibility divided between the public and private sectors?

Activity	Public sector	Private sector
Capital investment and maintenance		
Runways		
Terminals		
Intermodal connections		
Ground handling operations		
Cargo terminal operations		
Security		

4. What are the main impediments to efficient operations?
   ☐ Planning and budgeting procedures and funding
   ☐ Bilateral restrictions on aircraft
   ☐ Storage capacity available on the airport
   ☐ Cargo clearance procedures

5. What are the major routes served through this airport? _____

6. What models of passenger aircraft are used?
   Model: _____
   Freight capacity: _____

7. Which airfreighters are used?
   Model: _____
   Freight capacity: _____

8. What are the major commodities carried inbound and outbound on these routes? _____

9. What is the typical transit times for the principal airfreight routes?

_____

10. What are the typical rates for the principal airfreight routes? _____

11. Does the country have an Open Skies policy for scheduled airfreight?
    - ☐ Yes
    - ☐ No

12. If there is an Open Skies policy, does it extend to fourth and fifth freedoms?
    - ☐ Yes
    - ☐ No

13. If not, are there bilateral agreements on landing rights for scheduled services?
    - ☐ Yes
    - ☐ No

14. What regulations apply to airfreight charters? _____

15. What type of storage is available at the airport?
    - ☐ Cold storage
    - ☐ Warehousing for rent
    - ☐ Air cargo terminals with space for rent
    - ☐ Multistory cargo terminals
    - ☐ Cargo villages

16. Which types of cargo documents are transmitted electronically?
    - ☐ Airway master bill
    - ☐ Individual airway bills
    - ☐ None

17. What is the typical time required to clear import cargo, and how does it vary? _____

18. What is the typical time to clear export cargo, and how does it vary? _____

19. Is the airline allowed to
    - ☐ Select its ground handling agent
    - ☐ Manage its own storage
    - ☐ Operate its own storage facility
    - ☐ Interact directly with the shipper in booking cargo

20. Which of the following is a major impediment to the growth in airfreight services?
    - ☐ Low-value imports
    - ☐ Slow growth of high-value exports
    - ☐ Significant imbalances and cargo flow
    - ☐ Inefficient and costly ground handling services
    - ☐ Cumbersome customs and security procedures

□ Regulatory restrictions on introducing new flights

21. What air cargo handling services are provided?
    □ Ground handling services
    □ Storage
    □ Inventory management
    □ Leasing storage space
    □ Road transport
    □ Cold Storage
    □ Bonded storage

22. What is the size of the enclosed storage area?
    Normal: _____ (m²)
    Bonded: _____ (m²)
    Cold: _____ (m³)

23. What are typical handling charges? _____

24. Are these charges regulated? If so, by whom? _____

25. Which of the following causes significant delays in clearance procedures?
    □ Documentary requirements
    □ customs working hours
    □ Insufficient use of computer systems
    □ Inefficient customs procedures

26. What significant improvements are planned for the medium term?
    □ New facilities
    □ Improvements in cargo clearance procedures
    □ Improvements in coordination between airlines, cargo handling and storage service providers, customs and the airport authority
    □ Changes in airport management
    □ None

27. Rate the following:
    Airport authority: □ Good □ Adequate □ Poor
    Airlines: □ Good □ Adequate □ Poor
    Clearing and forwarding agents: □ Good □ Adequate □ Poor
    Customs: □ Good □ Adequate □ Poor

28. If poor, what are the reasons? _____

Notes

1. Dedicated cargo carriers are generally private in the developed world. In the developing world, state-run airlines can handle cargo, either through dedicated aircraft or through belly capacity in passenger aircraft. Malaysian Airlines is

a prime example. In this module, service provision is driven by demand from the private sector.

2. There are some multimodal examples of air and sea, such as Canada and the United Arab Emirates, but they are rare and found in fully developed hubs.

3. There are five Freedoms of the Air: (a) the right to fly across a country's territory without landing; (b) the right to land in a country's territory for nontraffic purposes; (c) the right to put down in the territory of the first country traffic coming from the home country of the carrier; (d) the right to take on, in the territory of the first country, traffic destined for the home country of the carrier; and (e) the right to put down and take on, in the territory of the first country, traffic coming from or destined to a third country.

References

Air Cargo World. 2010. *World News* 13 (7).

Boeing. 2010. "World Air Cargo Forecast 2010–2011." Seattle.

———. 2012. "World Air Cargo Forecast 2012–2013." Seattle.

Bofinger, Heinrich C. 2010. *Freight Transport for Development Toolkit: Air Freight.* Washington, DC: World Bank. http://siteresources.worldbank.org /INTTRANSPORT/Resources/336291-1239112757744/5997693-1266940498535 /air.pdf.

World Bank. 2009. "Air Freight: A Market Study with Implications for Landlocked Countries." Transport Paper 26, World Bank, Washington, DC. http://site resources.worldbank.org/EXTAIRTRANSPORT/Resources /515180-1262792532589/6683177-1268747346047/air_cargo_study.pdf.

———. 2011. "The Air Connectivity Index: Measuring Integration in the Global Air Transport Network." Policy Research Working Paper 5722, World Bank, Washington, DC. http://www-wds.worldbank.org/servlet/WDSContentServer /WDSP/IB/2011/06/30/000158349_20110630135825/Rendered/PDF /WPS5722.pdf.

Resources

Air Cargo Management Group. http://www.cargofacts.com.

The Air Cargo Management Group is a consulting and research firm specializing in airfreight globally and in the United States. The group issues two important reports on a regular basis: the U.S. Domestic Air Cargo Performance Analysis and the International Air Cargo Performance Analysis. These reports, which cost about $800 apiece, are considered the most comprehensive overviews of the industry. The group assembles data from many sources, including freight carriers. The analysis of international airfreight is one of the most important sources for industry insights.

Air Cargo World. http://www.aircargoworld.com.

Air Cargo World is a free monthly publication that covers the air cargo industry. Every year, one issue is devoted to the top global air cargo airports and another to the top global air cargo airlines.

The Airbus Global Market Forecast. http://www.airbus.com.
Airbus publishes each year a Global Market Forecast, which presents for a 20-year horizon estimates of the demand for civil passenger and freighter aircraft. The forecast offers valuable insights into growth trends and expected supply of aircraft in different markets, regions, and key countries.

Boeing Company. http://www.boeing.com/commercial/cargo/.
Boeing publishes a biennial World Air Cargo Forecast, which also provides an overview of global aviation markets, identifies major trends, and presents projections of world demand for freighter airplanes.

International Air Cargo Association (TIACA). http://www.tiaca.org.
TIACA represents the international air cargo organization globally. Its biannual event, the International Air Cargo Forum & Exposition, provides a key opportunity to talk to representatives of cargo airlines about schedules and routes.

International Air Transport Association (IATA). http://www.iata.org.
IATA acts as a clearinghouse for many freight transactions and maintains the Cargo Accounts Settlement (CASS) database, which can be purchased. However, many airfreight operations, especially those in developing countries, are settled outside this system. The data are therefore more valuable in measuring markets in developed than developing countries. IATA is also the publisher of the Air Cargo Tariff (TACT), which acts as a guide for determining airfreight pricing. As pricing is more market driven than it once was, the TACT should be looked at only as a guide.

International Civil Aviation Organization (ICAO). http://www.icao.int.
ICAO is the United Nations organization responsible for global air transport.

International Federation of Freight Forwarders Associations (FIATA). http://www .fiata.org.
FIATA represents about 40,000 forwarding and logistics firms. Among other objectives it aims to improve the quality of services provided to freight forwarders by developing and promoting uniform forwarding documents, standard trading conditions, and so forth and providing core training for freight forwarders on various topics, including liability insurance, tools for electronic commerce, and electronic data interchange.

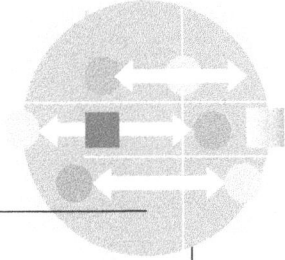

PART III

Corridor Impact Evaluation

This part of the Toolkit has only one module—a critical one that sets out the approaches to estimating the likely impact of a corridor project. The main objective of improvements to the performance of trade corridors is to reduce costs and increase trade. The module presents traditional approaches to estimating likely impacts as well as more recently developed and still evolving techniques that try to estimate the wider economic benefits of corridor projects. It does not deal with other possible impacts, such as reductions in carbon emissions from improved traffic flows or creation of employment, all of which can be important on specific corridors. The module uses examples from different projects to illustrate the likely impacts as well as the approaches that can be used to estimate them.

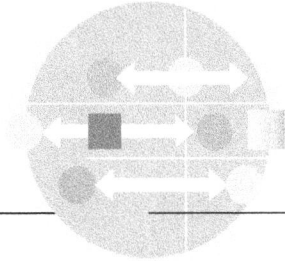

Evaluating the Economic Impact of a Corridor

The main objective of improvements to the performance of trade corridors is to increase trade and transport flows.[1] That increase can come from domestic trade flows in individual countries, bilateral or regional trade, from increased trade between landlocked countries in the same multinational corridors, or from increased trade in corridors that lead to the interior regions of coastal countries. Although the development objective is often expressed in terms of increasing export trade, many of the trade facilitation measures that are included in corridor improvement projects have a greater direct effect on imports, as for most low income countries imports exceed exports.

The economic evaluation of a corridor project attempts to determine whether the reductions in the cost of current trade and the generation of new trade are worth the investment needed to bring them about. Although the development objective of the project might be expressed in terms of export growth, the economic evaluation should also take account of the reduction in import costs, the generation of additional import volumes, and the cost reduction in and generation of exports and domestic commerce.

Changes in corridor costs are expected to serve as a stimulus for the reorganization of economic activity outside the transport sector. As a result of these changes, a manufacturer could change the source of inputs or the destination of exports or relocate production, thereby reconfiguring the topology of his supply chains. A retailer may centralize its operations to serve a larger market area; farmers may change their crops to a more marketable combination. (An example of a change by retailers is the emergence in recent years of a regional distribution industry in Uganda, which for security reasons is exploiting the easier connections to South Sudan to warehouse goods in Kampala instead of Juba, South Sudan.) Improvement of a corridor could result in firms relocating at some other node along the same corridor. In a network setting, such location decisions can be complex to model.

Transport networks have played a key role in the economic development of countries and regions for centuries. Transport links producers and consumers and has other impacts, including on land markets. It facilitates a wide range of economic activities and affects a wide range of economic decisions.

Although the presence of adequate transport is a necessary condition for economic development it is not a guarantee of it. For development to occur, other factors must also be present, including labor, land, politics, and a legal context. (Fujita, Krugman, and Venables 1999 maintain that clusters of skills and knowledge lead to endogenous economic growth.)

It is easy to make the argument for the restructuring effect of corridors where there is a strategy for a region served by a corridor. Corridors can be expected to create new opportunities for spatial competition and economies of scale. The challenge is to model the likely impact of corridor improvement beyond the transport effects to the wider economic impacts.

Most corridor projects are incremental. A transport and logistics network may already exist, in which case an assumption could be made that there are no significant wider impacts. Generally, however, corridor benefits will not capture all of the benefits to the economic system as a whole, or the final incidence of the benefits that will filter through the economy in terms of changes in prices, wages, and land rents. This module presents the main approaches to assessing the impact of corridor interventions and the conditions under which each approach might best be utilized.

This module is organized as follows. The first section identifies the objectives of impact evaluation. The second section examines the criteria for evaluation. The third section looks at issues to consider in an impact evaluation. The last section reviews various methods of economic evaluation.

Objectives of Impact Evaluation

There are three objectives of the impact evaluation of corridor projects:

- Optimize the design of each of the corridor components.
- Ensure that the package of project components is the most appropriate in achieving project objectives.
- Ensure that the sum of the benefits of the optimized components are worth the investment and other costs that must be incurred to achieve them.

The relative importance of each of these objectives for a particular corridor project can help determine which components are included in the economic evaluation and what evaluation methods are used to estimate the net economic benefits of the project.

Corridor projects typically include many more components than a single investment project (such as a highway development project) and even more than a typical policy-oriented project (such as a railway restructuring or a port reform project).

The evaluation of corridor improvement projects can be for the package of investment and policy components, for each of them separately, or both. It is possible that the benefits of the package of measures for the corridor as a whole will be greater than the sum of the benefits of the individual components.

Criteria for Evaluation

Before undertaking an economic evaluation of a project designed to improve the performance of a trade and transport corridor, it is helpful to review what is to be evaluated, what features should be included in the evaluation, and what evaluation method is most appropriate for these purposes.

Most corridor projects include a mixture of infrastructure investments, measures designed to improve operational performance of some parts of the corridor, and perhaps some regulatory changes and some institutional reforms. Some of these components are easier to evaluate than others; sometimes it is feasible to evaluate only some of them.

The following methods can be used to determine whether it is worthwhile to evaluate a particular feature of the corridor project (table 13.1):

- Ranking the cost of implementation of the various features, starting with the most expensive, and evaluating the features that account for a significant proportion of the total investment cost. This criterion is simple to

TABLE 13.1 Criteria for Selecting Project Components to Be Evaluated

Criterion	Degree of subjectivity	Ease of implementation
Contribution to project cost	1	1
Importance in achievement of project objectives	3	3
Contribution to expected project benefits	2	2

Note: A low rank implies less subjectivity and greater ease of implementation.

apply but runs the risk of including only infrastructure investments, omitting the regulatory, policy, and institutional features, which are less costly to implement, although they may be crucial to achievement of the objectives of the project.

- Prioritizing project components that are most crucial to achievement of the project objectives. This criterion is more difficult to apply than the first and involves much more subjective assessment in the ranking of project components by importance.
- Ranking project components by their expected contribution to the total benefits of the project. Implementing this criterion requires some prior assessment of the expected outcomes of the evaluation before it is made. Ranking the project components in this way and then evaluating the components that contribute most to the total benefits is similar to the first criterion but involves more subjective assessment (although less than the second criterion).

In practice, the choice of subcomponents to be evaluated generally involves a combination of all three criteria, but it is important that all of them be considered so that a rational choice of subcomponents is made and that the choice is not determined only based on of the ease of evaluation.

Issues to Consider in an Impact Evaluation

Selection of the characteristics to be included in the evaluation is related to the objectives of the project and can influence how easy it is to evaluate the project subcomponents. If the project objectives are relatively simple, such as reducing the costs of current trade and transport, then the characteristics to be evaluated can simply be the time and cost of transport. But even with these simple measures, some choices have to be made as to what times and costs are to be evaluated. These choices can be related to the selection of subcomponents to be evaluated.

Most corridor evaluations take account of the time and cost to transport traded goods from their inland origin in the corridor country to or from the deep water port where they are transferred to or from maritime transport. As argued in the Primer, it is preferable to include maritime transport in the specification of the corridor, even though no changes are proposed to the time or cost of the maritime transport sector. Including maritime transport is useful because the objective of the corridor project may be to increase the competitiveness of a country's exports. It is therefore helpful to know the delivered costs of those exports in the destination country and compare them with costs from competing countries and corridors.

The volume of trade to which these measurements are applied also needs to be considered. At a minimum, they should be applied to projections of the volume of trade through the corridor that would be expected even if the project were not to be implemented. Estimates of the growth of the underlying corridor trade then need to be made for all trade that would benefit from implementing the project.

Some corridor evaluations have been limited to imports, on the assumption that most proposed corridor improvements will apply much more to imports than to exports. Other evaluations have been limited to containerized products, based on the assumption that most trade facilitation measures apply more to containerized and general freight than to bulk products. Such limitations of the extent of an economic evaluation should be made only after analytical support of the assumptions has been made.

For example, one of the explanations sometimes given for focusing on trade facilitation in a project designed to increase exports, despite recognition that trade facilitation constraints can be a greater a barrier to imports than to exports, is that the cost of imports directly affects the cost of living, affecting wage rates, which in turn affect the cost of exports. Another frequent argument is that imports are an important input to many export products, so reducing the cost of imports reduces the costs of those exports. If these arguments are used in the project description, some simple analyses should be provided to support them. Analysis could include a review of the volume of imports to gross domestic product (GDP) (an indication of their effect on the cost of living) or a review of the type of products exported (manufactured exports are more likely to have a high import component than mining and basic agricultural exports).

Even if the evaluation is limited to projected volumes of currently traded products, some consideration should also be given to potential increased competition from other trade and transport corridors. If such competition is expected to increase, trade projections based on extrapolations of past trends may not be sufficient.

Several recent studies highlight the importance of reliability and confidence of traders in the times and costs of transport in a corridor.

To take account of these factors in the economic evaluation of a corridor, some measurement of the variability of time and cost should be included, as variability does not figure in the standard measures of economic benefit of a project (net present value or internal rate of return).

More ambitious project objectives include reference to stimulating trade in the corridor. Estimating the additional trade that would result from implementation of the project needs is not easy.

The main approaches that can be used in corridor impact evaluation are summarized in table 13.2 and reviewed below.

Economic Evaluation Methods

Impact evaluation approaches for a corridor can be grouped into four main types (table 13.3). Not all methods address all issues. Simple cost-benefit

TABLE 13.2 Link between Corridor Development Objective and Impact Evaluation Approach

Objective	Ease of measurement	Evaluation method
Reduce average times and costs of transport	1	Cost-benefit
Reduce variability of time and cost of transport	2	Adapted cost-benefit
Increase trade	3	Gravity model
Affect other aspects of national economy	4	Computable general equilibrium (CGE)

TABLE 13.3 Main Types of Impact Assessment Analysis

Type of analysis	Issues
Transport cost-benefit analysis	• Time and cost savings • Increased capacity and traffic volumes • Traffic reassignment across networks • Assumption: routes will be selected based on lowest generalized cost or based on policy choices of authorities
Supply chain assessment	• How corridor project will affect trade flows • Impact of corridor performance on reorganization of supply chains (change source of inputs or size of markets, relocate production) • Effect of higher inventory costs (20 percent increase in production costs, according to Guasch and Kogan 2003)
Analysis of trade impact	• Impact on trade of reducing the friction of distance. Studies suggest that each day saved through reduced travel time is equivalent to a 0.8 percent ad valorem tariff, 1 percent of trade, or 70 kilometers (Djankov, Freund, and Pham 2006). There are large distance elasticities in developing countries.
Macroeconomic (computable general equilibrium–type) modeling	• Use of improved access to markets and transformation of goods to unlock the inherent capital potential of specific spatial locations. Analysis requires inclusion of strategy to effect change at specific locations.

analyses that measure only the benefit to existing trade and its natural growth are the easiest to apply. If they show sufficient benefits to justify an investment, they may be sufficient. Gravity or other models provide estimates of the volume of additional trade deals. They can be used where trade impacts are particularly important. Supply or value chain analysis does not provide the same form of economic evaluation as the other methods, but it may provide more insight into how corridor improvements affect firms and trade flows. A macroeconomic (computable general equilibrium–type) model is the most comprehensive in assessing economywide impacts.

Cost-Benefit Analysis

The first, and by far most frequent, method is to estimate the savings in transport times and costs (and sometimes reliability) and to use these estimates in a cost-benefit analysis of the proposed improvements. This approach is best applied to the infrastructure components of a corridor project. It is more difficult to apply to the policy components. It is rarely used to evaluate a package of corridor improvements but is more frequently applied to individual components of such a package.

Cost-benefit analysis in corridor projects involves estimating the cost and time savings of implementing a proposed project rather than not implementing it.[2] Cost savings typically include savings associated with operating and maintaining vehicles (and maritime vessels and aircraft where appropriate) as well as reductions in the cost of deterioration and loss of goods in transit. Time savings can include savings related to vehicle operations (such as reductions in vehicle transit time) and the inventory costs of goods in transit and kept in storage to cover the risk of delays in transit and uncertainty of delivery times. Where feasible, time savings are converted into equivalent cost savings. These cost and time savings are compared with the infrastructure and investment and maintenance costs needed to achieve them. This comparison is usually made by comparing the stream of all cost and time savings and investment costs and either discounting the net annual costs to a net present value or calculating an internal rate of return for the stream of annual net costs. Other evaluation methods are not used much in corridor studies.

Cost-benefit analysis has been applied widely and successfully to many investment projects. It has been used less—and less successfully—to evaluate policy proposals. One of the principal reasons why is that it is difficult to determine the impacts of implementing a policy. There are many models available for cost-benefit analysis.[3] However, the approach is not particularly suited to analyzing policy interventions, neither is it suited to analyzing improvements in quality, for example, improving the reliability of logistics services. If these are important aspects of a project, then other techniques are needed, especially those with an emphasis on supply chain analysis, as described below.

Gravity Modeling

The second method is an analysis that takes account of new trade flows and diversion of trade flows from other corridors that might result from the corridor improvements. Trade generation and diversion impacts are usually estimated through the use of a gravity model. Such a model is difficult to apply to individual components of a corridor package, however, because each component has only a marginal effect on the level of trade. Where gravity models have been used, they have been applied to the package of proposed corridor improvements, where the expected trade impact is large enough to be estimated. A trade gravity model does not by itself provide enough information for an economic evaluation, as it does not include the costs of the investments in the corridor, only a possible reflection of these costs in the projected transport and trade facilitation tariffs to be charged in the corridors. It can therefore be considered as a complement rather than an alternative to traditional cost-benefit analysis.

There have been different formulations of the gravity model over the decades. Empirical studies have fitted a variety of augmented gravity models to international trade data, for various purposes. Frankel (1997) tests for the effects of a common border, per capita GDP, a common language, and membership in regional trading arrangements, as well as economic scale and distance. Rose (1999) extended Frankel's model by introducing colonial ties, exchange rate volatility, and a common currency. Soloaga and Winters (2001) add a control for effective distance by introducing a measure of generalized remoteness from all potential trade partners. Carrillo-Tudela and Li (2004) include the effects of a common border and trade association membership in their analysis of Latin American trade.

Gravity modeling approaches are generally useful to estimate likely trade volume impacts of a corridor improvement.[4] Nathan Associates (2011) used a gravity model in an analysis of corridors in East and Southern Africa (table 13.4). Their model takes the general form:

$$T_{ij} = k\left(X_{ij}\right)\frac{E_i^{\alpha_i} M_j^{\alpha_j}}{D_{ij}^{\gamma}}$$

where T_{ij} = trade volumes between areas i and j; E_i = economic scale of the exporting area; M_j = economic scale of the importing area; D_{ij} = a measure of

TABLE 13.4 Unconstrained Overseas and Regional Corridor Flows for East and Southern Africa, 2009–30

(Thousands of tonnes)

Corridor	2009	2015	2030	Average annual growth rate (percent) 2009–15	2015–30
Northern	9,060	15,092	36,547	8.9	6.1
Central	1,218	4,830	14,725	25.8	20.4
Dar	2,581	5,173	14,449	12.3	18.7
Nacala	1,181	2,262	4,887	11.4	13.7
Beira	5,406	9,037	25,154	8.9	18.6
Maputo	2,711	4,653	15,848	9.4	22.7
North-South	25,354	49,228	109,843	11.7	14.3
Trans-Kalahari	587	814	1,399	5.6	9.4
Trans-Caprivi	1,265	2,494	5,593	12.0	14.4
Trans-Cunene	461	796	1,028	9.5	4.4
Djibouti	5,835	9,120	14,783	7.7	8.4
Subtotal	55,659	103,499	244,256	10.9	15.4

Source: Nathan Associates 2011.

the disutility of shipping between areas i and j; and X_{ij} = a vector of other trade-cost-related variables, such as linguistic, political, and economic ties between trading partners; policy indicators that relate to trade; and so forth.

Nathan Associates (2011) applied a model of this basic form to model flows on corridors in Africa (the results appear in table 13.4). The flows respond to changes in the disutility of shipping (cost, time, and reliability) on each corridor.

Distance can be used to represent shipping disutility in developed countries; it performs less well in developing countries (Nathan Associates 2011). In developing countries, where road and rail transport conditions vary greatly, there is need for some adjustment to reflect differences in the quality of infrastructure. Disutility may be related primarily to cost (or price to the shipper), but it also includes transit time and the predictability of transit time (a measure of reliability). However, given the difficulties of obtaining data, it may be necessary to use coefficients estimated from other studies. Examples of some recent estimates are shown in table 13.5.

However, the inclusion of generated trade complicates the economic evaluation. If a project is expected to increase the volume of trade, it is possible that the estimated with-project transport cost will be greater than estimated without-project cost. A simple cost comparison would erroneously indicate that the project has a negative benefit. To overcome this problem, consideration needs to be given to the shape of the demand curve for the

TABLE 13.5 Gravity Model Estimates for Africa and Latin America

(Coefficients)

Study	Region	Exporter GDP	Importer GDP	Road distance	Road quality
Buys, Deichmann, and Wheeler (2006)	Sub-Saharan Africa	1.73 (14.08)	1.45 (11.75)	−2.29 (7.44)	2.06 (8.14)
Carrillo-Tudela and Li (2004)	Latin America	1.33 (15.35) to 2.13 (17.15)	0.69 (9.71) to 1.23 (17.56)	−1.13(4.95) to −1.68 (5.74)	—
Coulibaly and Fotagné (2004)	West Africa	1.40 (22.29)	0.83 (6.05)	−0.96 (4.93)	1.44 (4.34)

Source: Nathan Associates 2011.
Note: Figures in parentheses are *t*-statistics. — not available; GDP = gross domestic product.

products whose volume is projected to be greater with the project and the area under the relevant sections of the demand curve used to estimate the benefit to exporters from the additional trade. Even this does not go far enough, as there is a cost to producing the additional exported products that is not reflected in the transport demand curve. This production cost needs to be subtracted from the exporters' estimated benefit.[5]

Trade gravity models have rarely been used to estimate the potential impacts of improvements to specific trade corridors. Because of the nature of the data that are more readily available, especially in developing countries, such models are more often used to estimate the impacts of trade policy changes on the total international trade of a country.

Value or Supply Chain Assessment

Some corridor analyses make use of value or supply chain analyses. Supply chain analyses do provide an opportunity to add some other logistics and production costs to the transport costs used in most versions of the first two evaluation methods. They can also provide estimates of the volume of additional trade that may be generated by reducing these logistics and production costs.

The estimated logistics and production costs that result from supply chain analyses, together with the trade projections they provide, can be combined with the corridor investment costs in a cost-benefit analysis similar to those of traditional cost-benefit analysis (if there is no estimate of generated or diverted trade) or gravity modeling (if these estimates are provided). However, unlike the first two methods, supply chain cost changes and trade flow projections cannot usually be attributed to individual components of a corridor project.

Supply or value chain analyses typically analyze a sample of the chains that would benefit from implementation of the corridor project. They do not provide measures of the benefits that can be easily compared with estimates of the investment costs. Use of supply or value chain analyses requires a quite different approach from that of cost-benefit analysis. The analysis needs to include corridor investment costs as a component of the costs of the supply or value chain; estimating these costs is difficult and rarely done. Although supply or value chain analyses can add to the understanding of how the benefits of the corridor investment might be realized, they are not usually used as part of the economic evaluation of proposed corridor improvements.

For each unit of trade that uses the corridor, there is an average cost and transit time for the movement from origin to destination, only part of which may be in the corridor. There is also a level of reliability of the movement, which is equated with the variation in the transit time. These factors can be combined into a generalized cost function by assigning values to time and reliability. As reliability is measured as the additional time required to ensure on-time delivery, the values for the two can be estimated using the same value. The generalized cost, C_k, for a unit of trade k is

$$C_k = c_k + \alpha_k (t_k + \beta \sigma_{t,k})$$

where c_k = direct cost for the movement of a unit of trade k from origin to destination; α_k = value of time for a unit of trade k; t_k = average transit time from origin to destination; $\sigma_{t,k}$ = variation in transit time from origin to destination used to measure unreliability; and β = reliability criteria (for example, $\beta = 1.96$ means that 2.5 percent of delivery dates are missed).

Arvis, Raballand, and Marteau (ARM) (2010) developed a total logistics costs approach for a supply chain, building on the model originally proposed by Baumol and Vinod (1970). A supply chain approach provides a convenient conceptual framework for disentangling the logistics costs deriving from the sequence of transit operations and subsequently allows for the assessment of the impact of facilitation, regulatory, or investment measures. Their model is developed from the perspective of the shipper. It seeks to determine the total logistics costs associated with the time, cost, and reliability performance of a corridor. The end user supports costs directly or through fees paid to agents such as freight forwarders or transport operators. The model also takes into consideration whether the transport services industries are competitive or cartelized.

The ARM model estimates total logistics costs (C) as a function of transport costs, other logistics costs, and costs from delays:

C = transport costs + other logistics costs + delay-hedging costs

Transport costs are the actual costs paid by shippers of goods to transport service providers; logistics costs include payments of fees for procedures and other costs as well as the fixed costs of shipments; and hedging costs include the cost of capital tied up in moving inventory and the costs of unreliability. Unpredictability and uncertainty in shipment delivery time imposes a cost on shippers as they have to maintain additional stocks to minimize the risks of stock-outs as a result of uncertainties. However, for the same industry, volumes are typically lower in a landlocked country than a gateway country, which further increases inventory costs. Typically, the value of the optimal inventory is the quantity of stock necessary to satisfy demand between two shipments. The need to hedge inventory to account for unpredictability depends on variance in lead time.

The ARM model has been used to evaluate the impact of several corridor-based trade and transport facilitation projects financed by the World Bank. One example is the East Africa Trade and Transport Facilitation Project (box 13.1).

BOX 13.1
Evaluating the Impact of the East Africa Trade and Transport Facilitation Project

The Northern corridor is the main transport artery linking the landlocked countries of East and Central Africa (Rwanda, Uganda, Burundi, eastern Democratic Republic of Congo, and South Sudan) to the Port of Mombasa, in Kenya. Up to Kampala (Uganda), cargo moves by truck or railroad. Based on a diagnostic, the World Bank determined that the corridor's performance was hampered by two factors: the poor quality of Kenya's infrastructure and the weak performance of the railroad. Supply chain predictability was also found to be low, constraining processing activities in Kenya and Uganda.

The corridor governments, along with donors (the World Bank, the African Development Bank, and the European Union) sought to address these challenges through a multipronged project. The supply chain model was used to estimate the likely impact of the project, using various parameters as inputs.

As expected, average transport gains from the corridor facilitation initiative were modest: 2.2 days saved for the truck transport leg, at a cost of $130 day, which amounts to $286 per shipment. However, the inventory impact was significant, with the inventory level halved, entailing a cost savings of $1,000 per shipment (25 percent of the cost of transport).

Source: World Bank 2004.

The total logistics costs approach can be applied on a wider scale, as Transport Canada has done as part of the Canadian government's Transportation Gateways and Trade Corridors program.[6] Its approach takes a broad look at the time to market and reliability by developing systemwide performance measures of total delivery time, total delivery time variability, and the costs of shipping goods through gateways and corridors and between any two origin-destination pairs. This approach assigns a monetary value to the logistics activities associated with freight shipments. The core components of a total logistics costs model are direct transportation costs, in-transit carrying costs, ordering costs, cycle stock-carrying costs, safety stock-carrying costs and, stock-out costs.

Macroeconomic Models

A shortcoming of a supply chain approach is that the sum of impacts on an individual supply chain may not add to more than the total impact on a region served by a corridor. Rather, macroeconomic models are best suited to evaluating improvements along the corridor as a whole. The type of model sometimes used for this purpose is a computable general equilibrium (CGE) model. CGE models are a standard tool of empirical analysis. They are widely used to analyze the aggregate welfare and distribution impacts of policies whose effects may be transmitted through multiple markets or contain menus of tax, subsidy, quota, and transfer instruments. Examples of their use may be found in areas as diverse as fiscal reform and development planning (see, for example, Gunning and Keyzer 1995). They can be useful to evaluate packages of corridor improvements that include several policy changes, which are not easily included in conventional cost-benefit analysis or trade gravity models. However, because they depend on national economic and social statistics for their implementation, CGE models are difficult to apply to trade corridors that involve more than one country.

Although the traditional cost-benefit analysis is the most frequently used and easiest to apply, it does not directly address the corridor objective of stimulating trade (although it would be relatively easy to do so if elasticities of trade volume with respect to transport costs and times were readily available). Even where a transport gravity model is used to assess the increase in corridor traffic, it can provide only a partial measure of the trade benefits, as it does not take account of the cost of producing the additional goods that are traded.

Where a corridor is already well developed and economic rigidities are not very strong, cost-benefit analysis can be used to assess likely impacts. A basic rule is that an argument for wider economic benefits should not be used to justify schemes that would otherwise fail in transport terms.

There is, however, a common problem that is often faced with wider economic benefit assessment, posed by the double counting of transport impacts. The benefits are estimated in cost-benefit analyses and the impacts on other sectors under the wider economic benefit approach. General problems with availability of data often require that alternative approaches are adopted to assess wider economic impacts.

Transport Research Note 19 (World Bank 2005) recommends using a qualitative approach to explore two features. The first is the linkages between transport and the regional economy, with a focus on specific linkages affected by the project (possibly through supply chain analysis). The second is the competitive advantage of the regions connected by a corridor in traded sectors (for example, from natural resources and their role in agriculture or manufacturing). An assessment could then be made of the effect on employment and output.

In traditional cost-benefit analysis, user benefits are measured in the transport market itself. A key question is whether production should be included in the models (what is produced where and with what inputs). Spatial production models can yield useful insights into the linkages between transport and the local economy that would be helpful to policy decision making (box 13.2). However, these types of models are data hungry and require detailed spatial input-output matrices, which are not

BOX 13.2

Regional Impacts of Network Improvements

The Golden Quadrilateral (GQ) highway project upgraded the quality and width of 5,846 kilometers of roads in India, connecting many of the major industrial, agricultural, and cultural centers. The first phase of the project began in 2001 and was completed in 2007.

Ghani, Goswami, and Kerr (2013) investigated the impact of the project on India's organized manufacturing sector. Using difference-in-difference estimation based on enterprise data from four time periods (1994, 2000, 2005, and 2007), they studied how proximity to the GQ in nonnodal districts affected the organization of manufacturing activity, using establishment counts, employment and output levels, and firm entry and exit rates. They also considered industry-level sorting, the extent to which

BOX 13.2 *continued*

intermediate cities in India became more attractive for manufacturing plants, and the impact on sector performance through measures of average labor productivity and total factor productivity (TFP). Their study compared nonnodal districts 0–10 kilometers from the network to districts 10–50 kilometers away.

Their results showed the following:

- GQ upgrades had positive effects on the organized manufacturing sector, with substantial growth in entry rates in nonnodal districts within 10 kilometers of the GQ network. These patterns were absent in districts farther away.
- Labor productivity and TFP rose among manufacturing plants in nonnodal districts within 10 kilometers of the GQ network. These effects were not evident in districts farther away.
- Entry rates rose in nonnodal districts within 10 kilometers of the GQ network, especially in industries that are very land and building intensive. In nodal districts, the shift was toward industries that were less intensive in land and buildings.
- The timing of the improvements in the manufacturing sector was tied to the timing of the improvements in the GQ network. Impacts were absent from a similar network for which improvement was delayed.

These findings are consistent with findings of an earlier study by Datta (2011), who used enterprise survey data. That study found that that the GQ upgrades improved the inventory management and sourcing of manufacturing plants located in nonnodal districts along the GQ network by 2005. The two studies demonstrate the spatial development impacts and supply chain reorganization effects of corridor improvements. These effects have to be included in impact evaluation of corridor projects.

Source: World Bank 2013.

---

available in most developing countries. These models are better suited to networks than to individual projects.

The interaction of economies of scale and endogenous market size can lead to a cumulative process of agglomeration. Because corridors are about consolidation of flows to enable greater efficiency of movement, economies of scale are important and have to be reflected in how project impact is assessed.

Notes

1. This module deals only with economic evaluation, not with financial assessment. Financial assessments should be made for all revenue-earning public entities and all private sector operators whose main activity is in the corridor. As all of the financial appraisals are independent of the others, they do not raise any conceptual or technical issues that do not arise in single-investment projects.
2. For a concise but comprehensive summary of the use of cost-benefit analysis in transport projects, see World Bank (2005), particularly Transport Note 5.
3. The Highway Development and Management Model Version 4 (HDM4) is a typical cost-benefit-based transport tool. Details can be found at http://www .hdm-ims.com/hdm4.htm.
4. There are several reviews of gravity models, including Buys, Deichmann, and Wheeler (2006); Yamarik and Ghosh (2005); and Feenstra, Markusen, and Rose (1998).
5. For a more complete description of how to evaluate the benefits of trade generated by a corridor project, see World Bank Transport Note 11, particularly Annex 2 (2005).
6. Transport Canada is the government agency responsible for most transportation policies, programs, and goals in Canada. It maintains a major trade corridor monitoring and development program.

References

Arvis, J.-F., G. F. R. Raballand, and J.-F. Marteau. 2010. *The Cost of Being Landlocked: Logistics Costs and Supply Chain Reliability*. Washington, DC: World Bank.

Baumol, W. J., and H. D. Vinod. 1970. "An Inventory Theoretic Model of Freight Transport Demand." *Management Science* 16 (7): 413–21.

Buys, P., U. Deichmann, and D. Wheeler. 2006. "Road Network Upgrading and Overland Trade Expansion in Sub-Saharan Africa." Policy Research Working Paper 4097, World Bank, Washington, DC.

Carrillo-Tudela, C., and C. Li. 2004. "Trade Blocks and the Gravity Model: Evidence from Latin American Countries." *Journal of Economic Integration* 19: 667–89, Center for Economic Integration, Sejong University, Seoul.

Coulibaly, S., and L. Fontagné. 2004, "South-South Trade: Geography Matters." CEPII Working Paper 2004-08, CEPII Research Center, Paris.

Datta, S. 2011. "The Impact of Improved Highways on Indian Firms." *Journal of Development Economics* 99 (1): 46–57.

Djankov, S., C. Freund, and C. S. Pham. 2006. "Trading on Time." Policy Research Working Paper 3909, World Bank, Washington, DC.

Feenstra, R. C., J. A. Markusen, and A. K. Rose. 1998. "Understanding the Home Market Effect and the Gravity Equation: The Role of Differentiating Goods." NBER Working Paper 6804, National Bureau of Economic Research, Cambridge, MA.

Frankel, J. 1997. *Regional Trading Blocs in the World Economic System*. Washington, DC: Peterson Institute for International Economics.

Fujita, M., P. Krugman, and A. Venables. 1999. *The Spatial Economy: Cities, Regions and International Trade*. Cambridge, MA: MIT Press.

Ghani, E., A. G. Goswami, and W. R. Kerr. 2013. "Highway to Success in India: The Impact of the Golden Quadrilateral Project for the Location and Performance of Manufacturing." Policy Research Working Paper WPS 6320, World Bank, Washington, DC.

Guasch, J., and J. L. Kogan. 2003. "Just-in-Case Inventories: A Cross-Country Analysis." Policy Research Working Paper 3012, World Bank, Washington, DC.

Gunning, W., and M. A. Keyzer. 1995. "Applied General Equilibrium Models for Policy Analysis." In *Handbook of Development Economics*, vol. 3, edited by H. Chenery and T. N. Srinivasan, 2025–107. Amsterdam: Elsevier.

Nathan Associates. 2011. "Definition and Investment Strategy for a Core Strategic Transport Network for Eastern and Southern Africa." Report for the World Bank, Washington, DC.

Rose, A. K. 1999. "One Money, One Market: Estimating the Effect of Common Currencies on Trade." NBER Working Papers 7432, National Bureau of Economic Research. Cambridge, MA.

Soloaga, I., and A. Winters. 2001. "Regionalism in the Nineties: What Effects on Trade?" *The North American Journal of Economics and Finance* 12 (1): 1–29.

World Bank. 2004. "Project Appraisal Document for the East Africa Trade and Transport Facilitation Project." Washington DC.

———. 2005. Transport Research Notes 5–26. Washington, DC. http://web .worldbank.org/WBSITE/EXTERNAL/TOPICS/EXTTRANSPORT/0,,content MDK:20464962~menuPK:1323557~pagePK:210058~piPK:210062~theSitePK: 337116,00.html.

Yamarik, S., and S. Ghosh, 2005. "A Sensitivity Analysis of the Gravity Model." *International Trade Journal* 19 (1): 83–126.

Resources

CSIOR (Commonwealth Scientific and Industrial Research Organisation). 2010. "Implementation of the IR-CGE Model for Planning: IRSA-INDONESIA 5 (Inter-Regional System of Analysis for Indonesia in 5 Regions)." Townsville, Australia. http://www.csiro.au/~/media/CSIROau/Divisions/CSIRO%20 Sustainable%20Ecosystems/IR-CGEImplementation_CSE_PDF%20Standard .pdf.
The first computable general equilibrium (CGE) model for Indonesia was developed in 1980. Since then several other similar models have been developed. The paper describes one of the more recent attempts called IRSA-INDONESIA 5 where a dynamic CGE approach was used to model multi-region interactions within the country. The regions consist of multiple sectors that are interconnected through trade, movements of people and capital, and government fiscal transfers. Importantly, each region is also connected with the rest of the world and engages in import and export activities with other countries as well as participates in international money transfers. The model was used to model specific shocks to the economy. The model therefore has great potential for

modeling corridor type interventions, though the lack of data to develop such a model can be catastrophic in most countries.

Nathan Associates. FastPath Toolbox. http://www.nathaninc.com/resources /fastpath-toolbox.

FastPath is a commercially available and widely applied toolkit for assessing and evaluating transport corridors and their development. It includes an economic evaluation model that relies on a fixed trip matrix, although some of its more recent applications have included generated freight. Its corridor measurement features are described in Module 4. It also provides a comprehensive framework and module for economic evaluation of corridor project subcomponents and a land corridor as a whole. Different versions of the model have been applied to many trade corridors, including in Southeast Asia, South Asia, and East, West, and Southern Africa.

———. 2010. "East Africa Northern and Central Corridor Study." Washington, DC. Although gravity models have been used extensively in assessments of trade policies, such as tariff reductions, they have been little used in evaluating the trade impacts of corridor improvement projects, for at least two reasons. First, although they can be used to estimate trade growth impacts, most trade gravity models do not rely on estimates of reductions in transport costs and times as the basis for those impacts. Second, these models are very difficult and time consuming to apply and rely on massive trade and transport cost databases for their application. Few World Bank projects have the resources to develop and apply such models.

One of the few recent applications of a gravity model to predict the differences in trade flows that might arise through implementation of a trade and transport corridor project is the East Africa Northern and Central Corridor Study. This study uses a trade gravity model based on transport costs and times for the trade deterrence function (and on gross domestic product [GDP] and population estimates for the generation and attraction of trade flows between countries). As the model provides trade flows on an origin to destination basis and the competition between destinations and alternative corridors is expressed in terms of transport costs and times, the output of the model can be used in an evaluation making use of the "rule of half" method.

USAID (U.S. Agency for International Development). 2010. "Transport and Logistics Costs on the Tema-Ougadougou Corridor." West Africa Trade Hub Technical Report 25, Washington, DC. http://pdf.usaid.gov/pdf_docs /PNADU448.pdf.

This report provides a detailed assessment of transport and trade practices in the West Africa Trade corridor. Although it provides estimates of the reductions in logistics costs of more than 20 potential measures, it does not go to the next stage of undertaking a cost-benefit analysis that takes account of the costs of implementing the measures.

World Bank. 2005. "East Africa Trade and Transport Facilitation Project Appraisal Document." Report 34178-World Bank, Washington, DC. http://documents .worldbank.org/curated/en/2005/12/10932212/africa-region-east-africa -trade-transport-facilitation-project.

This evaluation is especially detailed in taking account of the reduced uncertainty in time and cost through the implementation of corridor components. It is not so good at estimating the value of time savings of goods in transit. The evaluation of the corridor development takes account of six subcomponents, including infrastructure investments, trade facilitation, and policy changes. Although the appraisal document provides extensive discussion of the trade impacts of the project, they seem to have been excluded from the economic evaluation, as no mention is made of their magnitude or how they were evaluated. The economic evaluation was based on target reductions in times and costs and their uncertainties, not on modeled estimates of the impact of the project subcomponents. Tables show the benefit attributable to each of the five measures that derive from the six subcomponents and their distribution among the four countries involved in the project. Though no sensitivity analysis of switching values is made, the impact of separately changing the values of four input parameters (operating costs, traffic volumes, value of time, and investment costs) by +20 and –20 percent is assessed. The base internal rate of return of 28 percent ranges from 14 percent (reducing the value of time by 20 percent) and 46 percent (reducing investment costs by 20 percent).

———. 2005. Transport Research Notes (TRN) 5–26. Washington, DC. http://go.worldbank.org/E6ZOPA73G0.

These Notes provide advice on dealing with some of the more controversial aspects of economic evaluation of transport projects. Most of them (with the exception of those specifically related to pedestrians and urban transport) have some application to the evaluation of corridor projects.

TRN-6 to TRN-10 provide criteria for selecting a particular evaluation technique or approach. TRN-11 to TRN-17 address the selection of values of various inputs in the evaluation. TRN-18 to TRN-26 deal with problematic issues in economic evaluation. The Notes are preceded by a Framework (TRN-5), which provides the context within which economic evaluation is used in the transport sector.

TRN-5 A Framework for the Economic Evaluation of Transport Projects
TRN-6 When and How to Use NPV, IRR, and Modified IRR
TRN-7 Risk and Uncertainty Analysis
TRN-8 Fiscal Impacts
TRN-9 Where to Use Cost Effectiveness Techniques Rather than Cost-Benefit Analysis
TRN-10 Relationship between Financial and Economic Evaluations for Different Types of Projects
TRN-11 Treatment of Induced Traffic
TRN-12 Demand Forecasting Errors
TRN-13 Treatment of Maintenance
TRN-14 Sources of Operating Costs
TRN-15 Valuation of Time Savings
TRN-16 Valuation of Accident Reduction
TRN-17 No Note was published under this number
TRN-18 Projects with a Very Long Life
TRN-19 Projects with Significant Expected Restructuring Effects

TRN-20 Evaluation of Public Sector Contributions to Public-Private Partnership Projects

TRN-21 Low Volume Rural Roads

TRN-22 Treatment of Pedestrian and Non-motorized Traffic

TRN-23 Evaluation Implications of Sub-optimum Pricing

TRN-24 Economic Appraisal of Regulatory Reform: Checklist of Issues

TRN-25 Evaluation of Resettlement Compensation Payments

TRN-26 Distribution of Benefits and Impacts on Poor People

———. 2008. "Project Appraisal Document for the Second Rijeka Gateway Project." Report 44539-HR, World Bank, Washington, DC. http://documents.worldbank .org/curated/en/2008/11/10177483/croatia-second-rijeka-gateway-project. This report is an example of conventional cost-benefit analysis applied to a port improvement project. Annex 9 describes the competing ports but does not show how the development of ports affects the projections for Rijeka. The report does compare the competitiveness of these ports as a group for container traffic destined for Central Europe with ports in Northern Europe, using a network and freight assignment model. The proposed development provides capacity only up to about 2015 (the analysis was undertaken in 2008); traffic projections beyond this date are capacity constrained and do not change. No sensitivity analysis is conducted of switching values, but a test with 25 percent less traffic through the port shows a reduction in the internal rate of return from 14 percent to 13 percent.

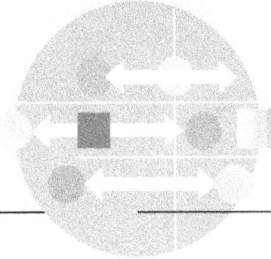

INDEX

Boxes, figures, notes, and tables are indicated by italic b, f, n, and t respectively.

Rift Valley Railways (RVR), 249*b*
Rijeka Gateway Project, Croatia, 323–24
risk management
    border crossing, 154–55
    cargo, 288
    shipping documentation, 78
road transport services
    freight operations, 205–6
    freight tariffs, 250*f*
    ICDs, 250*f*, 251*t*
    indicators for, 215–16
    infrastructure, 311–12
    questions, 225–34
    queueing systems, 202
    rail *vs.*, 239
roll-on-roll-off (Ro-Ro) stern berthing, 286
route attractiveness, 137*n*1, 137*n*5, 138
runway dimensions, 329–30, 337*b*
Russia-Kazakhstan-Belarus customs
    union, 90*n*1. *See also* Soviet Union
RVR (Rift Valley Railways), 249*b*

*SAARC (South Asian Association for
    Regional Cooperation) Preferential
    Trading Agreement (SAPTA) of 1993,* 84
SADC (Southern African Development
    Community), 14–15, 87
safety
    air transport, 330–31, 332–33
    of people, performance indicators
        for, 126, 133
*SAFTA (South Asia Free Trade Area) of
    2004,* 84
sanitary and phyto-sanitary (SPS)
    requirements, 146–47
*SAPTA (South Asian Association for
    Regional Cooperation Preferential
    Trading Agreement) of 1993,* 84
SARPs (Standards and Recommended
    Practices), 331
savings, transport time and cost, 353–54
seals
    customs, 180
    electronic, 183–84
secure load compartments, 179
security
    airfreight, 334
    of goods, 126, 133

self-financing, corridor
    management, 104
Sequence of TIR Operation, 187*f*
sequential activities, data collected for,
    58, 59
services, corridor, 16, 17*f*, 258–59
Shanghai
    container spot rates, 269*t*
    Containerized Freight Index, 269
shipping. *See also* air cargo; cargo;
    containers
    allocation system, 205
    break-bulk, 122, 137*n*3
    conventions for international, 77–78
    costs of, 131–33
    frequencies, 122–23
    maritime, 16–17
    packing types, 122–23, 137*n*2
    as performance indicator, 121–24
    quota systems, 205, 206, 207–8*b*
    reliability of, 130–31, 132*f*
    risk documentation, 78
    sizes, 122–23
    tariffs in Southern Africa, 250*f*
    time, 126, 129–30
    transshipping cargo, 263–64
    volume unit, 137*n*4
shipping lines
    amalgamation of, 272
    connectivity, 267–68
    container questions, 275–77
    Internet searches on, 268–69
    piracy impact on, 271–72
ships. *See* vessels
*SIECA (Central American Economic
    Integration Secretariat),* 82–83
Silk Road, trip diaries used for improving
    trade along, 48–49*b*
*Simplification and Harmonization
    of the Administrative Procedures
    and Port Transit within the West
    African Economic and Monetary
    Union,* 87
Singapore's Single Window, 158*b*
Single Window Repository, 175
single window system, 157, 158*b*, 175
Sokol, José B., 142
South America. *See* Latin America

www.ingramcontent.com/pod-product-compliance
Lightning Source LLC
Chambersburg PA
CBHW082128210326
41599CB00031B/5903